Exploring Scrum: The Fundamentals

Second Edition

Dan Rawsthorne with Doug Shimp

Forewords by
Ron Jeffries, Jeff McKenna, Johanna Rothman, Jeff Sutherland

Exploring Scrum: The Fundamentals

Dan Rawsthorne with Doug Shimp

Forewords by

Ron Jeffries, Jeff McKenna, Johanna Rothman, Jeff Sutherland

Many of the designations used by manufacturers and sellers to distinguish their products are claimed as trademarks. Where these designations appear in this book and the authors were aware of a trademark claim, the designations have been printed in initial caps, all caps, or with appropriate registration symbols.

The authors have taken care in the preparation of this document, but make no expressed or implied warranty of any kind and assume no responsibility for errors or omissions. No liability is assumed for incidental or consequential damages in connection with or arising out of the use of the information contained herein.

Cover illustration of "Explorer" by Phil Rawsthorne

First Edition publication date: July 23, 2011

Second Edition publication date: August 14, 2013

ISBN-10: 1461160286

ISBN-13: 978-1461160281

To Mel:
You gave us Lilly, and you left us all too soon...
We Miss You

This book is dedicated to:
Those we have coached and taught;
Those who will use this book;
Those whose shoulders we stand on.

And most importantly, it is dedicated to
Our Friends and Families,
without whom this book could not exist.

Contents

About the Authors -- xv

Preface to Second Edition --- xvii

Acknowledgements (for the First Edition) ------------------------------------- xix

Foreword by Ron Jeffries --- xxi

Foreword by Jeff McKenna -- xxiii

Foreword by Johanna Rothman -- xxv

Foreword by Jeff Sutherland --- xxvii

Section 1: Introduction --- 1
  1.1 About This Book --- 3
    What Scrum Is --- 3
    Purpose of Book -- 5
    My Goal -- 6
    How to Use This Book --- 7
    SirJeff's Problem -- 8
    Discussion Questions -- 8

  1.2 Scrum in a Nutshell-- 9
    The Team -- 9
    The Backlog -- 10
    The Release -- 11
    The Sprint -- 12
    Discussion Questions -- 14

Section 2: The People --- 15
  2.1 The Scrum Team --- 17
    Overview -- 17
    Team Members --- 18
    Other Scrum Team Roles --- 19
    Roles External to the Team -- 21
    Relationship Matrix -- 23
    Discussion of Project and Product Management------------------------------ 24
    Team Values --- 25
    Cross-Functional and Self-Organized--- 26
    Discussion Questions -- 28

  2.2 The Product Owner-- 31
    The Team's Relationship with the Product Owner---------------------------- 32
    Product Owner Examples--- 35
    Product Owner (Leadership) Teams --- 38
    Other Product Ownership Responsibilities------------------------------------- 41

Discussion Questions --- 42

2.3 The ScrumMaster -- 43
Role Unique to Scrum -- 44
Facilitate, Don't Manage --- 46
Organizational Constraints Must Be Honored ------------------------------ 47
Main Issues to Manage --- 48
Modes of ScrumMastering --- 52
Who Should Be a ScrumMaster? -- 53
Product Owner as ScrumMaster --- 54
Summary --- 54
Discussion Questions --- 55

2.4 Modes of the ScrumMaster -- 57
Trainer --- 57
Coach --- 60
Mentor -- 61
'Invisible' -- 63
Summary --- 63
Discussion Questions --- 63

2.5 People Outside the Team --- 65
Three Basic Patterns -- 65
Business Owner -- 68
Stakeholders -- 69
Subject Matter Experts --- 71
The ScrumMaster and Outsiders -- 73
Summary --- 74
Discussion Questions --- 74

2.6 The Team Swarm --- 75
Definition -- 75
Swarming Examples -- 76
Self-Organization and Self-Management ------------------------------------- 80
What Happens When a Story Gets Done? ----------------------------------- 81
Simplify the Story Board! --- 82
Summary --- 83
Discussion Questions --- 83

Section 3: The Product --- 85
3.1 What is 'Product'? -- 87
Stakeholders Want What They Want -- 88
It's All About the Feedback -- 89
Summary --- 89
Discussion Questions --- 90

3.2 The Backlog --- 91
Backlog Basics --- 91
Prioritization Buckets -- 92

Examples--- 95
Comments on Prioritization Buckets ------------------------------------- 97
Describing Progress to Stakeholders ------------------------------------- 98
A Simple Progress Report for Stakeholders---------------------------- 99
Backlog Terms--- 101
Discussion Questions --- 102

3.3 Capabilities and Chores --- 105
A Work Breakdown Structure (WBS) ------------------------------------ 105
Capabilities-- 107
Chores --- 108
Related Issues --- 109
Summary-- 111
Discussion Questions --- 111

3.4 Stories and Epics --- 113
Stories --- 113
Other Story Distinctions--- 115
Examples of Stories --- 116
Epics as Stories the Team Can't Agree to Do------------------------- 117
Epics as Containers-- 118
Summary-- 121
Discussion Questions --- 121

3.5 Technical Debt--- 123
Definition of Technical Debt --- 123
Discussion of Technical Debt --- 124
Primary Types of Technical Debt -- 126
Preventing Technical Debt -- 127
Removing Technical Debt -- 131
Summary-- 132
Discussion Questions --- 132

3.6 The Story's Agreement -- 135
Coding Stories -- 136
Non-Coding Stories-- 138
Examples for a Mature Team -- 142
Agreements on Epics -- 143
Other Topics about Story Agreements --------------------------------- 144
Summary-- 147
Discussion Questions --- 147

3.7 Velocity and Size --- 149
Acceptance-Based Stories and Ideal Effort --------------------------- 150
Actual Effort, Ideal Effort, and Velocity------------------------------- 151
StoryPoints and Velocity are Very Useful ------------------------------ 153
EffortPoints and WorkRate – an Aside---------------------------------- 156
Budgeting StoryPoints for Epics --- 157
Two More Issues -- 160

Summary -- *163*

Discussion Questions -- *163*

3.8 Organizing the Backlog -- *165*

Tags -- *166*

Themes --- *167*

Buckets -- *168*

Summary -- *169*

Discussion Questions -- *169*

3.9 Backlog Refinement --- *171*

Backlog Refinement Discussion --------------------------------------- *171*

Basic Prioritization Strategy --- *175*

Prioritization Factors -- *177*

Summary -- *180*

Discussion Questions -- *181*

3.10 Storyotypes --- *183*

Discussion --- *183*

Coding Storyotypes -- *186*

Analysis Storyotypes -- *192*

Other Storyotypes -- *196*

Summary -- *197*

Discussion Question -- *198*

Section 4: The Practices -- *199*

4.1 Planning Day -- *201*

Product Review (10am to Noon) ------------------------------------- *202*

Progress Assessment (Lunch, Noon to 1pm) ------------------- *204*

Team Retrospective (1pm to 3pm) ----------------------------------- *205*

Useful Metaphors about Changing the Team's Process -------- *208*

Sprint Planning (3pm to 5pm) -- *210*

Summary -- *212*

Discussion Questions -- *213*

4.2 Agreement-Based Planning --- *215*

General Strategy for Agreement-Based Sprint Planning -------- *215*

Stories Should Be 'Ready' for Planning --------------------------- *217*

Reprioritization --- *218*

The Team Agrees to the Stories -- *219*

Agreement and Technical Debt -- *220*

Plan of Action -- *221*

Appropriate Sprint Goals --- *222*

Sprint Planning and the Release Strategy --------------------------- *223*

Why I Like Agreement-Based Planning ------------------------------ *224*

Discussion Questions -- *225*

4.3 Adjusting Sprint Content -- *227*

Finishing Early -- *228*

Removing Something that's Not Necessary ------------------------------- 228
The Sprint Goal Needs to Change -- 229
The Team Can't Do what It Agreed to Do ------------------------------ 230
Changing Something that It Already Agreed to Do ------------------------------- 231
Negotiating New Work -- 232
Summary --- 234
Discussion Question -- 234

4.4 *PlaceHolder Stories* --- 235
General Budget/Planning Problem ------------------------------------ 235
PlaceHolder Stories to Manage Budget ------------------------------- 236
There Must Be a Sufficient Back Burner ----------------------------- 237
Discussion --- 237
Discussion Questions -- 237

4.5 *Cleanup Stories* --- 239
How Technical Debt Arises -- 239
Cleanup Stories --- 240
A Dream --- 242
Cleanup Stories and the Story's Agreement ---------------------------- 242
Summary --- 243
Discussion Questions -- 243

4.6 *Monitoring Sprint Progress* -- 245
The Sprint's TaskHour BurnDown -- 245
The Sprint's Checklist Item BuildUp ------------------------------------- 248
Discussion --- 250
The BurnDown Work-Around -- 251
Summary --- 253
Discussion Questions -- 253

4.7 *Kanban(ish) Variant* --- 255
Brief Description of Kanban --- 255
Integrating WIP into Scrum -- 257
The Sprint Is Still There -- 258
Discussion --- 259
Discussion Questions -- 260

4.8 *The Daily Scrum* --- 261
The Result Is Other Discussions --- 261
Other Questions -- 264
Focus on the Story --- 265
Who Attends, Who Talks? --- 265
Summary --- 266
Discussion Questions -- 266

4.9 *Other Sprint Issues* -- 269
Startup Sprint --- 269
Release Sprint --- 271

Sprint Length -- 274
Planned Mid-Sprint Re-planning Sessions ------------------------- 276
Cancelling a Sprint -- 276
Abnormal Termination of a Sprint -------------------------------- 277
Stories that Are 'Too Big' for One Sprint ------------------------ 277
Complicated Story Boards -- 278
Discussion Questions -- 278

Appendices --- 279
A.1 Glossary of Scrum Terms --------------------------------------- 281
Discussion Questions -- 293

A.2 Product Owner Definition -------------------------------------- 295
The Basics -- 295
The Product Owner Must Be Accountable -------------------------- 296
The Product Owner Should Be a Team Member --------------------- 297
Appeal to Authority -- 299
Summary --- 300
Discussion Questions -- 300

A.3 Evolution of Dan's Scrum ------------------------------------- 301
My History --- 301
Old Scrum (1997 to 2005) --------------------------------------- 303
Modern Scrum (2005 to present) . ------------------------------- 305
Future Scrum (2014 to ??) -------------------------------------- 306
Summary --- 307
Discussion Questions -- 307

A.4 Doug's Story --- 309
Recent History --- 309
Influences on Me --- 310
Painting --- 312
Self-Organizing Teams -- 313
Conclusion --- 314
Discussion Questions -- 314

A.5 Odds and Ends -- 315
Project Complexity --- 315
Lean Principles -- 317
Agile Manifesto -- 319
Benefit/Cost Curves -- 320
Some Simple Statistics --- 322
Discussion Questions -- 325

A.6 Estimation Games -- 327
Various Scales --- 328
What to Compare --- 328
Affinity Analysis --- 329
Is It Just about Stories? -- 330

Why It Works -- 330

A Complicated Example-- 330

Summary-- 331

Discussion Questions --- 332

Index --- 333

List of Figures

Figure 1: Parts of a Process --3

Figure 2: The Scrum Team--9

Figure 3: The Basic Backlog --- 10

Figure 4: A Simplified View of a Release Cycle--------------------------- 12

Figure 5: The Fundamental Process Flow of Scrum is the Sprint ------------------- 13

Figure 6: The Scrum Team in its Organizational Context --------------------------- 18

Figure 7: The 'Product H-12' Organizational Structure---------------------- 37

Figure 8: The 'Product H-12' Leadership Team ------------------------------ 39

Figure 9: Two Project-Level Leadership Teams ----------------------------- 40

Figure 10: The ScrumMaster's Goal --- 44

Figure 11: The ScrumMaster's Modes --------------------------------------- 57

Figure 12: PO 'All Alone' -- 66

Figure 13: PO Paired with BO --- 66

Figure 14: Product Owners in a Hierarchy -------------------------------- 67

Figure 15: The Team 'Swarming' through Time -------------------------- 76

Figure 16: The 'complete' Backlog with Transitions--------------------- 93

Figure 17: Graphing the Progress of 'Buy an e-Ticket'------------------ 100

Figure 18: UML diagram of Backlog Terms ----------------------------- 101

Figure 19: A Work Breakdown Structure for the Catalina Air Project ---------- 106

Figure 20: Sample Coding Story with Agreement ---------------------- 137

Figure 21: Sample Analysis Story with Agreement -------------------- 139

Figure 22: Sample Infrastructure Story with Agreement------------- 140

Figure 23: Sample Research Story with Agreement ------------------- 141

Figure 24: Sample Agreement for an Epic---------------------------------- 143

Figure 25: Agreement for an Epic that is a 'large' Story --------------- 144

Figure 26: Effort Distribution for a High-Performing Team ---------- 152

Figure 27: Effort Distribution for a Team in Trouble ------------------ 153

Figure 28: the [coding] Storyotype-- 187

Figure 29: The [use case] Storyotype --------------------------------------- 188

Figure 30: A [backbone epic] Storyotype ---------------------------------- 189

Figure 31: An Analysis Storyotype-- 194

Figure 32: Another Analysis Storyotype ----------------------------------- 196

Figure 33: TaskHour BurnDown Graph ------------------------------------- 247

Figure 34: Doneness Checklist Item BuildUp Graph --------------------- 249

Figure 35: Checklist Item BurnDown Work-Around Graph --------------- 252

Figure 36: WIP as Front Burner -- 257

Figure 37: Stakeholders Go Through the Product Owner ------------------ 296

Figure 38: Evolution of Product Owner's Relationship with Team ---------------- 297
Figure 39: the Stacey Diagram --- 315
Figure 40: The Agile Manifesto -- 319
Figure 41: The '80/50 Curve' -- 320
Figure 42: The 'Standard' S-Shaped Curve --------------------------------------- 321
Figure 43: Beta Normalizes -- 323
Figure 44: Simple Stories --- 324
Figure 45: Estimation Cards --- 328

List of Tables

Table 1: The RASCI Matrix Applied to Scrum -- 23
Table 2: The Team Values --- 25
Table 3: The INVEST Criteria for 'Good' Stories ------------------------------------ 114
Table 4: Reasons a Backlog Item May Be an Epic ---------------------------------- 117
Table 5: Decomposing the 'Buy an e-Ticket' Epic into Stories -------------------- 119
Table 6: Data for TaskHour BurnDown Graph -------------------------------------- 246
Table 7: Data for Doneness Checklist Item BuildUp Graph ----------------------- 249
Table 8: Data for Checklist Item BurnDown Work-Around Graph --------------- 251
Table 9: Distributions for Simple, Straightforward, and Complex Stories ------- 322

About the Authors

 **Dan Rawsthorne** has developed software in an agile way since 1983. He has worked in many different domains, from e-commerce to military avionics. He has a PhD in Mathematics (number theory), is a retired Army Officer, and a Professional Bowler and Coach. Dan is very active in the Agile/Scrum community and speaks quite often at conferences and seminars. He is a transformation agent, coaching Organizations to become more successful through agility. His non-software background has helped him immeasurably in his coaching: his formal training in mathematics guides him to look for underlying problems rather than focus on surface symptoms; his military background helps him understand the importance of teamwork and empowerment; and his work with bowlers has helped him understand that coaching is a two-way street.

 **Doug Shimp** has worked in the technology field since 1992 and has played many key roles on software teams, including Coder, Tester, Analyst, Team Leader, Manager, Coach, and Consultant. Doug's passion is for team learning to improve product development, and he is a leader in the area of agile/Scrum transitions and applied practices. He believes that the core basis for applied agility is that *'You must see the result for it to be real; otherwise it is all just theory...'* Much of his experience with teamwork and agility comes from outside the software field, including an earlier career as an owner/manager of a painting company – which enabled him to learn about small-team dynamics in a very hands-on way.

Preface to Second Edition

There have been many conversations about Scrum since the first edition of this book was published in 2011. These conversations have resulted in a number of changes about how the agile community thinks about Scrum, and this new edition reflects those changes. Specifically, this edition is current up to July 2013, the date of the latest *Scrum Guide*.

Some of the significant changes include de-emphasizing the *'As a... I want... so that...'* form of writing a Story, further deprecation of BurnDowns (they no longer exist in the latest *Scrum Guide*), and the changing of the term 'Grooming' to 'Refinement.' In addition, the Velocity chapter has been improved to emphasize the notion of Ideal Effort.

Of course, we have also given the book a thorough scrubbing, from front to back, to clean up text, tighten up ideas, and generally make it a better read.

One of the lessons of agility is that *'people change what they want once they experience the product,'* and that lesson applies to this book, as well. Based on requests from readers, there are some upgrades to the book itself, notwithstanding the changes in Scrum. These changes include:

- Discussion questions have been added to each chapter,
- The Glossary has expanded to include even more agility-related terms,
- The Index has been substantially improved, and
- Purely cosmetic changes have been made to improve the reading experience.

The bottom line is that this book describes Modern Scrum; the most current description of Scrum available in late 2013. Based on the discussions we've been having in the Scrum community, we believe that this version will remain stable for a while.

We hope you enjoy the new edition of the book!

Dan Rawsthorne
Seattle, WA

Doug Shimp
Racine, Wisconsin

Acknowledgements
(for the First Edition)

We have been lucky enough to have worked closely with some of the best and smartest agilists in the world, and they have helped shape our ideas through collaborations, conversations, arguments, and even fights. These people include: Alan Shalloway, Rod Claar, Scott Bain, Jeff McKenna, Rob Myers, Michael James, Tamara Suleiman Runyon, Angela Druckman, Jimi Fosdick, Kane Mar, Tobias Meyer, and many others.

Other agile experts we have collaborated with and whose shoulders we have stood on include: Alistair Cockburn, Ken Schwaber, Ron Jeffries, Kent Beck, Johanna Rothman, Jeff Sutherland, Grady Booch, Rebecca Wirfs-Brock, Mike Cohn, and Ivar Jacobson. We apologize sincerely if your name should be here and it isn't.

Dan thanks his wife, Grace, and his children, Derek and Catherine, for putting up with his traveling and taking the time to write this book. He gives special thanks to Alan Shalloway, Victor Szalvay, and Laszlo Szalvay, for paying him to do the things he loves. And, finally, Dan wants to thank Tommi Johnstone, Katie Playfair, and the rest of the crew at CollabNet (formerly Danube), for providing the logistical support he needed to be able to write this book.

Doug gives big thanks to his wife, Shakila, who is the most socially aware person that he has ever known; and to his children, Nathan and Kiran, who remind him of the thousands of little lessons he learned growing up that he forgot about.

And, of course, ultimate thanks to the thousands of students and clients who have given us the opportunity to test our knowledge and theories in the crucible of reality.

Dan Rawsthorne
Federal Way, Washington

Doug Shimp
Racine, Wisconsin

Foreword by Ron Jeffries

It's not always easy to reach agreement with Dan Rawsthorne, unless you happen to agree right off with what he says, or come to agree with him later. He rarely changes his mind. I have sometimes considered taking physical action but since he towers over me, this, too, seems fruitless. Fortunately, we don't disagree often.

In this book, I find little to disagree with. Dan has put together the most consistent and clear description of what Scrum is, and how to do it, that I have seen. He hews closely to the line of what Scrum is, and is a master at showing you how to do Scrum *in* your situation, rather than compromise Scrum *to* your situation. When you finish this book, you'll have an understanding of how to put Scrum into practice in almost every situation you may encounter.

In many cases, Dan will have addressed exactly your situation. Even where he hasn't directly addressed your world, his many examples will equip you to make decisions like his. Those decisions will help you stay within the spirit of Scrum.

Of course Scrum is not the only 'Agile' method, only the most popular. To help you find the way, Dan addresses a number of variant approaches and practices, and his thoughts will help you adapt those into Scrum, rather than deviate from Scrum. I believe that for most teams, for a good long time, it's best to stay inside the Scrum boundaries, and Dan will show you how to do that.

Dan mentions and strongly recommends solid software technical practices to teams who are using Scrum to build software, and that's good. I wish he had had the time and space to cover the practices, and the reasons for them, in more detail. Given the book's chosen scope and the amount of space available, it's a good decision that he didn't. Let me just say here that probably the second most common cause of Scrum trouble that I see is insufficient attention to technical practices. Look beyond this book for deep information on those practices.

You're probably wondering now what the most common cause of trouble is. In my observations, the most common cause of 'Scrum' implementations getting in trouble is that they aren't really doing Scrum at all: they are doing something Scrum-like but are missing out on key aspects of Scrum. Often, but not always, this dysfunction revolves around the lack of an empowered Product Owner with a business focus. The good news is that Dan's book addresses just about any situation you are likely to encounter, and tells you how to deal with it. You still need the will to do Scrum, and you need to develop the skill to do it well. The guidance you need is here.

Those who know me know that I call things the way I see them. I am not one to heap praise where it is undeserved. This praise is deserved: Dan and Doug have written the best Scrum book I have seen.

Read it, heed it, and prosper.

Ron Jeffries
www.XProgramming.com

Foreword by Jeff McKenna

This book has been quite a journey for Dan and Doug. It has been seven years since Dan and I first talked about it, and the gestation has been worthwhile.

Even though the title says 'The Fundamentals,' this book is not about the basics. It really is about the fundamentals. It is about the core ideas and principles of Scrum and how they are applied. Dan and Doug bring crystal clarity to why things are the way they are in Scrum – why certain practices work and others do not.

It is easy to see Dan talking to you while you read. His experiences in his life, especially his military experience, shine through as he brings those experiences into the world of Scrum. Some of the, shall we say, shortcomings of Scrum are clarified with direct recommendations that address them. As an example, the discussion of the role and function of the work breakdown structure is clear and compelling. And it is beyond the concerns of basic Scrum.

Throughout the book, the roles and responsibilities of the participants of Scrum are clear and detailed. Dan and Doug have expanded the scope of these beyond basic Scrum to address real concerns in real projects. At the same time, there is no diminishment of the central function of the team and the importance, in fact the criticality, of the team's self-organization. Of particular importance is the aspect of team maturity which shapes team function and ability.

The early stages of Scrum adoption were centered around the team with a particular emphasis on the soft skills needed to have performant teams. As Scrum is being more widely adopted, the hard questions of work definition and accountability are emerging as serious topics. Dan and Doug's book is a strong indicator of where we need to go to accomplish more.

Jeff McKenna
www.agile-action.com

Foreword by Johanna Rothman

I first met Dan Rawsthorne at a Software Development conference years ago. He was talking about how he managed projects. He made sense. We talked and struck up a friendship.

Years passed. I focused on more general management and project management issues. Dan focused on more agile and Scrum-specific issues. We still met at conferences, and ranted and raved, had loud conversations, especially about technical debt, and kept influencing each other's thinking, especially about how to make large agile programs work.

So when Dan told me he was writing a book about Scrum, I thought that book would make sense. I was right. Then he told me he was writing with Doug Shimp. Well, I'd met Doug at an Amplifying Your Effectiveness conference, and was impressed with Doug's experience troubleshooting project problems back in the mid-2000's and thought this book would be great. I was right.

Scrum is easy to describe. It's a lot harder to get right. Dan and Doug have given you a gift. They have written a book where you can get Scrum right. They have taken their vast experience and condensed it into stories, guidelines, and tips so you do not have to make the same mistakes that their colleagues and clients have.

Don't agree with them? No problem. Try it your way. When that doesn't work, come back to the book. Try it their way. Why? Because Scrum is easy to describe. It's a lot harder to get right.

See, you have a secret weapon in your arsenal of tools and techniques to use for your transition to Scrum. You have all of Dan's and Doug's experiences in *Exploring Scrum*. You don't just have your training, and (if you're lucky) your onsite coach, and any blogs or articles you're reading. No, you also have access to the experience from two of the most experienced guys in the business. And, you have a book that's easy to read, understandable, and can help you see where you might go off course.

I especially like the pragmatic, down-to-earth advice about the Scrum-Master, Product Owner, Backlogs, Technical Debt, and Chores. Okay, so that's just about the entire book, and the usual places that Scrum teams encounter problems. Like I said, Scrum is easy to describe. It's much harder to do right.

I know plenty of teams who use Scrum terminology but do not really use Scrum. If you want to use Scrum and use it to release systems and products that work without much technical debt, read this book. Cover to cover. Study it. If you have a sprint and you discover something you want to improve during a retrospective – or even better, an intraspective – *Exploring Scrum* will help you diagnose and fix your Scrum problems.

Use Dan's and Doug's experience and tips to help you master your Scrum implementation. Because Scrum is easy to describe. But it's not easy – at all – to implement well. And Dan and Doug can help. Use their experience and this book. You will be very happy you did.

Johanna Rothman
Rothman Consulting Group, Inc.

Foreword by Jeff Sutherland

Dan and Doug's book, with its focus on getting the people, products, and practices aligned, can help the reader build more effective Scrum implementations. I think studying this book can help overcome the biggest challenges that have occurred in the last 10 years as agile practices (75% of which are Scrum) have become the primary mode of software development worldwide.

Ten years after the Agile Manifesto was published, some of the original signatories and a larger group of Agile thought leaders met at Snowbird, Utah, this time to do a retrospective on 10 years of Agile software development. They celebrated the success of the Agile approach to product development and reviewed the key impediments to building on that success. And they came to unanimous agreement on four key success factors for the next 10 years.

1. Demand technical excellence
2. Promote individual change and lead organizational change
3. Organize knowledge and improve education
4. Maximize value creation across the entire process

This book focuses on technical excellence of both the Scrum implementation and engineering practices. Its discussion of team formation and transformation of the way of work facilitates organizational change. Carefully following the guidance laid out here can maximize value creation across your organization.

Demand Technical Excellence

The key factor driving the explosion of the internet, and the applications on smartphones, has been deploying applications in short increments and getting rapid feedback from end users. This is formalized in agility by developing product in short sprints, always a month or less and most often two weeks in length. We framed this issue in the Agile Manifesto by saying that "we value working software over comprehensive documentation."

The 10 Year Agile Retrospective of the Manifesto concluded that the majority of agile teams are still having difficulty developing product in short sprints (usually because of testing issues) because the management, the business, the customers, and the development teams do not demand technical excellence.

Lack of READY Product Backlog

The Product Owner is accountable for working with stakeholders and customers to develop a product backlog that is broken down into small pieces, clear to the developers, immediately actionable, estimated in points by the team that will implement it, and testable – acceptance tests are clearly defined that determine whether a backlog item is done. A strong definition of done that is continuously improved is a hallmark of a high performing agile team.

As I travel the world the majority of Scrum developers tell me they do not have good product backlog. The role of the product owner is not clear, the grooming of the backlog is not sufficient, the management of the stakeholders by the products owners is not working, and the result is slow implementation combined with poor quality product.

Dan and Doug go carefully through these issues and explain them clearly. Following their lead will save you an enormous amount of pain.

Lack of DONE Product at the End of a Sprint

The sum of the points for the product backlog items that are done at the end of each sprint is the Velocity of the team. This is used by the product owner to build release plans and a product roadmap. It is used by the teams to access performance improvement. And it is used by management and boards of directors to access the accuracy of product development plans and impact on revenue.

Lack of ready product backlog makes it impossible to get software done at the end of a sprint. Poor engineering practices such as lack of testing during a sprint, poor configuration management, failure to implement continuous integration and automated testing, or avoiding pair programming or code reviews leads to software that is not done. If software is not done, significant delays occur.

Following Dan and Doug's guidelines will spare you this pain and radically reduce the cost of your software implementation, improve quality innovation, and enhance the work environment for all concerned.

Promote individual change and lead organizational change

Agile adoption requires rapid response to changing requirements along with technical excellence. This was the fourth principle of the Agile Manifesto – "respond to change over following a plan." However, *individuals* adapting to change is not enough. Organizations must be structured for agile response to change. If not, they prevent the formation of, or destroy, high performing teams because of failure to remove impediments that block progress.

Dan and Doug share a lot of insights on how to set up your organization so it does not cripple your Scrum teams. Follow their advice.

Failure to See Impediments

The Daily Scrum is designed to surface blocks or impediments so that the team can remove them. Often, individual team members are trying to work in isolation on individual stories. When this happens, large numbers of items are open, almost nothing is done, sprint failure is almost certain, yet team members will say they have no impediments working on their own little piece.

In this situation, the team is actually a group of isolated individuals – not working as a team – and they fail to see that they are their own biggest impediment. They need to collectively and individually change their behaviors in order to work as a team.

Dan and Doug describe how the Scrum team can work together to overcome this problem. The book has a lot of good coaching advice on how to start up teams and coach them through the early stages when seeing impediments and overcoming them is critical to get the organization off to a good start.

Tolerating Defects

A second major pattern of failure is a team not seeing any impediments, yet they have many open defects that are not quickly repaired. Industry data show that fixing bugs the same day as they are discovered will double the velocity of a team.

Scrum is a continuous process improvement approach to identifying and removing impediments to performance on a daily basis. Teams need to identify impediments in both the daily scrum and retrospectives and remove them quickly. As many as 80% of the impediments found require management help to remove. Management needs to understand agile development and participate fully in its success.

Dan and Doug repeatedly lay out guidelines in this book that will enable your teams to strive for technical excellence and show how leadership teams can aid in this transition. Following their advice will make the transition to Scrum fast and easy. Pay attention or it could be slow and painful.

ScrumMaster Not an Agent of Change

The ScrumMaster *owns* the process, is responsible for team performance, and must educate everyone involved on how to continuously improve by removing impediments. When the ScrumMaster finds an impediment outside the team that is impacting team performance, the ScrumMaster is responsible for education, training, and motivating people to take action. A good ScrumMaster is a catalyst for change in the organization. This responsibility is embodied in the work of Takeuchi and Nonaka that inspired Scrum.

Dan and Doug spend a lot of time explaining the varied responsibilities of a ScrumMaster and how their role evolves as a Scrum team matures. They can help your ScrumMasters become better agents of change.

Organize Knowledge and Improve Education

There is a large body of knowledge on teams and productivity that is relatively unknown to most managers and many developers. Dan and Doug help remedy that problem.

Software Development is Inherently Unpredictable

Few people are aware of Ziv's Law, that software development is unpredictable. The large failure rate on projects worldwide is largely due to lack of understanding of this problem and the proper approach to deal with it. Dan and Doug describe the need to inspect and adapt to constant change. Their strategies will help you avoid many pitfalls and remove many blocks to your Scrum implementation.

Users Do Not Know What they Want Until They See Working Software

Traditional project management erroneously assume that users know what they want before software is built. This problem was formalized as "Humphrey's Law" yet this law is systematically ignored in university and industry training of managers and project leaders. This book can help you work with this issue and avoid being blindsided.

The Structure of the Organization Will Be Embedded in the Code

A third example of a major problem that is not generally understood is "Conway's Law." The structure of the organization will be reflected in the code. A traditional hierarchical organizational structure will negatively impact object oriented design resulting in brittle code, bad architecture, poor maintainability and adaptability along with excessive costs and high failure rates. Dan and Doug spend a lot of time explaining how to get the Scrum organization right. Listen carefully.

Maximize value creation across the entire process

Agile practices can easily double or triple the productivity of a software development team if product backlog is ready and software is done at the end of a sprint. This will create problems in the rest of the organization. Their lack of agility will become obvious and cause pain.

Lack of Agility in Operations and Infrastructure

As soon as talent and resources are applied to improve product backlog the flow of software to production will as least double and in some cases be 5-10 times higher. This will expose the fact that development operations and infrastructure are crippling production and must be fixed.

Lack of Agility in Management, Sales, Marketing, and Product Management

At the front end of the process, business goals, strategies, and objectives are often not clear. This will result in a flat or decaying revenue stream even when production of software doubles.

For this reason, everyone in an organization needs to be educated and trained on how to optimize performance across the whole value stream. Agile individuals need to lead this educational process by improving their ability to organize knowledge and train the whole organization. Dan and Doug's work can facilitate this process.

The Bottom Line

Many Scrum implementations make only minor improvements and find it difficult to remove impediments that embroil them in constant struggle. Work can be better than this. All teams can be good and many can be great! Work can be fun, business can be profitable, and customers can be really happy!

If you are starting out, Dan and Doug can help you. If you are struggling along the way, they can help you even more. And if you are already great, Dan and Doug can help you be greater. Improvement never ends and their insight is truly helpful.

Jeff Sutherland
Scrum, Inc., MIT Cambridge Innovation Center, 2011

.

Section 1: Introduction

This book explores the fundamentals of Scrum when developing software. At its core, Scrum is a simple development framework allowing a *single*, co-located, cross-functional, self-organizing Team to build high-quality software in an incremental, agile manner. In this book we focus on this simple, constrained view of Scrum because organizations that can't do *at least* this much successfully have no business trying to do Scrum on a larger scale.

Therefore, we focus on this relatively small topic in this book, and leave the study of bigger things to later books...

This introductory section sets the tone for the book. It includes an overview of the book itself and a simple description of Scrum that provides context for the rest of the book.

$\boxed{1.1}$

About This Book

Why does this book exist? This is a good question, and I'll try to answer it here. This chapter should be read before you continue to use this book to help you explore Scrum.

This book concerns applying Scrum to software development. Each of us (Doug and Dan) have trained and coached thousands of people, most of whom are already using Scrum. In spite of the fact that they have read about Scrum, have been trained or coached in Scrum, and are using Scrum, their most common complaint is that they need help to do it right. And, I must say, many (if not most) of them need some help.[1]

This book is for them and others like them.

This book is *not* an introductory text. I assume that those who read this book know, or think they know, something about Scrum. This book takes a deep, exploratory look into the Scrum framework, and offers advice about how to use it. Some of this advice is philosophical, some is pragmatic, some is practical, and some of it is controversial.

The controversies happen because I try to be brutally consistent and true to the essence of Scrum. This book is *not* the result of an academic exercise; every suggestion or conclusion in this book is grounded in real-life issues I have encountered, and suggestions that I have made for teams and people I have coached or trained. It is my intention that this book should contain both pragmatic advice and the philosophical underpinnings justifying that advice.

What Scrum Is

Let's get as basic as we can. There are three parts to a software development process: the People, the Product, and the Practices. As seen in Figure 1, these three things are related in a simple equation: *People use Practices to develop Product.* Our under-

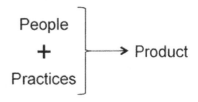

Figure 1: Parts of a Process

---

[1] The singular pronoun will be used from this point on, throughout this book, to indicate that Dan, or Doug, or both, are speaking. If we intend to differentiate, we will do so explicitly. In addition, the pronouns "you", "us", and "we" are used to include the reader in the conversation.

standing of the relationships amongst these three things shapes how we think about development. For example, in agile development there is a preference for People over Practices, and in standard development we often imagine that there is a preference for Practices over People.

Similarly, Lean principles tell us that Product should be developed by thinking from a user's point of view rather than a developer's – this is often referred to as the Pull, don't Push principle[2]. This, coupled with the People over Practices preference, gives us the proper mindset, or point of view, for using Scrum. Unfortunately, many people don't yet have this mindset. In fact, many people have exactly the opposite beliefs: a preference for Practices over People and the belief that a Product is *pushed* through the pipeline by the Practices.

Scrum is a development framework that is very demanding of its adherents. Scrum is easy to understand, but doing it successfully (one might even say 'right') is very difficult. Scrum requires a mental shift in the way people think of the relationships between People, Product, and Practices. It requires changes in 'process personality' – especially changes about how people think of themselves as members of a team, and how they think of their product and its production. Some of the beliefs (including the above) that Scrum requires are:

- A preference for People over Practices; understanding that solving complex[3] problems requires brainpower, not recipes;

- An understanding that the best Products are developed by having a Focus on User's Needs rather than relying on a requirements document;

- The acceptance that Reality Trumps Expectations, so when reality and expectations don't match, it is the expectations that must change;

- The preference for Self-Organizing Teams over either lone-wolf-ism or tightly controlled management; and

- The realization that each of us is part of a Team developing Product and that we are not simply People doing Work.

Scrum is such a *simple* framework that there are significant arguments about what it is. This is not surprising, as it is hard to separate the description of the framework from descriptions of particular implementations. Not only that, but Scrum is an ever-evolving framework – evolving over the years so

---

[2] The Pull, don't Push principle is discussed in the 'Lean Principles' section of Appendix A.5.

[3] The notions of Simple, Complicated, Complex, and Chaotic projects are discussed in the 'Project Complexity' section of Appendix A.5.

that its pieces and parts become more balanced and harmonious. And, just to make it more confusing, it is a part of the Scrum framework itself that a particular implementation *should* be changed based on the Team's (and Product's) needs and the realities it encounters.

Sometimes a Scrum Team's practices change *so much* it is hard to recognize that it is still a Scrum Team. This is because the simple Practices contained in the Scrum framework are merely 'training wheels'; their purpose is to be *barely* good enough to allow the Team to change its mental muscle memory while it is successfully developing Product. The main point of the Practices in the framework is to allow the Team to develop a 'scrummish personality' – to develop its mental agility. Once the Team has developed its scrummish personality, then it *modifies* its Practices to improve the way it works.

This is an interesting notion – the notion that Scrum requires a Team to change the way it works in order to improve. I have often wondered what the soul of Scrum is – what must be there for the Team to still be doing Scrum? I have decided that when I look at a Team and am determining if it is scrummish I am looking for the following:

- Self-organization and the ScrumMaster role;

- Strict accountability and the Product Owner role;

- Respect for the Product; and

- Agility in all things.

If I see these traits, then I'm looking at a Scrum Team. If I don't, then I'm not – but I may be looking at a Team that is *trying* to become a Scrum Team. I don't expect you to completely understand what I mean by these statements yet; helping you understand them is a significant goal of this book...

Purpose of Book

The *main* purpose of this book is to explore Scrum so that you can understand how to make Scrum work for you – what changes *you* need to make – and to give guidance about how to make the changes. There are five sections of this book, and they are presented in order of importance:

- **Introduction**: This section sets the tone for the book. It includes this introductory chapter and another containing a simple description of Scrum.

- **People**: Scrum focuses primarily on people. In particular, Scrum focuses on the Scrum Team and how it relates to the Organization and its Clients, Users, and Customers. This section discusses roles, responsibilities, values, and how people work together.

- **Product**: The Team is often producing Software, but it's not quite that simple. This section discusses the Product; complexities of the Backlog; Technical Debt; different kinds, types, and sizes of work that need to be done; prioritizing, sizing, and estimating the work; and how to know when you're done.

- **Practices**: The Practices are the *least* important part of the Scrum framework. This section describes the Practices *just well enough* to make a Team successful while its mental muscle memory changes to become mentally agile, and also describes several workarounds, tips, and tricks. With the exception of the Kanban chapter, this section contains guidance and corrects misperceptions about the basic Scrum Practices.

- **Appendices**: There are several appendices containing additional or optional material, including a glossary and discussions of Dan's and Doug's personal journeys and experiences with Scrum.

Ken Schwaber, who co-developed Scrum with Jeff Sutherland, wrote (or co-wrote) all of the seminal books about Scrum, and I use his writings as the jumping-off point for exploring Scrum in this book. In particular, the following three books (and two pamphlets) are referenced throughout.

[SB] Ken Schwaber and Mike Beedle, *Agile Software Development with Scrum*, Prentice-Hall, 2002.

[S1] Ken Schwaber, *Agile Project Management with Scrum*, Microsoft Press, 2004.

[S2] Ken Schwaber, *The Enterprise and Scrum*, Microsoft Press, 2007.

[SS] Ken Schwaber and Jeff Sutherland, *Scrum*, February 2010.

[SG] Ken Schwaber and Jeff Sutherland, *The Scrum Guide,* July 2013.

Each of these sources describes a slightly different version of Scrum (since Scrum evolved through time), but the essence of Ken's thoughts about Scrum shines through all of them.

My Goal

My goal in this book is to remain true to the essence of Scrum as I find it in Ken's books, in my discussions with other Scrum experts, and in the Teams that I work with. This book explores the framework of Scrum, and gives advice about what to do and how to do it within the framework. I have worked very hard to assure that the advice is logically consistent throughout the book. With the exception of chapter 4.7 (the Kanban(ish) Variant), everything in this book fits within the current framework of Scrum – that chapter is an extension that *only* applies to mature teams that already have scrummish personalities.

Scrum's 'out of the box' practices are *just good enough* to allow for successful development while changing the Individual's, Team's and Organization's mental muscle memories to become more scrummish – to develop their mental agility. Once their mental muscle memory has changed, then Scrum can be adapted for that Team or Organization. Many highly mature Scrum Teams follow a process that doesn't resemble 'by the book' Scrum very much – they have evolved the practices as they matured – but I can still see the essence of Scrum shining through.

However, pre-emptive optimization of Scrum (the *'that won't work here, so we will...'* kind of thinking) is the enemy, as it *almost always* means that the Organization is trying to 'do Scrum' before obtaining the scrummish personality – and thus losing Scrum's soul. This defeats the purpose of Scrum, and leads to doing Scrum "with waterfall goggles on."[4]

The simple framework already has lots of 'wiggle room' and this is largely what I explore. This book contains in-depth discussions and analysis of how to use the framework for real-life problems that arose from talking with my clients and students. It also contains pragmatic, explicit advice about how to do some particular things.

How to Use This Book

This book contains a series of short chapters, each with a fairly small, specific focus. My fondest dream is that this book will be used by reading and study groups who will discuss the book one chapter at a time. In order to aid these discussion we have included a few discussion questions at the end of each chapter. These questions are intended to be challenging and help you with your exploration of Scrum – so please don't skip them! This book is also useful for Coaches and Teams, as each of the chapters discusses one or two specific issues that they are likely to run into while practicing Scrum.

Many things are explicitly 'out of scope' for this book. This book is about basic, simple Scrum, so extending Scrum to large teams or projects is not included. Detailed guidance about Release Planning and sophisticated metrics is also missing, as well as requirements elicitation and analysis. These are advanced practices that are only useful to Teams that already have a scrummish personality, and I hope to have future books on these topics.

---

[4] A quote I got from one of my students.

Technical Development practices are also out of scope for this book, but they are occasionally referenced. I am a big fan of eXtreme Programming (XP) practices (and others like them), but I don't deal with these topics in any depth as they are adequately handled elsewhere.

Finally, I must say something about my writing style. As I have already mentioned, the words "I" and "me" refer to the authors (either Dan, Doug, or both), the word "you" refers to the reader, and the words "we" and "us" are used to draw the reader into the discussion.

In addition, I have a liberal interpretation of the rules of grammar and punctuation; I want my writing to reflect how I speak and make myself understood. Therefore, I capitalize technical terms, use lots of dashes, parenthetical expressions, ellipses, 'air quotes' (especially when introducing new phrases or words), and I might even throw in an emoticon or two – just sayin'... ;-)

SirJeff's Problem

Throughout this book I use a common development project to provide examples. This project is the building of a website for a boutique airline, Catalina Air. This airline is owned and operated by Sir Geoffrey Smithers (SirJeff) who is a multi-millionaire who made his money developing software in the Silicon Valley.

SirJeff likes to fly, and since retiring from developing software, he has been flying tourists around southern California and adjacent areas, with primary stops such as Burbank, Orange County, Catalina Island, Las Vegas, and so on. He has decided that he is going to buy four more planes, hire some pilots, and start a 'real' airline that focuses on the high-end tourist trade.

He has hired us (you and me and our company) to build his website for him. Whenever I need an example I'll hearken back to this project to find one. I assume that you know something about airline websites, and I'll just make up what I need as I go along.

Discussion Questions

1. What is the 'scrummish' personality and what might it look like in your organization?

2. What are the differences between a 'push' process and a 'pull' process? Find examples based on your experience.

3. Why is a simple framework so hard to describe and understand?

Scrum in a Nutshell

Scrum is about Teams developing complex Products in an agile way. Scrum Teams start with a simple framework and set of rules. Here is a short description of a Team using Scrum that sets the stage for what follows in this book.

Scrum is a very simple framework for agile development. Here is a quick overview of Scrum in action, which I present so that we can all have the same basic understanding of Scrum. This understanding will be explored and refined throughout this book.

The Team

The fundamental element of Scrum is the Scrum Team (Team), as seen in Figure 2 in its basic Organizational context. The Scrum Team is a small

Figure 2: The Scrum Team

(usually between three and ten) group of people that provides useful Products and Results for Stakeholders. The Team and others involved in Scrum are discussed in Section 2 of this book.

Arguably, the most important role involved in Scrum is the Stakeholder, as the Stakeholders are the ones who have desires, wants, and needs, and are the reason the Team is developing the Product and producing Results in the first place. There is a special Stakeholder, called the Business Owner (BO), who is often the Team's Sponsor or Champion and manages the budget for the Team.

While the Stakeholders are the most important people from the Product's perspective, the most important person on the Scrum Team is the Product Owner (PO). The Product Owner works with the Stakeholders, represents their interests to the Team, and is the sole team member held accountable for the value of the Team's Work Results. The Product Owner guides the Team to build Products that satisfy the Stakeholders' needs, wants, and desires. The Product Owner provides direction and goals for the Team, and prioritizes what will be worked on.

The Scrum Team Members (TMs) are the people that actually do the work that satisfies the goals and priorities the Product Owner has set for them. All Team Members are accountable to the rest of the Team for their perform-ance, even as the Product Owner is accountable to the Stakeholders for the Team's performance. The Scrum Team is cross-functional; that is, people on the Team (collectively) have all the skills and knowledge necessary to do the work (analysis, design, code, test, documentation, marketing plan, drawings, etcetera – whatever is required for the desired outcome). The Team is self-organizing and constantly trying to improve itself. The Team is value-driven; its conduct is largely based on values, not practices. The Team works on the priorities the Product Owner has set, and the Team practices its due diligence to do this work without undue influence from the Product Owner.

There is a role on the Team called the ScrumMaster (SM), who aids the Team in doing its work. The ScrumMaster is accountable to the business for the Team's proper use of Scrum. The ScrumMaster's responsibilities are to be a facilitator, moderator, and coach, with particular emphasis on helping the Team mature in its self-organization. The ScrumMaster helps manage the relationship between the Product Owner and the rest of the Team, and facilitates removal of impediments for the Team – often working with the Product Owner, the Business Owner, and other Stakeholders to do so. Impediments can come from either within the Team or outside the Team. The ScrumMaster understands the Scrum framework and how the Team is using it, recommends improvements in teamwork and practices, and assures that the Team Members are following the practices they have agreed to.

The Backlog

A Scrum Team's work is managed with a Product Backlog (Backlog), which is a collection of Product Backlog Items (Items). These Items represent the stakeholders' needs and wants – each of them is a request for something of value to be provided by the Scrum Team. These requests can be for *anything*, including software functionality, help with marketing, non-functional requirements, technical and infrastructure requests, business support, maintenance of existing systems, and so on. The Backlog

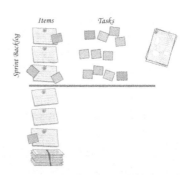

Figure 3: The Basic Backlog

and other Scrum topics involving the Team's Product are discussed in Section 3 of this book.

It is a rule of Scrum that the Team shouldn't do *anything* for *any* Stakeholder unless it's on the Backlog. The Team will be actively working on the top few items of the Backlog during the Sprint; this part of the Backlog is called the Sprint Backlog, which is often thought of as a separate list of its own. The Product Owner is accountable for prioritizing the Backlog and the Team is responsible for forecasting how many Items as it can do in a Sprint – thus creating the Sprint Backlog. From the Team's view, the Product Backlog is work that it might do *someday* and the Sprint Backlog is work the Team forecasts it can work on *now* – in the current Sprint.

The Backlog contains Items at *all* levels of fidelity, from vague wishes, wants, or needs to finely detailed requirements. The higher the priority of the Item, the more detailed the request needs to be, so that it will be ready for planning and execution – we call these 'Ready' Items[1].

When a Scrum Team starts a new project, the Product Owner should initiate the Backlog by working with the Stakeholders and other Team Members to capture their needs, wants, desires, and requirements as Backlog Items.

As the work progresses, the Product Owner and the Scrum Team should work with the Stakeholders *continuously* to prioritize the Backlog, identify new Items, eliminate noise, and refine and clean up the Items on the list to get them ready for Planning. This process is called Backlog Refinement, and must be done continuously because the Team's work often exposes new information that clarifies existing Items and identifies new ones.

Now that I have described the notion of the Backlog, let me describe a simple Scrum implementation, which involves discussion of Releases and Sprints.

The Release

The purpose of a Scrum Team that is working on a software *project* is to produce and release Product[s] that meet the goals and priorities that have been determined by the Product Owner by working with Stakeholders. Maintenance Teams can also use Scrum, but their Scrum implementation usually only contains Sprints that release updates, and not formal Releases.

Often, before a project formally begins, the project is given a Charter and there is a Visioning phase, when the Business Owner, Product Owner, and the Stakeholders produce a Product Vision and a Product Roadmap. The Charter 'gives permission' for the project to proceed, the Vision provides the overall focus for the Project, and the Roadmap gives guidance about Releases and their Goals. Even though they are very important, Chartering, Visioning, Roadmapping, and Release Planning are not a part of Scrum (see [SG]) and thus are not covered in any detail in this book.

---

[1] Ready does not imply *excessive* detail, but instead refers to *enough* detail. The Team, working with the PO, will determine how much detail that is.

The Scrum Team's purpose is to release Results satisfying the Stakeholders' needs, wants, and desires. Once the Visioning phase is over, the steps of a Release are relatively simple, as seen in Figure 4.

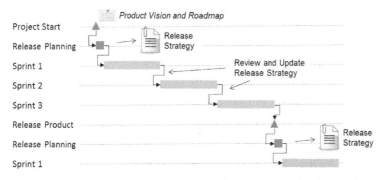

Figure 4: A Simplified View of a Release Cycle

Usually, the first thing that happens in a Release is Release Planning. The Stakeholders, the Product Owner, and (possibly) other members of the Team, get together and negotiate what should be accomplished in the Release. This negotiation takes the Product Vision and Roadmap into account, balances the needs and wants of the Stakeholders against the abilities of the Scrum Team, and the result is a set of Release Goals and a Release Strategy to achieve them. The Product Owner and Team must update the Backlog so that there are prioritized Items on the Backlog that support the Release Goals and Strategy and are being prepared for Planning.

Once the Team has a Backlog that supports the Release Goals and Strategy, the Team starts Sprinting. Each Sprint is a short, fixed-length time-box within which the Team works on Items. The idea is for the Team to do as many Sprints as the Release Strategy calls for, and then Release the Product. Each Sprint looks basically the same, but specialized Release Activities may be included as part of the last one.

The Sprint

The fundamental process flow of Scrum is the Sprint (Figure 5), which is a relatively short, fixed-length, period of time in which Backlog Items are converted into reviewable products the Stakeholders can provide feedback on. Most of the Practices discussed in Section 4 are about issues that occur in Sprints.

The first thing done in a Sprint is Sprint Planning. In Sprint Planning the Product Owner works with the Team to forecast what Backlog Items the Team should do in the Sprint in order to support the Release Goals and Strategy. Each of these Items has an agreed-upon meaning of Done, and collectively these Items are called the Team's Sprint Backlog. It is the

ScrumMaster's responsibility to assure that the Team forecasts a realistic amount of work without undue influence from the Product Owner.

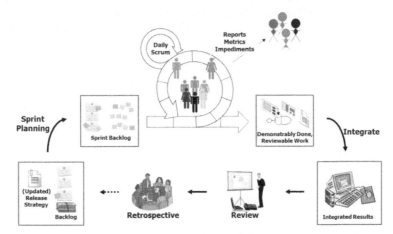

Figure 5: The Fundamental Process Flow of Scrum is the Sprint

Often, the Items on the Sprint Backlog are tasked out in order to give the Team confidence that it can do the Items, and thus agree to them. After forecasting the Items they can do, the Team and the Product Owner jointly agree to a single Sprint Goal that defines Success for the Sprint, and the Product Owner advertises this Sprint Goal to the Stakeholders.

It is important to note that the Team has *committed* to the Goal, but merely *agreed* to the Items; this provides a different 'sense of urgency' or 'criticality' for each of them. The idea is that the Goal defines Success and has been *promised* to the Stakeholders by the Team, while the Team is merely agreeing to *try their best* to get all the forecasted Items Done. This difference in criticality provides a measure of safety to the Team and allows it to do its due diligence without feeling pressured into producing Technical Debt.

Once Sprint Planning is over, the Team does work in the Sprint. The Team self-organizes to do the work and manages itself as it does the work. The Team's work pattern is often described as Swarming and can look chaotic from the outside. The Team's daily work is focused on getting Items Done while driving towards the Sprint Goal.

While the Sprint is in progress the Team has Daily Scrums that allow each Team Member to understand what the Team's status is and to enable the Team to re-organize for the work at hand. This re-organization usually occurs *after* the Daily Scrum (but can be thought of as an *extension* of the discussion), and it allows the Team to be as effective and efficient as possible.

During the Daily Scrum, and continuously throughout the day, the Team Members notify the ScrumMaster of any impediments they encounter. It is the ScrumMaster's responsibility to facilitate the removal of these impediments. Often, this requires working with Team Members, the Product Owner, the Business Owner, and other Stakeholders. The ScrumMaster must also ensure that the Team does enough Backlog Refinement to be prepared for the next Sprint's Sprint Planning session.

When the Sprint is over there is a Product Review, when the Product Owner and the Team review the Team's Results with their Stakeholders. This is done for three reasons: to *prove* to the Stakeholders that the Team is moving in the right direction, to get *feedback* from the Stakeholders about what they've done, and to *discuss* the next Sprint's Goal with the Stakeholders.

If necessary, the Release Goals, Release Strategy, and Backlog are updated as part of the Review (or soon thereafter), taking into account the Review and any changes in business reality the Stakeholders may have. When Projects or Organizations are small they can rely on intuitive reasoning to determine what the right direction is; however, as they get bigger they may see a need for more sophisticated techniques (including metrics, perhaps) to help them discover what to do next.

After the Product Review, the Team has an internal Retrospective to analyze its performance and practices. The Team, facilitated by the ScrumMaster, decides what changes, if any, it wishes to make to its practices based on this analysis. It is the ScrumMaster's responsibility to help the Team 'live up to' these decisions in future Sprints.

At this point the Sprint is complete, and the Team either begins the next Sprint, the next Release, the next Project, or disbands, as appropriate.

Discussion Questions

1. Scrum is a framework for developing complex products. What does it mean for something to be complex?

2. The Product Owner guides the Team to build products that satisfy the stakeholders needs, wants and desires. How does the Product Owner do this since we know that '*People do not know what they want until they experience your working product?*'

3. What does a cross-functional Team look like? How do cross-functional Teams work if they lack skill or knowledge needed for a Backlog Item?

4. Discuss what is meant by the quote: '*It is important to note that the Team has committed to the Goal, but merely agreed to the Items.*'

5. Release Planning, Project Management, and Scaling are not part of the Scrum framework, even though we often need to do them in our Organizations. Discuss what it might mean to do them in a 'scrummish' way.

Section 2: The People

The People are the most important part of the Scrum framework. If you don't understand how the roles are defined and how they balance and complement each other, you can't harness the power of Scrum.

Managing a project in Scrum is a *whole* Team effort: the Product Owner is responsible for maximizing the value of the Team's Product[s]; the ScrumMaster is responsible for the process being followed correctly; the Team Members are responsible for doing the best work they can do while working at a Sustainable Pace; and Stakeholders and other outsiders empower the Product Owner, help remove impediments, and provide the knowledge, feedback, and environment necessary to allow the Team to succeed.

In this section I explore the roles and responsibilities of the people in Scrum, and discuss how they work together.

2.1

The Scrum Team

*In this chapter I discuss the Scrum Team – the people who
actually do the work and develop the Product. The Scrum Team
is the basic building block in an Organization using Scrum*

A Scrum Team's mission is simple: to produce valuable Work Results, which for historical reasons are often referred to as 'Product' (I will use the terms interchangeably). A Scrum Team is made up of people with skills, not people playing roles. A Scrum Team is relatively small, usually having between three and ten people, although larger (and smaller) teams are sometimes necessary. The Scrum Team is self-organized and cross-functional, which is a fancy way of saying that the Team figures out how to do its work, manages itself as it does the work, and has all the skills it needs to get the work Done.

I discuss the basics about the Scrum Team in this chapter. This includes the roles and positions found on (and surrounding) the Team, what it means to be self-organizing and cross-functional, and the Values that the Team (and the people surrounding the Team) should have.

Overview

The Scrum Team is the fundamental development unit of Scrum, and it is important to realize that development in Scrum is about a Team developing Product, not People doing Work. This is an important realization because teams are more effective and efficient at solving difficult problems than individuals are, especially when the team members are sensitive to each other's emotions and needs and when they take turns speaking[1]. These behaviors are expected of Scrum Team Members, are an intrinsic part of the Team's self-organization, and are facilitated by the ScrumMaster.

A Scrum Team can only be understood within its organizational context. In order to simplify things, I look at the Scrum Team in a very simple and straightforward way, as seen in Figure 6. I also imagine the Team as a single entity, with the Product Owner as its head, and the ScrumMaster as its heart. It's a silly metaphor, but it works for me.

---

[1] Anita Williams Woolley, Christopher F. Chabris, Alex Pentland, Nada Hashmi, Thomas W. Malone, "Evidence for a Collective Intelligence Factor in the Performance of Human Groups," *SCIENCE*, 29 October 2010, VOL 330, pgs. 686-688.

The primary role on a Scrum Team is that of a Team Member, and there are five other roles for people involved in Scrum: two that are on the Team (Product Owner and ScrumMaster), and three that surround the Team (Business Owner, Stakeholder, and Subject Matter Expert).

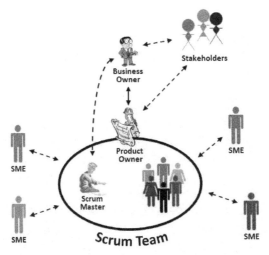

Figure 6: The Scrum Team in its Organizational Context

Each of these six roles is vital, and can be summarized quickly:

- Team Members (TMs) develop Quality Product at a Sustainable Pace,

- The Product Owner (PO) drives the Team and is accountable to the Business for the value of the Team's Work Results,

- The ScrumMaster (SM) is responsible for helping the Team improve through the use of Scrum,

- The Business Owner (BO) represents the Business and helps the Product Owner work with the Stakeholders,

- The Stakeholders (SHs) have the needs and wants the Team is trying to satisfy through developing Product, and

- The Subject Matter Experts (SMEs) have knowledge and expertise the Team needs but doesn't have on the Team.

Let me discuss these roles in more detail.

Team Members

Everyone on the Scrum Team is called a Team Member, which simply means that *every* member of the Scrum Team is responsible for the production of the Team's Products. There are no specialized *development* roles in Scrum; Scrum does not distinguish between Coders, Testers, Analysts, Usability

Experts, and so on. Every Team Member is simply that, a member of the Team; and each Team Member has the same primary goal – to work with the rest of the Team to do their due diligence and produce Quality Results at a Sustainable Pace.

Because the Team is seen as a single unit that works together, it needs to be small. The basic rules of Scrum say that the size of the Team should be 7±2, and I have found that the sweet spot is five people, because my experience is that this is the largest number of people that can be involved in a single conversation. However, the rules of Scrum also say that the Team should have every skill that it needs to have in order to develop its product [SG, pg. 5, for example]. These rules clash in two different ways:

- First, the Product the Team is building may require so many different skill sets that the Team needs more than nine (7+2) people. This is a reality many Organizations face, and causes a self-organization issue the Team must deal with – perhaps by having big Teams or by splitting Teams – and each Organization must deal with it in its own way.

- Second, there might not be enough skilled people to go around, so not every Team can actually have *all* the skills it needs within its (full-time) Team Members. Since this is so common I introduce the role of the Subject Matter Expert (SME).

The Team Members also have common secondary goals – to be good Team Members and to help the Team become a better Team. Scrum Teams *live* the Team Values, are self-organizing, and cross-functional. Each of these topics is discussed later in this chapter.

Other Scrum Team Roles

Everyone on the Scrum Team is a Team Member; Scrum has no specialized *development* roles. However, two of these Team Members have specialized *leadership* roles: the Product Owner and the ScrumMaster. These roles are central to the Scrum framework, and I'll discuss them now.

Product Owner

Every member of the Scrum Team plays the role of Team Member, but there is one (and only one) Team Member who is *accountable* to the Business for the success of the Team – for the value of the Team's Work Results[2]. This person is called the Product Owner (PO), and is the Team's formal point-of-contact with the 'outside world.'

---

[2] This is the most current definition of the Product Owner; see [SS, pg.4]. Appendix A.2 has a discussion of how the Product Owner role has been defined and redefined through the years.

Team Members are responsible for doing their due diligence and producing Quality Results at a Sustainable Pace, and the Product Owner's job is to make sure the Product the Team is developing is the 'right' one. In particular, it is the Product Owner's responsibility to balance the Team's Sustainable Pace with the Stakeholders' expectations of when the Results will be delivered. This requires that the Product Owner work with the Stakeholders and the Business Owner (as the Stakeholders' representative) to constantly scope the Product and negotiate delivery dates in order to 'make it fit.'

Since the Product Owner is accountable for the Team's Results, the Product Owner must be empowered to make sure that the Team has everything it needs to be successful. This means that the Product Owner must make sure the *right* Stakeholders are available to provide meaningful feedback, that *appropriate* SMEs are available to work with the Team, that the Team has an *adequate* development environment, and so on. Of course, this means that the Product Owner must work closely with the ScrumMaster and the rest of the Team to determine what is necessary, and also work with the Business Owner and other outsiders to make sure it is available.

The title Product Owner is a bit misleading, as it leads people to think that the Product Owner must be the expert on the Product, work with the Stakeholders, write the Stories, prioritize the work, and so on. It would be *nice* if the Product Owner had the knowledge and skills to do all these things, but there is *no guarantee* that this is the case – the Product Owner is defined by his or her accountability, not skill set. Because the Product Owner is not superhuman, it is the Team's responsibility to provide the Product Owner with *all* the information needed to make good decisions.

As a Team Member, the Product Owner has skills to use just like anybody else; the Product Owner is part of the self-organizing Team that gets high-value, high-quality, Products out the door. The only thing special about the Product Owner is the 'accountability thing' – which is quite a thing...

Chapter 2.2 is dedicated to the Product Owner, so I won't go into any more detail here.

ScrumMaster

While the Product Owner is the person who is accountable to the Business for the Team's Results, the ScrumMaster is accountable for making sure that Scrum is used correctly, that the Team uses Scrum in a positive way, and that the Team is constantly improving its use of Scrum. The ScrumMaster is a servant leader; leading by paying attention and reacting to the needs of the Team Members, the Team and the Organization.

ScrumMasters do not have managerial authority, but can assert moral authority when they need to. A ScrumMaster helps the Team and Organization get better by focusing attention on improving Team behaviors and working relationships. Because the ScrumMaster is a servant leader without managerial authority, Scrum requires that the ScrumMaster be a different person than the Product Owner [SS, pg. 7].

Since it is the Team's job to develop valuable Results, it is also the Team's job to deal with the constraints and impediments that arise when doing that. I can't remember where I heard this, but a great quote about this is: "if you don't deal with your constraints, they will certainly deal with you." Helping the Team deal with its constraints and impediments is one of the Scrum-Master's primary responsibilities.

The ScrumMaster is often a single person, especially on new Teams. However, as teams mature it is common for the ScrumMaster's respons-ibilities to be shared by multiple Team Members; and very mature teams may have diffused the ScrumMaster role to the point where the Scrum-Master is not easily identifiable – in that case I say that there is a little bit of ScrumMaster inside every Team Member.

Chapters 2.3 and 2.4 are dedicated to the ScrumMaster, so I won't go into more detail right now.

Roles External to the Team

As you can see in Figure 6, there are three roles for people surrounding the Scrum Team: Business Owner (BO), Stakeholder (SH), and Subject Matter Expert (SME). The following discussions are simplifications of these roles, but provide a solid basis for understanding them.

Business Owner

The role of Business Owner is used in order to discuss the Scrum Team's relationship with its Organization. The Business Owner refers to the person (or people) the Product Owner is (directly) accountable to for the Team's Work Results, and who often provides resources and assistance to the Team.

Both the ScrumMaster and the Product Owner have a relationship with the Business Owner. The ScrumMaster works with the Business Owner in order to help manage organizational impediments and constraints so that the Team can be more productive. The Product Owner works with the Business Owner in order to:

- Determine the priority of up-coming work in the Backlog;
- Consolidate the disparate needs of the Stakeholders;
- Modify the Release Plan as necessary; and
- Get resources for the Team.

The Business Owner is often thought of as the main (or lead) Stakeholder for the Team. As we'll see in chapter 2.3, in large Organizations there is often a hierarchy of Product Owners and, in that case, the Business Owner is usually the Product Owner's Product Owner.

Stakeholder

Stakeholders are the reason a Scrum Team develops Product in the first place; it is the Stakeholders that have the needs, wants, and desires that the Team is trying to satisfy with the work it is doing. Stakeholders are vital to the Team's success, as they review the Team's Product and provide ongoing feedback. There are many people that are interested in the Product, but not all of them are Stakeholders – some are merely interested bystanders.

The classic definition of Stakeholders is that they are people with 'legitimate interests' in the project. I have a tough time defining 'legitimate,' so I have a more pragmatic definition. I say that Stakeholders are people who should not be ignored; they are people who can have a negative impact on the Team if they are not attended to.

In this book I usually use the word Stakeholder (capital "S") to mean stakeholders that are *external* to the Team; it is true that Team Members are also stakeholders, but they are usually not the ones I am discussing or worried about.

Subject Matter Expert (SME)

Subject Matter Experts (SMEs) are people, external to the Team, with special knowledge or skills that the Team needs in order to do its work. They are a special sort of Stakeholder, and many Stakeholders are also SMEs. Each Scrum Team is supposed to have *all* the skills it needs within its Team Members, but this is often impossible – so the Team must work with external SMEs.

SMEs can have knowledge in technical or business areas. They can be experts on the Stakeholder needs (they could even be the Stakeholders with the needs), or they could have technical skills such as architecture, database, or user interface expertise. Whatever… all I know is that the Team needs their knowledge, but they're not on the Team.

SMEs work with Team Members to provide missing expertise, but since they are not on the Team, SMEs can be neither responsible nor accountable to the Product Owner for the work they do – they don't work for the Product Owner. This fact creates some interesting problems when working with SMEs, and this issue is discussed in chapter 2.5..

Relationship Matrix

The six roles I have discussed cause an interesting community of interactions. The following matrix, a RASCI[3] matrix, summarizes their relationships with each other with regard to the work the Team agrees to do.

Table 1: The RASCI Matrix Applied to Scrum

R esponsible	Team Members are *Responsible* for doing the work the Team has agreed to do and for providing the Product Owner with the information needed to make good decisions.
A ccountable	The Product Owner is the *only* Team member *Accountable* to the Business for the Products the Team builds and for the work the Team has agreed to do.
S upportive	The ScrumMaster is *Supportive* of the Team by facilitating its self-organization, coaching about Scrum, helping the Team remove its impediments, and so on...
C onsulted	External Subject Matter Experts (SMEs) are *Consulted* by Team Members if necessary. The SMEs are neither Responsible nor Accountable for work the Team has agreed to do.
I nformed	All external Stakeholders and the Business Owner are kept *Informed* of what the Team has agreed to do, and the progress the Team is making.

This matrix is intended to give a broad overview and summary of the relationships involved in Scrum. I find that discussing it with the Team and the Organization can help everyone understand the dynamics within and around a Scrum Team.

The RASCI matrix in Table 1 describes the relationships with regard to the work the Team agrees to do; that is, it is only about the Team's production. There are two other Accountabilities on the Scrum Team, as well:

- Each Team Member is *Accountable* to the other Team Members (to the Team) for living the Team Values (discussed later in this chapter), following the Team's agreed-to Practices, making their own agreements and commitments, and developing Quality Results; and

- The ScrumMaster is *Accountable* to the Business to teach Scrum to the Team, facilitate the Team's self-organization, help the Team manage its impediments, and assure that the Team follows its own, agreed-to, process.

Since the Team's process is inherently malleable through retrospection (see chapter 2.3), these relationships are only intended as a guide – the realities of a Team will vary based on Team norms, culture, and so on. However, I

---

[3] The RASCI matrix is often used to document the interactions among people/roles involved in a project, activity, or task. See http://en.wikipedia.org/wiki/Responsibility_assignment_matrix.

firmly suggest that you follow these guidelines with your Team until they have been proven *not* to work... and only then consider changing them.

Discussion of Project and Product Management

Now that I have described the primary roles involved in Scrum, let me discuss two roles/positions that people often ask me about: the Project Manager and the Product Manager. There are no roles named Project Manager or Product Manager in Scrum, but many Organizations have people in these positions. This causes issues and questions about what happens to these people when an Organization moves to Scrum.

First of all, here are common definitions of the Project Manager and Product Manager positions:

- The Project Manager is the person accountable to the Business for the Project's objectives (including the Team's Work Results), and

- The Product Manager is the person accountable to the Business for delivery of the Product to the marketplace.

These may not be the definitions used in your Organization – and that's ok – but all of the definitions I've seen include the notion that these are people who are accountable to management for delivering Results.

Because of this accountability for delivering Results, the only role they *could* play on a Scrum Team is that of Product Owner – since there can only be one Team Member accountable for the Team's Work Results, and that person is the Product Owner. One specific consequence of this is that the Project Manager *cannot be* the ScrumMaster... unless the role of Project Manager is drastically redefined to explicitly *exclude* accountability for Work Results.

In chapter 2.2 I give examples that show these roles in an Organization using Scrum. Please take a look there for further information about how formal Project and Product Managers could be involved in an Organization using Scrum.

On a Scrum Team the project management responsibilities are carried out by the Team itself, which includes the Product Owner and ScrumMaster. Project management usually includes managing both the Product *and* the Team, and this is just too big and too difficult (and schizophrenic) for one person to do well.

So, on a Scrum Team the Project Manager (PM) role is essentially divided into two pieces, one focused on the Product and one focused on the Team. These two pieces are the Product Owner and ScrumMaster roles, respectively. In some simplistic way, we have the equation: PM = PO + SM. Of course, this is not *technically* correct since the other Team Members are each involved because of the Team's self-organization, but it is a simplistic truth, none the less.

Team Values

Scrum is successful largely because it is based on values. The collection of Team Values listed here are ones I want Scrum Teams to have, and it would be nice if the Team Members have them (as individuals), as well. It would be even nicer if the people surrounding the team (and the Organization as a whole) had them, but that's often too much to hope for. The Black Book [SB, pgs. 147-154] described the first five of these Values, and called them the Scrum Values. Based on my experiences with Scrum, I have added two more Values to the list. Collectively, I call these Values the Team Values.

I believe that these Values are tightly coupled to one another; there is significant overlap between/among the Values. For that reason, it is *not* my intention to describe exactly what these Values mean; the way each Team interprets these Values is its own. In any case, Table 2 lists the Values and presents some of my comments about them. It *is* my intention that you reflect on these Values taking my comments into account in order to help you make yourself, your Team, and your Organization, better.

Table 2: The Team Values

Openness	There should be no secrets between/amongst Team Members about things relevant to Production; the Team Members should be open to suggestions from others.
Focus	Everything that the Team does must have a focus; and the Team Members must focus on what is important in everything they do.
Commitment	The Team makes and keeps its commitments/agreements; and the Team Members must have commitment to the Team and the Product itself.
Respect	Team Members believe that people are always doing the best they can do at any given moment; they respect all points of view, including those of their Stakeholders.
Courage	The Team must have the courage to make reality visible, the courage to say No; and Team Members must have the courage to be open with each other.
Visibility	The Team must make the current state of the Product visible; that is, the details of production belong to the Team, but the state of the Product is available to all.
Humor	Since everyone is always doing the best they can, everyone needs a sense of humor; I believe that if we can't laugh at the things we do, we'd have to cry.

In particular, Respect is an interesting value. Since Respect means that each of us believes that people are *always* doing the best they can, and since a person's behavior is a function of the person and the environment,[4] this says that in order to change a person's behavior, the person's *environment* must change. The environment can be changed in many ways, including modifying practices, providing training, emphasizing the Team Values, removing impediments... whatever it takes. The focus should be on fixing the environment – not on fixing the people – when trying to change behavior.

Keep in mind that these Values exist because teams that have them are usually good teams, and thinking about them will help teams improve. I believe that a Team's *actual* values can only be determined by looking at what it actually does. Therefore, I believe that discussion of the Values should be an integral part of every Team Retrospective and Intraspective (see chapters 4.1 and 2.3).

These are not the *only* values the Team should pay attention to. The Organization itself has values, and the Team should understand them as well. Often, when an Organization is new to Scrum, the Organization's values will be in conflict with the Team Values I have listed here. In particular, the Organization may not value 'safety' and thus not provide a safe environment for the Team, which will make it very hard for the Team to live the Team Values I just discussed. I firmly believe that safety for the Team must be present (to some minimal degree, at least) in order for a Team to be *capable* of living the Team Values.

When the Team's and Organization's values clash, it is the ScrumMaster's job to have discussions with the Team and the Organization, in order to resolve these differences and/or help the Team decide what to do. In other words, the ScrumMaster should help the Team resolve its differences with the Organization. In many cases, these differences in values are the primary impediment to becoming scrummish, and hence effective as a Team.

Cross-Functional and Self-Organized

According to the Rules of Scrum, Scrum Teams are cross-functional and self-organized ([SB, pgs. 36-38], [S2, pg. 76], and [SS, pg. 4] for example). Well, that's nice, but what do these things mean? In this section I give a quick definition of these terms.

Cross-Functional: this simply means that the Scrum Team has all the skills and knowledge necessary to get the work Done; there are people who can test, there are people who can code, there are people who do analysis and understand the Product, there are people who write documentation, and so on. It does *not* mean that everyone on the Team has *all* the skills; it means that the Team has all the skills as a collective – so a cross-functional team is

---

[4] Lewin's Equation, developed by Kurt Lewin, the founder of social psychology.

often referred to as "self-contained." The notion of cross-functionality is in opposition to the notion of having teams of testers, teams of analysts, teams of coders, and so on... each of these teams focuses on a relatively small set of skills. Since most Scrum Teams can't be *completely* cross-functional, the Team often needs external SMEs to help out. This is particularly true when the Team lacks knowledge about the Product itself.

Self-Organized: a Team is self-organized when the Team determines *how* it's going to do its work, and that's really all it means. To be precise, the Team determines how it's going to do its work *within the constraints* the Business has given it. The Organization may have rules, standards, and procedures that affect how work is done, and the Team can't violate them. However, the Team should feel free to do whatever seems necessary within these constraints (see chapter 2.3 for more on this).

The term 'self-organized' could lead you to believe that each person determines what he or she should do, but that isn't what this means. It means that the Team frequently re-organizes itself for the work at hand – no one from outside the Team tells them how to do their work. It's not about individuals independently deciding what they will do – that would be anarchy – and that's *not* what we're talking about. We're talking about the Team changing the way it does work based on the work it's doing.

In other words, the Team does not require an external manager to tell the Team Members what to do, and when to do it – the Team is self-managing. Now, that doesn't mean that there is no *external* management – the Team as a whole is managed as a unit through the prioritizations in the Backlog, but the internal workings of the Team are managed within the Team. So, we can say that the Team is self-organized and self-managed, but *not* self-directed – it figures out the 'how' and 'who,' but *not* the 'what' or the 'why' – those are supplied by the Product Owner through working with the Business Owner and Stakeholders.

One of the major issues with self-organization is what I call 'pre-emptive self-organization' – when a Team changes its practices because of reasons usually stated like *'we don't do it that way'* or *'that won't work here.'* This is not scrummish behavior; what *should* happen is that the Team should start with basic Scrum and modify its practices based on information obtained through Retrospection and Intraspection (see chapters 4.2 and 2.3).

Discussion: I like to think of cross-functionality and self-organization in terms of roles and responsibilities. In typical 'process geek' terminology, when a person plays a role, it is as if that person puts on a coat that represents the role, and inside the coat's pockets are slips of paper listing all the responsibilities that 'belong' to that role.

There are many potential 'role coats' for a Scrum Team, but for simplicity's sake let's just assume that there are three: the ScrumMaster coat, the Product Owner coat, and the Developer coat – and each Team Members is wearing the appropriate one. Because the Team is self-organized, once they are all together in the Team Room the Team Members empty out their pockets onto the floor, and the ScrumMaster says *'that pile of responsibilities belongs to the Team. How are we going to deal with them?'*

In other words, *all* the responsibilities (except for the special accountabilities of the ScrumMaster and Product Owner) belong to the Team as a whole, and the Team self-organizes to figure out how to get them Done. Because the Team is cross-functional, it should have all the skills and knowledge it needs to do them, and it uses external SMEs to fill in the gaps.

As you can see, self-organization and cross-functionality are coupled, and when combined with the Team Values, can result in extraordinary Teams. In fact, this combination is so potent that I use the term "well-formed team" to refer to teams like these. I believe that one of the major lessons of Scrum is that *all* teams (not just Scrum Teams) should be well-formed teams – especially when working in complex domains. As my friend (and fellow CST) Michael James said when comparing teams 'doing it for money' versus Scrum Teams: "People who contribute out of love for the work, shared vision, and team camaraderie will surely out-innovate people who think of themselves as wage slaves"[5]. I couldn't put it any better ;-)

Discussion Questions

1. The term 'due diligence' means using the appropriate Standard of Care when doing work. What do you think are some of the factors involved when a Team Member is doing his or her due diligence while developing software?

2. What are the implications of *'believing that people are always doing the best they can do at any given moment'*? Discuss this issue and the rest of the Team Values. Which of the Values appeal to you the most?

3. If there is no SME available to the team, what might happen?

4. Do you think the RASCI Matrix will help you discuss how Scrum will work (and how it will be implemented) within your Organization?

5. Scrum says that the Team's Product Owner and ScrumMaster roles *must* be played by different people. Why do you think this is?

---

[5] Scrumdevelopment user's group, 12/29/2009 12:46 PM.

6. Why does Scrum suggest we limit Team size to 10 or fewer? What does this imply if we need more than 10 people to do a job?

$$\boxed{2.2}$$

The Product Owner

In this chapter I discuss the Product Owner, who is the most important person on a Scrum Team, and the key to the Team's success. Product Ownership is one of the most commonly misunderstood topics in Scrum, so this discussion is vital.

As stated in the last chapter, the Product Owner is the one and only *"Team Member who is accountable to the Business for the success of the Team – for the value of the Team's Work Results."* To put it succinctly:

- The Product Owner is *the* Team Member who is accountable to the Business for the value of the Team's Work Results.[1]

In other words: the Product Owner is the one and only Team Member with a 'bull's-eye' on his or her chest. It is important to emphasize that the Product Owner is a single Team Member; this accountability is not something that can be shared. Basically, here is the deal that is struck with the Product Owner: *'You prioritize the Team's work, and in exchange you have to take the blame for the Results.'*

Because of the 'is accountable' part of this definition – the fact that the Product Owner is the "single, wringable, neck" [S2, pg. 6] – the Product Owner *must* have the final say over what the Scrum Team does, in order to be able to protect said neck. Therefore, the definition of the Product Owner can also be stated as:

- The Product Owner is the Team Member who has the *final say* over what the Scrum Team does.

This 'final say' business can cause problems with the Business Owner, the Stakeholders, and the Team. The Business Owner and Stakeholders often believe that they, and not the Product Owner, get to determine what the Team does – they might not actually want an *empowered* Product Owner. However, the Product Owner's main responsibility is to balance the Team's Sustainable Pace with the Business's expectations, and to make the necessary decisions about the Team's priorities.

The Product Owner should work with the Business Owner and Stakeholders constantly in order to scope the Product and negotiate delivery dates – and

---

[1] Please see appendix A.2 for a thorough discussion of this definition and how the Product Owner role has morphed through the years.

Scrum states that the Product Owner is empowered to make the final decisions. In case there is any doubt about this, Ken was quite emphatic [SB, page 34] when he said: "For the Product Owner to succeed, *everyone* in the Organization has to respect his or her decisions." It can't get any clearer than that. The Product Owner makes the final decisions, and then makes sure that the resulting reality is visible outside the Team.

On the other hand, the Product Owner is often told that reality is not acceptable, and that the Team better start working faster and harder. Clearly, bending to this pressure can cause problems with the relationship between the Product Owner and the rest of the Team. Since the Product Owner has the final say and is being pressured by the Business, it is very tempting for the Product Owner to boss the Team around – and this could prevent the Team from self-organizing and applying their cumulative brainpower to the problems at hand. It is the responsibility of the ScrumMaster (who is described in chapters 2.3 and 2.4) to manage this relationship between the Product Owner and the rest of the Team. This is difficult, and I like to summarize the key points of the relationship thusly:

- The Product Owner has the *right* to be involved in every decision the Team makes, but has an *obligation* not to micromanage;

- The Product Owner *has* veto power at all times, but should *control* the urge to use it;

- The Scrum Team is required to give the Product Owner *all* the information needed in order to make good decisions and be able to work effectively with Stakeholders; and

- The ScrumMaster works with both the Product Owner and the Team to manage this relationship and keep these things in balance.

These points *should be* self-evident because the Product Owner and the Team are supposed to live the Team Values given in chapter 2.1, but they are certainly worth stating explicitly here.

The Team's Relationship with the Product Owner

As you can imagine, the Team's relationship with the Product Owner is a tricky one, and managing this relationship is an inherent, and important, part of the Scrum Team's self-organization. Therefore, this relationship must be facilitated and managed by the ScrumMaster. In this section I'd like to explore this relationship further.

Command and Control (C&C): The relationship between the Product Owner and the rest of the Team can be largely understood by considering the issues of Command and Control (C&C), which is a phrase invented by the military[2]. Most of us think of C&C as being a *bad thing*, and refer to micro-managing managers as being 'Command and Control.' However, one thing people need to know is that the military *invented* the phrase in order to *separate* the concepts of Command and Control, *not* combine them.

Military officers are constantly reminded that they have Command over their Units, but don't have Control over their Troops. Specifically, while Officers can issue orders to their Units, it is their Sergeants that organize the Troops to get the work done. This is very similar to Scrum, where the Product Owner provides goals and priorities to the Team, and the ScrumMaster helps the Team self-organize to accomplish them.

This explicit separation of Command and Control is one of the genius elements of Scrum (the other major genius element is the self-organizing Team). Most leadership training tells leaders that they should separate the concepts of Command and Control but, as far as I know, Scrum is the only management framework (outside the military) that *explicitly* separates them – which it enforces by having the two roles of Product Owner and Scrum-Master to provide the necessary balance.

Closeness to the Team: Many people ask me questions about how close the Product Owner should be to the other Team Members. Common questions are:

- 'Should the Product Owner be with the Team all the time?'
- 'Our Product Owner is very bossy. What can we do?' and
- 'Is it ok for the Product Owner to be nosy and pestering Team Members with questions like: 'How are you doing?' or 'What're you working on now?' and so on?'

So, should the Product Owner have this close a relationship to the rest of the Team? Is it ok for the Product Owner to be bossy? Is it ok for the Product Owner to be nosy? What should the ScrumMaster do about it? Good questions, and there's a balance that must be met.

First of all, remember that the Product Owner is accountable for the Team's performance and Work Results, and that the Team has an obligation to provide the Product Owner with all the information needed to make good decisions and be able to work with Stakeholders. If the Product Owner isn't getting this information, then there is a problem. If the Product Owner is getting 'too close' to the Team it may indicate that the Product Owner isn't getting the necessary information.

---

[2]   Dan is a retired US Army Officer, and has spent many years studying and analyzing this topic.

Similarly, the Product Owner is responsible *to* the Team Members to make sure they get all the information and support they need from the Business to get *their* jobs done. In practical terms, this means that the Product Owner is accountable to the Team for having the right SMEs available when the Team needs them, for getting logistical and infrastructure support the Team needs, and so on. The Product Owner and the Team must work very closely to make sure these things happen.

These are only two of the reasons the Product Owner *must* work closely with the Team – you can probably think of many others. In general, it is my experience that a Product Owner needs to spend at least three hours a day with his or her Team in order to be effective...

On the other hand, the Product Owner must avoid having negative impacts on the Team. Often the Product Owner is seen as being too bossy or nosy; the Product Owner is constantly 'pestering' the Team. Now, being bossy is a bad thing, and I discuss it in the next section, when talking about the Product Owner as a Team Member.

Being nosy is a different issue, though. The Product Owner may be asking a lot of questions about things the other Team Members think is *'none of your business...'* This is a difficult issue for the Product Owner to manage, so helping the Product Owner manage it is a significant ScrumMaster responsibility. It often seems like there is a choice between having a nosy Product Owner or an efficient Team. If I must make that choice then I usually choose the nosy Product Owner as the lesser of two evils.

The reason for this is that the Product Owner needs to have a lot of information in order to be effective, and if the Product Owner is ineffective, the Team will be ineffective – which is much worse than the Team being inefficient. Of course, the Product Owner may feel the need to be nosy in order to get needed information, but the Product Owner shouldn't try to *control* the Team. This can be a really difficult balance for the ScrumMaster to manage... just sayin'...

Product Owner as a Team Member. Another thing that complicates the relationship between the Product Owner and the rest of the Team is that the Product Owner is also a Team Member. That is, the Product Owner is not always in a command position with respect to the Team, sometimes the Product Owner is just another Team Member helping to get work Done. After all, the Product Owner is a person with skills, and those skills are put to use by the Team as part of its self-organization. This does not give the Product Owner permission to be bossy about it, though...

This could cause problems because the Team needs to know when this person is speaking as a Team Member, and when this person is speaking as the Product Owner. Now, the ScrumMaster is supposed to help with this, but the Team needs to have a way of knowing what role this person is playing at any given moment. Until the Team has established its norm in this area, here is a simple set of rules I recommend the Team uses:

- The Product Owner is acting as the *Product Owner* during Sprint Planning and Review; and

- The Product Owner is acting as a *Team Member* at all other times; unless

- Another Team Member is *asking* for 'Product Owner' support, and the Product Owner reverts to *Product Owner* mode to give it.

These simple rules will help the Team become more cohesive, and limit the confusion the Team can have when dealing with the Product Owner. Some Product Owners have a hard time with this relationship, and their Teams may need to set some additional boundaries that define how the Product Owner will interact with the rest of the Team when acting as a Team Member. This is a Retrospective issue, and is discussed in chapter 2.3 when discussing the ScrumMaster's main issues to manage.

Now let's look at some examples of Teams and their Product Owners.

Product Owner Examples

Let's look at three examples:

- An existing team moving to Scrum,

- A team that has been assembled to do a Scrum project, and

- A relatively large Organization doing Scrum.

Through these examples you can get a better understanding of the Product Owner role, and who is the Product Owner on your Team.

Existing Team Moving to Scrum. Let's take a look at the easy case first. Let's say there is an already-existing Development Team with a Team Leader, Chet. This Team works for a Product Manager, Grace. And Grace has told Chet that she wants his Team to work the next project using Scrum.

This is pretty straightforward. Since Chet is already Team Leader, and thus is already accountable to Grace for what the Team does, Chet will be the Product Owner of the Team once it moves to Scrum. Assuming that Chet is not a Subject Matter Expert on the project, Grace may have to assist the Team in the role of SME, as well as be the Team's Business Owner.

And that's really all there is to that.

Make a New Team. Now, let's look at a slightly more interesting case. Assume there is a matrix Organization that likes to assemble teams together to work on projects. Assume further that this Organization is using Scrum. Now, they assemble a new team for their next Scrum project. This Team consists of:

- Pete, a Project Manager from the PMO,

- Mary, from Sales, to act as the Subject Matter Expert,

- Ted, a Technical Lead, to head up the development efforts, and

- A number of coders, testers, analysts, and so on, to actually do the work.

There would seem to be three possible choices for the Product Owner on this Team: Pete (the Project Manager), Ted (the Technical Lead), and Mary (the Subject Matter Expert). I can imagine valid reasons to want to choose each of them – but let's just look at the definition.

Assuming that Pete will actually be doing what is defined as the Project Manager role (by the PMI) then Pete is "the person assigned... to achieve the project objectives."[3] This would make Pete the Product Owner of this Team by definition, because he is accountable to the Organization for the Product. It is likely that Pete is not a SME, but there is Mary (from Sales) on the Team to provide advice and assistance – and that's all that Scrum requires.

This example does lead us to an interesting realization, however. It's is not really *enough* for the Product Owner to be accountable to be successful; it also requires three additional things:

- That the Product Owner realizes, and accepts, that he or she has accountability for the Team's Results,

- That *no other* Team Member believes that he or she is accountable to the Business for the Team's Results, and

- That the Business Owner and other Stakeholders *acknowledge* that the Product Owner is the *single* Team Member who is accountable for the Team's Results, and that they give the Product Owner the *authority* to do the job.

Without this social contract in place, a Team will have big problems. In this example, it may be that the Organization, or Business Owner, thinks that someone besides Pete (the Project Manager) is the Product Owner. Maybe somebody would rather have Mary (the SME) be in charge. Maybe this is ok in this Organization because people called Project Managers aren't *actually* accountable in this Organization; it's up to the Organization. Whoever is *actually* accountable becomes the Product Owner, even though it may not be

---

[3] Pg. 13, A Guide to the Project Management Body of Knowledge (fourth edition), PMI, 2008.

the *right* person according to my (or somebody else's) definitions or guidelines. Remember, it's all about who *really* has the bull's-eye on his or her chest – no more, no less.

Product Owners in a Large Scrum Organization. Okay, now let's look at a large team. There are many ways that Organizations organize themselves into teams, and Figure 7 shows a simple example. This Product-focused Organization has a Product Management Team that has associated (technical and business) SMEs and a staff; some Project Teams, one of which has a single embedded Development Team; and some Development Teams working on the Projects.

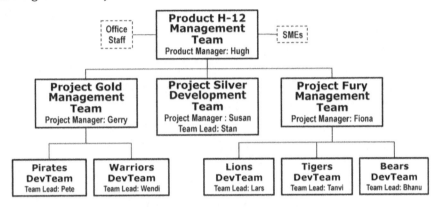

Figure 7: The 'Product H-12' Organizational Structure

Where are the Product Owners here? Well, people who are accountable are all over the place. There are DevTeam Leads who are accountable to Project Managers, there are Project Managers who are accountable to the Product Manager, and the Product Manager is accountable to the Business. So there are lots of *potential* Product Owners.

Actually, it's really that simple. *Each* of these people could be a Product Owner, as long as they have Scrum Teams to be Product Owners of. But first we need to know their spans of accountability. Let's make a list:

- Hugh, the Product Manager, is accountable to the business for the Product. He is accountable from 'cradle to grave' and is supposed to be an expert on both the market for the Product as well as the Product itself. So, in some sense, Hugh should be the Product Owner for 'Product H-12.' I'm not sure exactly who his Scrum Team is yet – I'll discuss that later. I'm also not sure who his Business Owner is, but it's probably somebody at a Program or VP level (maybe even the CEO...).

- We have three Projects, each of which has a Project Manager. Each of these Project Managers is accountable to Hugh for his or her

Project. So, I would say that each of these Project Managers (Gerry, Susan, and Fiona) should be the Product Owner for their Project, and they each have Hugh as their Business Owner. Again, I'm not sure exactly what their Scrum Teams are.

- We also have many Development Teams, each of which has a Team Lead. Each of these Team Leads is the Product Owner for his or her Team (which is a Scrum Team, as it's the right size), and has the appropriate Project Manager as his/her Business Owner. In the case of 'Project Silver' there is an embedded Development Team, whose Product Owner is its Team Lead (Stan), with Susan (the Project Manager) as the Business Owner.

This is actually pretty simple, and illustrates one of the strengths of Scrum. In a large, well-organized, Organization, there should be a clear hierarchy of Product Owners. Each of them has a team (be it large or small), and each of them has a Business Owner, all the way to the top. But, as we'll see in the next section, there is an issue to deal with...

Product Owner (Leadership) Teams

Okay, so far so good. There are lots of Product Owners, each accountable for his or her own 'piece of the pie.' But, just how big is each of their pieces of pie? Let's look at Hugh, the Product Manager. There might be 50 or more people working for Hugh, and this raises a problem. The problem is this:

- Hugh is a Product Owner, which means he heads up a Scrum Team.

- Scrum Teams are small – they don't have 50 or more people in them.

- So... what's up?

Well, it's not really that hard. There is the concept of a Product Owner Team (also called the Leadership Team or Management Team), which consists of a Business Owner, the Product Owners that are accountable to him or her, and maybe a few others to round out the Team.

So, let's take a look at Hugh. Hugh is the Product Manager of the whole Organization, and is also the Product Owner of the 'Product H-12 PO Team,' which is a virtual Scrum Team (shown in Figure 8) that has Hugh as the Product Owner, and the Project Managers (Gerry, Susan, and Fiona) as the primary Team Members. The Team will also probably have some of the SMEs that are assigned to Hugh on it, as well – this will be determined by Hugh and the primary Team Members as part of their self-organization. For example, it may be that Hannah the Architect and Harry the Systems Analyst are on the Team. And, of course, it needs a ScrumMaster, who is probably just one of the people already mentioned.

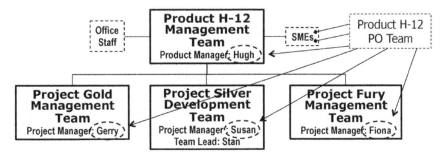

Figure 8: The 'Product H-12' Leadership Team

What does this Leadership (Product Owner) Team do? What is its Product? What are its Work Results? In this case, the 'Product H-12 PO Team' has the job of coordinating the three Project Teams, and its Product is 'Coordinated releases of Product H-12' or 'Project Teams that work well together' or something. It really doesn't matter that much what you call its Product... this is a case when we talk about Results.

What *does* matter is how this Team acts. Its existence causes the Project Managers to talk together every day (this Team's Daily Scrum) and talk out their issues. It causes this Team to remove impediments for the whole Product Team, and gives the Project Managers responsibility for under-standing the big picture (of course, Hugh is still accountable to the Business...). It causes them to negotiate how they will use the SMEs amongst the Teams. It causes them to do 'load leveling' of the Product's Backlog across the Projects (see chapter 3.2). It causes them to discuss the sharing or transfer of people across Teams. And it does it with Hugh (their Product Owner) in the room to prioritize things.

This Leadership Team may have its own Backlog, its own Sprints, and so on – it is a Scrum Team after all. It does coordinated and consolidated Planning across all the Projects. It may do Portfolio Management in order to help determine what the next Projects for Product H-12 will be. It does whatever Hugh needs it to do in order to manage getting the Product out the door.

And, it allows Hugh to manage a large team without micromanaging. Each Project Manager is part of the 'Product H-12 PO Team,' and Hugh works *through* this Leadership Team and these Project Managers. When Hugh wants to influence and guide the Project Teams (and he will surely want to do this), he does it by mentoring and coaching the appropriate Project Managers, not by directly micromanaging the Development Scrum Teams.

In practice, this means that when Hugh visits a Project Team he should be accompanied by the Project Manager – he should not be left alone to wander around. If Hugh has some guidance for a Team (or a Team Member), he issues this guidance *through* the appropriate Project Manager – he doesn't do it directly. Of course, Hugh is a Stakeholder/SME for each of these Teams, and may be present at the Product Reviews and make comments directly in that capacity.

Now, when looking at the Product hierarchy, it is apparent that there are two other Leadership (PO) Teams: the 'Project Gold PO Team' and the 'Project Fury PO Team' (I assume that Project Silver's Susan and Stan can just talk together...). These Product Owner Teams at the Project level, seen in Figure 9, have the job of coordinating Development Scrum Teams.

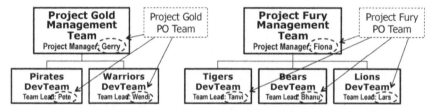

Figure 9: Two Project-Level Leadership Teams

Since the DevTeams are actually developing software, this often means that these Product Owner Teams:

- Help Refine and Prioritize the DevTeam's Backlogs (chapter 3.9),

- Help with Integration, Validations, and Exploratory Testing,

- Work on cross-cutting technical issues, and

- Whatever else the Project Manager thinks they should work on.

The experts necessary to do these things may not be on the Product Owner Team, so they may incorporate some of the DevTeam's experts into the Team (as Team Members or SMEs) in order to do the work as part of the Product Owner Team's Backlog. The Product Owner Team's Team Members could also negotiate amongst themselves and determine which of the DevTeams will do these things, and have that Team's Product Owner take the appropriate Stories back to the Team and prioritize them into the next Sprint.

In general, these Product Owner (Leadership) Teams are the mechanism for tying large Organizations together. At each node of the Organization's Org Chart there is a Product Owner Team that consists of a Business Owner and his or her Product Owners as its core Members. This core needs to get together, decide what their goals will be, and make sure they have the additional Team Members or SMEs they need that will enable them to achieve those goals.

These additional Team Members should come from within the part of the Organization that the Business Owner controls. Remember that this is a

Scrum Team, and must be cross-functional and self-organized, just like any other. If appropriate Team Members can't be found that 'close to home' it creates a need for SMEs from further away, and obtaining them could be difficult. In practice, I've often seen consultants hired specifically to work on these Teams.

One of the issues that keeps coming up when I coach Organizations about Leadership Teams is: *'Do Leadership Teams have Daily Scrums just like real Scrum Teams?'* The answer is *'Yes, they do.'* I expect the sub-teams to have their Daily Scrums, and then (immediately afterword, probably) the members of the Leadership Team get together for their Daily Scrum. In this discussion they handle issues that came up in their Team's Daily Scrums – as well as discussing the Items on their own Backlog.

Other Product Ownership Responsibilities

So, there is a Product Owner on every Scrum Team. What would this Product Owner likely do? The Product Owner is wearing the bulls-eye – that's the main thing – but what else does the Product Owner do? When reading what people write about the Product Owner, you can find a long list of things they *want* the Product Owner to do, including:

- Determine what Product the Team will build, and drive the Team at a Sustainable Pace to build that Product;

- Work with the Business Owner to make sure the Team has all the support and resources it needs;

- Be the primary interface with the Stakeholders, and be a Subject Matter Expert (SME) on the Product;

- Write *all* the Stories, do all the analysis, populate and prioritize the Backlog;

- Do the Release Planning for the Team;

- Be the acceptance tester for the Team, determining if Stories are Done;

- Know the Business Value of each of the Stories;

- And so on...

Well, Product Owners have a bulls-eye on their chest, not a big, red 'S' – they aren't Superhuman – they are just people; but they are people on cross-functional, self-organized Teams. If the Team and the Product Owner agree that something is necessary to do for the success of the Team, then the Team must make it happen. Whether it's 'PO stuff', 'ScrumMaster stuff', or

'Developer stuff', the Team is on the hook for it, not any individual Team Member – including the Product Owner.

After all, the Product Owner may not have the skills necessary to do all these things – but somebody has to do them, either a Team Member or a SME who is working with the Team (see chapter 2.5 for a discussion of SMEs). All the Product Owner is required (by Scrum) to do is:

- As the Product Owner, make prioritization decisions and work with the Team in a 'scrummish' way; allowing the ScrumMaster to provide guidance, help, and support; and

- As a Team Member, work with the Team to provide quality product while living the Team Values.

Remember that the only thing that *defines* the Product Owner is that bulls-eye on the chest, not what skills the Product Owner has or may need.

Discussion Questions

1. Scrum provides a minimal framework that enables agility. However, it won't be *actually* agile until it is *mentally* agile – it actually uses the framework in an agile way. How much of a Team's mental agility is embodied in the Product Owner?

2. Who invented the phrase "Command and Control"? What did they mean when they said they should not be combined? How does this concept relate to Scrum? Does Scrum as a management framework have an explicit separation of Command and Control?

3. Scrum says that the Product Owner has final say over the priorities for the Scrum Team? Why? What do you think would happen if the Product Owner is overruled? Who grants the Product Owner the authority to do his or her job?

4. Remember that the term 'due diligence' means using the appropriate Standard of Care when doing work. What does it mean for the Product Owner to be doing due diligence?

5. The Product Owner can't do everything we wish he or she would. Who do you think will pick up the slack on your Team? In your Organization?

6. If there is a leadership team, does it have a Daily Scrum? What might you find in a leadership team's backlog? What would they discuss daily?

| 2.3 |

The ScrumMaster

The ScrumMaster is the Team Member who is accountable for the Team using Scrum correctly, and is the secret to successful use of Scrum. The ScrumMaster helps the Team improve its ability to deliver the Results the Product Owner needs from it.

While the Product Owner is the Team Member who is accountable to the Business for the value of the Team's Results, the ScrumMaster is accountable to the Business for making sure that Scrum is used correctly, that the Team uses Scrum in a positive way, and that the Team is constantly improving.

The ScrumMaster is seldom a 'master of Scrum'; but the ScrumMaster *is* the Team Member whose primary responsibility is to help the Scrum Team use and improve its use of Scrum. This isn't simply for Scrum's sake; it's because the Team needs to get better at doing what the Product Owner needs it to do. In practice this means that the ScrumMaster works with the other Team Members to help the Team produce Quality Results at a rapid, though sustainable, pace.

In this chapter I will describe the ScrumMaster's role in the context of the team maturity model[1], which says that as a team matures it goes through four phases: forming, storming, norming, and performing, which are briefly defined as:

- **Forming**: when the Team is getting together, figuring out what its objectives are, and the Team Members are getting to know each other;

- **Storming**: different ideas compete for consideration, Team Members compete with each other for dominance, Team Members figure out what behaviors *don't* work, and so on;

- **Norming**: Team Members start to adjust to each other and develop work habits that allow them to work together, they figure out what *does* work for them, and they become capable of actually getting work Done;

- **Performing**: the Team functions as a single unit and works without inappropriate internal conflicts or with the need for supervision.

---

[1] Bruce Tuckman, "Developmental sequence in small groups," *Psychological Bulletin* 63 (6), 384-99.

This model makes it easy for me to describe the ScrumMaster's primary goal, which is depicted in Figure 10. This goal is to get the Team Performing as quickly as possible, and then keep it there, or maybe even push it further towards hyper-Performance, which is when the Team is doing so well the ScrumMaster becomes 'invisible' (see the discussion in chapter 2.4). In any case, this means that the ScrumMaster is constantly helping the Team Members deal with, and fight through, the environmental forces inside and surrounding the Team, in order to help them improve.

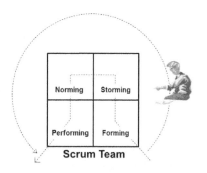

Figure 10: The ScrumMaster's Goal

The ScrumMaster helps the Team mature to become a performing unit in many ways. One of them is to help the Team Members achieve and maintain focus – on both Product and Practices. The Product Owner's job is to prioritize what part of the Product to focus on, and the ScrumMaster's job is to help the Team achieve a well-balanced set of Practices. Teams consist of people, and the ScrumMaster role is to help them become a performing unit as fast as possible so that they can maximize their performance in the direction set by the Product Owner.

Now, this is actually a pretty simple description of the ScrumMaster's job, but it leads to some significant discussions about what it means and how to do it – and the purpose of this chapter is to have some of those discussions.

Role Unique to Scrum

The ScrumMaster is a new leadership role that is unique to Scrum. Even though it's a leadership role, it comes with no management power; that is, a ScrumMaster has no actual management authority over the people on the Scrum Team. Any authority that the ScrumMaster has is moral authority that is granted to the ScrumMaster by the Team.

The ScrumMaster uses this moral authority to help the Team improve its internal processes; to help the Team become more cross-functional, self-organized, self-managed, and self-aware; and the ScrumMaster works with the Organization and the Team to manage the impediments and constraints that are affecting the Team.

Not only that, but there are many aspects (sub-roles or responsibilities) of the ScrumMaster role. Each of these sub-roles is familiar to us, but the combination of them is special. There is no official list of these various responsibilities, but here are some of them that I talk about when coaching ScrumMasters:

- **Facilitator**. The ScrumMaster is constantly working with the Team, helping it get better, facilitating its self-organization, and assuring that it follows the Scrum process.

- **Teacher**. The ScrumMaster teaches the Team what Scrum is and how to use it. The ScrumMaster is constantly working with the Team Members to help improve their knowledge and use of Scrum. The ScrumMaster also helps the Team Members improve their technical abilities in any way that he or she can.

- **Referee**. The ScrumMaster acts as a referee in most internal disputes on the Team. This is a special case of the Facilitator role, but is common enough that it needs to be called out separately.

- **Conscience**. The ScrumMaster acts as the conscience of the Team, especially when it comes to the Team Values I described in chapter 2.1. When a Team Member (or the Team as a whole) is not living the Values it is the ScrumMaster's job to make this fact visible and try to do something about it. This often, but not always, causes the ScrumMaster to call for an Intraspective (discussed later in this chapter) to discuss the issue with the Team.

- **Canary**. The ScrumMaster acts as the 'canary in the coal mine' when it comes to process. That is, when the ScrumMaster notices a 'process smell' the ScrumMaster should talk to the Team about it in order to resolve and correct it.

- **Impediment Manager**. One of the primary responsibilities of the ScrumMaster is to manage the impediments or constraints that are getting in the way of the Team. Often, the ScrumMaster does this by facilitating the Team to manage its own impediments and constraints, but sometimes the ScrumMaster must work with the Product Owner, Business Owner, or others in the Organization to help deal with them.

- **Team Member**. The ScrumMaster is a Team Member, and brings his or her own skills to the Team, working on the Team's Stories and Tasks. Often, the ScrumMaster understands how the Organization works; so helping the Team adapt to the Organization and helping the Organization adapt to the Team becomes one of the things the ScrumMaster usually does – often in tandem with the Product Owner.

The ScrumMaster is not simply a collection of these sub-roles, though. The basic idea is that the ScrumMaster will do 'whatever it takes' to help the

Team get better so that the Team can do the work the Product Owner requires of it. When I coach ScrumMasters, I constantly enjoin them to 'make it work' no matter what is going on.

Because of this 'make it work' attitude the ScrumMaster often needs to take the cultures of the Team and the Organization into account. There is no 'one size fits all' guidance to give a ScrumMaster – it is all situationally dependent. Not all ScrumMasters are appropriate for all Teams, and ScrumMasters must be constantly self-evaluating to determine if they are being effective. If they are not, they owe it to their Teams to get themselves replaced.

Facilitate, Don't Manage

No matter what the ScrumMaster sees that the Team needs to do, it is up to the Team to actually do it – the ScrumMaster merely assists and facilitates. That is, the ScrumMaster is involved in identifying problems and issues, and then helps the Team resolve them. Remember that the Team *owns* the problem, so the Team *owns* the solution – one of the basic premises of self-organization and Scrum. The primary tools the ScrumMaster has for this are the Retrospective and Intraspective[2].

The Retrospective is a formal discussion, built into the Scrum process, which requires the Team to improve its Practices every Sprint (see chapter 4.1). Intraspectives are discussions called *within* the Sprint to address specific issues. The Daily Scrum (see chapter 4.8) is a good time to discover issues that need to be intraspected, but they can be discovered at any time.

One of the purposes of both the Retrospective and Intraspective is for the ScrumMaster to help the Team Members identify and resolve their issues and problems through self-awareness, self-organization and self-management. These issues and problems can be about almost anything, including (but not limited to) interactions between Team Members, working with SMEs, keeping Stakeholders informed, refining standardized Definitions of Done for Stories, or the need for improved development environments. In any case, the Team must make changes consistent with the Organizational constraints, rules, standards, and procedures the Team is working under.

I think that Retrospectives require different techniques in order to keep them fresh every Sprint, and it's not my goal to cover the topic in any depth[3], but my Intraspectives tend to follow a specific pattern:

---

[2] This is not a typo, I *don't* mean introspective... An introspective is to look inside oneself, and an Intraspective is a Team reflecting upon itself within a Sprint: 'intro-' vs. 'intra-' vs. 'retro-'... I invented the word, so I get to determine how it's spelled... ;-)

[3] See, for instance, Esther Derby and Diana Larson: *Agile Retrospectives: Making Good Teams Great*, The Pragmatic Bookshelf, 2006.

1. Identification by the ScrumMaster of the problem or issue to be addressed,

2. Agreement amongst the Team Members that the problem or issue needs to be addressed,

3. Discussion of the Values that were violated; as this usually causes a good discussion,

4. Asking the Team Members what they want to do about it,

5. Facilitating the Team to come up with an action plan, and agreeing to try it, and

6. Going back to work, with 'one more thing' that the ScrumMaster has to look out for...

Now, this is just *my* pattern. If you like it, use it when you are a ScrumMaster. But remember, it is *your* Team, and as its ScrumMaster you must find your own path – your own way – to get your Team to improve.

The '-spectives' (both Intra- and Retro-) are the major reflective practices to use when moving the Team through the maturity phases. These are the primary tools for self-organization. Note that Team self-organization is *not* about the individual; it is about the Team organizing itself to more effectively and efficiently accomplish its goals. Since these goals are constantly changing, we *expect* a Team to be constantly adapting and self-organizing to meet them – hence the need for frequent Intraspectives.

Remember that it is *always* about the Team and not the ScrumMaster; the ScrumMaster is merely the facilitator and catalyst for the Team's self-organization, self-management, and self-improvement efforts.

Organizational Constraints Must Be Honored

Many Organizations place constraints upon their Teams; they impose rules, standards, and procedures that the Teams might find unreasonable and think of as impediments. Self-organization does *not* mean that the Team can ignore these constraints; they are *not* impediments that the Team can unilaterally remove or ignore.

For example, if the Team has compliance rules it must conform to, it can't unilaterally decide to modify them. There could be rules and standards based on CMMI compliance or security policies; there could be regulatory compliance issues based on Sarbanes-Oxley, FDA, FAA, or other regulations; there could be 'best practices' that are imposed by a process or architectural group within the Organization; there could be procedures that need to be followed when releasing a Product, and so on.

These things usually manifest themselves in one of two ways. The first way is that the Team is required to produce additional Product; for example, a compliance document, training materials, or some other documentation. The second way it can constrain the way the Team works is by adding specific procedures or practices that must be followed. In either case, these constraints provide good candidates for storyotyping, and could show up as storyotyped Definitions of Done, Doneness Stories, or even Doneness Epics (see chapters 3.6 and 3.10).

Many things that seem like unreasonable impediments to the Team are actually rules, standards, or procedures based on legitimate Organizational needs. The Team's initial response should not be rebellion; the Team must respect the Organization and *assume* that these needs are legitimate. Of course, it is *reasonable* for the Team to ask for clarification of these issues (through either the ScrumMaster or Product Owner). It can ask the Organization for relief or dispensation of some of these constraints (see the discussion of 'not us' changes in the Retrospective portion of chapter 4.1), but it can't unilaterally make the changes itself – that is mutiny, *not* self-organization.

I *expect* the Organization to constrain things through rules, standards, and procedures – this is the nature of Organizations – but I also expect these constraints to be about 'whats,' not 'hows.' In other words, I expect them to constrain *what* the Team has to do (manifested as new Product or Doneness issues), and I expect that the Team has the *right* to decide *how* to meet these constraints – *this* is the essence of self-organization. This tension between 'whats' and 'hows' is often a topic of near-continuous discussions between the Team and the Organization.

Main Issues to Manage

Well, so now we know that the ScrumMaster's job is to help the Team get better while working within the constraints the Organization has given them. That's a great summary of the job; now let's discuss some particular issues that I find the ScrumMaster often has to deal with. First, I'll discuss my 'top three' issues that I find particularly vexing, and then just mention some others. The first three are listed in priority order based on how big a problem the Team has if the issue isn't dealt with.

First, the ScrumMaster must get good technical development skills into the Team. If the Team can't produce Clean Code, then it's going to have a tough time being effective. And by Clean Code I mean code that is extensible, modifiable, maintainable, and can be quickly integrated and verified with extensive unit, functional, and performance regression tests. Basically, it's code the Team is not afraid to change... it's code that has little or no Technical Debt (see chapter 3.5)[4].

This means that the Team must have good development, testing, and integration environments, practice strong configuration management, and (most probably) use something like the eXtreme Programming (XP) practices for actually designing and building the code. Personally, I think that Test Driven Development (TDD), relentless refactoring, and all the rest of XP's technical practices are brilliant stuff. In any case, the specifics of what the Team needs to do in order to achieve Clean Code for a particular Story are captured in the Definition of Done part of the Story's Agreement or in the Agreement section of the Story's Storyotype (see chapters 3.6 and 3.10).

The ScrumMaster must do whatever it takes so that the Team is not afraid to modify its code. If there is fear of changing the code it will be a major impediment to agility. In my opinion, a Team that writes software must write Clean Code in order to call itself a functional Scrum Team.

Second, the ScrumMaster must help manage Product Ownership issues. I believe that these issues extend outside the team – it's not only about the Team's Product Owner. The Organization should value accountability and give people the authority and empowerment they need; it is hard to imagine a Scrum team thriving if the Organization doesn't do so. The Organization needs to provide safety and a nurturing environment for the Team, and it is the ScrumMaster Community's job to work with the Organization to foster this environment. As a member of this ScrumMaster Community, your Team's ScrumMaster is instrumental in having the Organization provide this safe, nurturing environment.

Within the Team, the ScrumMaster must assure that there actually *is* a Product Owner – a single, identifiable, Team Member who is accountable to the Business for the value of the Team's Results. There must be *nobody* with authority *between* the Product Owner and the Team – not even somebody *appointed* by the Product Owner – as this would make the Product Owner actually be (at best) the Business Owner. If these things aren't true, the ScrumMaster must work with the Business Owner and others outside the Team to make sure it becomes true.

The ScrumMaster must manage the Team's relationship with its Product Owner. This can be particularly difficult, because the Product Owner, as a person, really plays two distinct roles on the Team: The Product Owner is a Team Member, but is also the Team's single, wringable, neck. As the Team's

---

[4] See Martin, Robert, *Clean Code*, Prentice-Hall, 2009, for a thorough description of Clean Code, at least as it pertains to Java. In my opinion, passing a top-end Code Review means that it has none of the 'code smells' defined in the book.

single, wringable, neck, he or she may be tempted to be bossy, to control, or micromanage, the Team.

In fact, an argument could be made that the Product Owner has the moral *right* to micromanage the Team, as it his or her neck on the line. However, the Product Owner has an *obligation* not to micromanage, and the ScrumMaster must work closely with the Product Owner to help maintain the proper balance in the working relationship.

The Product Owner must also respect the Team and the Team Members. For example, assume that the Product Owner is really upset at the Team – it's not performing very well – and the Product Owner is tempted to say some harsh words to the Team. What the Product Owner should say is something like*: 'I know you guys are doing the best you can, but it looks like this problem has gotten the better of you. What can we do about that?'* Of course, asking the Product Owner to be this reasonable may be an unreasonable request, and that leads to the Product Owner and ScrumMaster playing 'good cop – bad cop' with the Team – with the ScrumMaster being the good cop. The Product Owner will be harsh to the Team, and the ScrumMaster will have a respectful discussion with the Team about how the Team can improve.

Third, the ScrumMaster must facilitate the Team's self-organization. This will be difficult to do if the Organization has not provided a safe environment for the Team. Therefore, I recommend that the ScrumMaster focus on Product Ownership issues until this safety is assured; and then the ScrumMaster can focus on the Team's self-organization.

Self-organization has two aspects: the first is that the Team changes its work patterns based on the work in progress, and the second is that the Team modifies its practices and procedures in order to get better at doing its work.

The first aspect of self-organization says that the Team should organize and manage itself differently based on the work that it's doing – based on the Stories being worked on – this is also called 'task-organization.' The main purpose of the Daily Scrum is to provide information about how the work is progressing, which includes progress on the Product and impediments that arise. Based on the state of the work, and what the Stories need, the Team will rearrange itself to optimize its efforts for the day. One common pattern is for the Team to Swarm on the work that is available (see chapter 2.6). Additionally, the Team (often assisted by the ScrumMaster) will remove or work around the impediments that are obstructing the work in progress.

The second form of self-organization is longer-lasting, and normally happens though the use of –spectives, as I discussed in the previous section. This process consists of the Team Members modifying their practices and procedures in order to get better at what they do, while conforming to whatever constraints the Organization has placed on them. To put it simply, the Team must adapt to Organizational realities and constraints without compromising its 'scrummish' personality.

The Rest: of course, these are not the *only* things the ScrumMaster needs to worry about – they are just the ones that I think are the most important. Here are some of the other things I think are important (if not crucial) for the ScrumMaster to do:

- The ScrumMaster must make sure that the Team has an Agreement on Done for everything it has agreed to on the Backlog (see chapter 3.6). Without a good Agreement on Done the Team may founder and either do too much or too little on any given Story. If it does too little, the Results may suffer; if it does too much, it is stealing time from the future and, decreasing the Team's capability to be agile.

- The ScrumMaster must make sure Team Members focus on the present and immediate future, and leave the worrying about the near and far future to the Product Owner. The Team Members must remain focused on the Goals and Stories they have already agreed to, and make sure they follow the practices they have agreed to while doing so.

- The ScrumMaster must protect the Team from 'wolves,' who are external Stakeholders who want to directly interact with Team Members. While Team Members have the ability to ask for help from external SMEs, this does not mean that external Stakeholders have the right to meddle with the Team – it's a one-way street.

- The ScrumMaster must manage the relationships within the Team itself. The Team is constantly self-organizing in order to be more effective and efficient, and the ScrumMaster must keep track of who is doing what – what the Team's current practices and organization actually are. At any given time the ScrumMaster might be the *only* Team Member who completely understands these relationships.

- The ScrumMaster must help the Team live the Values, especially the Values of respect and courage. Remember that Respect, in our context, means that everybody believes that everybody else is *always* doing the best they can, which implies that improving people's performance is more of an environmental issue than a people issue. That is, in order to help people improve, their environment must be improved so that they have room to improve. Then, once they *can* improve, they *will* improve. And Courage is always important, especially the Courage of a Team Member to respect him- or herself enough to say '*No*' when it's required.

- The ScrumMaster helps the Team remove its impediments, and takes the ones the Team can't remove to the Business Owner for help. It is not the ScrumMaster's job to remove the Team's impediments single-handedly; it is the ScrumMaster's responsibility to make sure they *get* removed. Usually, the Team Members who are impeded are the people who know best how to remove the impediments, so they often actually do the removal. If necessary, it is the ScrumMaster's responsibility to get the Product Owner to prioritize their removal and renegotiate the Team's Agreements so that the appropriate Team Members can have the time to work on them.

- The ScrumMaster makes sure the Team does enough Backlog Refinement (see chapter 3.9) to have Stories ready for Sprint Planning – to have each Story no more than a single '10 minute conversation' away from being agreed to. It is not the Product Owner's responsibility to get the Stories ready for Planning; it is the Product Owner's responsibility to do the initial prioritization and work with the rest of the Team to get the Stories Refined.

Even though I've given a reasonably comprehensive list of things the Scrum-Master must deal with, this is not all you're going to have to deal with as a ScrumMaster. Your Team will run into problems you and I can't even imagine right now, and you must remember your fundamental goal – to *'make it work anyway.'* As I stated in the last section, the major tool the ScrumMaster uses is the -spective, as the ScrumMaster works with the Team to help the Team resolve its own issues and impediments.

And, just to make it interesting, I don't think you can make the problems go away. In my experience, every time you solve a problem, another one shows up. What you are trying to do as a ScrumMaster is trying to turn the big, ugly, problems into lots of little, manageable ones. When I'm coaching I call this the 'conservation of crap' law; the problems never really go away, they just get spread around thinner and thinner and thinner. The hope is that the crap will get thin enough that it can be avoided or managed through the Team's self-organization.

Modes of ScrumMastering

The ScrumMaster's Team will run into many issues, and the ScrumMaster must try to resolve them so that the Team can work better. As the Team matures, the ScrumMaster usually changes methods of working with the Team, moving through the modes of Trainer, Coach, and Mentor. As the Team gets very mature – even hyper-performing – the ScrumMaster tends to become invisible; the ScrumMaster can't be differentiated from the other

Team Members; I like to say that Team Members on very mature Teams have a little bit of ScrumMaster in each of them.

There is another mode the ScrumMaster often has that is different from Trainer, Coach, and Mentor, and it's *not* based on the maturity of the Team. This mode is the Change Agent mode, and is a mode that every ScrumMaster should be in most of the time. Most ScrumMasters are Change Agents only for their own Teams; their primary job is to help their own Team increase its maturity and become more cross-functional, self-aware, self-organized, and self-managed.

Some ScrumMasters go further, and become Change Agents for the Organization. These ScrumMasters become full-fledged members of the Scrum-Master Community and work to change the Organization to make it better for all its Scrum Teams – and for Scrum in general.

The different modes of the ScrumMaster will be discussed in more detail in chapter 2.4.

Who Should Be a ScrumMaster?

Finally, I want to discuss one of the more common questions I get involving ScrumMasters, *'how do we find a ScrumMaster?'* I won't beat around the bush, let me just tell you what I think the main points are.

First of all, I think that many ScrumMasters are born to it, that Scrum-Mastering is a calling. ScrumMasters are people that value the Team before themselves, they are people who realize that development is a Team, and not individual, effort.

ScrumMasters are people who must gain the trust and respect of their Team, and I think they do this by *living* the Values. The ScrumMaster cannot expect his or her Team to live the Values if he or she does not. ScrumMasters are not perfect, but they must be viewed as honest in their belief that the Team comes first.

Let me tell you a story about how I get my Teams to accept me as a ScrumMaster. I'm certainly not perfect, so at some point early in the process I will overstep my bounds and be a little too bossy, or maybe I'll say some harsh words to my Team.

As soon as I can, after I calm down, I will ask my Team to gather around, and I say something like: *'I'm sorry that I snapped at you guys yesterday; I was completely out of line. That didn't work out so well for us, did it? Let's see if we can figure out how you guys can help me not do it again.'* At this point my Team usually has a discussion with me about how we can set up an arrangement between us so that I can better ScrumMaster them.

Now, let's just look at what just happened. My Team has just agreed to ScrumMaster me a *little bit*, so that I can better ScrumMaster them *all the time*. This is a social contract we can all live with, and because it was negotiated in good faith, with everybody's benefit in mind, it will likely be a lasting one.

Product Owner as ScrumMaster

There is one final thing I like to say about the ScrumMaster before ending this chapter. As I have stated before, it is a rule of Scrum that the Scrum-Master may not be the Product Owner, and this should be clear to you since one of the primary responsibilities of the ScrumMaster is to manage the relationship between the Team and the Product Owner – and how could he possibly protect the Team from himself?

However, there is one common case where the ScrumMaster *starts out* as the Product Owner, so I want to describe this very quickly. This situation arises when an Organization decides to convert an already-existing (or new) team to Scrum, so it sends the Team's Team Leader to Scrum training.

The Team Leader, once back from Scrum training, will act as the Team's Training ScrumMaster in order to get the Team up and running. However, this person is already the Team Leader, and thus the Product Owner, because of the 'accountability thing.'

This isn't all that bad, really. A ScrumMaster acting in Training mode is often a little bossy and controlling, because the Team is not yet self-organizing. However, the Team Leader must surrender the ScrumMaster responsibilities as soon as the Team is trained enough to begin its self-organization, and revert to being simply the Product Owner as quickly as possible.

I recommend that the Team Leader (Product Owner) selects a Team Member with the right personality to take over as ScrumMaster. The handoff is simple, and consists simply of saying *'You are now the ScrumMaster. Protect this Team from me. I'll be here to give you advice when you need it. Good Luck!'*

Summary

The ScrumMaster is a leadership role that is unique to Scrum. It comes with no management power; any authority that the ScrumMaster has is moral authority that is granted to the ScrumMaster by the Team.

The ScrumMaster has a very difficult job, with lots of facets and sub-roles that I have described in this chapter. Just remember that the ScrumMaster is the Team Member who is accountable to the Business for making sure that

Scrum is used correctly, that the Team uses Scrum in a positive way, and that the Team is constantly improving.

Also remember that the ScrumMaster is human. All the ScrumMaster can do is the best he or she can, and that's really all we can hope for or expect from anyone.

Discussion Questions

1. Does the ScrumMaster have to be a single person? What happens if there is no designated ScrumMaster?

2. How does maintaining focus on both Product and Practice help a team mature?

3. How does the ScrumMaster help the team navigate organizational constraints? Does Scrum give the team permission to ignore external process demands? Can the team skip documentation if they don't want to do it but, and someone outside the team says you do?

4. Two of the important concepts discussed in this book are 'due diligence' and 'mental agility'. What do these concepts mean when applied to the ScrumMaster's job?

5. Who is responsible for getting good technical skills into the team? What happens if the team is afraid to modify code?

6. As a ScrumMaster what are the two kinds of change agents you can be? Which one should you be exceptional at first and foremost?

7. The ScrumMaster needs to: 1) help the Organization provide a safe environment for the Scrum Team, and 2) help the Scrum Team write Clean Code. When would you have the ScrumMaster do these things: *before* the Team starts work, or *as* the Team does work? Discuss the pros and cons of each approach.

$\boxed{2.4}$

Modes of the ScrumMaster

The ScrumMaster is responsible to move the Team through the phases of the Team Maturity Model. While doing this, the ScrumMaster will likely change modes, from Trainer to Coach to Mentor, and may eventually become Invisible. This chapter describes these modes and transitions.

As I discussed in chapter 2.3, it is easy to describe the ScrumMaster's role in the context of the team maturity model, consisting of the phases of Forming, Storming, Norming, and Performing. The ScrumMaster's primary goal is to get the Team Performing as quickly as possible, and then keep it there – or maybe even push towards hyper-performance, which is when the ScrumMaster becomes invisible.

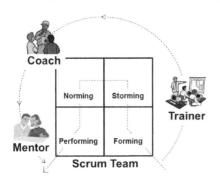

While moving the Team through these phases, the ScrumMaster will run into many issues that the Team has, and the ScrumMaster must try to resolve them so that the Team can work better. As the Team matures, the methods the Scrum-

Figure 11: The ScrumMaster's Modes

Master uses to work with the Team will change, tending to move through the modes of Trainer, Coach, and Mentor (Figure 11) – and eventually becoming invisible. This chapter is about these modes and transitions.

Trainer

When a Team is in the early stages of maturity – when it is in the Forming and Storming phases – the ScrumMaster often acts as a Trainer, as opposed to a Coach or Mentor.

During these early phases the Team is not *really* knowledgeable enough to know how to self-organize to use Scrum, and the ScrumMaster must simply train the Team in the basics. At this stage of maturity, I could truthfully say that the ScrumMaster *owns* the process. At this stage I expect the Team's Retrospectives to be difficult, and I expect the Team to have many Intraspectives throughout the Sprint.

Many Organizations new to Scrum are tempted to preemptively modify it because they believe that basic, out-of-the-box Scrum just won't work for them. While in Training mode, the ScrumMaster must work hard to avoid succumbing to suggestions for changing Scrum.

During the Forming Phase the ScrumMaster *must* insist that Scrum will be implemented in its most basic form, and convince the Organization that it will naturally evolve as the Team matures. Forming should be relatively short and, except for this insistence on not changing Scrum, really doesn't involve Scrum all that much – it's purely a Team's 'getting to know you' phase.

During the Storming Phase the ScrumMaster should train the Team to do basic, out-of-the-box, Scrum. The Team should focus on getting better at the basics, and many of the overall improvements will be because the Organization changes to be safer – more nurturing and supportive of Scrum. This will happen because using Scrum will expose issues in the Organization that need to be corrected if the Organization is to mature. That is, Scrum exposes issues that need to be corrected *whether or not* the Organization uses Scrum. By helping the Organization with these issues the ScrumMaster is also acting as a Change Agent.

So, how does the ScrumMaster work with the Team during the Storming Phase, when he or she is in this Training mode? Well, the ScrumMaster is bound to be a little bit bossy and controlling, because the Team really isn't ready for the self-organization that the ScrumMaster would like to eventually see.

The ScrumMaster will teach the basics of Scrum, set up the Team's initial Scrum process, set Scrum adoption targets for the Team, and monitor the Team's progress as it adopts Scrum. How aggressive should the Scrum-Master be with the Team? Should he or she go *all out* and be very forceful with introducing technical practices and the Scrum process, or should the Trainer do it more slowly and incrementally?

On the one hand, an incremental move will be easier on the Team. Team Members may want to maintain some of their non-agile behaviors, such as thinking of themselves as role players like JustaCoders or JustaTesters, or some such. They might not feel that they can put good technical processes in place yet; there could be many ways in which they have yet to mature. It would seem that an incremental ramp-up would be less stressful and avoid the temporary disruption and inefficiencies inherent in an aggressive approach.

On the other hand, Jeff Sutherland (one of the co-founders of Scrum) has evidence that shows that moving aggressively to Scrum, immediately introducing solid technical processes and robust Definitions of Done – and sticking to them – can increase a Team's productivity by 300% in less than two months[1]. It would seem that the temporary inefficiencies caused by aggressive change can almost immediately be overcome with a dedicated, hard-charging, Training ScrumMaster who 'takes no prisoners.'

Ultimately, though, it's the ScrumMaster's Team. What is he or she comfortable with? What will the Organization be willing to put up with? These are questions that must be addressed, and thought hard about, before deciding on a strategy. Of course, I recommend the aggressive approach, because the faster the Team becomes mature, the sooner the Organization will reap the benefits.

No matter what style is used, one of the things that the ScrumMaster trains the Team to do is self-organize. In particular, the ScrumMaster helps the Team discover what forms of organization work in which situations – this is called task-organization, or organization for the tasks at hand. For example:

- If the Team is bug-bashing, it might be good to just break up into individuals or pairs and work in parallel;

- If the Team is doing some typical production work on a number of fairly complex Stories, they would probably want to be Swarming with a Coordinator for each Story (see chapter 2.6); or

- If the Team was doing some serious exploratory work like architecture or analysis, maybe brainstorming sessions with a few SMEs would be appropriate.

No matter how they go about it, at the end of a Team's Storming phase, the Team begins to self-organize and self-manage, and the ScrumMaster will be ready to move into the Coaching mode. Typically, a ScrumMaster can tell the Team is ready for this once it is changing its task-organization by itself based on what it is working on. For example, it may be breaking itself into TeamLets that are Swarming on work – the Team Members are self-organizing (and re-organizing) within these Teamlets and the roles are starting to blur (see chapter 2.6 for more about this).

By the way, ScrumMasters that specialize in working new Teams through the Forming and Storming phases (and into Norming) are often referred to as 'Training ScrumMasters.' Within the Scrum community there are many ScrumMasters that take on this challenge, and if you have a large Organization you may want one (or more) of these Training ScrumMasters to help with your Scrum transformations.

---

[1] Jeff Sutherland, Scott Downey, Björn Granvik, "Shock Therapy: A Bootstrap for Hyper-Productive Scrum," *Proceedings Agile 2009*, pp.69-73.

Coach

Once the Team has settled down and it has worked itself through its Storming phase into the Norming phase, the ScrumMaster usually moves into the mode of Coaching the Team (of course, it could also involve a handoff from a Training ScrumMaster to a new ScrumMaster who will carry on as the Coach). The ScrumMaster, while working as a Coach, is helping the Team become more self-aware, self-organized, self-managed, and cross-functional. The idea is that the Team knows enough to understand *what* it needs to do, but it needs some coaching help to actually do it.

The ScrumMaster becomes less of a guide, and more of a facilitator. This is a very similar process to what happens with young athletes[2]; in the beginning we must *train* them so they understand how to play the game, and as they mature we *coach* them so they can have their own talents emerge in their own way.

I like to think of this transition from Trainer to Coach as 'loosening the reins' – and believe that the looser the reins the faster the Team can move. However, loosening the reins too much too soon may increase the speed in an undirected, unfocused, and non-useful way. Holding tight to the reins provides more direction and loosening the reins provides more speed – it is a delicate balance – and it is the ScrumMaster's job to manage this balance by constantly working with the Team.

Once the Team has moved out of the Storming Phase into the Norming phase, it knows enough to know what doesn't work, and so it can make some slight modifications to its Scrum process in order to improve things. Usually these changes are suggested by the Team, through facilitated discussions (Retrospectives or Intraspectives) led by the ScrumMaster, and the changes must be approved by the ScrumMaster before actually being put into place. During the Norming phase it can be said that the Team's process is *jointly* owned by the Team and the ScrumMaster.

When the ScrumMaster is acting as a Coach, he or she is offering advice rather than giving direction. This means that the ScrumMaster starts conversations about things that *may* lead to advice. Basically, the ScrumMaster and the Team are in a long-running series of discussions using the Socratic method[3]. When I'm working as a Coach and an issue comes up that I think should be addressed, I call the Team around for an on-the-spot Intraspective, and use the following three phrases:

---

[2] The authors know a little about training young athletes. Doug coaches his son's soccer team, and Dan is a Certified Silver-Level coach for bowling... these experiences have helped them with their ScrumMastering.

[3] The Socratic Method is "The pedagogical technique of asking leading questions to stimulate rational thinking and illuminate ideas," *Frameworks Glossary*, Nebraska Dept. of Education.

1. *'How's that working out for us?'* which I use to point out that there is an issue, or problem, that I think should be addressed. Once the Team agrees that something *bad* happened, then we go to;

2. *'What should we do about it?'* which I use to start a Team discussion about possible solutions; and

3. *'Just Sayin'...'* which I use to throw the decision back onto the Team, reminding them that they are self-organized and that this is really their problem to solve.

Sometimes this leads to quite interesting circular, repetitive, discussions, often ending with the Team asking me *'Well, what would you suggest?'* which gives me what I call a 'training moment' because the Team has *asked* me for direction and I have the ability to go into Training mode for a short while. Note that I only give direction if asked; most of the time I am simply giving advice.

At this point, I better have a suggestion – that's my job as the Scrum-Master/Coach. I don't have to know that the suggestion will work; I'm just giving them something to try. Remember, it is not expected that the Scrum-Master be perfect, only that the ScrumMaster helps the Team improve in whatever way he or she can.

Even though the ScrumMaster (in Coaching mode) is trying not to give direction, that does not mean that the ScrumMaster is not working very hard to change the Team. In fact, quite the opposite is true. The ScrumMaster *must* (and I mean **must**) work hard to get the Team to mature: to get the Team Members to step out of their Justa- roles, to get the Team to be more self-aware, to self-organize, and get the Team to modify its process in order to become completely Normed. It's just that the ScrumMaster does this in a non-controlling, facilitative, fashion. Basically, what the ScrumMaster is looking for is opportunities that can turn into training moments; the best thing is for the Team to figure it out itself, but the ScrumMaster is always ready with a Training Tip if needed.

Eventually, through near-continuous dialogue with the Team, the Team improves itself to the point where it can be said to be fully Normed. A fully Normed Scrum Team will be cross-functional, self-aware, self-organized, and self-managed. It will be able to do work and is often said to just be able to 'crank stuff out.' It has now entered the Performing phase of its maturity.

Mentor

Once a Team enters the Performing phase, the ScrumMaster usually becomes a Mentor to the Team, rather than either a Trainer or a Coach. The Team will still have improvements to do – it can still get better – but it needs to do it through mentoring, which is a state in which the Team is clearly improving *itself* and only using the ScrumMaster for advice, and only when the Team wants it. Basically, when the ScrumMaster is mentoring, the ScrumMaster only calls for Intraspectives when the Team *asks* for one – this is what differentiates it from Coaching.

When a Team is Performing it is capable of getting work Done, so the mentoring that takes place focuses on improving the Team and moving it towards hyper-performance, which is when the ScrumMaster seems unnecessary. That is, the Team is trying to become *more* cross-functional, have *better* technical skills, become *more* self-aware, become *more* self-managed, become *more* self-organized, and so on.

It is tempting for a Team that is Performing to get complacent. After all, they are pretty good at getting stuff Done. However, even though the Team is Performing, that doesn't mean it should stop improving. The ScrumMaster (in the Mentor mode) will need to make sure the Team doesn't get *too* comfortable. People think that they work better when they are comfortable – and comfort is important – but I think being *too* comfortable is a force for inertia. Teams that are *too* comfortable may not mature any further; in fact, they may become complacent and actually get worse.

Therefore, the ScrumMaster must keep the Team from getting *too* comfortable in order to get them to improve. Like my strength coach used to tell me, "you're only going to get stronger if you lift weights you can't lift yet," which was his way of saying that you get better only by stepping out of your comfort zone, becoming comfortable in that new place, and then repeating the process. The ScrumMaster helps the Team improve – and takes it out of its comfort zone – by constantly looking for small things to improve, by having challenging Retrospectives, and continuing to have Intraspectives when little things go wrong and the Team asks for help.

Just as when the ScrumMaster moved from Training Mode to Coaching Mode, the ScrumMaster may change when moving to Mentoring Mode. Often, the original ScrumMaster has left the Team to either work with another Team or focus on becoming a Change Agent for the Organization.

If the original ScrumMaster is gone, the ScrumMaster that is left behind on the Performing Team may not be *all that good* at ScrumMastering; after all, the Team barely needs a ScrumMaster. In cases like this, if the Team can't solve its problems itself, the Team's ScrumMaster may simply call for help. That is, the Team's ScrumMaster's job is to call for help from the expert ScrumMasters when the Team needs help – and maybe the expert being called is the ScrumMaster that just left the Team but has moved to another. I find this to be a common pattern, and a very good way for Organizations to grow when they only have a few expert ScrumMasters.

'Invisible'

Eventually, if the Team gets mature enough, it may happen that the Scrum-Master role dissolves into the Team Members; the ScrumMaster is no longer identifiable as a single person, but ScrumMastering is done by the Team as a whole – everybody looks out for everybody else. At this point we could say that the ScrumMaster has entered the 'invisible' mode, and the Team is now hyper-performing. I use the term 'hyper-performing' to indicate that it has gone beyond merely performing; it has basically removed *all* of its internal impediments and has found smooth sailing.

This is likely a temporary phase, as something is bound to happen to perturb the Team's balance and equilibrium. Therefore, the ScrumMaster must still be there in case the expert needs to be called, or the Team needs some tuning up with an Intraspective. Most of the responsibilities can be shared, but a Team Member (besides the Product Owner) must be *accountable* for the Process in case the Team slips back to a 'lesser' phase.

Summary

The ScrumMaster must adapt his or her methods to the maturity level of the Team. Teams that are less mature need a heavier hand; and Teams that are more mature need a light touch. When a Team is very mature the touch can be so light as to be virtually invisible, but the ScrumMaster must always be there, watching and ready to jump in to help when needed.

Discussion Questions

1. How do you think Retrospectives and Intraspectives will change as the Team moves through the Stages of the Maturity Model?

2. When the Team is Storming it may need some technical training in order to improve. Does this mean that the ScrumMaster must be technical?

3. Team Members start self-organizing as the Team moves from Storming to Norming. What affects would a blame-setting organization – one that punishes failure – have on this transition?

4. Why do Teams and Organizations often look at the Scrum Framework and say *'this won't work here, we'll have to change it?'* Should the ScrumMaster fight this tendency? How does the ScrumMaster fight this tendency?

5. What would happen if scrum is aggressively adopted with no compromises including clean coding practices like XP? What happens when scrum is weakly adopted without solid leadership support?

6. The ScrumMaster uses Retrospectives and Intraspectives to help the Team get better. Why is this sort of reflective thinking important, and how does it work?

7. What would happen if Scrum were aggressively adopted with no compromises – including clean coding practices like XP? What happens when scrum is weakly adopted without solid leadership support?

People Outside the Team

There are three roles outside the Scrum Team: Business Owner, Stakeholder, and Subject Matter Expert. Working with each of them has its own issues. In this chapter I discuss these issues, and provide some guidance about how to resolve them.

In the last few chapters I've talked about the Scrum roles that are *on* the Scrum Team: the Team Member, the Product Owner, and the ScrumMaster. In this chapter I'll talk about the three roles that are *outside* the Team, as described here:

Business Owner (BO): represents the 'formal' part of the Organization or Business. The Business Owner represents the Business, empowers the Product Owner, provides resources to the Team, and helps the ScrumMaster remove impediments.

Stakeholders (SHs): these are the people that have a 'legitimate' interest in the Team, Product, or Process, who shouldn't be ignored, and who provide priorities and meaningful feedback to the Team. I use the word Stakeholder to represent the *external* Stakeholders to a Team; I do not use the term to refer to the Team Members themselves, even though they are clearly stakeholders.

Subject Matter Experts (SMEs): these are people that are outside the Team, but have skills that the Team needs in order to produce its Results.

These are just the simple descriptions of these roles; and the rest of this chapter will describe them, and how the Team interacts with them, in more detail.

Three Basic Patterns

From the standpoint of a member of the Scrum Team, these concepts are easy enough to understand. What is important for a Team Member to know is how to interact with people playing these roles. However, in order to get a full understanding of these issues, you need to have an understanding of the different situations that a Scrum Team may find itself in. In my opinion, there are three basic patterns, which are briefly described here.

Pattern 1: Product Owner Stands Alone

The first pattern (Figure 12) is one in which the Scrum Team finds itself 'all alone' and the Product Owner is working *directly* with each of the Stakeholders. In this case the Team and its Product Owner have no management support to help control the Stakeholders.

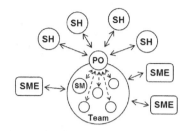

Figure 12: PO 'All Alone'

The Product Owner in this situation has a very tough job, as he or she must work both with the Stakeholders to help sort out their priorities and with the Team on a day-to-day basis – and this often feels like two full-time jobs.

Pattern 2: Product Owner Paired With Business Owner

The second case (Figure 13) is the one I'm focusing on in this book, as it provides a useful abstraction. In this case the Product Owner has a Business Owner who sits *between* the Team and the Stakeholders, and is helping the Product Owner manage the Stakeholders.

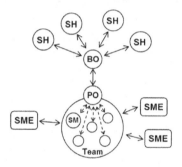

Figure 13: PO Paired with BO

This case is quite common, and arises in many situations:

- It happens when a contract Scrum Team is working with a Client, and there is a Client's Representative working closely (as the Business Owner) with the Team's Product Owner;

- It happens when a Scrum Team in an Organization has a Sponsor (playing the Business Owner role) who is helping the Team's Product Owner work with the Stakeholders;

- It happens for each piece of the Hierarchy in 'Pattern 3' shown below in Figure 14;

- It happens when a single DevTeam splits into many DevTeams and the original Product Owner becomes the Business Owner for each of the new Teams;

- It happens when a Product Owner is working as in 'Pattern 1' (Figure 12) and the job becomes overwhelming and the Product Owner role 'splits into' a Product Owner and a Business Owner;

- and so on.

Pattern 3: Formal Hierarchy

The third common situation is when there is a hierarchical structure; for example, when there are Product Managers, Project Managers, Development Scrum Team Leads, and so on, arranged in a hierarchy like you see in Figure 14 (Figure 7 of chapter 2.2 is another example of a Formal Hierarchy).

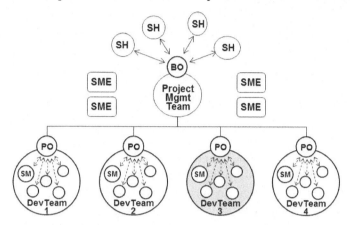

Figure 14: Product Owners in a Hierarchy

Figure 14 shows a simple hierarchy, representing a Project Team that has four Development Scrum Teams, and we are looking at it from the point of view of 'DevTeam 3,' the 'grayed-out' one. Of course, the Business Owner is probably the Project Manager, and the Product Owners are actually the Team Leads, I'm just using their roles here rather than their actual positions or titles...

There are a number of things that are interesting about this structure:

- The Project Manager (BO) is the Project's Product Owner as well as the Product Owner of a PO Team made up of all of the DevTeam's Team Leads (POs) along with some of the SMEs and members of the Project Management Team. This Product Owner Team helps manage the whole Project (see chapter 2.2 for more details on this).

- Each of the Development Teams has a *built-in* set of Stakeholders, including the Team Leads of their 'sister' Development Teams, the Project Manager, members of the Project Management Team and some of the SMEs, and (at least some of) the Stakeholders that the Project Manager is dealing with.

- The SMEs are likely shared across the DevTeams, and (at least partially) managed by the Product Owner Team. I'll discuss this later...

Well, now that you've seen these three patterns, let's discuss the roles. When discussing the roles I will refer back to these as 'Pattern 1', 'Pattern 2', or 'Pattern 3', since some of the discussions are relevant only in certain circumstances.

Business Owner

As you can see, not every Scrum Team has a Business Owner; and the Business Owners we *do* have come in two basic types:

- Business Owners who are really only *lead* Stakeholders, and

- Business Owners who are the individuals the Product Owners are officially accountable to; in other words, the Product Owner's Product Owner.

This *shouldn't* be a big deal, since the Product Owner is supposed to be accountable to *all* the Stakeholders for the Team's Product, but it can *turn into* a big deal when things go wrong. In the first case, it is the Product Owner's job to work with all the other Stakeholders when they are dissatisfied; and in the second case this task belongs to the Business Owner.

In either case, though, the Business Owner helps the Product Owner work with the Stakeholders in order to get their combined priorities, help with Release Planning, determine who the SMEs are, and so on. In some strange way, you can think of the Business Owner as being the Product Owner for a 'Stakeholder Team' whose purpose is to supply priorities and guidance to the Development Scrum Teams. This is especially true for 'Pattern 3' Organizations (Figure 14), but is often true for 'Pattern 2' Organizations (Figure 13), as well. I'll discuss a little more about how to work with Stakeholders in the 'Stakeholders' section later on in this chapter.

There are two perspectives going on here. From the Team's perspective, the Product Owner is the person who has the priorities, and is in charge of the Team. From the Stakeholder's perspective, however, it may look as if the Business Owner is the person to work with when requesting new work. In either case, it is the joint responsibility of the Business Owner, the Product Owner, and the Team's ScrumMaster to keep the Stakeholders from meddling with the Team Members.

This use of the two perspectives makes both the Product Owner's and Business Owner's jobs easier; the Product Owner can focus on the Team, the Business Owner can focus on the Stakeholders, and the two of them can jointly work on producing the best possible Results. The way they work together is largely determined by the accountability – is it the Business Owner who is accountable to the other Stakeholders, or is that still the Product Owner's responsibility? In the first case the Business Owner is in charge of their relationship, and in the second case it's the Product Owner that's in charge – follow the accountability...

Even when the Business Owner is in charge, the Business Owner must remember to work with the Team *through* the Product Owner and not go around him. Going around him is called micromanagement, and is bad in its own right. However, it's *really* bad, even *forbidden*, in Scrum, since Scrum doesn't allow *anyone* to direct the Team to change its priorities other than the Team's Product Owner – even the Business Owner (see chapter 2.4). Remember that the defining characteristic of a Product Owner is making prioritization decisions that *can't* be overruled by *anybody* else, even the Product Owner's bosses. Their bosses can replace them if they continue to make bad decisions, but they can't overrule them.

Stakeholders

Stakeholders are people outside the Team who have a legitimate interest in the Product, the Team, or the Process – these are people that the Team cannot ignore. I will discuss the ones that are interested in Team and Process in the 'ScrumMaster and Outsiders' section of this chapter; for now I'm only interested in the Stakeholders that are worried about the Product the Team is developing.

These Stakeholders are the reason the Team exists; they are the ones that have the needs, desires, wishes, and so on, that provide the reasons for the Team's production of Results. These are people that provide meaningful feedback at Product Reviews, and who we try to co-opt to be Subject Matter Experts (SMEs) to help us do our work. As I just said, there may or may not be a Business Owner that represents these Stakeholders to the Product Owner; so for now are just going to assume that there is an entity/role (call it the PO/BO) who is working with the Stakeholders to provide information for the Team. This role (the PO/BO) could be filled by:

- The Team's Product Owner, when there is no Business Owner;

- The Team's Business Owner, when the Business Owner is the person the Product Owner is accountable to, and the Business Owner is representing *all* of the Stakeholders to the Product Owner; or

- The Product Owner and the Business Owner, working together, with the joint goal of eliciting good information from the Stakeholders.

In any case, the PO/BO could be augmented by others (such as a facilitator, Analysts, Architects, or a ScrumMaster) in order to work with the Stakeholders to provide the Team the information that it needs to develop Quality Results. The main reasons that the PO/BO works with the Stakeholders are:

- Stakeholders provide information to the Team for use for planning and prioritization,

- Stakeholders provide meaningful feedback on the Team's Results, so that the Team can 'inspect and adapt,' and

- Stakeholders (as SMEs) provide ongoing support to the Team while it is doing development.

At the beginning of development (or even before), there is often a Visioning Phase. The Stakeholders *must* be available during the Visioning phase in order to help provide the 'shape' of the Product – to help produce the Product Vision, the Product Roadmap, and the initial Backlog. During the Project, Stakeholders must be available to help the Team with Release and Sprint Planning. Scrum does not have formal discussions that require this support from Stakeholders, so the PO/BO must have these discussions *outside* of the basic Scrum framework.

That's just the way it is – don't worry about it – just make sure it happens. What I recommend is that during Visioning the PO/BO gets the key Stakeholders together for a few hours (at most) a day, and discusses the *big* issues. Perhaps the PO/BO plays some games with the Stakeholders, such as the ones found in Luke Hohmann's book[1] – I particularly like the 'Remember the Future' and 'Product Box' games when exploring what the Product might be or do, and the 'Buy a Feature' game when getting the Stakeholders to help prioritize for planning purposes.

Stakeholders also provide feedback on the Product. The Scrum framework contains the Product Review, which is the primary feedback mechanism the Stakeholders have (see chapter 4.1). As part of this feedback, I like the Team to get some guidance on planning for the next Sprint; in particular, I like the Team to discuss the next Sprint's Goal with the Team's Stakeholders.

At the Review the Team also gets help from the Stakeholders on things that it cares about, such as who the SMEs are for the Stories that are likely to be in the next Sprint, what the Stakeholders want to see in the next Product Review, any guidance they might have on what the Acceptance Criteria should be for some of the Stories, and so on. Because of their importance in the Review, it is the BO/PO's job to make sure the 'right' Stakeholders are available for the Review.

The Stakeholders are less active *during* the Sprint, although the BO/PO often goes to see some of them for guidance and advice during the Sprint. This

---

[1] Luke Hohmann, Innovation Games: *Creating Breakthrough Products through Collaborative Play*, Addison-Wesley, 2006.

should be informal, and could involve advice about who some SMEs are for Stories that are being worked on, for example.

Of course, the Stakeholders are *always* free to add new Items to the backlog; they are *always* free to lobby the PO/BO for things that they want; but they *must not* meddle with the individual Team Members. The Team Members *will* be getting help from some of the Stakeholders – the ones that are actually Subject Matter Experts (SMEs) – and I'll be discussing that in the next section.

Subject Matter Experts

Okay, so let's talk about SMEs, which I define as *people that are not on your Team who have skills that your Team needs*. Now, these Subject Matter Experts can be experts in many different fields: they can be experts in the problem domain (business analysts, people who use your software, client representatives, and so on), they can be experts in the solution domain (architects, back-end database gurus, usability experts, and so on), they can be experts in process, environment, infrastructure, whatever...

Your Team's SMEs might have started off as Stakeholders who were co-opted to help you. Your SMEs have their hearts in the right place – they really want to help you develop a Quality Product. However it is important to realize that the SME's priorities are *not* your Team's priorities – the SME is *not* accountable to the Team; the SME is accountable to his or her own boss. This means that whenever the Team requires the use of a SME, it is taking a risk. It is taking a risk because the Team's Product Owner is accountable for delivering the work, the Team Members are accountable to each other (and the Product Owner) for doing the work, and the SME (who the Team is depending on) could have different priorities. In other words, you can't trust a SME. ;-)

So, how do you manage this risk?

The best thing to do would be to get the SME assigned to your Team for the Sprint; to make the SME a temporary Team Member. If you can't do this officially, do it unofficially – make the SME *feel* like one of the Team. One of the Organizations I work with calls this extended team the 'Sprint Team,' which has a nice ring to it. It's not official Scrum, but I like it... so I define the Sprint Team to be the Scrum Team *along with* any external SMEs who are (either officially or unofficially) members of the Team during the Sprint.

If you can't make the SMEs part of the Scrum Team, you do all the obvious things to mitigate the risk. You try to make sure that the SME will be available during the Sprint; you get assurances from the SME's boss that the SME has your work as his number one priority, and you assign somebody on your Team to watch him like a hawk. This often won't be enough... if I had a nickel for every time a ScrumMaster has told me that his number one impediment was that SMEs don't deliver what they promise, I'd be a zillionaire by now. ;-)

So, if those things are not enough, what is? Well, nothing provides a sure-fire guarantee, but I propose using the 'Buddy-Up' pattern. This pattern is pretty simple. What the Team does when it agrees to a Story that requires a SME is make an *existing* Team Member (the SME-Buddy) accountable for what the Team wants the SME to do.

Then there are two cases: either the SME does the work, or the Team's SME-Buddy does the work as best he or she can. In the second case, the situation is explained to the Stakeholders during the Product Review, and there are three sub-cases:

- The resulting work is fine as is, and we're actually Done;

- The resulting work satisfies the Stakeholders from a Business Value perspective, but is not good enough technically; that is, it causes Technical Debt. In this case the Team needs to add a Cleanup Story to the Backlog (see chapter 4.5); or

- The result is not good enough for the Stakeholders to live with, so a new Story is added to the Backlog, and the Team tries to get the Stakeholders to help get the SME 'freed up' to actually do the work next time.

There are some further nuances with the Buddy-Up pattern:

- When the SME is actually doing the work, the Team Member (the SME-Buddy) who is accountable should actually work with the SME. The best case is that the SME-Buddy actually *does* the work under the tutelage of the SME, because this eventually causes the SME to be unnecessary and removes the risk entirely. In other words, you are using the SME's expertise, but not his manpower.

- There are often many Teams that are competing for the same SME. When this happens you can think of the collection of each of the Teams' SME-Buddies as its own team whose job it is to share the SME. This leads to self-organizing and self-management of this small virtual team as it cooperates to share the SME.

- If the SME is responsible for some part of the Story's Agreement, it could lead to a situation where the Story is not technically Done, but the Team can't do anything about it. So, what I suggest you do is have the Team's SME-Buddy do the work as best he or she can, add a Cleanup Story to the Backlog, call the Story Done for now, and discuss the issue at the Product Review (there is a discussion of this issue in chapter 3.6).

- In the hierarchical 'Pattern 3' arrangement (Figure 14), the SMEs are often controlled by somebody higher up the Organization, perhaps the Business Owner. In this case the Team uses the appropriate Product Owner Team to help apportion the SME's time amongst the Teams that require it. It is likely that part of the Product Owner Team's Daily Scrum will be taken up discussing apportionment of SMEs.

Okay, that's almost enough about the SME for now. Let me make two more comments:

- It is the Product Owner's responsibility to know who the SMEs are. Usually the Product Owner works with the Stakeholders or the Business Owner to figure this out, and

- When agreeing to a Story that requires a SME, it's a good idea to document who the SME is as part of the Story's Agreement (see chapter 3.6).

That's it for SMEs that are needed to help develop Product.

The ScrumMaster and Outsiders

Finally... it's not just about Product. A Team's ScrumMaster often works with people who are outside the Team, because the ScrumMaster is responsible for the removal of the Team's impediments. As I will discuss in chapter 4.1, one of the categories of impediments requires the ScrumMaster to get some help from outside the Team.

This means that the ScrumMaster will have his or her own collection of SMEs (and Stakeholders) who deal with things like Team and Process issues. These SMEs often include people who work in Finance and Human Resources; they usually include the Functional Managers of the Team Members, and so on.

In order to get impediments removed, the ScrumMaster often needs to go work with somebody who has legitimate power and authority within the Organization. This person is often called the Team's Champion (or Sponsor), and this Champion is often also the Team's Business Owner. Of course, it could be somebody else; the Champion might even be the Team's Product Owner. However, there is an interesting 'wrinkle' to this idea in a 'Pattern 3' (strict hierarchy, Figure 14) type Organization.

In a hierarchical structure like this one, the ScrumMaster usually goes to the ScrumMaster the next level up for help. For example, rather than going directly to the Business Owner, the ScrumMaster might go to the Business Owner's ScrumMaster. Then the Business Owner's ScrumMaster can ask the Business Owner to do something, or could continue up the ScrumMaster hierarchy, which is parallel to the Product Owner hierarchy made up of Product and Business Owners.

This ScrumMaster hierarchy manages itself the same way the Product Owner hierarchy does, with ScrumMaster Teams that work on impediments, people, and process issues rather than product-based ones. If the ScrumMasters need to use some actual power to make something happen, the appropriate ScrumMaster whispers guidance into his Product Owner's ear, and this Product Owner uses his or her inherent Organizational power to take care of the problem.

This issue of how the ScrumMaster makes stuff happen with help from outside the Team is a very interesting topic all in itself, but I'll just leave it for now...

Summary

The Scrum Team doesn't live on an island. It lives within an Organization of some kind, and in order to get its work Done, it must work with people outside the Team. In this chapter I have given a quick overview of some of the issues involved. However, every Organization is different, so when it comes right down to it, you'll have to figure out what works for yours.

Discussion Questions

1. The Roles of Business Owner, Stakeholder, and Subject Matter Expert are not part of the Scrum Framework. Why do I spend so much time talking about them in this book?

2. The Business Owner is often the person the Team's Product Owner is accountable to. Discuss some examples of this sort of arrangement in your Organization.

3. SMEs are 'people that are not on your Team who have skills that your Team needs'; and SMEs are typically shared across Teams. How is this managed? What do you think the 'scrummish' way to do this is?

4. Who can add items to the Backlog? Anyone? Who keeps the Backlog 'clean'? How do you avoid and eliminate confusion in the Backlog?

5. Which Stakeholders should be invited to the Product Review? Does 'who gets invited' change based on the results of the Sprint?

6. What happens if SMEs do work that is not 'good enough'?

The Team Swarm

Scrum is about Teams producing Results, not people doing work.
The best way that Teams can produce Quality Results is by
working together, helping each other out, having conversations,
and just plain 'getting it done.' This pattern of work is called the
Team Swarm, and I discuss it in this chapter.

Ever since I started developing software I have noticed that Teams that work well together are quite noisy; there are lots of conversations going on. Team Members work together, help each other out, and have an almost continuous conversation. Some people move from Story to Story, helping out whoever needs help; some people stay put and concentrate on a single Story. Years ago, when I worked at Net Objectives, I identified this pattern of behavior and called it the Team Swarm; the name caught on and has been used by many people ever since.

In this chapter I'd like to talk about the Team Swarm and related topics.

Definition

First of all, let's define what I mean by Team Swarm. It does *not* mean that the *whole* Team Swarms on one Story until it's Done (even though this an option); what it means is that the Team Swarms on *each* Story until it is Done, but it may be Swarming on several Stories at the same time.

At any given time the Team consists of a few TeamLets, each of which is working on a single Story. The Team is constantly self-organizing these TeamLets, in order to best work on the Stories the Team has agreed to. One of the ScrumMaster's primary responsibilities is to make sure that the Team does this (see chapter 2.3). Let me make some definitions first, and then give some examples. Then we'll move on to other issues involving the Team Swarm. First, the basic definitions:

TeamLet: The TeamLet is the collection of people that are working on a given Story. Every Story being worked on has a TeamLet working on it, even if the TeamLet consists of only one person. The TeamLet is made up of no more than one Coordinator and (possibly many) Swarmers.

Coordinator: The Coordinator is the Team Member who is 'in charge' of the Story being worked on. Sometimes there is not a single person 'in charge' of a Story; the whole Team (as a collective) is 'in charge.' In this case there would be no Coordinator – only Swarmers. A person can be a Coordinator for only one Story at a time, but could be a Swarmer on other Stories. (The Coordinator is also called the Story's Point Person, Captain, or StoryBoss.)

Swarmer: A Swarmer is a person who is moving from Story to Story, working with those Story's Coordinators and other Swarmers, in order to offer his or her expertise and efforts wherever they are needed.

We can see what this looks like in the following diagram, where we see a 7-person Team's division into 2 or 3 TeamLets at any given time. This picture shows the Team's structure through time, with the 'C's being Coordinators, the 'S's being Swarmers, and the 'clumps' representing the TeamLets working on Stories. As you can see, the Team Members are moving from Story to Story as the situation warrants.

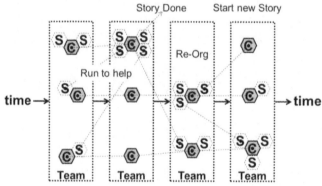

Figure 15: The Team 'Swarming' through Time

Now that we have the definitions, let's see some examples.

Swarming Examples

In general, people can either be specialists or generalists, and the Scrum Team may be made up of either or both. In what follows, however, when I refer to a person as a coder or an analyst, I'm not referring to a specialist, but rather to a person who has those skills. A Scrum Team is made up of people with skills (each of whom is simply called a Team Member or Developer) and it is those people that are involved in the Swarming. Of course, there are also SMEs involved, who act as a kind of honorary Team Member, or member of the Sprint Team, while they're working on Stories...

With that in mind, let's look at some examples of Swarming.

Pairing of Developers: Pairing is a practice often associated with eXtreme Programming (XP), in which each Story is worked on by two Developers, working side-by-side at one computer, collaborating on the same design, algorithm, code or test. This has been practiced in industry with great success for years[1]. Many Teams have found it useful to rotate Pairs every 1-2 hours, which is referred to as Polygamous Pairing. Both Pairing and Polygamous Pairing are stylized forms of Swarming; however, only in the Polygamous case are there actual Swarmers.

In basic Pairing, where the Pair is fixed for the duration of the Story, the TeamLet is the Pair, one of the Pair is the Coordinator, and there are no Swarmers. In the Polygamous case, the Coordinator is the developer that stays with the Story (if there is one – sometimes nobody stays put for the duration of the Story's development), the Swarmers are the developers who come by and Pair on the Story, and the TeamLet consists of everybody who worked on that Story (basically, the whole Team). Of course, the Team could self-organize to form a hybrid of the two – Pairing is pretty flexible, and I like it... but it's not the only way to go.

Stay-at-Home Coder: It is generally accepted that coders have a tough time context switching; that is, when they are buried deep in a piece of code and they have to come out to do something else, it then takes them awhile (sometimes a long while) to get back 'into the code.' Therefore, one of the patterns of Swarming is the Stay-at-Home Coder pattern.

In this pattern each coding Story gets a coder as its Coordinator (remember that not all Stories are coding Stories). The non-coders on the Team (analysts, testers, and so on) then become Swarmers that share their expertise across all the coding Stories as well as work on the non-coding Stories.

In other words, these non-coders will be Coordinators for non-coding Stories and Swarm on the coding Stories, while the coders will stay-at-home with their individual coding Story – they will only Swarm after their story is Done.

The Team will probably need a coder to be a Swarmer in order to give technical support to the other coders and help others with the non-coding Stories. Since this coder should not be Coordinating a coding Story at the same time, we say that the Team has kept one coder *in reserve* to act purely as a Swarmer.

This pattern is very similar to the Polygamous Pairing pattern, except that the Swarming is not limited to a Pair of Developers at a time. Sometimes the Coder works by him or herself, and at other times it is useful for a coder, an analyst, and a tester (or some other combination) to all be working together at the same time – and that's what this pattern allows.

---

[1] For further information on Pairing, see Williams, Laurie. *Pair Programming Illuminated*, Addison-Wesley, 2003

Single Item Flow: Single item flow (also called 'single piece flow' or 'one piece flow') is a lean manufacturing concept that says that each individual Item will move through the manufacturing process *all at once* with no waiting between steps. On software teams, this means Stories don't wait for people who have skills they need – the people are available when they're needed.

So, on software teams, Single Item Flow has usually been taken to mean that the whole Team has all the skills it needs (no need for SMEs), and works on a Story until it's Done – and then the team moves on to another Story. In our Swarming terms, this would mean that there is a Coordinator for each Story, and that everybody else on the Team is dedicated to that Story, as well. This seems wasteful to most people, so most Teams don't want to do it.

But that's ok, since Single Item Flow doesn't necessarily *require* the whole Team. To be more specific, I think that Single Item Flow really means that a TeamLet Swarms on a Story until it's Done, and the TeamLet must have *all* the skills necessary to get that Story Done. In other words, there can be no Swarmers that have skills that are required by more than one TeamLet *at a time*. This takes some careful coordination between the TeamLets, in order to use these specialists without interrupting the flow of any of them – but this is why the Team self-organizes all the time, isn't it?

When looked at this way, strict Pairing of Developers is a form of Single Item Flow, since nobody but the Pair works on the Story, and that's all the Pair works on until it is Done – there are no required Swarmers. This can also be true of Polygamous Pairing, as long as none of the Developers are Specialists required by more than one Story at the same time.

Having multiple TeamLets each doing Single Item Flow is a fine idea, and is basically what the Team Swarm concept is trying to achieve. It will work reasonably well as long as the Team is not overly constrained by the availability of required Swarmers – including the SMEs.

Professional Swarmers: Some people that do the Team's work shouldn't be Coordinators of Stories; they should only Swarm *(technically, many of them should Mostly Swarm, but let's look at it simply first – then see the follow-up section)*. We refer to these people as Professional Swarmers; and their primary production responsibility is to augment, support, and provide expertise, brainpower, and additional muscle to existing TeamLets. Some of these people are:

- **Product Owner:** The Product Owner has significant responsibilities that are conducted external to the Team, and we are usually safe in assuming that the Product Owner could be pulled away any time to work with Stakeholders or the Business Owner. Therefore, it is unwise to have the Product Owner be a Coordinator because the

Product Owner can't be dedicated to a Story. However, the Product Owner is a person with skills who acts as a Team Member, so the Product Owner is often used as a Professional Swarmer.

- **ScrumMaster:** The ScrumMaster's basic responsibilities are to be a trainer, coach, mentor, impediment remover, facilitator, and so on. Therefore, at any moment, the ScrumMaster may be called upon to do something other than work on a Story as part of a TeamLet. Therefore, the ScrumMaster should not be used on a Story in a Coordinator role, but should only be used as a Swarmer. Like the Product Owner, the ScrumMaster is a person with skills and is used as a Team Member – so the ScrumMaster should be a Professional Swarmer.

- **External SMEs:** SMEs are people from outside the Team who have skills that the Team needs. Because they're not Team Members, they can only be Swarmers; but there's more to it than that. In chapter 2.5 we saw that we can't really trust the SMEs to stay focused on the same priorities that the Team has, so we Buddy them up with a Team Member while doing work for the Team. In a Swarming situation, a SME could Buddy up with a Team Member permanently, and the Pair of them work as a unit Swarming from Story to Story, or the SME could buddy up with somebody on each of the TeamLets. Either way, what the Team gets is the SME's expertise and Buddies that are smarter. What the Team doesn't get is the actual extra manpower.

- **Tech Leads:** Technical Leads, Development Leads, and so on, are an interesting issue. These Team Members should be used more as mentors, trainers, or coaches than they are used as actual developers – that is their job now. For example, Tech Leads don't usually *write* code anymore, they work with others to help *them* get better at writing code. Therefore, folks like these should work as Professional Swarmers, and move from Story to Story doing the mentoring, coaching, and training that they are supposed to do.

- **Internal SMEs:** Even though we officially use the term 'SME' to refer to *external* Subject matter Experts, we probably have experts on our Team (Technical Writers, Database Gurus, and so on). These people will be in demand by many different Stories and TeamLets, so they should be used as Professional Swarmers. Unlike external SMEs, however, they *do* have the Team's priorities in mind and therefore don't have to be Buddied Up. The Team might decide to Buddy them up anyway, so that the Team can spread the expertise around, but this knowledge sharing usually happens naturally because of discussions that happens inside the TeamLet.

***Mostly* Swarmers:** Many of the Professional Swarmers I mentioned in the last section are actually *Mostly* Swarmers. Let me give you an example, and leave it at that. Let's look at the Technical Writer. It is likely that most Stories have a requirement something like 'Tony the Tech Writer reviews the online documentation' as part of its Definition of Done, so we could reasonably assume that Tony would be a Swarmer on each of these Stories. In fact, he probably helps write the online documentation for each Story, and also gathers whatever else he needs for the other documentation he is responsible for (User Manuals, Marketing Materials, and so on).

Tony may also have his own on-going Stories like 'Produce the User's Manual' and 'Help Marketing with Advertisements' that he does more-or-less by himself (from the Team's perspective), so he's the Coordinator for them. He probably spends some time in every Sprint on these Stories (so they are officially Epics), but only when he's not Swarming. In other words, his *first* responsibility in most Sprints is to Swarm, but he may have ongoing background Stories he's the Coordinator for. These Stories may move to the foreground once in a while (like during a Release Sprint), when they may actually be Swarmed on by other Team Members.

I call people like Tony 'Professional Swarmers' even though they are also Coordinators. This is because their primary responsibility is to Swarm, and their own Stories are of secondary concern in most Sprints.

The Kanban(ish) Variant: Chapter 4.7 of this book is on the 'Kanban(ish) Variant,' and I'd like to simply note that using it results in Team behavior that is very similar to the Swarming behavior I am discussing here – the only significant difference is that the Stories that are eligible to be Swarmed on next are not already agreed to. That is, when a Story is Done and the Team is deciding what to do next, the Stories that are eligible to Swarm on next can come from anywhere in the Backlog – not just from the Sprint Backlog. Typically, though, they come from the Back Burner, as the Back Burner is full of Stories that are ready to be agreed to (see chapter 2.1).

Self-Organization and Self-Management

The previous section contains examples of Team Swarming behavior – there are many more. Team Swarming is the core behavior resulting from the Team's self-organization and self-management – and is managed in many different ways. The key thing to remember is that it's about the Story; *'What does the Story need?'* is the *primary* question that self-organization is responding to. It's not about the people: *'What do you want to do?'* has got to be a question of *secondary* importance to a Scrum Team.

The Daily Scrum is a formal discussion in which this Swarming behavior is managed. During the Daily Scrum each Story's Coordinator could discuss the status of his or her TeamLet, and talk about whatever needs the Story has today. With this information the Team decides how to re-organize the Team in order to support all the TeamLets (see chapter 4.8).

If the Team is doing Polygamous Pairing, the Team can have the Swarmers move by the clock – like speed dating. For example, you might have the Swarmers all pick up and move to the next TeamLet every 90 minutes or so.

Of course, as Teams mature, they will Swarm on their own. It will be a nearly continuous activity with Team Members moving from TeamLet to TeamLet as the Stories' needs change. This movement is what causes the constant conversation and buzz that typifies the Team Swarm, and is something the ScrumMaster is facilitating (if not orchestrating) at all times.

What Happens When a Story Gets Done?

One of the obvious questions that comes up when a Team is Swarming is *'what happens when a Story gets Done?'* What happens when a Team has done its job and has finished a Story? There is a TeamLet now that is out of a job and needs something to do.

Well, it's actually pretty easy, but it does require the Team to self-organize. Basically, when the Story gets finished there is one Coordinator who has been freed up, and all the Swarmers are Swarming on one fewer Story – but they're still Swarmers. So there are a couple of choices:

- The Coordinator can just convert to Swarming, and all the members of the TeamLet that just finished now start Swarming on other Stories, with other TeamLets; or

- A new Story can start, with its Coordinator either being the Coordinator of the TeamLet that just finished or any of the Team Members that are currently Swarming.

In either case, the Team figures it out with the ScrumMaster's help. One common thing to do is have the finished TeamLet's members start Swarming on the unfinished Stories, and just raise the issue at the next Daily Scrum. At that time, the Team will probably decide to have a short discussion to re-plan and self-organize in order to continue to optimize its Story production. They could continue to Swarm, or select a Story from the Sprint Backlog (Front Burner) to Swarm on next. If the Team is using the Kanban(ish) Variant of Scrum (chapter 4.7), the whole Team must have a short Planning discussion and agree to a new Story from the Backlog – probably from the Back Burner.

Simplify the Story Board!

As you can see, when the Team is a Team that Swarms, a Story really only has three states: 'Not Started' (there is no TeamLet), 'In Progress' (there is a TeamLet Swarming on it), or 'Done' (the TeamLet is disbanded). There are a couple of other (error) states – 'Interrupted' or 'Impeded' – but these are treated either as a kind of 'Done' (if the TeamLet has been disbanded, and we'll pick the Story up again later) or is a kind of 'In Progress' (when the TeamLet is working to get the Story unimpeded, so that *real* Swarming can continue).

In any case, the Story Board (the stickies on the wall or in the tool) should represent the simple reality, and only have the three states: 'Not Started', 'In Progress', and 'Done'. In my experience, when a Team has more states than this, it's because they really don't want to Swarm, so they are artificially building in a series of handoffs – a form of waterfall.

For example, one of the states most teams use when it gets complicated is the 'To Verify' or 'For Testing' state. This is actually a *bad* thing, as it is intentionally trying to remove the Swarming behavior that happens between coders and testers. Don't do this! These particular communications, when the tester is helping the coder with coding and the coder is helping the tester with testing, are some of the most powerful and useful Swarming behavior a Team can do. And, of course, an analyst should help them both...

Not only that, but when there is a Story Board with many different states on it, the Team invariably starts concentrating on moving tasks across the Board rather than concentrating on what Done should mean. The Team should not do this, as the Story's Agreement (see chapter 3.6) is what drives the development of the Story – not the movement of Tasks across the Story Board. If the Team needs to see progress, turn the Doneness Agreement into a Checklist, and have a ceremony of checking off Doneness Checklist Items (see chapter 4.6 for more on this.)

One could argue, and many have, that by putting the states on the Story Board you are actually *helping* the Team by making the Story Board represent the Story's Agreement. That would be a good idea, if it were true. However, different Stories' Agreements can be fundamentally different, so there can't be a *single* Story Board that would work for all of them. Either the Story Board will be too simple to be useful, or it's just plain wrong for some of the Stories, and the Team will get confused. Either way it's bad, so don't do it!

Summary

The Team Swarm is a pattern that most successful Teams use, even many non-agile ones. The main reason that it's good is that it focuses on the needs of the Stories, and adapts the Team's organization and behavior based on those needs.

The Team Swarm encapsulates the Lean Concept of Single Item Flow and uses constant Team self-organization and self-management to keep the flow optimized. The Daily Scrum is largely concerned with the Team's self-organization in order to maintain an effective Team Swarm, and it is the ScrumMaster's responsibility to facilitate, orchestrate, and organize the Swarm.

Discussion Questions

1. Some Organizations say they don't micromanage because they don't assign *Tasks* to individual Team Members. However, they often assign *Stories* to individuals. Is this ok? Does this interfere with the Team's Swarming behavior?

2. Do Stories *need* somebody to Coordinate their getting Done? Is having a person *appointed* as Coordinator a good thing, or a bad thing?

3. Have you ever seen spontaneous Swarming behavior? If so, when and why? Do you think it would work *all* the time?

4. What are professional swarmers? Who do think should be professional swarmers?

5. In this chapter I said that a Team's self-organization is often based on asking the question *'What does the Story need?'* How do you feel about this, and how does it affect the Team's Swarming behavior?

6. Discuss the similarities, differences, and relationships among the following concepts: swarming, self-organization, self-management, and self-determination.

Section 3: The Product

The purpose of a Scrum Team is to produce Results that satisfy Stakeholders' desires, needs, and wants. These Results are built incrementally, with each piece being pulled from the Team by its Agreement on what Done means, rather than being pushed out by the Process. This is a Lean concept that is incorporated into Scrum by design (see appendix A.5).

Because of this emphasis on Doneness, Scrum generally considers quality to be more important than quantity, which leads to interesting issues that are discussed throughout this book.

In this section I explore issues about the Product (the Team's Work Results), the Stories that represent work the Team will do to produce these Results, the Backlog of such Stories, and so on.

$$\boxed{3.1}$$

What is 'Product'?

Throughout this book I talk very glibly about the Team's Product
or Work Results, as if it was obvious what that means. It isn't. In
this chapter I have a short discussion about the topic...

In this book I use the words Product, Work Results, and Results almost interchangeably, in order to signify that there is some ambiguity about what a Scrum Team should produce. In this chapter I'd like to discuss this issue.

When it comes to Scrum Teams that actually develop software, Ken Schwaber has some strong words to say about what a Team should deliver – what its Product should be. He says that Scrum requires teams to build a Done (or Potentially Shippable[1]) Increment every Sprint, which means that *"the increment consists of thoroughly tested, well-structured, and well-written code that has been built into an executable and that the user operation of the functionality is documented... This is the definition of a 'done' increment"* [S1, pg. 12].

The reason for this definition of Product is simple. Ken wants to make sure we don't ship poor quality software, and I agree. Since the Product Owner has the *authority* to ship anything he or she wants to ship, the only way we can *guarantee* we don't ship poor quality software is to make sure the Team *doesn't produce* poor quality software.

This notion of delivering 'quality stuff' is ubiquitous in Scrum. Since the Product Owner has the authority to ship anything he or she wants, the Team must make sure that *anything* they build has the technical quality that should be in a shipped product. Ken uses the phrases *potentially shippable* and *potentially releasable* for this purpose, and the concept of the Definition of Done (see chapters 3.6 and 3.10) was developed to make sure that anything we call 'done' actually has the technical quality we want.

Since the phrase 'potentially shippable/releasable' is confusing (*the Product Owner has the right to release something that isn't potentially releasable?!?*), I prefer to use a phrase something like *'the Team uses its due diligence to deliver product that meets the Definition of Done.'*

Anyway, let's get back to discussing Product...

---

[1] The phrases 'Done Increment', 'Potentially Shippable Increment', and 'Potentially Releasable Increment' are synonyms in Scrum. In order to avoid confusion, I will stick to the phrase 'Done Increment' in this book.

Not producing a technically inferior product is a noble goal, and I agree with it completely. However, Ken's definition is specifically about software, so his definition of what the Team delivers won't work for *all* Teams and *all* Products. In fact, even for Teams that *do* deliver software it's not quite that simple, for two major reasons:

1. Stakeholders want what they want, and

2. It's all about the feedback.

In this chapter I will discuss these two issues so that you can understand what I mean when I talk about Product/Results. This discussion will start by talking about Teams that have software as their ultimate product, and we'll see where it goes from there.

Stakeholders Want What They Want

So, let's assume that we *are* in an Organization that *is* developing software, and consider our Stakeholders. Stakeholders want what they want, and as I said in chapter 1.2, *"the Product Owner must guide the Team to build Product[s] that satisfy the Stakeholders' needs, wants, and desires."*

What if the Stakeholders *don't want* software – what if they want something else? What if they want something we might consider perverse, like a software design description? Would the Team give it to them? Or would the Team go on strike?

Well, I'd probably try to talk them out of it. I'd patiently explain that having real, working, software would be better... and they would patiently explain to me that they need a detailed design document because the ultimate clients have asked for one; this is their Product for now, the software will come later.

I'm probably not going to win this argument, so my Team will deliver a design document, with numerous caveats indicating that this is only a potential design, it may change, etc., etc., etc... Ultimately, though, the Team will deliver the design document – that's its job, after all, to give the Stakeholders what they desire.

So, even in an Organization whose ultimate deliverable is a software Product, we see that the idea that the Team's Results should always be Done *software* is too constraining and simplistic. The Team needs to deliver what the Stakeholders care about; they might be asking for a Deliverable that is not software.

So, let's expand our scope to become more general, and assume that our Team's goal is to release a Product made up of Deliverables. For a software Product these Deliverables may include executable software, user documentation, training materials, and so on. For Teams developing other sorts of Products, the Deliverables are something else. Now, with this understanding, would it be reasonable to conclude that the Team should deliver a Done Increment of Deliverable every Sprint? (I know, that sounds funny, but you know what I mean...)

It's All About the Feedback

Unfortunately, the answer is still 'not always.' Logically, the *best* thing to deliver every Sprint *would be* a Done increment of Deliverable, so that it could be released if the Stakeholders said it was complete enough. For most Teams, however, not every Sprint is a potential Release Sprint – the purpose of *most* Sprints is to gather meaningful feedback about what the Stakeholders want in order to progress towards a Release in the future.

In situations like this, the Product the Team needs to deliver each Sprint is a Product that will elicit meaningful feedback about what the Stakeholders want and need – and this isn't always an increment of a Deliverable. To make it simple, let me discuss this in the context of the Deliverable being running software. Perhaps the most meaningful feedback (for the money) could be obtained with a StoryBoard, a Prototype, a Simulation, a Usability Study, or through some other means. If so, then that is what the Team should build as its Product in these (non-Release) Sprints.

Now, I'm not talking about Requirements Documents, Design Documents, or any other sort of *intermediate artifact* produced as part of the development process. Unless these are Deliverables *specifically* asked for by the Stakeholders, I wouldn't want to deliver them because it is unlikely that they are a good way to elicit meaningful feedback about the actual (final) Product. These intermediate artifacts are mainly about increasing the detail about *how* the Team is going to develop the Product; they are not about getting meaningful feedback about *what* the Stakeholders need and want. I *am* talking about something that simulates, demonstrates, or describes the actual Product, and that the Team is using to elicit meaningful feedback in a timely, efficient, manner.

In these situations we can see that the Team's Product every Sprint is not restricted to Done Increments of deliverables, but can also be other products used to elicit meaningful feedback about what the ultimate Deliverables should be.

Summary

Ok, that's enough to give you the general idea. Let me summarize. First of all, listen to your Stakeholders. The Team's job is to deliver Product[s] that satisfy them, and the Product Owner is accountable for delivering them.

Through the iterative process, the Team is gathering feedback every Sprint that helps the Stakeholders, the Product Owner, and the Team determine what the final Results should be.

Therefore, the Product[s] that are delivered and demonstrated every Sprint should be *either* increments of the final Result or *other* (possibly completely different) Products that provide meaningful feedback about *what* the final Result should be or do.

Discussion Questions

1. In this book, we use the phrases 'Work Results' and 'Product' almost interchangeably. What does this mean to the applicability of Scrum?

2. Can software be released every Sprint? Who determines if software is releasable – the Developers, the Product Owner, or the Stakeholders? Who determines if software is Done? Can software that is not Done be released?

3. I have observed the following Law: *"People do not know what they want until they experience your Product."* What is the implication of this Law on what we ship?

4. The purpose of most Sprints is to gather meaningful feedback from Stakeholders about what they want from us. Why don't we just get this information up front so that all we have to do is build the correct thing the first time?

$$\boxed{3.2}$$

The Backlog

The Backlog is the collection of 'stuff' that somebody wants the Team to do someday. In this chapter I provide an overview description of the Backlog that will be explored further in subsequent chapters...

With the exception of the Product[s] that the Team produces, the Backlog is the most important artifact involved in Scrum. Conceptually, the Backlog is very simple; it is merely a list of Items that "represents everything that anyone interested in the product or process has thought is needed or would be a good idea..." [SB, pg. 33] This is a simple concept, but, as we'll see, the Backlog itself can be quite complex.

The Backlog is used in two ways:

1. To drive development by being a prioritized list of Items representing work Stakeholders want the Team to do, and

2. To inform Stakeholders about the Team's work and progress in order to give them the information they need to understand, and participate in, the project.

In other words, the Backlog is used both to prioritize the work, and to enable understanding of the work in progress. The Backlog is an interesting beast, and in this chapter I'll discuss some of the things that make it so.

Backlog Basics

The primary purpose of the Backlog is to help manage the work the Scrum Team is doing, or will do. To be precise, it is used to manage *all* the Team's unallocated time – time that is not used by an intrinsic part of the Team's process. The Backlog is *owned* by the Scrum Team, and it consists of Items describing all the work that stakeholders[1] want the Scrum Team to do someday. This work that stakeholders want includes Items describing product functionality, bugs that need to be fixed, issues that need to be considered, problems /risks/fears that need to be addressed, improvements in environment and infrastructure, and anything else a stakeholder can think of.

---

[1] In this chapter I use the word 'stakeholder' to represent both external Stakeholders and Team Members. If I mean external Stakeholders, the word will be capitalized...

The Backlog is the place where *any* stakeholder can make a formal request for work from the Team. If the Team has more than one list where stakeholders (including the Team Members themselves) can make requests of the Team, then *all* of these lists are considered part of the Backlog. Obviously, it is best to have a Backlog that is all in one place; as having multiple places makes the prioritization murky – but multiple lists sometimes happen. In fact, it is quite common (even though we don't like it) to have a list of bugs, a list of risks or issues, and yet another list of requested features. In this case, it is the Product Owner's responsibility to have a single prioritization across all these lists (at least for the Items near the 'top' that might be worked on soon).

The Backlog should be visible to all stakeholders, and any stakeholder is allowed to add Items to the Backlog. Sometimes this adding of Items is filtered through the Product Owner, but I prefer that most (if not all) stakeholders have direct access to the Backlog. Adding an Item to the Backlog does not *guarantee* it will be worked on; but adding it to the Backlog is the proper way to *request* that it be worked on. However, it is only the Product Owner who prioritizes the Backlog (see chapter 3.9 for more guidance on prioritization).

By the way, when Scrum uses the word 'prioritize' with respect to the Backlog, it does not mean how *important* something is. Prioritization (in Scrum) is the *order* in which the Team does things – the Item we do next is the highest priority Item. This ordering is indicated by where an Item sits in the Backlog; Items that are near the top of the Backlog are likely to be worked on sooner than Items near the bottom. This concept of prioritization is what makes multiple places for holding Backlog Items a bad idea, as there will be multiple 'number one' priorities – one for each list.

Prioritization Buckets

Since the Items that are near the top of the Backlog will be worked on sooner, they must be better understood. It is tempting to want to understand *all* the Items on the Backlog, but this is just reinventing the detailed Requirements Document that has got us in trouble in the past. From a development point of view, the *main* purpose of the Backlog is to prioritize the work the Team will do. That is, the Backlog is used to allow the Product Owner to prioritize the use of the Team's time and to focus their efforts and attention. The Backlog naturally falls into five prioritization buckets that I will describe shortly. However, before I do that, I must introduce two terms that describe different 'sizes' of Items. These terms will be described and discussed in chapter 3.4, but here is what you need to know for now:

- **Story** – an Item that is small enough that the Team could actually do it all at once (in a single Sprint), and

- **Epic** – an Item that is 'too big' to get Done 'all at once' and, therefore, must be decomposed into Stories (we say that the Stories are *extracted* from the Epic or that the Epic is *decomposed* into Stories).

Now that I have these definitions, I can define, describe, and discuss the prioritization buckets that make up the Backlog and the state changes between them. Figure 16 gives a visual overview.

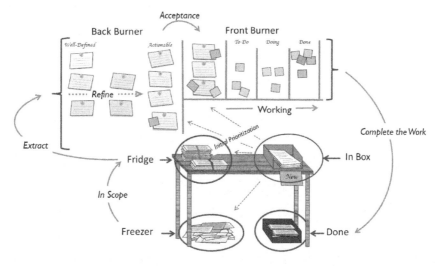

Figure 16: The 'complete' Backlog with Transitions

I have found the cooking metaphor a powerful and popular one, and I define the buckets within that metaphor:

- **Front Burner** – Stories that the Team has agreed to do in the current Sprint (traditionally called the Sprint Backlog…);

- **Back Burner** – Stories that are being made Ready so that they will be ready to be taken to Sprint Planning; these Stories are small, defined well enough to think about making them Ready, and of high priority;

- **Fridge** – Items (either Stories or Epics) that are in scope for the Release but not yet ready to be taken to Planning, either for prioritization or readiness reasons;

- **Freezer** – Items (either Stories or Epics) that are out of scope for the Release;

- **InBox** – Items that have not yet been prioritized into one of the previous Buckets; and

- **Done** – Stories that have been completed – usually not considered part of the Backlog proper, but discussed here for completeness.

There are basic state changes as Items move from one bucket to another, as follows:

- **Initial Prioritization** – when an Item is first identified to the Team, the Product Owner places it into the correct Bucket based on when it needs to be worked on, its readiness, and so on;

- **In Scope** – Items that are in scope for the current release are placed in the Fridge;

- **Extract** – the process of placing Stories in the Back Burner, either by extracting them from Epics, or by simply moving an existing Story;

- **Refine** – the process of refining Stories *well enough* so they are Ready and can be taken to Planning;

- **Acceptance** – once the Team Accepts a Story (in Sprint Planning) the Story is moved to the Front Burner to be worked on; and

- **Completing the Work** – actually doing the work (getting it Done, see chapter 3.6) moves the Story to the Done pile.

I would like to note that in some circumstances, such as a maintenance project, there are actually fewer prioritization buckets than we define here. For example, a Maintenance Project may only have a Front Burner and Back Burner, since every defect is already small enough to do, and all of them are eligible to go to Planning if the list is short enough. Of course, a Maintenance Project could also have all five buckets – even some defects that are big enough to be Epics.

Crazy Idea: maybe the Freezer is actually just the Trash Can – we don't keep *anything* unless it's in scope for the current release. This is rather extreme, but it has the advantages of keeping the Backlog manageable and preventing Items from hanging around forever. It's also consistent with a lesson I learned a long time ago that goes something like this: *'if you don't know when you're going to deal with it, throw it away – it'll show up again if it's actually important'*. Ron Jeffries documented a pattern similar to this in 2002, with his 'Petition the King' parable[2]. With all this going for it, maybe this isn't such a crazy idea, after all. Just sayin'…

---

[2] http://xprogramming.com/xpmag/petitiontheking/

Examples

Let me present some examples from the Catalina Air backlog in order to explain the Buckets and State Changes in more detail. The examples are simplified and simplistic, but they give a good overview of how Items enter, and move through, the Backlog.

Example 1: Renting Bicycles on Catalina Island. SirJeff just can't stop thinking about new things he wants to do on his CatAir website, and one day, early in the first Release, he comes up with the bright idea that he would like to have bicycles for his passengers to use when they arrive on Catalina Island. This idea precipitates the following actions.

1. SirJeff sends an e-mail to Dan (the Product Owner for the CatAir Project) asking for this new Capability. At this point it has entered the project's InBox, and Dan takes a look at. He gives SirJeff a call and they have a short discussion about it.

2. After this discussion, Dan summarizes this new Capability as follows:

    > 'Rent Bicycles on Catalina Island: If a Passenger is going to Catalina Island, we'd like to be able to have a bicycle waiting for him at the airport. SirJeff has a friend who will carry as many bicycles as we need to the airport in his truck. We don't actually rent the bicycles on the website, all we do is reserve them, and SirJeff's friend will do the rental at the time of delivery. We also don't need to worry about handling payments from SirJeff's friend, as this will be done off-line.'

    Since this new Capability is not in scope for the current release (Release One), Dan puts it in the Freezer, where it sits waiting for further review and analysis.

3. During the Release Planning for Release Two, SirJeff and the Team decide that this Capability is in scope for Release Two, so it is moved to the Fridge.

4. As the Team is analyzing the Capabilities that are in scope for Release Two, they realize that this one is an Epic and must be decomposed. The Team discusses the Epic and extracts the following Stories:

    *   'If the Flyer's destination is Catalina Island, add a 'Rent a Bicycle?' option on the Reservation Page,' and

    *   'Keep a running total of how many bicycles are needed for each flight landing on Catalina Island.'

These two Stories are now moved to the Back Burner, and the 'rest of' the Capability remains in the Fridge, as there might be more Stories needed to make this Capability releasable. While these two new Stories are in the Back Burner, they may be further refined in order to make sure they will be ready for Sprint Planning.

5. Finally, during Sprint Planning for the third Sprint of Release Two, the Team accepts the 'If the Flyer's destination is Catalina Island, add a 'Rent a Bicycle?' option on the Reservation Page' Story, so it moves to the Front Burner.

6. The Story is completed during Sprint 3 of Release Two, and at the end of the Sprint it is moved (with all the other completed Stories) to the Done pile.

Example 2: SCUBA tanks. At the Product Review for the third Sprint of Release One, SirJeff realizes that he needs to know if passengers going to Catalina Island are planning to take their own SCUBA tanks, as it will affect his luggage weight calculations – SCUBA tanks are *heavy*.

1. He brings this up to the Team during the Product Review, and it is at this point this new request has entered the Team's InBox.

2. Since the Main purpose of Release One is to 'Sell an e-Ticket on the Web,' this new request is in scope for this release. Therefore, it is immediately moved to the Fridge and is added to the 'Buy an e-Ticket' Capability that is already there. (Note that by this time *many* Stories for this Capability have *already* been extracted and completed, but the Capability is still in the Fridge in order to hold *new* information about this Epic/Capability.)

3. During its periodic Backlog Refinement activities, the Team realizes that this new request actually consists of two new Stories:

    • 'Get number of SCUBA tanks from Flyer,' and

    • 'Update luggage weight calculations to include SCUBA tanks.'

These new Stories are moved to the Back Burner where they can be refined for consideration for Sprint Planning sometime in this Release. Note that there is *no guarantee* that the Stories will actually be worked on in this Release, merely that they are *eligible* to be considered for this Release. In other words, these Stories are *in scope* and the Team believes they are *small enough* to be agreed to and accepted.

Example 3: Talking with a Pilot Timesheet Expert. One of the things that the Team has agreed to do in Release One is 'Investigate Pilot Timesheets' to see just how hard it would be to implement them on the CatAir website. The

Team did not expect to do this work until late in the Release, but SirJeff contacted Captain Jack, an expert on Pilot Timesheets, and scheduled a discussion with him two days from now, in the middle of the current Sprint (Sprint three).

1. So, SirJeff calls up Dan and tells him he's scheduled this discussion, thus putting the request for the discussion into the Team's InBox. Since this discussion had not been planned for, but will be in, the current Sprint, it sets off a flurry of activity.

2. The Team believes that this discussion with Captain Jack (along with internal follow-up discussions) will take a full day from two of their Team Members, and is thus a significant amount of work. There is no doubt that they will do the work, only that the current Sprint's Backlog (the Front Burner) must be adjusted and reprioritized in order to make it fit.

3. So, Dan and the Team sit down to negotiate how this will work. The result is that they move an already-accepted (but not started) Story from the Front Burner back to the Back Burner in order to make room for the discussion with Captain Jack, and they put a Story that represents this discussion directly into the Front Burner. (For discussions on renegotiating a Sprint's content, see chapter 4.3.)

4. The Team Members then have the discussion with Captain Jack as scheduled, discuss, analyze, and document the resulting information, and move the Story to the Done Pile.

Comments on Prioritization Buckets

I trust that these three examples have explained enough about the Prioritization Buckets to give you a good idea how they are used to drive development. In this section I will make some additional comments on the Buckets to explain some nuances that are not clear from looking at the examples.

InBox. Sometimes there is an actual section of the Backlog artifact called the InBox; I often add it in order to have a formal place for external Stakeholders to add new Items that they come up with. However, the InBox is usually only *virtual*; that is, when an idea is either presented to (or discovered by) the Team it is in the InBox even though it will be almost immediately prioritized into the appropriate section of the Backlog.

Freezer. It seems as if the Freezer could be simply an unorganized collection of Items. This is *sometimes* true, but in many Organizations the Freezer has its own organization in order to allow the Stakeholders and the Product Owner to analyze it in preparation for the next Release. However, it is a good idea for Team Members to be insulated from the Items in the Freezer as much as possible so that they won't be confused by looking ahead too far into the future.

Fridge. The Fridge contains Items that are in scope but not yet ready for Planning. In practice, this includes Epics that have not been completely decomposed, and Stories that are either ambiguous or that the Product Owner and Team do not think should be worked on right away.

Back Burner. The Back Burner contains Stories that are ready (or becoming ready) for Planning – they require additional refinement before going to Planning. When a Story moves into the Back Burner, I expect the Story to already answer the question: *'who wants what, and why?'* I also expect the Team to believe that the Story *can* be done all at once (within a single Sprint). However, the Story's Agreement (see chapter 3.6) may still need to be nailed down. The Stories in the Back Burner are Inventory (in the Lean sense, see appendix A.5) as there is an expectation that they will be worked on – and thus are waste and should be minimized. I suggest that you keep the number of Stories in the Back Burner small – usually no more than two or three Sprints' worth.

Front Burner. This is what is usually called the Sprint Backlog in the Scrum literature, and consists of Stories the Team has agreed to do. I like the term Front Burner because it fits with my cooking metaphor and sounds cool, and also because it *emphasizes* the fact that this is work the Team has agreed to do. Furthermore, if the Team is doing a Kanban(ish) version of Scrum (see chapter 4.7), the Front Burner represents the Work in Progress (WIP).

Describing Progress to Stakeholders

As I mentioned at the beginning of this chapter, the Backlog is also used "to inform Stakeholders about the Team's progress in order to give them the information they need to understand, and participate in, the project." Let me give you a short description of how the Backlog does this (see chapter 3.8 for a discussion about organizing the Backlog in order to make this discussion easier).

First of all, you can see that the Capabilities, Issues, and Risks that Stakeholders care about move into the Fridge once they are in scope – usually as Epics. In order to help the Stakeholders understand what is going on, they need to be able to maintain their focus on these Epics, and be able to tell what their status is throughout the Release. By having this understanding, the Stakeholders become knowledgeable enough to be capable of being full participants in the Product Reviews.

By looking at the structure of the Backlog, the Team and Stakeholders can see how the Stories that implement the Capability (or deal with the Risk or Issue) are extracted from the Epic (in the Fridge) and moved through the Back Burner to the Front Burner to being Done. By tracking and monitoring these Stories (for each Epic) as they move through the levels of the Backlog, everyone can understand what the status of the Capability, Issue, or Risk is.

In practice, as I'll discuss in chapter 3.7, the Team often puts a budget/quota of Stories (or StoryPoints) on each Epic indicating how much work the Team expects this Capability, Epic, or Risk will require (or consume) during the Release. As Stories are extracted from the Epic and completed, this quota is consumed throughout the Release. So, at any given point, we would have the following information about an Epic:

- How much work has been completed (the Epic's Stories that are in the Done pile);

- How much work is in progress (the Epic's Stories that are in the Front Burner);

- How much work is 'ready to go' (the Epic's Stories that are in the Back Burner);

- How much un-allocated work remains in this Capability's quota; and

- What work is considered out of scope for this Release (the Epic's Stories that are in the Freezer).

This information, coupled with Velocity calculations (also discussed in chapter 3.7), gives the Team and Stakeholders the ability to monitor the current situation, and (possibly) produce reasonable projections to the end of the Release. We really can't ask for too much more than that, can we?

A Simple Progress Report for Stakeholders

Since 'hard core' Release Planning and Monitoring are out of scope for this book, let me give you a simple example of a Capability's progress report, as seen in Figure 17.

I will discuss the 'Buy an e-Ticket' Capability. In the story I'm telling, this Capability was briefly analyzed before the project started, and there were 72 StoryPoints (SPs) worth of Stories already in the Back Burner at the start of the project – ready for the first Sprint's Sprint Planning. The Team believed that it would take 108 SPs of Done Stories to produce a releasable version of the Capability (the 72 SPs they already know about plus an additional 36 SPs worth of Stories they expect to find along the way...). This information, the data that the Team had at the beginning of the release, is represented by the 'Beg' column in the chart.

As the (7 Sprint) release progressed, a new column was added (each Sprint) in order to show the Capability's progress at the Product Review of each Sprint. Since the CatAir website was released after Sprint 7, the last column is labeled 'Rel' (for Release) rather than 'Sp-7.'

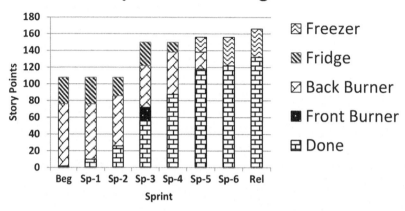

Figure 17: Graphing the Progress of 'Buy an e-Ticket'

Here's what this Chart is telling us:

- In Sprint 3 it was realized that 108 SPs was not enough to get a releasable version of the Capability, so the quota of SPs was raised to 150 SPs. This is a classic example of agility in action – of adapting to reality;

- From Sprint 1 to Release, the Team did 132 SPs of 'Buy an e-Ticket' Stories. At that point it was considered releasable – it didn't actually require all the SPs allocated as the Capability's ultimate quota;

- There were 12 SPs of work completed on this Epic in the last (release) Sprint. Some of this work (the Story 'Add User Help to the Website') was expected, but most was not. There was unexpected interface cleanup and bug fixing that was found to be necessary. This is not an ideal situation, but it happens;

- The number of 'Buy an e-Ticket' Stories that were ready to go (in the Back Burner) started out at 72 SPs and was about 40 SPs or less throughout the Release. This isn't too high, since the Team was getting about 20 SPs or so of this Capability completed each Sprint – so there was not *too* much waste;

- In Sprint 3 there were 16 SPs of 'not Done' work that needed to be carried from Sprint 3's Front Burner over to the Front Burner in

Sprint 4. This is *not* a good thing, but it happens, and it's necessary to report on it;

- In the last two Sprints there were more known Stories than there was quota. So, Dan (the Product Owner) moved Stories back to the Freezer as he realized they were nice-to-haves that weren't going to get worked on in this Release. The grand result was that at Release all the Stories were either Done or out of scope (in the Freezer); and

- The ones in the Freezer at the end of the Release are ready to be moved to the Fridge for the next release (if required), and the project continues...

As you can see, this report is both easy to generate and understandable. Give it a try; I think you'll like it.

Backlog Terms

Finally, let me show you a diagram showing the Backlog-related terms that you will find in this section on Product. Figure 18 gives a UML diagram of the terms I use concerning Backlogs and Backlog Items, as well as the relationships between them.

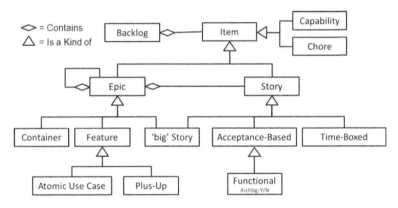

Figure 18: UML diagram of Backlog Terms

Here is an explanation of what this means, along with some short definitions and simple examples:

- A Backlog is made up of Items that represent valuable Work Results.
- Items can be either Capabilities or Chores.
- Items can be either Epics or Stories.
- Epics are Items that the Team can't agree to do 'all at once'.
- Epics contain Stories and (possibly) other Epics.
- Stories are Items that have a well-defined Agreement on Done.

- 'big' Stories are Stories that are too big to bring into a Sprint as a whole, and thus are also Epics.
- Features are Epics that are released as a whole, and don't have a well-defined Agreement on Done; their Doneness is usually 'fuzzy'.
- Containers are Epics that are used to hold (relatively) independent Stories, such as a 'Collection of SouvSite Bugs'.
- Atomic Use Cases are Features representing functionality achieved by a user in a single session with the system, such as 'Buy an e-ticket' or 'Rent a Hotel Room'.
- Plus-Ups are Features that add functionality to an existing Use Case, such as 'Add Hotel-Renting functionality to Buy an e-Ticket' or 'Make Buy an e-Ticket more robust'.
- Acceptance-Based Stories are those that have their Doneness defined by explicit Acceptance Criteria, and the effort it takes to do them is a byproduct of getting to Done; non-Functional examples include 'Release Buy an e-Ticket to the Production Server' and 'Install junit on all the Team's machines'.
- Time-Boxed Stories have their Doneness defined by a time-box, and the actual Results produced are limited to what can be completed in that time-box; examples are 'Spend two days investigating Pilot Timesheets' and 'Do one day of exploratory testing of Buy an e-Ticket'.
- Functional Stories are Acceptance-Based Stories that are defined by an Acceptance Test, like 'Get List of Flights from CUTLASS' or 'add new Passenger to existing Itinerary'.
- In addition, some Functional Stories are architecturally-significant.

These topics will be discussed in the remainder of this section. As you go along, I recommend that you periodically come back to Figure 18 and this list in order to judge your understanding...

So, let's get going...

Discussion Questions

1. Assume that you are a landscape crew. Describe how the request 'I want my front yard fixed up' could work its way through the Backlog.

2. What sorts of things would you expect to see in a Product Backlog? How does a Team handle 'overhead' tasks?

3. Any stakeholder can add Items to the Backlog. Can Items only be removed by the Stakeholder that put them there? What happens when the backlog becomes messy and overwhelming?

4. How does the Backlog inform the stakeholders about the progress of development?

5. What is the difference between extraction and refinement? Explain it to someone out loud by using a concrete example. Keep your book closed when you do this.

$$\boxed{3.3}$$

Capabilities and Chores

There are two types of work that a Scrum Team does: work that provides value to Stakeholders, and work that provides value to the Team or Product. I refer to these two types of work as Capabilities and Chores, and discuss them in this chapter.

The purpose of a Scrum Team is to provide value to its Stakeholders and, from a Team Member's point of view, the Backlog is very simple – it contains a prioritized list of Items that represent the work that needs to be done. As you probably know, it's not *really* that simple, but for right now I'm going to pretend that it is.

Well, almost. The reason we do work *at all* is because it provides value to *somebody*. Basically, we can divide the work into two categories based on who gets the value. We ask ourselves the question: *'Is the primary value the work produces for external Stakeholders, or is the primary value for the Team or the Product itself?'*

In the first case, when the value is to Stakeholders outside the Team, we say that the Item provides a Capability, and we often refer to the value as *Business Value*. In the second case, when the value is primarily to the Team or the Product itself, we say that the item is a Chore. There are a lot of nuances involved in these definitions, and we'll be discussing some of them in this chapter, and more of them in later chapters. But for now let's just go with the following definitions:

Capability: an Item that provides (business) value for external Stakeholders.

Chore: an Item that provides (internal) value for the benefit of the Team or the Product.

Now, let's discuss this a little more.

A Work Breakdown Structure (WBS)

Let's have a simple example. To take a simplified version of things, there are three reasons that a software Development Team does work:

- To develop Software Product[s], which includes
  - Adding or enhancing features to a Product, and

- o Improving the technical quality of a Product;

- To enable the Team to develop Software Product[s]; and

- To enable the Business to 'consume' the Software Product[s].

Figure 19 shows this Work Breakdown Structure (WBS) for the 'Catalina Air Project,' which is a project to develop the Catalina Air Website. As you recall, I am using this project for the examples throughout this book. This WBS breaks down into legs that represent the different reasons for doing work, and you might notice that each leg contains its own Issues/Risks bucket, along with the others you would expect.

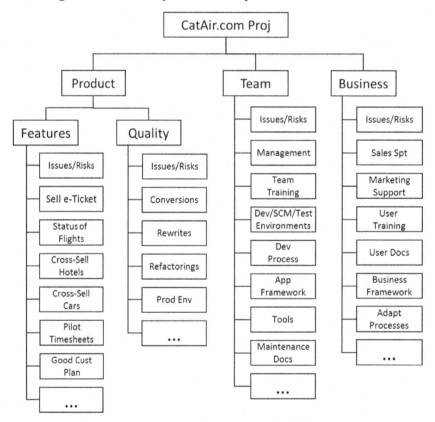

Figure 19: A Work Breakdown Structure for the Catalina Air Project

Now, let's take a closer look at this. If the primary Stakeholder is SirJeff (the owner of Catalina Air), and we look at this WBS from *his* point of view, then we can see that the Features and Business legs of the WBS are of primary interest to him. That is, these are the parts of the WBS that provide Business Value to SirJeff and thus we would consider them Capabilities.

The middle two legs of the WBS are not of *primary* value to SirJeff, and provide value to either the Product or the Team, and thus would be considered Chores. Now, I *know* that *all* of this work actually has value to SirJeff, and he's going to wind up paying for it, but we're talking about primary, *I really want it*, value.

In other words, Chores are things our Stakeholders know they need to pay for, but they don't *really* want to. They'd be just as happy if the code was magically written in the middle of the night by the 'coding faeries,' they're not *really* interested in the Team having a whiz-bang development environment, and so on.

And, then, there are the Issues and Risks. Issues and Risks lead to work the Team has to do in order to deal with them, and they occur all over the place. I have put a bucket for them in each leg of the WBS because Issues and Risks spring up in virtually every context, and we want to make sure we've captured them. They will eventually be decomposed through Backlog Refinement (see chapter 3.9) into Stories that can be dealt with, just like everything else...

Ok, so let's get into some more details.

Capabilities

First of all, let's talk about Capabilities. Basically, a Capability is something that an external Stakeholder has asked for; and it is something that provides value for that Stakeholder. When it comes to the Software Product[s] we're building, we're often talking about Features that provide value to End Users.

Capabilities are the things we talk about with our Stakeholders, and we talk about them in the Stakeholder's language. As we'll see in chapter 3.4, Capabilities are often Epics: large, hard to validate, chunks of work that must be decomposed to Stories to give to the Team to work on. The reason that we don't give these big Capabilities to the Team all at once is simple; they are large, hard to validate, chunks of work and lead to elongated feedback cycles – and having long feedback cycles is one of the things that gets us into trouble (think about the basic waterfall and its feedback cycle...).

Also, strictly speaking, Capabilities themselves are of secondary concern to the Team, as the Team Members will be working on individual Stories, not the overall Capability itself. However, the Product Owner must be able to talk to the Stakeholders about the work in progress, and therefore must be able to talk about Capabilities in the language the Stakeholders use and are thinking in. Talking about the Capabilities, in the language Stakeholders understand, helps everybody understand the Product the Team has built and is, therefore, a major contribution to the 'inspect and adapt' cycle.

As we know, Stakeholders can ask for virtually anything. Therefore, Capabilities can be virtually anything, from small bugs that need to be fixed to extremely large wishes and dreams. For example, each of the following statements describes a Capability because a Stakeholder has specifically asked for it:

- 'Remove the extra linefeeds in the presentation of the list of flights on the 'Choose a Flight' page' (a bug);

- 'I want to be able to specify that I need a special meal for my flight' (a new feature);

- 'I'm worried about the website not being fast enough' (an Issue that could lead to an extremely large, ambiguous request).

Another important thing to know about Capabilities is that the business value of a Capability comes from the Stakeholders. This has a major impact on the prioritization of the Backlog, even though the actual priorities are modified by dependencies that the developers see, as well as other factors (see chapter 3.9). Since Scrum requires a prioritized Backlog to work on, we can see that much of the ordering of the Backlog is derived from the Stakeholder's Capabilities and their business value.

Chores

It would be nice if *all* the work that the Team does was to develop Capabilities – but it isn't. The Team has to do a lot of work just because it is needed so that the Team can do *real* work. We call these things Chores, which basically are things that the Team needs to do, but the external Stakeholders would be more than happy that it didn't do.

Chores are work that just *needs to be done* in order to be successful at developing actual Product. One way I look at it is that Capabilities are things we do in order to provide value to Stakeholders, and Chores are things we do in order to maintain the Team's ability to provide those Capabilities.

More specifically, Chores are things we do in order to enable our Team to do work, or to improve the code base so that it can be worked with more easily, and so on. Here are some examples of Chores:

- 'Improve the build script to incorporate module ABC,'

- 'Re-arrange the Team room so that the testers and coders are sitting together,'

- 'Add a new test box to the lab so that we can do dedicated perform-ance testing,'

- 'Refactor the FlightInfo module so that it'll be easier to use,' and

- 'Have Joe spend some time coaching Diane and George on SQL.'

Another way to look at Chores is like this. The Team actually has two jobs: to produce Capabilities, and to maintain its Capacity to produce Capabilities. We can think of the Chores as work the Team does to maintain its Capacity, either by keeping the Code cleaner and easier to work with, or by improving the Team and its Environment.

Related Issues

The overall concept of Capabilities and Chores is relatively simple; however, there are some 'sticky bits' that have confused many of the people I have coached. I'd like to discuss some of these issues quickly.

Business Value. One of the things we often talk about is the concept of Business Value. This concept is closely related to the notion of Capabilities, since we have *defined* Capabilities to be those things that provide value to external Stakeholders.

Basically, then, saying that something is a Capability is equivalent to saying that it has Business Value. This doesn't mean that we know what the actual value is, just that it has some. Sometimes, we'd like to put a numerical value on the Business Value of the Capability, and we must work with our Stakeholders in order to do that.

Personally, I think that Business Value is intrinsically subjective, and not something that can be objectively determined. If we need to have a value, then, I think that the best way to do this is to play some sort of Estimation Game (see appendix A.6) with the Stakeholders. One thing I often suggest is to play the 'Buy a Feature' game from Luke Hohmann's book[1], which will produce relative business values for the Features being compared.

Risks and Issues. Both Stakeholders and Team Members have Fears, can see Risks and Problems, or have Issues, and they need to be captured on the Backlog. Generally speaking, Risks and Issues are Epics, because they are too complicated or ambiguous to deal with all at once. Sometimes they just sit there to remind the Team and Stakeholders to watch out for something. Sometimes they lead to changing Definitions of Done (see chapter 3.6). Sometimes they lead to Ready Stories as they get analyzed and refined. There is no clear-cut guidance of how to deal with Issues and Risks other than to document them, refine them, and work on any actionable bits that arise – just like any other Epic.

---

[1] Luke Hohmann, *Innovation Games: Creating Breakthrough Products Through Collaborative Play*. Addison-Wesley, 2006.

What if Stakeholders care about Chores? In general, I do not consider *anything* that a Stakeholder asks for to be a Chore. Therefore, if one of the Team's Stakeholders is asking for refactoring as a specific request, then it would be a Capability; but if the Team needs to do the refactoring so that it has Clean Code to work with, it is a Chore. It all depends on who is requesting it...

Sometimes this is confusing, but it doesn't matter *all* that much, as it's all work that our Product Owner has to prioritize anyway. If you are really worried about it, think of it this way: if the Product Owner will be held to account by the Business Owner (the person the Product Owner is accountable to) if the work isn't done, then it's a Capability; otherwise, it's merely a Chore.

If the Product Owner doesn't have a Business Owner to determine which things are important, and there are multiple Stakeholders holding the Product Owner to account for different things, then the Product Owner must 'make the call' and determine what is a Chore, and what is a Capability. Of course, this determination must be visible to all the Stakeholders, and the determination of the Product Owner must be respected.

Generally speaking, we would prefer that Stakeholders *not* care about what would normally be considered Chores. When Stakeholders define these things to be Capabilities it constrains the Team by removing some of the wiggle room the Product Owner normally has when prioritizing work. When the Product Owner can balance the efforts spent on Capabilities and Chores the Product Owner can do a *better* job of maximizing the value of the Work Results the Team produces and, as we know, this is the main responsibility of the Product Owner.

Prioritizing Chores. Many of my clients say to me*: 'My Product Owner isn't technical enough to prioritize Chores. What do I do?'* Good question... As a general rule of thumb, we would expect a Team to spend between 20% and 50% of its time doing Chores (depending on the quality of the codebase and other factors), with a number of around 30% being a good average.

If the Product Owner doesn't want to prioritize the Chore directly, here are three ways to get them done:

- **Orphan Tasks**: Every time a Capability is agreed to by the Team, a (hopefully relevant) Chore is *adopted* by that Capability as a Task. For example, if Capabilities A and B both need refactoring in Module X, the first of them to be worked on adopts the 'Clean Up Module X' Chore as a Task (also called the *First One in Buys* pattern).

- **Leftover Time for Chores**: The actual number of StoryPoints completed in a Sprint has a wide variance[2], often ±25%. Therefore, the only way to guarantee a *constant* Velocity is to agree to do 25% less than the Team can actually normally do, and stop doing work when you have met your agreements. So, have the Team only agree to Capabilities, and use the 'leftover time' each Sprint to work on Chores. This should result in between 0% and 50% of the Team's efforts on Chores each Sprint, which is approximately the right amount on average.

- **70/30 Rule**: During Sprint Planning the Team agrees to use 70% of its efforts to doing Capabilities, and 30% to doing Chores. In practice, this is often based on StoryPoints; 70% of the agreed-to StoryPoints are for Capabilities, and 30% of them are for Chores (of course, the actual numbers are up to your Team).

I prefer the 70/30 Rule because it actually *forces* the Product Owner to make the prioritization decisions (even though it provides some firm guidance about how to do so), and keeps the Product Owner clearly in charge of prioritization. But, no matter what method the Team uses, the goal is to get past many of the conflicts Scrum Teams have about prioritizing Chores.

Summary

The work a Scrum Team does, and the Items on the Backlog, comes in two types: Capabilities and Chores. Items that provide value primarily for external Stakeholders are called Capabilities, and Items that provide value primarily to the Team (or Product) are called Chores.

Understanding this difference is important when prioritizing, organizing, and understanding the Backlog, and will continue to be discussed throughout the following chapters.

Discussion Questions

1. Provide examples (with explanation) of Capabilities and Chores involved in landscaping the front yard or throwing a party. Now take one of those Chores and argue that it is actually a Capability.

2. What are some risks and problems inherent in landscaping the front yard? How might some of these risks and problems turn into Capabilities or Chores?

---

[2] This range is predicated on the Team doing approximately 10 stories in a Sprint. See the 'Some Simple Statistics' section of Appendix A.5 for a discussion.

3. If you are a landscaper you need to maintain your tools. Is maintaining tools a Capability or a Chore?

4. Chores do not provide business value, so who should pay for them? Should the Stakeholders who want Capabilities have to pay for Chores? Does the rule *'The Capability that finds the Chore should pay for it'* make sense to you? What other ways could we handle it?

5. What is the purpose of a WBS? How does this help us organize the work and consider the different risks/issues?

Stories and Epics

The Team's Backlog contains Items that represent work to be done, and value to be produced. Some of these items are small and well-defined, and some are large, ambiguous, and chunky. In this chapter I describe and define Stories and Epics. This topic is not as simple as it looks, and it is important that you understand the content of this chapter as you do Scrum.

The purpose of Scrum is to produce valuable Work Results (Product) based on Items in the Backlog. In the last chapter I talked about Capabilities and Chores, which are two big categories of Items. In this chapter I'm going to talk about Stories and Epics, which concern the 'size' of the Items that are in the Backlog.

From a development point of view, the most important type of Item is the Story, which is the small, well-defined, unit of work that the Team agrees to do and gets Done. From a Stakeholder point of view, however, the more important Items are usually Epics representing Capabilities, Risks, or Issues.

So, let's discuss Stories and Epics.

Stories

The most important unit of work that a Scrum Team does is the Story. The Story is a small unit of work (Item) that the Team does 'all at once' and is used to provide small units of value. This value could be a complete or partial Capability, a Chore, resolution of an Issue or Risk, or anything else.

In general, I think of a Story as simply a request for the Team to do something of value. This does not mean releasable value; that's what Capabilities are for. It does mean demonstrable, testable, verifiable value, as the Team needs to be able to inspect and adapt based on the results.

A Story is an extension of the User Story, which is a concept introduced in eXtreme Programming (XP) to represent work that provides value to users. Since not all work items the Scrum Team does provide value to users, I extend the concept to represent work that provides value to some stakeholder, not only the user. For this reason, I just call them Stories and often add a modifier, as in 'Analysis Story' or 'Infrastructure Story' or 'Coding Story.'

In spite of the fact that not all our Stories are User Stories, it is useful to look at the INVEST acronym, which Bill Wake[1] originally introduced to describe good User Stories:

Table 3: The INVEST Criteria for 'Good' Stories

I ndependent	Stories should be internally independent during their execution; the success of one Story should not depend on the success of another being worked on at the same time.
N egotiable	Stories are the negotiation units in Scrum; It is Stories that are agreed to in Planning and are delivered; and the Team negotiates actual content of Stories during development.
V aluable	Stories are, by definition, units of value that are requested by Stakeholders or Team Members. The value can be external or internal – for Stakeholders or the Team.
E stimable	The Team needs to be able to agree to the Story, which implies that the Story's effort could be estimated. However, some Stories are ambiguous and must be time-boxed.
S mall	Stories should be small enough that there is little confusion about what they mean, and so they can be completed relatively quickly. I recommend a single focus per Story.
T estable	Stories should be testable; more precisely, each Story needs to be verifiable, so that the Team can determine when it is Done. Doneness takes different forms for different Stories.

While the acronym needs to twist a *little* bit to fit when we expand the concept from User Story to just plain Story, the basic ideas are good. Basically, a good Story is one that is small and well-understood enough for the Team to agree to and not be confused by it.

There are two kinds of 'small' that I use when I describe Stories; and which kind of small applies to a particular Story is based on whether that Story is functional or non-functional. Functional Stories are those that provide functionality in the code, and are Stories that we typically think of when we discuss software development; basically, these are the User Stories we find in the XP process.

- If we are talking about functional Stories, the definition of small I like to use is 'one thread' or 'one positive test' or 'one state of the system' or something like that.

- For non-functional Stories, I often define small in terms of a time-box. That is, many non-functional Stories will be completed after a certain amount of effort has been expended – their Doneness is not determined by results, but by time and effort.

---

[1] Xp123.com, blog on INVEST in 2003.

Another thing I like to stress about a functional Story is that the business analysis (explaining the requirement) and the verification (testing to see if it is Done) are both *intrinsic* parts of the Story. That is, the Story contains *all* the work to get the Story from Idea to Done, not just the coding. The Story should be agreed to by the Team with the minimum possible information that allows them to agree; then the remaining analysis and other work happens *inside* the Story itself. This is an example of the lean principle of *delaying decisions until the last responsible moment*, as discussed in appendix A.5.

The concept of the Story is both *simple* and *brilliant*:

- What makes it *simple* is that at its core a Story is just a request for something of value, and the purpose of the Story is to start a conversation. The Story fills the same ecological niche as a requirement, but it has a completely different tone. Whereas the requirement has the tone *'here's what I want, just go do it'* the Story has the tone *'here's what I want, let's talk.'* As Alistair Cockburn has said, "a Story is a promise for a conversation"[2].

- What makes a Story *brilliant* is that not only does it replace a requirement, it also replaces the low-level activity; a Story is not only the *request* for value, it is also the activity, or work, that it will take to *provide* the value. In practice, this means that as a Team is doing analysis in order to find requirements (Stories) it is also developing its units of work. All the Team has to do is order the Stories and add Agreements about what Done means for each of them, and their planning is finished.

Stories come in many different types and forms, but all of them are requests for value of some sort. As the Team moves the Story into the Back Burner (see chapter 3.2), we expect the Story to answer the question: *'who wants what, and why?'* Before it can move from the Back Burner to the Front Burner, the Story's Agreement (see chapter 3.6) must be nailed down, and the Story must be agreed to.

Other Story Distinctions

In the previous section I distinguished functional and non-functional Stories. These are not the only distinctions I'd like to make. Stories come in many different forms, and exist for many different reasons, and here are some of the other common distinctions to make between and amongst Stories:

---

[2] This is according to Ron Jeffries, as noted in Jeffries, Anderson, and Hendrickson, *eXtreme Programming Installed*, Addison-Wesley, 2001, pg. 28.

- **Architecturally Significant Stories:** functional Stories that cause the Team to make architectural decisions – which are then validated by the fact that there is existing, working code using the decisions – thus proving that they are reasonable decisions.

- **Spike**: Stories that figure out answers to tough technical or design problems. A spike addresses only the problem under consideration and ignores all other concerns. Most Spikes get thrown away, which differentiates them from Architecturally Significant Stories.

- **Analysis Stories**: Analysis Stories exist because they find other Stories. There are many different kinds of Analysis Stories, and the most common ones find Functional Stories. However, there are also Risk Analysis Stories (finding risks and fears that need be dealt with), Process Analysis Stories (finding process improvements), and so on.

- **Infrastructure Stories**: Stories that add to, or improve, the infrastructure the Team is using. The value of these Stories is that the Team improves its ability to develop.

For further information about different kinds of Stories, see chapter 3.10 on Storyotypes.

Examples of Stories

As we can see, there are many different types and kinds of Stories. Some examples of Stories include:

- 'As a <passenger>, I want to <be able to select my seat online>, so that <I don't have to do it at the airport>' – a functional Story[3];

- 'Get a list of available Flights from CUTLASS,' – an Architecturally Significant Story because it causes the Team to decide how to interface with CUTLASS (assuming this is the first Story that does so);

- 'Go talk to the pilots and find out what they think about pilot compensation' – an Analysis Story that should be time-boxed;

- 'Review the suggestions the pilots have submitted to see if there's anything interesting there' – another Analysis Story that needs to be time-boxed; or

---

[3] This Story is in the Connextra format created by Rachel Davies in 2002 and popularized by Mike Cohn. This is not Scrum dogma; many Scrum Coaches no longer recommend it.

- 'I need somebody to spend an afternoon with the pilots, to explain to them how the pilot compensation page works' – yet another non-functional, time-boxed, Story – more of a 'train the users' Story.

There are other things we want from our Stories, as well, and we'll be discussing them throughout this book. For now, though, this is enough.

Epics as Stories the Team Can't Agree to Do

Stories are small and cute, but not all requests for value are like that. Some requests (Items) are large, ambiguous, and confusing. These are the ones we call Epics. Many people think that Epics are simply large Stories, but I like to define an Epic as an Item that can't be agreed to by the Team. I like this definition because it points out that Planning is based on agreement, not size. The Team could be unable to agree to an Item for a variety of reasons, most of which are captured in the acronym CURB:

Table 4: Reasons a Backlog Item May Be an Epic

C omplex	The Item might be too complex to be understood well enough to be agreed to.
U nknown	Maybe nobody on the Team knows enough about the Item to even make a guess whether or not it can be agreed to.
R isky	There are too many unknowns; it is too risky to agree to the Item without further investigation or a mitigation strategy.
B ig	The Item could just be too big to do in one Sprint, even though it is well understood.

In any case, an Epic is an Item that contains at least one Story, even if the Story is just an investigatory one. Usually, a functional Epic contains analysis Stories that produce functional Stories that also belong to the Epic. For Epics that represent Issues or Risks, the internal Stories represent actions the Team will take in order to investigate or mitigate the Issue or Risk. In any case, an Epic is a container of Stories, and we often refer to *any* container of Stories as an Epic.

Since an Item becomes an Epic if the Team can't agree to do it, sometimes an Item that was thought to be a Story turns out to be an Epic during Planning; it only becomes an Epic when the Team declines to agree to do it. This is not unusual, because the Team can't know whether or not it can agree to it *for sure* until it knows what Done means for the Item, how much Technical Debt is involved, who is available to actually work on it, and so on.

Most Capabilities are Epics rather than Stories; the main counterexamples being bugs or trivial features. If we think of a Use Case as being a typical Capability for our software, then it is an Epic, with the individual scenarios of the Use Case being potential Stories. Of course, some of the scenarios might actually be big enough to be Epics of their own.

Some examples of Epics are:

- 'We want the system to be able to manage the pilots' schedules,'

- 'We're going to need to train all our users on this new release,'

- 'As a <tourist>, I want to <fly to Catalina for the weekend>,' or

- 'I need you to translate the website to Spanish, because I'm planning to do a lot of marketing of Catalina Air in Mexico.'

Epics as Containers

So, Epics are Items that the Team can't agree to do all at once. Because of this, an Epic contains more than one Story, and this fact is often used as the defining characteristic of an Epic. That is, an Epic is often considered to be simply a *container* of Stories, which allows Epics to be used to do interesting things with the Backlog.

In particular, Epics can be used to help manage Releases, or help in organizing the Backlog. As an example of using Epics to organize work, the Work Breakdown Structure that I showed in the last chapter (Figure 19) could be thought of as a collection of Epics, which the Team would throw the appropriate Stories into as they were discovered.

Let me give you a simple Release Management example, which will illustrate how a Team could manage the development of a Capability. Let's say that in Release One the Team wanted to release a 'Buy an e-Ticket' Capability; that is, it wants the website's users to be able buy an e-ticket online. Now, nobody knows *exactly* what this means, but it's clearly an Epic, since it's large, ambiguous, and can't be done all at once. So what does the Team do? Here's a simple sequence of events:

1. The Team defines an Epic called 'Buy an e-Ticket (Release 1)' and puts it in the Fridge section of the Backlog, which indicates that it is in scope for the next release. Now, since this Epic is actually a Use Case, I have coached the Team to expect it will take between 10 and 40 Stories (based on my experience) to be able to deliver a minimal releasable version of it.

2. Then the Team starts doing analysis of this Use Case in order to produce Stories, and puts them in the Epic. Normally, I would expect this process to be ongoing, and not have all the Stories up-front. These Stories are going to *live in* the Epic that was just defined.

3. What makes things interesting is that these internal Stories will move from the Fridge, to the Back Burner, to the Front Burner, to being Done, even while the Epic just *sits there* in the Fridge as a placeholder. Some of the Stories may even move to the Freezer as they become out of scope for this Release. (See the discussion at the end of chapter 3.2 for more on this. Figure 17 summarizes the information that follows here.)

What this means in practice is that Epics used as containers are *not only* members of the Backlog, but can also be thought of as an orthogonal *organization* of the backlog. Table 5 looks at the Epic (Use Case) 'Buy an e-Ticket (Release 1)' from the point of view of the Epic. Let me explain it a bit:

- Each Story is labeled with its Storyotype, which is discussed in chapter 3.10.

- This Table shows the six Sprints of Release 1 of the CatAir website, and focuses on the 'Buy an e-Ticket' Use Case.

- The 'Sprint Found' column indicates which Sprint the Story was extracted from the Epic and added to the Back Burner – when it was discovered – and '0' means it was found in up-front analysis before Sprint 1 (see the 'Startup Sprint' section of chapter 4.9). This list is organized by 'Sprint Found,' and shows the order in which the Stories were added to the Backlog

- The 'Sprint Done' column indicates which Sprint the Story was Done – when it was moved to the Front Burner and completed – and a blank means the Story was not Done in this Release – and thus moved to the Freezer. As you can see, some Stories that were found later were Done earlier than others, and that some Stories found earlier than others were not Done in the Release – that's what frequent reprioritization does for you.

- The 'Size' column indicates the Size of the Story or Epic, in Story-Points. See chapter 3.7 for more information on sizing.

Table 5: Decomposing the 'Buy an e-Ticket' Epic into Stories

Backlog organized by Epic and Sprint Found	Sprint Found	Done	Size
[use case] Buy an e-Ticket (Release 1)			
[work with SMEs] Determine 'Buy an e-Ticket' Backbone	0	0	2 SP
[backbone epic] Buy an e-Ticket Backbone			
[backbone] Capture Itinerary Information	0	2	8 SP
[backbone] Get List of Flights from CUTLASS	0	1	8 SP
[backbone] Capture Passenger Information	0	2	4 SP
[backbone] Reserve Flight in CUTLASS	0	2	4 SP
[backbone] Pick Flight and Pay for It (stub out CC widget)	0	3	12 SP

Story			
[backbone] Hook Up Actual Credit Card Processing Widget	3	4	4 SP
[backbone] Issue email Confirmation to Customer	0	4	8 SP
[alt] Handle Round Trip Flights (ugly Interface)	0	3	8 SP
[beefup] Close Reservations when Plane is Full	0	4	8 SP
[alt] Reserve Flight to Pay Later	0	4	4 SP
[alt] Handle multiple-Passenger Parties	0	5	8 SP
[beefup] Add User Help to CatAir Website	0	7	2 SP
[work with SMEs] Analysis Discussion with SirJeff	1	3	2 SP
[alt] Modify CUTLASS to Understand When Flight is Full	2	3	8 SP
[spt] Make sure SirJeff's Marketing Materials are correct	2	6	2 SP
[interface] Improve Interface for Flight Selection	3	4	4 SP
[alt] Add Payment with PayPal (note: really straightforward)	3	4	4 SP
[alt] Pay with Coupon	3		4 SP
[alt] Pay with AMEX	3		4 SP
[alt] Select Seat online	3		4 SP
[alt] Change Seat online	3		4 SP
[alt] Web Interface for Adding/Modifying Flight Info	3	5	8 SP
[beefup] Get Luggage Info, including Scuba Tanks	3	5	8 SP
[beefup] Seat Belt Extender Needed for 'large' Passenger	3		2 SP
[analysis] Exploratory Testing to 'See What's Left'	4	5	2 SP
[redo] Fix Error in Luggage Weight Calculations	5	6	2 SP
[bug] Fix Small List of Bugs found in Exploratory Testing	5	6	4 SP
[alt] Bring Pet on Board	5		4 SP
[alt] Comfort Seat for 'really large' Passenger	5		8 SP
[beefup] Special Meals	5		2 SP
[beefup] Special Needs (wheelchair, etc.)	5		2 SP
[interface] 'Pretty Up' 'Capture Itinerary' window	7	7	2 SP
[interface] 'Pretty Up' 'Choose Flight' window	7	7	2 SP
[bug] Fix Bugs found in Exploratory Testing of 'live' Website	7	7	4 SP

Hidden in Table 5 is an interesting story. The [backbone] Story 'Pick Flight and Pay for It' was originally sized at 16 SPs, and its Agreement included connecting a Credit Card Processing widget. While discussing the Story during Planning, the Team decided that was too much to do all at once, agreed to stub out the Credit Card widget, downsized the Story to 12 SPs, and created a new [backbone] Story 'Hook up actual Credit Card Processing Widget' which was then sized at 4 SPs. This is classic *on the fly* Epic decomposition, forced by the fact that the Team couldn't agree to do a Story during Sprint Planning (see chapter 4.2).

By looking at Table 5, you can see how the Epic is used as a container of Stories as they are extracted from the Epic. In addition, a lot of good information can be gathered from this table about the ongoing analysis and discovery that was happening throughout the Release. This table, showing the Epic and its decomposition into Stories, is a good tool for the Product Owner to use to explain to Stakeholders the Capability's development as the Release moves along.

Summary

The work a Scrum Team does, and the Items on the Backlog, come in two sizes: Stories and Epics. Epics consist of work that can't be done all at once, and thus contains other Items (Epics and Stories). The notion of an Epic is usually extended to mean *any* Container of Items, which allows the Team to use Epics to put some structure on the Backlog.

This structure must be understood as *orthogonal* to the linear prioritization the Backlog provides, and this can cause confusion – especially if the Team is not using a tool that supports this kind of structure. However, Epics are very important from a Stakeholder's point of view, in order for them to understand the Backlog and the progress of the Team.

Discussion Questions

1. Provide examples (with explanation) of Epics and Stories involved in landscaping the front yard or throwing a party. Now take one of those Epics and argue that it is actually a Story. Take one of the Stories and argue that it is actually an Epic.

2. Does the INVEST model only apply to User Stories? Or are there other kinds of work we do that the INVEST model is still useful for?

3. What are the differences between Epics, Stories and Tasks?

4. Capabilities and Chores are about types of value. Epics and Stories are (essentially) about size. Discuss these two types of distinctions.

5. If a Story represents both a requirement and an activity how does this impact our understanding of a classic WBS?

6. Describe the CURB acronym. Give examples of Epics of each type.

Technical Debt

Technical Debt is what makes code hard to work with and deliver. It is an invisible killer of software, and must be aggressively managed. In this chapter I define Technical Debt and describe some of the issues. The topic of Technical Debt recurs throughout the book.

In chapter 2.3 I mentioned that the ScrumMaster's #1 issue on a Team is likely to be getting the Team to write Clean Code, which is code that the Team can change easily. I noted that we (as an industry) know how to write such code, by using XP-like practices. Unfortunately, we often fail to do so.

Technical Debt includes the stuff in and around the code that keeps it from being Clean Code – that makes it hard to change. In other words, the term 'Technical Debt' usually refers to the debt that is owed to the code before it can become Clean Code. Often, people use the term 'legacy' (or even 'instant legacy') to refer to code with large amounts of Technical Debt.

I usually think of Technical Debt as being the *viscosity* of the code; it is what makes the code hard to wade through. One of the best metaphors I have for Technical Debt is that of going for a run. Working with Clean Code is like running in the park, in good weather, with shoes that fit. It is comfortable, and the Team can move quickly and with confidence. I like to refer to this as '6-minute code' since it takes about 6 minutes to run a mile when it's nice out, the course if flat, and you're a pretty decent runner...

On the other hand, there is '4-hour code,' which refers to how long it takes to trudge a mile in the swamps, with a pack on your back and water up to your belly-button. The ratio of 6 minutes to 4 hours is 40, which is a reasonable (if anything, too low) estimate of how much more difficult it is to work with terrible code than it is to work with Clean Code. If you're a Coder, you know what I mean...

Anyway, the issue of Technical Debt is so ubiquitous in this book that it deserves its own chapter, with its own discussion. So, here it is.

Definition of Technical Debt

So, let's take a closer look at Technical Debt. The overall concept is pretty clear; it's the stuff that makes code hard to change and deliver. As you can imagine, this is a tremendous drag on agility, and having high amounts of

Technical Debt is probably the number one impediment to Teams being agile. In fact, I think that having code that the Team is afraid of *is* the number one killer of agility, as I discussed in chapter 2.3.

Technical Debt is not just about the code, though; there are other factors that come into play. For example, the code can be hard to change because of the quality of the code itself, lack of technical documentation, the development environment, 3rd-party tools, procedural impediments, Organizational issues, and even the skill-level of the Team itself.

Since it is the ScrumMaster's job to help the Team remove impediments, each of these issues is something the ScrumMaster should worry about. However, in this chapter I will restrict the issues I discuss to the ones that are either in, or near, the code. So, my definition of Technical Debt is:

> **Technical Debt** consists of deficiencies in the code, technical document-ation, development environments, 3rd-party tools, and development practices, which makes it hard for the Team to modify, update, repair, or deliver the Product.

Now that we have a definition, let's get some more discussion going...

Discussion of Technical Debt

It is important to note that Technical Debt is *invisible* from outside the Team; people who are looking only at the Product can't see the Technical Debt – it is only *clearly* visible to the Team Members working with the Code. For example, a bug is not Technical Debt – it is a bug. Performance issues are not Technical Debt – they are performance issues (but improving the Code's design sometimes mitigates them...). A bad interface is not Technical Debt – it is a bad interface. And so on...

On the other hand, Dirty Code (Code with poor design, lack of tests, and so on) *is* Technical Debt; a slow, inefficient, build process *is* Technical Debt; technical documentation that lies to you *is* Technical Debt; and a develop-ment environment that is hard to work with *is* Technical Debt.

Each of these things (bugs, performance issues, bad interfaces, dirty code, bad tools and environments, etc.) should be managed with Backlog Items, but they are different kinds of Items – some are visible from the outside, and some aren't – some have value to external Stakeholders, and some only provide value to the Team. We had this discussion in Chapter 3.3, when we talked about Capabilities versus Chores. The management of Technical Debt is discussed in many places in this book, including chapters 3.6 and 4.5.

One of the major sources of Technical Debt is Dirty Code; some even equate Technical Debt with Dirty Code. So, before going too much further, I must give the eXtreme Programming (XP) community its due. Since the very beginning, the XP community has focused on the production of Clean Code because they realized that the Team needed Clean Code in order to be agile. In the first XP book[1], Kent Beck states that the main reason to write Clean Code is to flatten the cost of change curve; that is, to assure that adding a feature in the future will not be significantly harder or more expensive than adding it now. In other words, the Team is not writing Clean Code just because it's the 'right thing to do,' but it is writing Clean Code for legitimate business reasons.

Flattening the cost of change curve is what makes the Team predictable, as it makes the Team's Velocity essentially constant[2]. Predictability is also improved if the Team is relentless in its writing of Clean Code, as it helps minimize the variations between Stories. These are the promises of XP and, historically, most software Organizations that have been successfully agile have "either used XP or done something very much like it"[3]. If you look carefully, you can see the influence of XP throughout this book.

Unfortunately, most Teams don't write Clean Code, and they create more and more Technical Debt as time goes on. This means that their Velocity (or Capacity) will continue to decrease as the code gets harder and harder to work with, and eventually there will be a lot of fear of working with that code. When that happens everyone can see that the agility has been seriously impeded, the code seldom gets modified, and that *that* code is dead code.

Is producing Technical Debt always a bad thing? No. There could be perfectly good business reasons for creating Technical Debt. For example, if there was a start-up company with a brilliant idea for the next Killer App I would expect them to create a lot of Technical Debt early on. This is not a bad thing; the goal of the first release of this new App is to capture market share, and 'hacking out' the code as fast as possible (and thus creating Technical Debt) is an appropriate business decision.

Of course, the enlightened company knows that it is creating Technical Debt, and has promised itself that it will fix it once it has established its market presence and has the time and money to do so. Too many times, however, the company won't grab enough market share with version 1, and will be forced to hack out version 2 as well. If the second version doesn't catch on, the Company often dies, and its product dies along with it.

---

[1] Kent Beck, *eXtreme Programming Explained*, Addison-Wesley, 2000.

[2] Private data from Capers Jones indicates that the velocity decreases as the size of the code base has 'order of magnitude' increases in size; this is an active research area.

[3] Jeff Sutherland, personal conversation.

Is this a bad thing? I don't think so... the company just didn't get lucky. If they had truly developed a Killer App like they hoped, and had cleaned up the code for version 2, they could have had a long lived and successful company. They made correct business decisions from their point of view, they adapted to reality like they should, and they just lost the game... stuff happens.

Now, one could argue (and I have at times) that they could have delivered the first version just as fast while creating Clean Code and using a great development environment. That may be true, but I'll also accept that the company in question *couldn't* believe that argument – so it was *incapable* of making the decision to have a great development environment and produce Clean Code from the beginning. I may believe they made bad decisions, but I also know that the decisions they made were (at least) reasonable and understandable – and the best they could do.

Primary Types of Technical Debt

I don't pretend to be an expert on Technical Debt; and even if I was, this book would not be the right place to have a thorough discussion of it. However, I'd like to list what I think are the four most common types of Technical Debt: lack of tests, bad design, lack of technical documentation, poor readability, and deficient tools.

Lack of tests. Code that is not protected by tests is very hard to change, as developers should have little or no confidence that they have successfully made a change unless they have tests proving that they didn't break something. This lack of tests is such a big deal that Michael Feathers *defined* legacy code by the statement "legacy code is simply code without tests."[4]

Bad Design. The second biggest problem that causes Technical Debt is bad design of our code. And when I say bad design what I really mean is that the code is poorly structured in some way. There are three structural issues that I focus on:

- The code should follow the 'once and only once' rule, which means that the same behavior is not duplicated many times throughout the code base;

- The code should be highly modular, with each of the modules being highly cohesive, and the modules being loosely coupled to each other; and

- Each of the modules should have an intention-revealing name, allowing developers to quickly grasp what they do, and why they are there.

---

[4] Michael Feathers, *Working Effectively with Legacy Code*, Prentice-Hall, 2004, pg. xvi.

Lack of Technical Documentation. Even if there is nothing wrong with the code, it might still be hard to understand because of a lack of technical documentation. In order to change code, a developer needs to be able to find the code that needs to be changed. I don't believe in *exhaustive* documentation, but I do think that some might be necessary. It doesn't need to be on paper – maybe the documentation is imbedded in the code, maybe it's in a Wiki, whatever... But, in any case, it is likely that some sort of technical documentation is needed to make the code understandable.

Poor Readability. A lot of the code currently being written will be around for 5, 10, or 20 years and it will be continuously maintained and changed throughout that time. The sheer size of the code, as it grows, will make its maintenance harder and harder as time goes by. Making the code easy to read makes it easy to understand, which makes it easier to modify or change – so we should want to do that. So how can the Team make it easy to read? Here are some suggestions:

- Team Members can have other developers read it to make sure that *somebody* else understands it;

- The Team can break the code into *virtual* modules by using comments explaining what the developer's intent is for the next piece of code;

- Team Members can use common, well-known, coding practices to make future developers comfortable with reading the code; and

- The code can be made self-documenting by using intention-revealing names for the variables, methods, and classes.

There is no way to *guarantee* readability, but these suggestions should help.

Deficient Tools. Software developers use a lot of tools, but the ones that are the *most* important for the prevention of Technical Debt are testing tools. For reasons I discuss in the next section, Unit Testing, and other Regression Test tools are very important.

Preventing Technical Debt

So, now you know what Technical Debt is, and that it kills your Team's code, what are you going to do about it? How does the Team prevent the development of Technical Debt in its code?

First of all, let me say that I think that the prevention of Technical Debt is both a 'process' issue and a 'pride in craft' Issue. That is, it is something that must be done by both the Team and the Team Members; the Team must have processes (a Standard of Care) in place to help prevent Technical Debt, and the Team Members must do their due diligence and follow them faithfully and continuously look for ways to improve them. This is the essence of self-organization when it comes to development, which, as we know, is at the core of Scrum.

The prevention (and reduction) of Technical Debt could require additional tools or training for the Team. This isn't free. Either the Organization must be progressive and enlightened enough to provide them, or the Team must do it itself by doing Chores that are prioritized by their Product Owner. Since the prevention of Technical Debt requires effort beyond the effort needed to simply provide working software, there is clearly a prioritization issue.

It takes courage to prioritize preventing Technical Debt over the need to develop Product. This courage can erode when the Team is under pressure to develop Product quickly, and the result is added Technical Debt.

This tension between reducing Technical Debt and providing Business Value is always there. It is the ScrumMaster's job to try to convince the Product Owner and Organization that Technical Debt prevention and removal should have priority, and it is the Product Owner's job to prioritize work that will enable that.

And, of course, the ScrumMaster should try to reduce the pressure on the Team to develop Product quickly. The focus should be on getting to Done, not going fast. In my experience, focusing on fast *always* creates Technical Debt.

In any case, here are some of the things that the Team could do to help prevent Technical Debt.

Many Eyes on the Code: It is well-known and accepted that reviews are the best way to keep quality up. So, have lots of them: architecture reviews, test reviews, design reviews, code reviews, and so on. Have the Team Members work in groups or Pairs (see chapter 2.6).

Stories are *promises for conversations*, so make sure the Team Members have the conversations, and that appropriate SMEs are involved. This is not simply a matter of doing Pair Programming, which is a brilliant technique; it should go well beyond that. These conversations not only increase the quality of the code, but they increase the knowledge of the Team and the Team's lottery metric.[5] This is all good stuff...

Not only is this good stuff, but it is fairly low cost, and usually something the Team can decide to do itself. As a ScrumMaster I constantly push the Team (through frequent -spectives) to improve in this area.

---

[5] The lottery metric is a count of how many people need to win the lottery (leave the team) before the project is in trouble.

Test Coverage: Putting many eyes on the code creates a better product and smarter people, but it doesn't solve the problem about what to do for the future – what does the Team do to protect the code from future developers? The best way to make the code easier to use for future maintainers and extenders is to have extensive automated test coverage. This gives future developers a better understanding of the code and less fear of changing it – and the code itself will not fear the developers.

There are two types of tests that one should have. There are Black Box tests that illustrate the externally-visible behavior of the system, and there are Unit Tests that protect the internal components. Each of these kinds of tests has its own purpose, and both are important.

Black Box tests can be thought of as executable requirements; they represent a highly-detailed statement of what the system actually does. I think it's fair to say that the very best (detailed) documentation of the system is an extensive, exhaustive, spanning collection of Black Box tests.

Unit Tests, on the other hand, are about the design of the system. They illustrate what each of the components actually does, and how they all fit together. One of the best development paradigms, Test Driven Development (TDD), focuses on testability as the primary motivator for component design; this paradigm not only provides code that is protected by unit tests, but also components that are highly cohesive and whose coupling is well understood. I highly recommend TDD, and I recommend that you look into it for your Team[6].

The problem with the simple statement that *'we need our code to be protected by tests'* is that it leads to a plethora of issues. In order to have code that is effectively protected by tests, the tests must be automated and easily run, usually as part of frequent integrations. In order to protect code with tests, developers must learn how to design and write effective tests.

It is an easy thing to say that all developers should do TDD, but is a completely different issue to get developers to *learn* the skills, and still another to get Organizations to *allow* developers to learn the skills. It is easy to say the Team needs Continuous Integration with regression testing, but it is quite another thing to get the tools paid for, installed, and used.

Therefore, getting the Team to protect its code with tests may be a difficult, and expensive, proposition. As a ScrumMaster, I often need to go outside the Team to the Business Owner and beyond in order to get the 'muscle and money' to institute these practices. And remember that Rome was not built in a day; it can take a long time for a Team to be good at this.

---

[6] see, for example, Kent Beck, *Test Driven Development: By Example*, Pearson Education, 2003.

Continuous Cleanup: In order to produce and maintain Clean Code, it is necessary to do continuous cleanup. The key word here is 'continuous' – it's not something the Team does 'every once in a while.' Experience shows that once the amount of dirty code gets too big, it is very hard (if not impossible) to clean it all up.

In software this cleanup activity is called Refactoring, which is defined as "changing a software system in such a way that it does not alter the external behavior of the code yet improves its internal structure"[7]. Test Driven Development, Refactoring, and unit testing are intricately linked. The three of them usually go together, and the ability to do them is considered part of the core competencies of an Agile Developer[8].

Once you have the tools you need to do unit testing with continuous integration, becoming good at refactoring is purely a matter of training, practice, and experience. Trying to do refactoring without adequate unit testing, on the other hand, is very scary – and it will probably be nearly impossible to do.

Technical Documentation: In order to change code easily, the developers need to find their way around the code so they can find what needs to be changed. They also need to understand what they are actually looking at when there is some code in front of them. The code itself can't tell you what design decisions were made, and why; it can't tell you what the logical groupings of entities into modules are; and it is often hard to discern the intent of some complicated snippets of code. Because of these issues, the code often requires some sort of technical documentation. At the very least there needs to be comments imbedded in the code to help the developer understand what is going on. However, this documentation must be kept current – it requires its own refactoring as the code changes. Having no documentation is bad, but having incorrect documentation is worse.

XP Practices: Finally, there is eXtreme Programming (XP). XP contains a set of development practices that produce Clean Code in an object-oriented environment. It is quite common for successful Scrum Teams to be using the XP practices when working on Stories that produce code.

I like XP, and I'm not afraid to say so. However, it might not be for everyone. As a ScrumMaster, however, I'm usually striving to get my Team to adopt as many of the XP practices as they can. Learning and using XP practices is a classic example of the 'pick-up sticks' metaphor I will discuss in chapter 4.1.

---

[7] Martin Fowler, *et al*, *Refactoring: Improving the Design of Existing Code*, Addison Wesley Longman, 1999, pg. xvi.

[8] These competencies are being explored and defined by a group of coaches and trainers led by Ron Jeffries and Chet Hendricksen. See http://www.AgileSkillsProject.com.

In my experience, and based on what I hear from other Scrum coaches and trainers, virtually every successful agile software Development Team is either doing XP or something like it. The simplest thing to do in order to produce Clean Code is do the XP practices – they are well-defined, and many coaches exist. It's simple, but not easy... like so much in Scrum.

Removing Technical Debt

So, now you know what could be done to *prevent* Technical Debt. In most Organizations, however, it will take a while for a Team to get good at it. Among other things, this means that there will be Technical Debt in the code that the Team develops first – before it got good at preventing Technical Debt. The Team may also be working in older code that is rife with Technical Debt. How can the Team reduce its codebase's Technical Debt in order to be able to work with the code more easily?

First of all, don't even *think* about paying off *all* the Technical Debt – that would be *way* too expensive. There are many strategies for working with debt-ridden code, and I suggest you look at Michael Feathers' book *Working Effectively with Legacy Code* for guidance. However, let me give you an idea of some of the things you can do in the following few paragraphs.

First of all, *stop producing* Technical Debt; as my friend Scott Bain[9] says "first, do no harm!" Then, pay down the debt in that part of the codebase that is *active*; that is, in the stuff you are working in right now. More specifically, you want to protect the code *near* the code you are getting ready to add or change. You can pay down the Technical Debt in a number of ways:

- **Refactoring:** You can refactor those parts of the code that are 'near' the code you're going to work with, protecting it with unit tests as you do so. This will allow you to add new code with little fear of messing up your existing code.

- **Rewriting:** Sometimes the code is so messy that refactoring would be essentially hopeless. In a situation like this you may need to rewrite the section of the code you're working in. This is an extreme measure, but might need to be done for clarity's sake. It might also need to be done in order to bring the code up to current standards like moving from VB to C# or DB2 to Oracle.

- **Documentation:** Add a little in-line (or external) documentation to the code so that other developers can tell what's going on. Document the big design decisions, the metaphors, and the patterns that are

---

[9] A friend I worked with at Net Objectives, author of Scott Bain, *Emergent Design: The Evolutionary Nature of Professional Software Development*, Addison-Wesley, 2008.

being implemented in the code. The code probably doesn't need a lot of documentation, but a few well-placed signposts along the way would be useful.

- **Add Black Box Tests:** At the very least, you should add Black Box tests to your system in order to document and protect its externally-visible behavior. There are many tools that will allow you to capture existing behavior in a regression test suite, and I suggest you get one. This will have no effect on the quality of the design, but should reduce the fear of change.

In each of these cases the fix could be expensive. This work is managed with Chores that could be either Epics or Stories, and may be documented with Cleanup Stories (see chapter 4.5). It is up to the Product Owner to prioritize the work, which means that the ScrumMaster and the rest of the Team must work closely with the Product Owner to determine which Technical Debt is *really* important to get rid of so that it can be prioritized for removal.

Summary

This chapter is a brief description of Technical Debt: the problems it causes, how to prevent it, and how to remove it. However, the issue of Technical Debt is ubiquitous, and is touched on by many other sections and chapters of this book.

It is important to note that every Scrum Team Member is involved in preventing or reducing Technical Debt:

- The Developers must strive to increase their proficiencies in Test Driven Development, Refactoring, and other practices that prevent or remove Technical Debt,

- The Product Owner must prioritize Chores that either reduce Technical Debt or enable the Team to better prevent its production, and

- The ScrumMaster must consider Technical Debt as a primary impediment to production, hold frequent -spectives on the issue, and push for practices that produce Clean Code.

Discussion Questions

1. Does Technical Debt in the code really *matter*? Can an application or product containing large amounts of technical debt be viable in the marketplace? What does a large amount of technical debt mean for the evolution of the product?

2. Is Technical Debt visible from outside the Team? Can another developer spot technical debt in code if they are not working in that code?

3. What type of Story helps remove Technical Debt? Prevent Technical Debt? Describe some examples.

4. Technical debt has been described as the *'mother of all problems in software development.'* Why?

5. The code being written today will probably be around 1, 5, 10, or even 20 years from now. What is the price of change for software that has a long lifecycle? How many times have you heard the statement *'we will be getting rid of this code next year, so you don't have to worry as much about it'?*

6. How does a team improve its agreements on what Clean Code looks like?

3.6

The Story's Agreement

*During Planning the Team negotiates with the Product Owner
and they agree which Stories the Team will attempt in the next
Sprint. For each Story the Team agrees to do, the Story's
Agreement is what it has actually agreed to. This is a potentially
complex issue, and I discuss it in this chapter.*

One of the distinguishing characteristics of Scrum is that the Team *owns* its effort – nobody tells the Team how much work to do each Sprint. The Sprint Backlog represents an agreement between the Product Owner and the rest of the Team about what will be attempted in the Sprint. In order to come to this agreement the Team Members need to know what 'Done' means for the Stories they are agreeing to, in order to feel confidence they *can* get them Done while still doing their due diligence and producing Quality Results.

This agreement on what Done means has been a major topic of conversation within the Scrum community since 2005 or so. Various aspects of the topic have been described by many names – including Acceptance Criteria and the Definition of Done – but I'll refer to the whole concept as the Story's Agreement; which represents how the Team Members will know when they are finished with the Story.

This Agreement can take many forms, but there are two things that are necessary for an Agreement to be a good one:

1. The Agreement must be (reasonably) objective and clear enough so that the Team can determine if the Story is Done or not; and

2. The Team Members themselves determine whether or not the Story meets the Agreement; people outside the Team do not determine if the Story is Done (remember that the Product Owner is a Team Member).

The Story's Agreement is *officially* agreed to during Sprint Planning, though it usually will have been an item of discussion during the Refinement process (see chapter 3.9). The way I express it to the Teams that I coach is: *'the Agreement you bring to Planning should be good enough so that you need no more than a single 10-minute discussion to agree (or not) to the Story.'*

Coding Stories

First of all, let's take a look at a Coding Story; that is, one that produces code as its main result. What *should* be true when a Coding Story is Done? Well, I think we could agree that whatever functionality the Story was requesting would be verified as being there, probably by passing some acceptance tests. I think that's fairly obvious...

What isn't as obvious, though, is that the Team should also be able to verify that it mitigated the risk of producing Technical Debt – we want to know that the Team did its due diligence when it wrote the Code. We want the Team to write Clean Code, so the Story's Agreement should indicate that fact in some way. Remember, the Team needs Clean Code in order to be confident that it is easily modifiable, verifiable, and maintainable in the future (see chapter 3.5 for more discussion).

Each of these two things is crucial. However, I actually divide a Coding Story's Agreement into *three* pieces, as follows:

- **General Agreements**: Agreements about who the SMEs are for this Story, who the Story's Coordinator will be (see chapter 2.6), simplifying assumptions that refine the scope of the Story, discussion of what is explicitly out of scope, and so on.

- **Acceptance Criteria**: How the Team Members will verify that they have produced the Story's value. Typically, this is an informal description of the Black Box test[s] that will pass (remember that it is best to have only one of them) and the list of additional artifacts (such as documentation and training materials) that need to be developed along with the code. A Story is said to be *well-defined* once its Acceptance Criteria are known.

- **Definition of Done**: What the Team will do in order to mitigate the creation of Technical Debt; these are usually procedural verifications or reviews that will take place in order to assure the development of Clean Code. The Definition of Done is often common across Stories that are of the same Storyotype (see chapter 3.10).

Note that the Story's Agreement can be quite specific about *what* needs to be done; but it is silent on *how* it should be done. The Team owns its work – Team Members should not be micromanaged – but the Agreements can constrain the work in order to maintain quality. In other words, one shouldn't micromanage the People, but it's ok to micromanage the Product.

The phrases 'Acceptance Criteria' and 'Definition of Done' are already in common use in Scrum, so I am simply reusing them. The phrase 'Acceptance Criteria' describes what must be *externally* visible (what tests must pass) for the Stakeholders to accept the Story. Similarly, the Scrum community uses the phrase 'Definition of Done' to mean what the Team does in order to mitigate Technical Debt and produce Clean Code. (Note: This last is particularly important, as many Teams have documented a generalized Definition of Done for Coding Stories – this is a first step on the way to storyotyping, which I describe in chapter 3.10.)

Unfortunately, this causes an overloading of the word 'Done.' On the one hand, we have *'a Story gets Done'* means that the Story meets its Agreement on Done; and on the other hand we have *'a Story gets Done'* to mean that the Team has done its due diligence and produced Clean Code. In this book, I will *always* use the phrase 'a Story is Done' to mean that the Story met its Agreement – it satisfies the Acceptance Criteria *and* consists of Clean Code.

Here is an example…

Get List of Flights from CUTLASS

Size: Medium   Type: [coding]

I want to have a list of flights that matches my itinerary

General Agreements:
1. Joe is the SME on CUTLASS
2. Sue will be the Coordinator for this Story
3. Note: don't worry if the flights are full or not, just return all of them that match dates and places…

Acceptance Criteria:
❑ Pass in an itinerary and get a list of (at most 10) Flights back
❑ User Documentation is Updated

Definition of Done:
❑ Did a half-hour of pre-factoring on way in
❑ Passed Design Review
❑ Passed Review of Functional Test Cases
❑ Passed Review of Unit Tests
❑ 85% Unit Test Coverage
❑ Verified all Tests passing on Development Machine
❑ Tied up all the 'loose ends'
❑ Passed Code Review
❑ Verified all Tests passing on Integration Box
❑ All Tests (Functional and Unit) added to Regression Test Suite
❑ Technical Documentation is Updated
❑ Did a half-hour of refactoring on the way out

Figure 20: Sample Coding Story with Agreement

In this example, the CUTLASS system is a back-end system for the CatalinaAir website that contains all the information about flights. As you can see, this example has a number of parts, including the three parts of the Agreement I mentioned above. It also has a Title, a basic statement of need, and a Size and a Type. These last two are here to display a *complete* Story, and will be discussed in chapters 3.7 and 3.10.

You will also notice that the Acceptance Criteria and Definition of Done are shown with checkboxes. I do this so that it is easy to check off these Checklist Items when things are finished, and it provides a simple, visual clue about how the Team is progressing with this Story. This is further discussed in chapter 4.6.

Also note that Joe (the SME) is not mentioned in either the Acceptance Criteria or Definition of Done. This is because, in general, Joe (as a SME) is neither responsible nor accountable to the Team, and the Team can't make agreements on Joe's behalf. In this particular Story the Team is agreeing to do the work with or without Joe's help, even though they know that Joe is the expert to seek advice from. See chapter 2.5 for a discussion of the Team's relationship with SMEs.

Non-Coding Stories

When most people think about Agreement on Done they are thinking about Coding Stories. As I have just demonstrated, the Agreement for a Coding Story is actually fairly straightforward. It is with the non-Coding Stories where things get really interesting. As before, I will illustrate this with a few examples – one is not enough here!

As in the Coding Story, I think there are the same three parts of the Agreement. However, the Definition of Done has a slightly different purpose. Most of the time with non-Coding Stories, it's not about mitigating Technical Debt, because the concept isn't applicable. Therefore, I use the Definition of Done to document the internal agreement that the Team Members have with each other, describing their strategy for actually doing the work.

Let's just look at the examples.

Analysis Story: Most Analysis Stories find or produce Coding Stories, and add them to the Backlog. Some Teams don't have Analysis Stories; they just do this work as a part of Backlog Refinement (see chapter 3.9). However, I usually need more analysis than that, and I need this additional analysis to be done with Analysis Stories that are explicit so that the Product Owner prioritizes them, and is aware of when they are being done.

There are many types of Analysis Stories, ranging from doing paper analysis to working with SMEs to doing Exploratory Testing, with many things in between. The example I give here is a simple one that involves talking to SMEs about the 'Shopping for Flights' Use Case. The purpose of this Story is to find some Stories that are part of the Use Case's primary scenario (called the Backbone) and get them on the Back Burner so that the Team can refine them for future Sprints.

Well anyway, here it is.

```
┌─────────────────────────────────────────────────────────────┐
│ Determine 'Buy an e-Ticket' Backbone                         │
│ Size: 2-day Timebox              Type: [work with SMEs]      │
│                                                              │
│ Find the backbone for the 'Buy an e-Ticket' Use Case         │
│                                                              │
│ General Agreements:                                          │
│  - Amir (the analyst) is the Coordinator                     │
│                                                              │
│ Acceptance Criteria:                                         │
│ ❑ The backbone Epic is in the Backlog                        │
│ ❑ There is at least one valid backbone Story, based on this  │
│    backbone Epic, in the Back Burner ready to be groomed     │
│    for Planning                                              │
│                                                              │
│ Definition of Done:                                         │
│ ❑ Identified SMEs and documented them in Use Case            │
│                                                              │
│ Met with the SMEs and:                                       │
│ ❑ Discussed the Use Case and documented the results in the   │
│    Wiki                                                      │
│ ❑ Generated, and validated, the backbone Epic for this Use   │
│    Case                                                      │
│ ❑ Decomposed the backbone into at most 10 Stories            │
│ ❑ Worked with SMEs and Team to prioritize and move at        │
│    least one of these Stories into the Back Burner for        │
│    further refinement                                        │
└─────────────────────────────────────────────────────────────┘
```

Figure 21: Sample Analysis Story with Agreement

As you can see, the Agreement for this Story has the same general form as that for the Coding Story, and is also in the form of a checklist. As before, the Size and Type attributes are discussed in other chapters.

Also note that the Team will *fail* to complete this Story if the SMEs will not meet with Amir. This makes agreeing to do the Story at Sprint Planning risky unless (at least some) SMEs have already agreed to the discussion. This early coordination with the SMEs is considered a part of Backlog Refinement, and is usually done by (or through) the Product Owner (see chapter 3.9).

Environmental Story: There are many different kinds of work that need to be done for a Team to succeed. One of these things is to maintain its development environment. In the following Story, we see the Team requesting to have its own copy of CUTLASS in the development lab.

Here it is.

Install Copy of CUTLASS in Lab
Size: Medium   Type: [enviro]

As a ‹developer› I want ‹to have my own copy of CUTLASS to play with› so that ‹I can figure out how it works and run realistic tests›

General Agreements:
- Joe (SME) is expert on CUTLASS
- Sam is Coordinator, and will be Team's expert on CUTLASS

Acceptance Criteria:
❑ CUTLASS is 'up and running' in the lab

Definition of Done:
❑ Got CUTLASS install from Joe
Worked with Joe to:
❑ Set up clean machine
❑ Installed CUTLASS
❑ Did Smoke Test and verified that it worked

Figure 22: Sample Infrastructure Story with Agreement

This example is interesting for a couple of reasons:

- The Story relies on Joe, who is an external SME. This will probably take a lot of Joe's time, and this must be arranged with Joe and his supervisors before agreeing to this Story.

- The last part of the Definition of Done requires the 'Smoke Test' of the system, as opposed to a full 'Regression Test' or something else. This is an example where the Definition of Done is limiting internal scope creep; as opposed to the normal (externally imposed) scope creep that is limited through the use of the Acceptance Criteria.

Research Story: Let me give you just one more, slightly trickier, example. This is an example that involves doing research, which could lead to a never-ending Story if we didn't manage it somehow. By using the Definition of Done to describe the work strategy we have controlled the amount of time this Story will take.

Here it is.

Figure out how to work with CUTLASS
Size: up to 40 person-hours   Type: [research]

As a <developer> I want <to know how to work with CUTLASS>
so that <I can do my job>

General Agreements:
 - Joe (SME) is expert on CUTLASS
 - Sam will be the Team's expert on CUTLASS

Acceptance Criteria:
❑ Either the Team believes that Sam has a 'good enough'
   understanding of how CUTLASS works, or the Team has
   added a new Research Story to the Backlog

Definition of Done:
1. Sam will meet with the Team for 15 minutes after the
   Daily Scrum to discuss the issues they are worried about
   (2 total hours)
2. Sam will spend 4 hours exploring CUTLASS to resolve
   these issues, and will have a one-hour discussion with the
   Team about what he finds and to discover further issues
   (12 total hours)
3. Sam and the Team will repeat Step 2 at most 3 times until
   the Team is satisfied with Sam's knowledge.
Note: if this isn't enough, the Team will work with the PO to
add another research Story.

Figure 23: Sample Research Story with Agreement

In the Story the Team has not committed Joe to anything; it is relying on Sam to figure things out. However, both the Acceptance Criteria and Definition of Done are squishy:

- The Acceptance Criteria is squishy because there is no guarantee that the Team will be satisfied with Sam's knowledge, and

- The Definition of Done is squishy because the Team can repeat Step 2 up to three times.

This Agreement is objective and can be agreed to. It *does* limit the amount of effort the Story will take, but it seems somehow unsatisfying – and there's just one check-box indicating that the Team is finished. I once forced myself through three months of research one Story like this at a time, where each Story was basically 'Do one more week, with a report.' I thought of the whole effort as a Research Epic, made up of Research Stories. I can't think of a better way to do this stuff and manage it in an agile fashion… what do you think?

Examples for a Mature Team

So far this chapter I have defined Story Agreements in a very robust way. For mature Teams this can be unnecessary, as they have normed on what these agreements should be. So, now let me go to the complete opposite end of the spectrum of defining an Agreement, and just document a couple of conversations I have heard during Sprint Planning.

Conversation 1.

PO:	*'… and I'd like you to do blah-blah-blah. How long will that take?'*
Team:	*'Five days or so…'*
PO:	*'That's too long, what I'd like is for you guys to do the best you can for three days. Make sure that it works, and then add the appropriate Cleanup Stories to the backlog. Is that OK with you?'*
Team:	*'Yep, we can do that…'*

Conversation 2.

PO:	*'Guys, you Know that thing we did on Page ABC?'*
Team:	*'Yeah…'*
PO:	*'Okay, do it again for Page XYZ…'*
Team:	*'Yeah, that works for us.'*

As you can see, these conversations achieve everything the Team needs to achieve: the Team has agreed to do the work, and nobody is confused about what the work is. However, it takes a long time for the Team and the Product Owner to develop the ability to have conversations like these. Therefore, I recommend that you do something like the Agreements that have been discussed so far – at least until the Team is performing at a fairly high level.

Not only that, but you always have this robust method of documenting Story Agreements that I'm describing to fall back on if it looks like your Team is getting a little lackadaisical in its approach to Technical Debt… or if you need a robust Agreement for compliance reasons. Just sayin'…

Agreements on Epics

So far, I've been talking about Agreements for Stories. That is, after all, what this chapter is about. However, it also makes sense for Epics to have Agreements. There are two reasons for an Epic's Agreement: to hold things that are inherited by *all* the Stories extracted from (or belonging to) the Epic, and to hold requirements at the Epic (Capability) level that will need to be satisfied before the Capability is considered Done, or Releasable.

The first idea is that an Agreement for an Epic contains things that are inherited by all the internal Stories. This is particularly useful if one wants to have a list of SMEs for the Epic, or for documenting simplifying assumptions that apply to all the Stories.

The second idea is about Doneness for the Epic itself, and could contain requirements for internationalization, usability testing, performance testing, and the like. The following example shows an example of a large, ambiguous, Epic that represents a significant Use Case for the system.

Shop for Flights
Size: 150 SPs (budget)   Type: [use case]

This Story represents the complete searching and shopping Use Case for the Catalina Airlines Ticketing website

Agreement:
1. The following are the primary SMEs for the various areas covered in this Epic:
- Joe, expert on CUTLASS, the back-end system we interact with
- Tom, for specials, discounts, coupons, and all things about costing
- Sandra, for luggage, special needs, pets, etc.

2. The following should be done before the Use Case can be released:
❑ Usability Testing done and passed
❑ Performance Testing done and passed
❑ The Use Case is available in both Spanish and French

Figure 24: Sample Agreement for an Epic

Note that there are 'requirements' here that may be moved out of scope later. For example, the Product Owner may decide that it actually doesn't need to be in both Spanish and French to be released. This emphasizes the fact that a Story (or Epic) is malleable – it merely documents the reality that was known at the time it was written, and can change as reality changes.

This second example shows an Epic that represents a large Story – one that is just *too big* to do all at once. In this case the Agreement involves the simplifying assumptions that define the particular scenario that will be decomposed into individual Stories.

Shop for Flights Backbone
Size: 48SPs (rollup)   Type: [backbone epic]

This Epic represents the architecturally significant scenario for the 'Shop for Flights' Use Case

Agreement: simplifying assumptions: One Way, Single Leg, No Seat Selection, Single Passenger, Full Fare, Pay with VISA™, No Luggage, ...

Figure 25: Agreement for an Epic that is a 'large' Story

I hope that these two simple examples you some ideas about how to use Agreements for Epics.

Other Topics about Story Agreements

There are many other things I would like to say about Agreements for Stories and Epics. However, saying it all would be overkill, unnecessary, and boring. So I'll restrict myself to making some short notes about various additional topics I hope you will find interesting.

Time-Boxing: You may have noticed that two of the Story Agreement examples in this chapter are time-boxed; that is, the Team agreed that they will be Done when a certain amount of time has passed, no matter what the actual result was. We do this in order to keep a Story that doesn't have an obvious endpoint (such as a passing test) from becoming infinite in duration through analysis paralysis and similar things. Time-boxing is typically used for exploratory Stories such as analysis, architecture, research, and so on.

Time-boxing is a very powerful technique for managing scope creep, and is often applied to Stories and (sometimes) parts of Stories. For example, the Team may decide that the amount of analysis on a Story could be time-boxed, or that the amount of time the Team spends working with the SME should be time-boxed, or that the amount of refactoring should be time-boxed, and so on.

The time-box does not have to be a fixed period of time such as hours or days; it can also be a squishy duration such as 'one StoryPoint's worth' of time. This last is useful because it leaves it up to the Team *exactly* how much effort to spend, but definitely states that there should be an upper bound. I like this latter method of time-boxing because it gives the Team more freedom, but keeps it out of trouble. Not only that, but it is easier to add to the Velocity, since it's in StoryPoints. This topic is discussed in chapter 3.7.

The Team didn't Meet the Agreement: Sometimes the Team completes a Story without actually completing the Agreement. This should be 'illegal' but it sometimes happens because the Product Owner says *'that's enough, it's done!'* In a situation like this, the Team may need to add a Story to the Backlog in order to make up the difference. In particular, if the Team believes Technical Debt was created, there needs to be a Cleanup Story added to the Backlog to make it visible that the Story was short-changed (see chapter 4.5).

Compromising the Agreement: Similarly, the Agreement itself may not be strong enough. Maybe the Definition of Done was compromised at Planning because the Team agreed there wasn't enough time to do it right. In this situation the Team needs to add a Cleanup Story to the Backlog right away, during Planning itself, to make sure it's visible that the Team did so.

You Can't Always Get What You Want: Sometimes the Team can't agree to what will *actually* provide value to the Stakeholders. For example, there might be a Story something like 'I want Page ABC to render in <.1 seconds.' The Team could say: *'That's nice, but we can't agree to that – it's too risky...'* So, the Story just became an Epic, and the Story the Team could agree to may be: 'Try XYZ algorithm and see how fast it renders' or 'Spend 4 hours making it faster, and then see where we are' or something. In other words, the original Story is now very much like the Research Epic I discussed earlier.

Agreements and Story Size: The Agreement and Story's Size could be tightly linked. For example, in the Agreement for the Infrastructure Story shown above, the Definition of Done included: 'Do Smoke Test to see if it works.' If this part of the Definition of Done had actually been 'Do a full regression test' it is likely that the size of the Story would go from a Medium to a Large – if not bigger.

This is important to note because sometimes the Agreement is finalized *long after* the Size is determined, and the Agreement may change the Size. In a situation where the Team is working with a budget of StoryPoints, this could have a significant impact. Let me give you a simple example. Let's say that a Story is sized as a Small (2 SPs), but when the Team is discussing the Agreement during Sprint Planning, it is clear that the Agreement is being expanded so that it's actually the Agreement for a Large (8 SPs) Story. Then the Team must have a discussion about whether this Story is consuming 2 SPs of the budget, or 8 SPs of the budget (I usually recommend going for 8). I've seen quotes like: *'we budgeted for a Yugo, but you're describing a Cadillac – that's cheating!'*

External Constraints on the Definition of Done: Many Organizations want consistency of the Definition of Done for functional Stories, in order to manage Technical Debt in a uniform way. They may even want to manage the Definition of Done of other Stories, as well, for consistency of process. This could mean that the Definition of Done for Stories (or at least some of the Stories) is determined from the outside – possibly by an architecture or process group.

I think that this is a reasonable thing, and is one of the reasons that a Team does Storyotyping (see chapter 3.10), but the Team should always feel free to *strengthen* the standard Definition of Done if they think that the Organization is not going far enough. In fact, Teams should be *encouraged* to experiment with strengthening the Definition of Done so that the Organization might learn something useful that it may want to standardize in the future.

Verification versus Validation: The Story's Agreement *verifies* that a Story is Done, it does not *validate* that the Results are fit for use. This is an important distinction – the distinction between verification and validation – and not everybody understands it. Verification is assuring that something has met its specification; that it does as it was *intended* to do. Validation means that is fit for use; that it does what it *needs* to do. Stories need to be verified, and Capabilities need to be validated before they are released.

This validation can be done either by the Team itself, or by somebody outside the Team – often an Integration or Test Team. Validation is usually done as its own Story, conducting some sort of testing (e.g., exploratory testing, acceptance testing, or usability testing) in order to prove the Capability is fit for use. The results of Validation Stories are either:

- Validation of being fit for use, or
- New Stories to try to correct the defects found.

Therefore, validation is actually a form of analysis (since it produces new Stories), and I always look at it that way...

Retrospecting on Agreements: Finally, there is the issue of reflecting on Story Agreements, either through retrospectives or intraspectives. I believe that Agreements are a constant source of reflection; the Team is continuously trying to get better and better Agreements. In particular, the Definition of Done for functional Stories is a constant issue, as the Team has to work hard to attain and retain the appropriate level of Technical Debt mitigation.

Summary

In Scrum a Team's work is broken down into fairly small chunks called Stories. In order for the Team's efforts to be managed successfully, each of these Stories must be defined *well enough* so that the Team will know when it is finished with the Story and can move on to the next one. The definition of the Story, however, is not provided by a detailed specification; it is accomplished through an Agreement about what Done means. Each Story has an Agreement that defines, in an objective way, how the Team will know when it is finished with the Story.

In this chapter I have described a robust way of defining and documenting these Story Agreements. All the different kinds of Stories that a Team will do should have Agreements about Doneness. They don't always need to be as robust as the ones I have presented in this chapter, but I think that what I have presented is a good place to start. As your Team gets more mature, the Team Members will automatically start to do their own storyotyping (see chapter 3.10), and the way they define their Story's Agreements will be refined and tuned to the Team and the Organization.

Discussion Questions

1. A Story's Agreement allows the Team to determine whether or not a Story is Done. What would happen if people *outside* the Team determined if a Story was Done or not?

2. Under what circumstances can the Team change a Story's Agreement during the Sprint, as the Story is being worked on?

3. Is a Story Done if it meets Acceptance Criteria but the Team didn't do its due diligence to produce Clean Code?

4. An Epic consists of multiple Stories. Is it possible to have each of the Stories verified as Done, and yet the Feature/Epic is not validated as Releasable?

5. What is the purpose of Analysis? What does a typical Analysis Story produce? What stops an Analysis Story from taking 'however long it takes?'

6. What should be true when a Coding Story is Done? Describe the difference between a Story's General Agreements, Acceptance Criteria, and Definition of Done. Give an example based on your experience.

3.7

Velocity and Size

*A Team's Velocity is a very important metric because it
measures a Team's throughput. In order to calculate a Team's
Velocity one needs to have a Story's Size, which is often
estimated in StoryPoints. These are complicated issues, and I
discuss them in this chapter.*

Whenever I'm developing software, two of the most common questions I get
when referring to Product development are *'how long will this take?'* and
'when will you be done?' As a Coach and Trainer, the most common question I
get from developers is *'how do I answer those questions?'*

Now, these are really good questions, and Scrum itself gives essentially no
guidance on how to answer them. As of the 2013 Scrum Guide [SG] (and
even before), all *explicit* guidance about Release Planning, predicting
completion dates, or monitoring progress from Sprint to Sprint, has been
removed from the Scrum Framework.

However, even though they are *not* part of Scrum, everybody agrees that
those questions in the first paragraph are important questions; and in order
to answer them one needs to know something about how fast a Team does
work – how much product it can crank out... in other words, one needs to
know a Team's production rate.

The terms we use when discussing size and production rates are:

- **StoryPoints**, which measure the relative sizes of Items (Stories,
  Epics, Features, etc.), and may be written as *StoryPoints*(Item).
  StoryPoints are usually determined by the Team using an Estimation
  Game (see appendix A.6).

- **Velocity**, which *measures* how fast a Team *has* produced Results, and
  is defined as the number of StoryPoints *earned* in a Sprint (#Story-
  Points per Sprint), where a Story's StoryPoints are earned once the
  Story is Done (it meets its Agreement – *no partial credit*).

- **Capacity**, which is an assumption about how fast StoryPoints *will* be
  produced. Capacity assumptions should be verified or re-baselined
  every Sprint based on current Velocity.

I assume you already know these things, but I want to make sure we're on
the same page before we begin our exploration of size and velocity issues.

Acceptance-Based Stories and Ideal Effort

There is no accepted definition of what a StoryPoint represents, other than that it is a unitless, relative measure of size to be used for both Stories and Epics.[1] I want to give definitions I consider useful, and that's what I'll be doing in this chapter. First I will deal with Acceptance-Based Stories – those Stories that are defined by Doneness Criteria – rather than a Time-Box:

> *StoryPoints*(Story), for an Acceptance-Based Story, is a relative measure of Ideal Effort, which is the effort it would take to develop the Story (meet both the Acceptance and Doneness Criteria) if everything were as it *should* be.

What does 'as it *should* be' mean? Good question. Here is what I mean:

- Your Team has the people it needs, and they are all top-notch; the Team has the domain knowledge, the skills, and the development environment it needs to do its job – there are no impediments due to a lack of **Team Ability**.
- Your Code is Clean, protected by both Unit and Functional Tests, and the Technical Documentation is both minimal and sufficient – there is no **Technical Debt**.
- The Organization provides a safe, learning environment; Team Members are allowed to focus on their Team's work and are not sidetracked by excessive meetings and other distractions – there is no **Organizational Noise**.
- There are Subject Matter Experts available who have the knowledge or expertise you need, when you need it – there are no impediments based on **SME Availability**.

In other words, when estimating Acceptance-Based Stories we need to *ignore* Impediments caused by Environmental Variables (Organizational Noise, Team Ability, Technical Debt, SME Availability, and others specific to *your* environment); we ignore the portion of the effort that is based on the Team and the Organization and focus only on the Story's Intrinsic Difficulty.

On the other hand, 'as it *should* be' doesn't mean you can expect magic or miracles: the laws of physics have not been repealed; you haven't suddenly been gifted with transporter technology; Superman, the Hulk, and Einstein aren't suddenly going to show up as Team Members; and so on. It's *'as it **should** be'*, not *'as it **might** be if only ABC and XYZ were true'* where *ABC* and *XYZ* are fanciful, non-realistically-attainable, things.

I hope you understand what I'm getting at here...

---

[1] See Mike Cohn, *Agile Estimating and Planning*, Prentice-Hall, 2006, pgs. 36-39.

This definition is a natural extension of XP's Ideal Time[2], which is the *"amount of time it would take to develop the Story if there were no distractions or disasters."* I like this definition, and I am merely extending it to be a relative (not absolute) estimate, to *explicitly* exclude consideration of *any and all* Impediments, and to make sure we're not expecting miracles…

This definition is a complicated expression of a simple idea; that *all* Story-Points *should* take about the same amount of relative effort if everything were the way it *should* be. A two point Story *should* take about half the effort of a four point Story, all small Stories *should* take about the same amount of effort, and so on. However, because of impediments, some StoryPoints are *harder* than others; some two-point Stories may take more effort than some eight-point Stories – those darned Environmental Variables often get in the way.

This notion – that Stories with the same StoryPoints value *should* take the same amount of effort – leads to a discussion of Time-Boxed Stories. It will be short and sweet…

We use Time-Boxes for ill-defined Stories – those Stories with 'mushy' or non-existent Acceptance Criteria. Examples of such Stories include 'Refactor Module ABC,' 'Analyze Use Case XYZ' and 'Make page 123 faster.' Generally, Stories like these need to be time-boxed, or there's no guarantee they'll ever get finished. These Stories can be time-boxed in Days or Hours, but I recommend that they be time-boxed with StoryPoints, like 'Do 1 SP's worth of Analysis of Use Case XYZ,' as this allows the Team to self-organize and self-manage while doing the Story. It is the Team's job to figure out *exactly* how much Actual Effort to spend, based on their experience about how much Ideal Effort a StoryPoint should take. I find that the 'StoryPoint Time-Box' concept allows the Team to do what it feels necessary to provide the demonstrable value the Story represents, without going overboard, and while spending the right amount of effort.

In any case, StoryPoints represent a relative measure of Ideal Effort, and I will refer to *StoryPoints*(Item) as the 'Size' of the Item, and it will be determined through an Estimation Game as we see appendix A.6.

Actual Effort, Ideal Effort, and Velocity

Of course, when working on a Story the Team is expending Actual Effort, not just Ideal Effort. The Actual Effort spent on a Story falls into three pieces:

1. The Ideal Effort for the Story – the Time it *should* have taken to develop the Story if everything was as it should be – this is what is

---

[2] Kent Beck, *eXtreme Programming eXplained*, 2000, Addison-Wesley, pg. 178.

measured by the StoryPoints and is represented by the Team's Velocity.

2. The Effort spent dealing with Impediments – dealing with the Drag caused by the Environmental Variables – this is what the Scrum-Master is trying to minimize through facilitation and reflective practices such as Retrospectives and Intraspectives.

3. The time for Slack, which is time when Team Members are not *actively* busy on the Story. A certain amount of Slack is proper and necessary in order for the Team to maintain a Sustainable Pace[3].

The following two Velocity graphs illustrate these concepts (in a conceptual way) for Teams that have been developing for a few Sprints. The graphs show the Actual Effort expended in each Sprint, divided into Ideal Effort, Environmental Drag, and Slack – this is for *all* the Stories completed in the Sprint. The Ideal Effort is also labeled as 'Velocity', since the Velocity from Sprint to Sprint will be proportional to the Ideal Effort part of this graph.

The 'Slack' and 'Environmental Drag' portions of the graphs are *greyed out* because there is *no way* you could know how much time is *actually* being spent on dealing with Environmental Variables (this effort is *baked in* to the work you're doing), and it is very unlikely that you know how much actual Slack Time there is. These graphs are *purely* conceptual...

Figure 26 represents a High-Performing Team; it improved its performance between Sprints 1 and 2, and has been relatively consistent since then. We can see that relatively little of its time is spent dealing with Environmental Variables, and we would probably be willing to assume that its future Capacity will be approximately 50 SPs/Sprint.

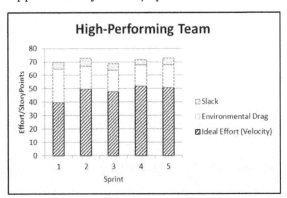

Figure 26: Effort Distribution for a High-Performing Team

---

[3] See Tom DeMarco, *Slack: Getting Past Burnout, Busywork, and the Myth of Total Efficiency,* Broadway Books, 2001.

Now, in Figure 27 we see a similar graph, but this time it's for a Team in trouble. It improved between Sprints 1 and 2, but *something bad* has been happening since then – its time is being *gobbled up* by Environmental Drag, and its performance has been steadily decreasing.

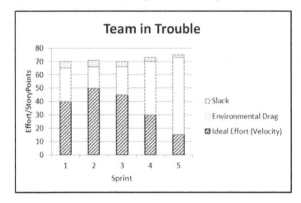

Figure 27: Effort Distribution for a Team in Trouble

This Team is producing fewer and fewer StoryPoints, in spite of the fact that it is working more hours and cutting back on Slack Time. If they are developing Functional Stories, the most likely culprit for this is increasing Technical Debt; the Team is probably writing *bad* Code, and it is becoming harder and harder to work with as time goes on. We don't *really* know, though – the graph alone can't tell us – and figuring out what is causing the problem is something for the ScrumMaster to work with the Team on. Because the Team's Velocity has *not* settled down, we should probably not be willing to assume a Capacity for this Team – we really don't have a clue.

By looking at these graphs we can see (if we ignore Slack), that the Ideal Effort is proportional to the Actual Effort spent if (and only if) the percentage of time dealing with Impediments (caused by Environmental Drag) is constant. This is an important observation, because it means that a Team with a steady Velocity (Velocity [proportional to] Actual Effort) is not seeing major changes in the impediments it is facing.

StoryPoints and Velocity are Very Useful

As you can see (if we ignore Slack), the definition of StoryPoints separates the Actual Effort expended while working on a Story into two pieces: the piece spent producing the value the Story represents (the Ideal Effort), and the piece spent dealing with impediments, including Technical Debt (the Environmental Drag). There are three big things this separation of concerns does for us:

- We can make Capacity assumptions (or not),
- Velocity becomes a useful indicator, and

- The Environmental Variables must be managed explicitly.

Let me briefly describe these for you. While I'm going through these discussions, it may help you to think of Functional Stories – Stories whose main result is Code that passes tests. These are not the *only* Stories that we have, but focusing on them may help make the discussions more pointed and understandable to you.

We can make Capacity assumptions (or not)

We make Capacity assumptions in order to be able to make predictions. These Capacity assumptions should be verified or re-baselined every Sprint based on current Velocity calculations. As we see in Figure 26, sometimes this is easy to do; unfortunately, as we see in Figure 27, sometimes it isn't. And yet, we must do the best we can – and our best may be to admit we can't make a Capacity assumption that we can justify.

Velocity becomes a useful indicator

What's *supposed* to happen on a Project is that the Environmental Variables settle down and become steady-state – this leads to a more-or-less constant Velocity (as we see in Figure 26), and allows more-or-less accurate Capacity assumptions (as stated above). When this happens, the Team is constantly dealing with an *expected* number of Impediments; it's the same thing over and over again – the cost of a StoryPoint (in Days or Hours) is essentially constant. The Team is Performing at a steady rate, the Team is predictable, and this is a good thing.

But, what happens if the Environmental Variables don't settle down?

For example, what happens if the Team is getting *better* at development? The *Team's* improvements don't change the number of a Story's StoryPoints, since Team Ability is ignored when estimating StoryPoints. However, the improved Team will produce StoryPoints faster, and this means that Velocity will increase. This resolves the Alan Atlas[4] conundrum that he posed years ago: "*How come if my Team is getting better their Velocity doesn't increase?*" – which often happens when the impacts of the Environmental Variables are allowed to factor into the StoryPoint estimates.

Conversely, what happens if the Team starts producing an *abnormal* amount of Technical Debt? When this happens, developing new Functional Stories becomes harder and harder and harder, and since the existence of Technical Debt is *ignored* when estimating StoryPoints, Velocity will tend to decrease over time (as we see in Figure 27). Since this decrease in Velocity is visible,

---

[4] Alan Atlas is a Certified Scrum Trainer and a good friend of mine.

the Stakeholders are likely to ask questions about it, and the creation of Technical Debt will be exposed to the light of day.

A special note on this... I have seen many Teams (perhaps unintentionally) *hiding* the existence of Technical Debt by assigning more and more StoryPoints to Stories in order *to take care of* the extra effort needed to deal with the Technical Debt *they are currently creating* – and this fools the Stakeholders into thinking everything is ok because the Velocity 'looks right.' This is *very, very wrong*, and is one of the main reasons I *insist* that we ignore Environmental Variables when estimating a Story's StoryPoints.

In general, then, if Velocity is trending up or down, this tells us that something might be happening with the Environmental Variables – they are not in steady-state. This is something the ScrumMaster needs to investigate, and have the Team retrospect on (see chapters 2.3 and 2.4). Importantly, because StoryPoints are *independent* of the Environmental Variables, this trend in Velocity *can't* be disguised by re-estimating the StoryPoints to account for changes in Team Ability, Technical Debt, or any of the other Environmental Variables. Therefore, it is there for all to see, and ask questions about. This is a very good thing, from a Scrum perspective – it helps everybody live the Team Values.

This isn't perfect, though. Imagine the following scenario: the Team is new, and their Velocity is essentially constant. Things look good, right? Maybe not... what if the Team is getting better (synergizing better, better self-organization) and they are also creating Technical Debt? Then the two factors could be cancelling each other out. Eventually, the Team will stop getting better, the Technical Debt that has been produced will dominate, and the Velocity (and Capacity) will plummet. So, don't assume that a constant Velocity is always a good thing... just sayin'... ;-)

The Environmental Variables must be managed explicitly

Since there are no StoryPoints earned for simply *dealing with* impediments, it is unreasonable to expect that the impediments will be *removed* as part of simply working on an impeded Story. Some impediments *may* be removed through conversations, negotiations, agreements, and other inexpensive human-based processes. However, other impediments, such as Technical Debt and the Team's lack of training or tools, will take time and effort to rectify and remove. Specifically, I don't expect large amounts of Technical Debt to be removed simply because the Team is working in Code infested with Technical Debt.

In other words, it is likely that some impediments (like Technical Debt or needed Team training) won't be removed unless there are Stories explicitly set aside to do so. This is a good thing for two reasons. First, it makes the fact that the impediments exist, and are being removed, visible to everybody.

Second, because they are being managed with Stories, they are actually *being managed* – they are being prioritized, they are being discussed, they have their own Agreement about Done, and so on. This issue of removing Technical Debt with Cleanup Stories is discussed in chapter 4.5.

EffortPoints and WorkRate – an Aside

So far I've been talking about a Story's size and that this size must ignore Technical Debt, Organization Noise, SME Availability, and Team Ability. Sometimes this seems unreasonable, especially when it comes to Technical Debt. What if a Team Member says something like *'This Story would be pretty simple if there was no Technical Debt, but in real life it's going to be hard... I can't, in good conscience, call this a Small Story'* – what would I do then?

Well, I might reply with *'It looks like Technical Debt is becoming a big issue, and we need to track it somehow. How about if we have another measure, call it EffortPoints, which is a relative measure of how big the Story is <u>including</u> Technical Debt. Then StoryPoints will be size without Technical Debt, Effort-Points will be size with Technical Debt. By looking at the difference between EPs and SPs, we can get a measure of how much Technical Debt we have.'*

Note that this is doing two important things:

1. It is respecting the Team Members' need to take the Technical Debt into account, and

2. It is allowing the Team to somehow quantify the amount of Technical Debt in the system.

For example, let's say there was a simple Story that needed to be implemented in a module that was full of bad code. Then it would be reasonable for the Story's size to be 2 StoryPoints and also be 8 EffortPoints, which would indicate that there are 6 EffortPoints worth of Technical Debt imbedded in the Story.

Of course, there is a velocity-like metric to be used with EffortPoints, let's call it WorkRate, which is defined by *earned EffortPoints per Sprint*. The WorkRate metric could be useful for Sprint Planning, as it would help the Team know how many EffortPoints they could expect to get Done in a Sprint. Unfortunately, it's not very useful for Release Planning (and re-Planning), when we need to know how much Product is being developed, not how many Impediments have been dealt with.

Is this really a big deal?

Well, StoryPoints are about Ideal Effort, which is the amount of work spent developing what we want - not dealing with Impediments. In other words, StoryPoints (Ideal Effort) are *only* about the Product, not about the difficulty (or ease) of development. In other words, earned StoryPoints are measuring the Effort we spend on the *stuff we want* – they represent value-producing effort or Benefit. By the way, for all you Project Managers out there, this is what Earned Value is all about...

On the other hand, EffortPoints and WorkRate are measuring how much total Effort was spent, which is about total Cost. In other words:

- Earned StoryPoints are a measure of Benefit, and

- Expended EffortPoints are a measure of Cost.

These are fundamentally different issues.

The terms EffortPoint and WorkRate are not standard within the Scrum community, nor are the actual terms important. What *is* important is that you understand that size and cost are *not* the same thing, that they shouldn't be confused, and that StoryPoints and Velocity need to measure size – while Actual Effort is about cost.

This understanding is especially important when considering using Story-Points to budget for Epics, which is discussed next.

Budgeting StoryPoints for Epics

So far, I have discussed the sizing of Stories, and the calculation of Velocity as the Team gets these Stories Done. Remember that the Team is doing this because they'd like to be able to use this Velocity to estimate their future Capacity for developing Product, and then use this Capacity estimate to predict (guess) how much longer the remaining work will take.

However, if the Team is managing its Backlog correctly, much of it could consist of Epics that have not yet been decomposed into Stories. In order for the Capacity estimates to do the Team *any* good with predicting into the future, there must be StoryPoint sizes for these Epics, as well – so that there is a notion of how much work (in StoryPoints) remains.

Sizing Epics is a fundamentally different issue than sizing Stories, because Stories get Done (an objective measure), while Epics get Releasable (a subjective measure). This is not just a subtle distinction – not understanding this difference has got a lot of Teams into trouble. Let me discuss this issue in the context of Use Cases, which are a kind of Epic (Feature or Capability) I assume most of you understand.

Let's take a look at the Use Case 'Buy an e-ticket,' which is something I've been using throughout this book as an example. The Team wants to know how big this Use Case is in StoryPoints. So, let's go back to first principles. Use Cases consist of scenarios, with each scenario being a particular interaction a user might have with the application. Some of these scenarios are successful; some are unsuccessful, and so on. In any case, though, each scenario can be defined by a *single* acceptance test – it is a single thread. Because of this fact, an individual scenario of a Use Case is a good candidate to be a Story, because we like Stories whose Acceptance Criteria consists of a single test (see chapter 3.4). Therefore, in order to have an estimate of how big the Use Case is (in StoryPoints) we would need to answer two questions:

1. How many scenarios do we think it will take to release this Use Case? and

2. How many StoryPoints (on average) does each scenario have?

The second question is a lot easier to answer than the first; and is based on the StoryPoint estimation scale being used, and how big a typical scenario is expected to be. For example, if I am using the S/M/L (2/4/8 SPs) scale, I may just decide to allocate 5 StoryPoints for an average scenario – the average of Small, Medium, and Large. No big deal...

It's the first question that causes trouble, because the answer is inherently subjective. There are many issues involved in answering this question – here are some of the most obvious:

- **Complexity of the Use Case:** How many entities are involved? For example, buying an e-ticket involves itineraries, passengers, seats, luggage, pets, meals, payments, coupons, mileage plans, etc. It's reasonably complex – it's not a simple 'Buy a t-shirt' Use Case...

- **How good the Product Owner is at Prioritizing:** The Product Owner must be able to differentiate between must-have scenarios and nice-to-have scenarios – the Product Owner must make sure all the must-haves are developed before the Use Case *will* be released, and the fewer nice-to-haves that are developed along the way, the sooner the Use Case *can* be released.

- **Willingness of the Stakeholders to Compromise:** The Stakeholders help our Product Owner determine must-have versus nice-to-have scenarios... and if there is no compromise in them, there are lots of must-haves that could have been nice-to-haves... just sayin'...

- **The Kind of Application we are Writing:** For example, a client-server application must have more scenarios *actually implemented* in code than a web application does. This is because a client-server application must implement *all* the must-have scenarios, while a web application usually has the 1-800-UCALLUS number that allows an actual person to help the client with the less common (but still must-have) scenarios. In the 'Buy an e-Ticket' Use Case these may include scenarios involving extra-large people who need a comfort seat, wanting to sit across the aisle from your friend, needing a second seat for your cello, bringing a live pet on board, having a phobia about being within four rows of the lavatory, special meals, having a weapon in your luggage, etc.

Ok, so let's say the Team is willing to guess how many scenarios will be needed in order to make the Use Case releasable. They're still not finished... they will need to know how many *extra* StoryPoints to throw in there for buffer, for unexpected rework, for Analysis Stories, for nice-to-haves that turn into must-haves, for refactoring, for improving the interface, for other risk mitigation, and so on.

As you can see, sizing a Use Case is a nontrivial problem, especially if the Team is looking for an *accurate* size. This is a version of the *'we can't get all the requirements right up front'* problem... So, don't do that. Have the Team look for an *adequate* Budget of StoryPoints for the Epic. Then simply give the Product Owner the task of spending those StoryPoints wisely in order to get a releasable version of the Use Case. In other words, rely on the People, not the Process. This is what agility and Scrum is all about, anyway. Let the Product Owner take the Team up the S-Shaped curve of delivered value (see appendix A.5).

How does the Team get an *adequate* budget for a Use Case? With an Estimation Game, of course! They play the Small/Medium/Large game with a *'How big is this Use Case?'* question – and do it with their Stakeholders, who are the ones that understand the Use Cases. In my experience, a releasable Use Case in a web application has between 5 and 20 must-have scenarios. If we assume that the must-have scenarios consume about 1/3 of the Epic's budget (see the S-Shaped curve discussion in appendix A.5), and that each of these scenarios is worth 5 SPs, we would get a standard range for an Epic's budget as 75 SPs to 300 SPs. So the Team might go with budget values like: Small Use Case = 75 StoryPoint budget; Medium Use Case = 150 StoryPoint budget; and Large Use Case = 300 StoryPoint budget. Note that these StoryPoints are to be consumed by *all* the Stories involved in the Use Case, not just the functional ones.

These numbers are borne out by the 'Buy an e-Ticket' Use Case that I have presented many times in this book. It was sized as a medium-sized Use Case, and it was budgeted for 150 SPs. It actually took 132 SPs to produce an initial releasable version (see the info in Table 5, chapter 3.4) – the Product Owner was good at eliminating nice-to-haves (note that neither 'Select Seat Online' nor 'Change Seat Online' made it into the Release). Of course, this is only one example, and your mileage may vary.

Also, no matter which of these numbers you use, it is only a starting point for discussion. The number may be adjusted based on the factors given above, with special emphasis on the willingness of Stakeholders to compromise.

And, finally, these Epic sizes are *budgets* of StoryPoints, and these Story-Points are *fungible*. They can be moved around (from Epic to Epic) when needed. That is, if one Epic is getting finished quickly, and another is lagging behind, it is the Product Owner's responsibility to move the StoryPoints from one Epic to the other. This *balancing the load* is one of the agile tools the Product Owner has when planning and budgeting. Of course, this means that Epics shouldn't be decomposed too much too soon – the StoryPoints are harder to move if they are already allocated to existing Stories – it is easier if they are unallocated.

Ok, enough about Epics already...

Two More Issues

There are two more 'Velocity and Size' issues that I'd like to discuss; these issues are ones that I often get asked about and I think they deserve a short discussion. The first issue comes from the question *'How do I compare Velocities between Teams?'* and the second comes from the question *'What do I do when a Story's Size changes?'*

Comparing Velocity Between Teams: A Team's Velocity measures how fast the Team develops Product, and it is reasonable to want to combine Teams' Velocities to determine how fast an Organization develops Product. It is also reasonable to want to compare the productivity of Teams in the same Organization. In order to do this, we need to know if there is some way that we can combine, or compare, Velocities for different Teams?

Let's go back to the basics of Velocity and StoryPoints as I have described in this chapter. As you recall, in order for Velocity to have the appropriate properties, StoryPoints need to measure (for well-defined Functional Stories) the Ideal Effort needed for the Story, and ignore the Technical Debt, Team Ability, Organizational Noise, and other Environmental Variables.

So, if the Team's units of Ideal Effort were the same, it *would be* possible to compare the StoryPoints for well-defined Functional Stories. This can be accomplished if the exemplar Stories used by the Teams for the Estimation Game were either the same, or had the same Ideal Effort, and the Teams used the same Estimation Game script.

However, not all of the work a Team does provides well-defined function-ality, and StoryPoints for other types of Stories would likely *not be* compar-able. For example:

- If two Teams each did 8 SPs worth of well-defined Functional Stories, they had the same exemplar Stories, and they used the same Estimation Game, we *would* expect that each Team produced about the same amount of Product, but

- If each Team did 2 SPs worth of refactoring, we would not expect that the Teams had refactored the same amount of code. This is because refactoring is a time-boxed Story whose SPs are based on effort, so the productivity is not comparable across Teams.

Since a Team's Velocity combines the StoryPoints of all sorts of Stories, it would *not be* reasonable to combine or compare the Velocities directly.

However, if we separated the amount of the Velocity that involved *only* the well-defined Functional Stories (and called it Functional Velocity, perhaps…) we *could* compare and combine that metric, if the Teams are in the same codebase and used the same exemplar Stories and script for the Estimation Game.

If we did this, Functional Velocities for different Teams *could* be added together to provide an overall Functional Velocity, and Functional Velocities could be compared between Teams. The differences between Teams' Functional Velocities would be primarily determined by differences in the Environmental Variables each Team runs into. This is reasonable, and differences in Velocity will allow the Stakeholders to ask interesting and reasonable questions about the impacts of the Environmental Variables on the Teams.

I can imagine Organizations that would want to do this, but I advise against it unless both the Organization and its Teams are *very* mature in their self-organization and quality development practices – this is *not* something to try until a Team has been performing for a good while. Remember, first People, then Product, then Process (see chapter 1.1).

Changing Story Sizes: The second issue I'd like to discuss is what to do when a Story's Size changes. This is actually a fairly straightforward issue, as long as we keep our focus on what a Story's Size is. If what we're really asking is *'What do I do when the effort for a Story increases beyond what I expected?'* then it's fairly simple. The StoryPoints don't change in this instance, because StoryPoints are based on Ideal Effort, not Actual Effort, and don't change unless the Acceptance Criteria change.

What happened is that this Story just got hard… maybe there was significant new Technical Debt, maybe the Team lost a Team Member with necessary expertise, whatever… the StoryPoints didn't change, and the Velocity will indicate that something interesting happened. So, this situation leads to a discussion of what happened to make it hard, but not a change in StoryPoints. Of course, if the Team is using EffortPoints, the EffortPoints would change, and the fact that the EffortPoints changed could also lead to this discussion.

But what if the Story's Acceptance Criteria changed and the StoryPoints are based on a misunderstanding of the Story itself? This could happen if the Team estimated the Story's Size before the Story's Acceptance Criteria was finalized (see chapter 3.6) or if the Story's Acceptance Criteria changed (see chapter 4.3). In these cases the Team might need to change the number of StoryPoints because the Team's understanding of the Story had been fundamentally changed – its Ideal Effort could have been changed. This discussion is tightly related to Backlog Refinement (see chapter 3.9).

This could wind up being an interesting issue, and let me tell you why. There are two things to worry about:

- First, if the Team realizes that this change is symptomatic – that it will be common to many more Stories in the Backlog – this can be a *real* problem for future predictions. For example, if *all* 2 SP Stories of a given type are *actually* 4 SP Stories, because all their Acceptance Criteria had a fundamental change, this can mean there is more Product (Ideal Effort/Intrinsic Difficulty) in the Backlog than was originally thought – even though the number of Stories has not increased.

- Second, the Team has a problem if the Story has been extracted from an Epic that has a budget of StoryPoints. If it turns out that the Story's new Acceptance Criteria need more Ideal Effort than the original Acceptance Criteria, the Team needs to make sure that the correct number of StoryPoints is deducted from the Epic. In other words, if the original estimate was that the Story was using 4 SPs of the Epic's budget, and it turns out that the Story is actually an 8 SP Story, then the Team must make sure that 8 SPs are subtracted from the Epic's StoryPoint budget.

In practice, from the *development* point of view, this changing of a Story's size is not much of an issue as long as the Team is doing Agreement-Based Planning (chapter 4.2) and is basing its development on the Story's Agreement, as the Agreement *includes* the Story's Acceptance Criteria. This makes the Story's StoryPoints basically irrelevant to the Development Team – at least from the viewpoint of actually *doing* the work. However, if the Team is also using EffortPoints, the EffortPoints for a Story *could* be relevant to the Development Team, as they are a relative measure of the Actual Effort needed to do the work – which is something the Team 'owns.'

Contrariwise, StoryPoints and Velocity could be *very* important to the Product Owner when discussing progress and expectations with the Stakeholders. So, as a part of Backlog Refinement and Retrospectives, this issue should be discussed and managed (see chapters 3.9 and 2.4).

Summary

Philosophically, sizing an Item (Story or Epic) is a complex issue. I hope that this chapter has convinced you of that. As a practical matter, however, a Team will quickly settle on sizing mechanisms that works for them. Many Teams want to consider actual effort as well as size when they estimate a Story, and I recommend that the Team estimate both StoryPoints and EffortPoints in this case. In appendix A.6 I present an Estimation Game that allows a Team to estimate a Story's size for all Stories.

You may believe that I am *thinking too hard* about this issue, and you may be right. However, I'm only doing it because questions about Story Sizing, StoryPoints, and Effort come up *all* the time, with every Team I've ever worked with. So, be warned, it's a mess. I hope that this chapter helps you with it.

Discussion Questions

1. How long will this take? When will the Team be done? Are these legitimate questions to ask? If you were spending your money would you want to have answers to these questions? If so, who would you ask? What can we measure to understand these questions?

2. What is the difference between Team's Capacity and a Team's Velocity?

3. How can Velocity be used in a way that is useful and not weaponized as a tool to push work onto the Team?

4. What happens to Velocity if Technical Debt is increasing? What happens to Velocity when the Team is getting better? What happens to Velocity when Organizational Pressure/Noise increases? What is happening when Velocity is holding steady? What is the impact on Velocity when the work is simpler to do (i.e., it takes a much time but not as much thought)? Can Velocities from different teams be compared in a meaningful way?

5. Does the amount of data you have impact decision-making based on Velocity measurements? What happens when people draw conclusions from small data sets?

6. Draw four quadrants on a piece of white flipchart paper. Write down the Environmental Variables (Team Ability, Technical Debt, SME Availability, and Organizational Noise), one in each quadrant. Put the word "Story" at the intersection of the axis. Discuss concrete examples of each Environmental Variable as they relate to experiences you have had. Which ones can you influence? Which ones cannot be easily altered, if at all?

7. Can we change a Story's understood size? What reasons might cause a Story's size to change? When should we not allow it to change and why?

8. What happens if the Backlog has more Intrinsic Difficulty (takes more Ideal Effort) than we originally expected? Does this matter? If it matters what do we do about it?

Organizing the Backlog

There is no intrinsic organization of the Backlog other than its order. In this chapter I describe tagging mechanisms that provide ways to organize the Backlog that makes it easier for Stakeholders to understand.

In chapter 3.2, when I defined and introduced the Backlog, I indicated that one of its uses was "to inform Stakeholders about the Team's work and progress in order to give them the information they need to understand, and participate in, the project."

From the Team's perspective of *work* the Backlog is a simple list, but from the Stakeholder's perspective of *understanding* it is more complicated. In any case, the Stakeholders need to know what they need to know, and the Backlog has to give it to them – probably accompanied by conversations with the Product Owner and other Team Members.

For example, Stakeholders may think of the Backlog in terms of a Work Breakdown Structure like the one for the **CatAir.com Project** given in Figure 19 in chapter 3.3; they may think of the Backlog in terms of an Organization Chart like Figure 7 in chapter 2.2 showing the **Product H-12 Organization**; they might want to know how much progress is being made on the 'Buy an e-Ticket' Use Case with a report like Figure 17 at the end of chapter 3.2; they may want to know which Items and Stories belong to a given Epic as shown in Table 5 at the end of chapter 3.4; they might want to know which Items are dependent on each other; they may want to know the Items that are resolving a particular Issue or Risk; they might want to know which Items are bugs; they might want to know which Items Dan wants to work on; there are lots of things they might want to know.

Whatever it is the Stakeholders want to know about the Backlog, it is the Team's (and in particular the Product Owner's) job to give it to them. This could involve a lot of conversations and take a lot of time, and I would prefer if the Backlog, itself, provided the necessary information. In order to allow the Stakeholders to understand the Backlog in the way they want to understand it, I have found three concepts to be very useful: Tags, Themes, and Buckets. These concepts are related, and here's a brief description of each of the three concepts:

1. **Tags:** Some information should be readily apparent from just *looking* at the Item: what kind of Item it is, who's planning to work on it,

which Stakeholders are interested in it, and so on. This requires an *ad hoc* tagging mechanism that attaches information *directly to* the Item.

2. **Themes:** Items are often *related* to each other in interesting ways; they may be inter-dependent, they may be involved in resolving the same Issue or Risk, or they could be related in some other way. Themes allow the relationship itself (Dependency, Issue, Risk, etc.) to be its *own Item* in the Backlog, and for the Theme to tie together the other, inter-related, Items.

3. **Buckets:** Some Items *belong* to other Items. For example, Epics *contain* Stories (and other Epics), Products *contain* Capabilities (a kind of Epic), Organizations and Programs *contain* Projects and Products, and so on. Many Stakeholders want to see these relationships represented in the Backlog, and Buckets allow Items that contain (or own) other Items to be displayed.

These three concepts can be implemented in many different ways. If your Team uses a tool to manage its Backlog, the tool may have method[s] to use. If the Team is using 'stickies on the wall,' a spreadsheet, or its tool provides no methods to do these things, have the Team try naming conventions like the ones described in this chapter.

For each of the naming conventions I will present simple examples, and I hope that this will give you some ideas for your own Team. Generically, I refer to this naming convention as 'Tagging the Items,' as it adds useful information of various types.

Tags

The simplest Tagging is adding Tags to the Stories; these Tags provide additional information, and allow for filtering of the Backlog. For example, I have already used Tags that represent the Story's Storyotype (chapter 3.10) in some of my examples:

- '[usecase] Buy an e-Ticket,' which indicates that the Item is a Use Case, which is a kind of Epic;

- '[backbone] Pick One and Pay for It,' which indicates that the Story has the [backbone] Storyotype, which has special meaning for the Story's Agreement; and

- '[redo] Fix Error in Luggage Weight Calculations,' which shows that the algorithm is calculating things incorrectly and both code and (at least one) Acceptance Test must be changed.

Note that an Item could have several Tags that represent different things. For example:

- '[CUTLASS][beefup][arch-sig] Close Reservations when Plane is Full,' which indicates that the Story is *beefing up* an existing scenario, is architecturally significant, and is dependent on the CUTLASS system; and

- '[Tigers][epic][SH-George] Pilot Timesheets,' which shows that 'Team Tigers' *owns* the 'Pilot Timesheets' Epic and that there is a Stakeholder named George who is particularly interested in it.

Of course, in each of these cases the Stakeholders need to know what the Tags mean; there is no intrinsic way to tell from the Backlog. I like the *ad hoc* nature of Tags, as it allows the Team to add new Tags when needed, for whatever reason they have. New Tags are typically added through negotiations with the Stakeholders, in order to provide added information to help them understand what the Backlog is trying to tell them.

Themes

Simple Tags are nice because they add meta information to particular Items in the Backlog. However, the Stakeholders often need information that connects many different Items together. In this case the Team can use Themes and Buckets. In this section I'll introduce the Theme, and I will discuss the Bucket in the next section.

Basically, a Theme is a Tag that is *also* its own Item in the Backlog; that is, there is an Item in the Backlog that describes the relationship of other Items in some way – it provides context and helps Team Members and Stakeholders understand the relationship amongst the other Items. Generally, though, this relationship is not a whole-part relationship – we reserve that relationship for the Bucket. Let me give a simple example.

One of the most common reasons to use a Theme is to document a dependency. For example, if the CUTLASS System is commonly depended on, we could add the Theme:

- '[dependency-12] CUTLASS System,'

to the Backlog as an Item. This Item would describe the CUTLASS system, and what elements of it other Items could depend on. Then this would allow Items like:

- '[12] Stop Accepting Passengers if Plane is full,'

where the '[12]' indicates that this Story is dependent on the CUTLASS System, and that the dependency itself is described in the Backlog. If it were simply tagged '[CUTLASS]' it could indicate a dependency, but the fact that it's a '[12]' indicates that there is an Item that describes the dependency. This is useful information for Stakeholders and Team Members alike.

Themes can also be used to indicate that Items are related by Teams or individuals that will need do to the work; they can be used to show that the Items are required for a given release or other events (like a trade show); or for any other reason your Stakeholders can think of. That's the strength of Themes; they can be used to document the relationships among Items, and is used like a Tag so that we know which Items are inter-related. Because of their ability to contain information, they are much more powerful than Tags.

Typically, these Themes (as Items) will live in the Fridge or Freezer (depending on whether items related by the Theme are in or out of current scope), while the Items that are related by this Theme will move up the Backlog, through the Back Burner to the Front Burner and actually get Done. As you can imagine, the numbering of the Themes must be unique, no matter the type of Theme, so that there will be no confusion – and it also allows a given Item to be related to several Themes.

Buckets

Whereas Themes are used for relating Items together in general ways, the Bucket is used specifically when there is a whole-part or belongs-to relationship between the Bucket and the Item. The most obvious example is when the Bucket represents an Epic, which contains its Stories (and sub-Epics). Let's look at our old friend, the Use Case 'Buy an e-Ticket.' This Use Case could be documented in the Backlog as the Item:

- '[usecase-1] Buy an e-Ticket,'

which shows that this Feature is a Use Case, and is also Bucket #1. This Item is used in the Backlog to document specific information about this Use Case as a whole, such as its brief description, SMEs, Personas and Actors, and so on.

But that's not all.

In chapter 3.7, when discussing sizes, I mentioned that Epics often have a budget of StoryPoints in order to help manage releases. When a Bucket is used to represent an Epic, it often has a budget of StoryPoints – this is one of the ways that a Bucket differs from a Theme. So, it could be:

- '[usecase-1] Buy an e-Ticket' (size=150SPs).

If this Bucket/Epic is in the Backlog, the Epic's sub-Stories are labeled as:

- '[backbone][1] Pick One and Pay for It' (size=8SPs), and

- '[redo][1] Fix Error in Luggage Weight Calculations' (size=2SPs),

In this case, the Epic not only knows who its children are (because of the labeling), but it also has a StoryPoint budget that can be compared to its children's sizes – this allows Stakeholders to understand what Stories the Epic's Budget is being spent on.

This is a very powerful mechanism. By using it, it is possible to create lists like that found in Table 5 at the end of chapter 3.4, graphs like Figure 17 at the end of chapter 3.2, and even have understanding of more complicated WBSs and Organizations. These are important things to be able to do for our Stakeholders so that they can understand what is going on, and I recommend this method for doing so.

Summary

In this chapter I have presented simple – even trivial – Tagging methods that provides additional information in the Backlog. This Tagging can be used for many reasons, including identifying Epics that can then *roll up* information about their internal Stories. These Tagging techniques are both simple and powerful, and are often enough to give Stakeholders what they need to know about the progress of the Team. In fact, discussing what sorts of Tagging to use in order to make it easy on Stakeholders is a common subject of Retrospectives, and are an easy thing to proceduralize.

Discussion Questions

1. Describe Tags, Themes and Buckets. What is the difference between them and how are they related?

2. What is the simplest mechanism described in this chapter to start organizing your Backlog?

3. Can you add Tags to Epics? Stories? What is the difference? What kinds of differences do you expect to see between Tags?

4. What are the differences between Themes and Buckets? Give examples of each.

Backlog Refinement

Backlog Refinement is the process of getting Stories ready for Planning. It includes extracting Stories from Epics, defining Done for Stories, and Prioritization – both the prioritizing of the Epics and Stories to be Refined, and the prioritizing of the Refined Stories for Planning. In this chapter I discuss these topics and some of the issues that are found...

The Backlog consists of Items representing work that stakeholders want the Team to do. The most important part of planning is forecasting which of those Items the Team will do in the next Sprint. In between putting an Item on the Backlog and deciding to do it is Backlog Refinement (also called Grooming, Backlog Maintenance or Story Time), which consists of activities that order the Backlog and turn Backlog Items into Ready Stories: small, well-defined and ready to take to Planning.

My standard, and what I recommend to the Teams I coach, is that a Story is Ready when all it will take is a short (less than 10 minute) conversation *during* Planning in order for the Team to finalize the Agreement, agree to do the work, task it out, and move on to the next one (see chapter 4.2). Based on this definition of Ready it is clear that Backlog Refinement is a fairly substantial activity.

Activities of Backlog Refinement fall into two basic categories: prioritizing the Items (moving them up the Backlog into the Back Burner), and preparing the Items in the Back Burner for Planning – making Stories Ready. In this chapter I will discuss both of these categories. First, I'll discuss Backlog Refinement in general – including preparation for Planning – and then I'll discuss various factors involved in Prioritization itself.

Backlog Refinement Discussion

You will recall from chapter 3.2 that Backlog Refinement includes moving Stories into the Back Burner and further refining them until they are Ready to go to Planning. In order to do this there are some basic things that must be done:

- It must be determined if Backlog Items are to be worked on soon; if they are, then they are candidates for moving to the Back Burner. Note that these Items can come from the Fridge, the Freezer, or the InBox.

- There are a number of factors to consider when moving Items to the Back Burner:
    o If the Item is already 'small' enough to be a Story, it may be moved to the Back Burner directly for further refinement, or
    o If the Item is an Epic, Stories must be extracted from it and moved to the Back Burner. In either case,
    o The Stories that are moved should be examined, and rewritten if necessary, so that their goals are simple, clear, and correct.

- Once Stories are in the Back Burner, they are further refined to make them Ready for Planning.

These things should be obvious, but you'd be surprised how confusing it can get once you start doing it. By concentrating on one thing at a time, it gets easier. Nevertheless, there are a number of issues involved, which I will now discuss.

Refinement, Waste, and Targets: First of all, we don't want *too many* Stories on the Back Burner, as this is inventory (and hence waste) in the Lean sense (see appendix A.5). By moving Stories to the Back Burner, the Team is predicting what they will be working on soon. This prediction is non-agile (as all predictive behavior is), and is (at least partially) reinventing the notion of having a detailed requirements document. In practice this could be ok, but philosophically, this bothers me... just sayin'...

Therefore, I recommend that a Team has no more than two or three Sprint's worth of Stories in the Back Burner at any given time, and sometimes I think that even this is a bit much.

On the other hand, the Team needs *some* predictability – they usually feel better if they have some targets to *shoot at*. Since the Team is usually working within the context of a Release, these targets often take the form of fixed (even if ambiguous) Release Goals. Having Release Goals as targets that put bounds on what the Team does allows the Team some mid-term predictability and stability.

This tension between the Team wanting to know what's going on and needing to keep the inventory down is an ongoing issue for all Teams, and resolving it in favor of smaller inventory is a good sign of Team maturity – the more work on the Back Burner, the more immature the Team usually is.

Activities of Backlog Refinement: Now let me be a little more specific about what Backlog Refinement is, and expand on the basic responsibilities I presented above. Each of these activities is the responsibility of the Team, led by the Product Owner, and may involve help from the Stakeholders and

SMEs. Many Teams view this as a 'PO thing' – and it is – but the Product Owner must *feel free* to use the Team and SMEs as his or her staff to help with this. Anyway, here they are:

Prioritize Items in the Backlog for further Refinement: The first thing to do is figure out which Items need to be in the Back Burner to be Refined. These Items could come from the Fridge (the usual source), the Freezer, the InBox, or just 'show up.' This prioritization is based on many factors, including which Capabilities are in scope, how close to releasable each of them is, and the prioritization strategies discussed later in this chapter. We usually do this prioritization with input from Stakeholders, and is clearly a responsibility of the Product Owner.

Place Stories in the Back Burner for further Refinement: Once the Items have been prioritized for moving to the Back Burner, the Team (with input from SMEs) analyzes each Item, (possibly) rewrites it, and actually moves it to the Back Burner. If the Item is already a Story (not an Epic) the Story may be moved over as-is or re-written and moved. If the Item is an Epic, Stories must be extracted from the Epic and placed in the Back Burner. This extraction could involve various forms of analysis (Use Case analysis, State-Based analysis, User Experience analysis, and so on), often assisted by SMEs. The resulting Stories should be small and, if functional, defined by just one positive test. It is likely that this analysis is something the Product Owner and Stakeholders will need help with – that this analysis usually requires expertise that these people don't have.

Draft the Story's Agreement and/or Tasks: In order to make the Story '10 minutes away' from being finalized during Planning, the Team often needs to draft the Story's Agreement and/or Tasks. It is natural for the Team to discuss how the Story will get Done, and these drafts are just documenting these conversations. However, remember that the Agreement and Tasks are not *finalized* until the Sprint Planning itself and that this is, therefore, merely a draft. Storyotypes are very useful in preparing these drafts, as Storyotypes contain standard Agreements and may contain sample Tasks (see chapter 3.10).

Size the New Stories: If your Team requires it, it may also need to size the new Stories in StoryPoints, EffortPoints, or both (see chapter 3.7). The sizing in EffortPoints may be useful for the Team's Sprint Planning (see chapter 4.2), and the sizing in StoryPoints is necessary if it is tracking the expenditure of budgeted StoryPoints. In the latter case the Team must also re-size the Epic it is extracting the Story from, in order to keep the Epic's StoryPoint budget current (see chapter 3.7). The sizing of a Story should be done as the Story's Acceptance Criteria and Agreement become clear, and should be re-done if they change in any significant way.

Preparing SMEs for Sprint Planning: Refining Stories should include getting commitments from SMEs ahead of time (before agreeing to the Story at Sprint Planning) if their participation is necessary for completion. For example, this is often true of Analysis Stories or Architectural Stories, where getting info from SMEs could be the whole point. This *is* a bit of predictive planning, and could be replaced with verifying the SMEs availability during Sprint Planning itself, but it seems to me that setting it up ahead of time is reasonable mitigation of the risk of them not being available. It seems to me that giving the SME a 'heads up' is a simple matter of manners and living the Team Values.

Finding new Capabilities: Even though it's not actually in scope for Backlog Refinement, it often happens that the Team working with SMEs will find new Capabilities. These Capabilities should be placed in the Fridge, the Freezer, or the InBox (whichever is appropriate), in order to be dealt with later. I recommend that these new Items not be dealt with in detail as they're found, but sometimes it's tempting to do so because the SMEs are with you. It certainly seems reasonable to get a one paragraph description of the Capability as long as the SMEs are there, and if the Team *must* do it, it should keep the conversation short.

Refinement Sessions versus Refinement Stories. I just discussed some of the activities that take place during Backlog Refinement, but when do we do it? Basically there are two choices: Refinement Sessions as part of the Team's process, and Refinement Stories that are prioritized as part of the Backlog. Each of these methods has its strengths and weaknesses, and I recommend that most Teams do both.

Specifically, I recommend that the whole Team, as a group, has 4 hours of Refinement sessions a week, probably in two 2-hour bursts. These sessions could include SMEs and should focus on Items that will be coming up soon. I recommend that the Team should have a maximum of two or three Sprint's worth of Stories ready to go in the Back Burner, so this limits the extent of these Sessions.

I also recommend that the Team have specific Refinement Stories that are worked on by one or two Team Members working with SMEs. These Stories should be used when either the SMEs are not available for Refinement Discussions, or when the Refinement itself is complex. Refinement Stories are a specific kind of Analysis Story, and usually focus on extracting and refining Stories from Epics, rather than finding new Items – which is the focus of other types of Analysis Stories.

Basic Prioritization Strategy

Prioritization is arguably the most important thing in Scrum, as Scrum is about incremental delivery in order to provide value and feedback – and the prioritization determines the order in which the value is produced, and thus what feedback is sought. There are at least three layers of prioritization, as Items are moved from the InBox *up through* the Backlog to be Done:

1. The first layer of prioritization is determining whether or not an Item is in scope for consideration for the current release. If it is, then the Item is moved to the Fridge part of the Backlog.

2. The second layer of prioritization is to determine whether or not the item is going to be worked on 'soon' or not. If it is, then the Item must be moved to the Back Burner to be refined and the result will be Ready Stories in the Back Burner, ready for Planning.

3. Finally, the third (and final) layer of prioritization is to determine whether or not the Ready Story is going to be worked on 'now' or not. This is done as part of Planning or, more rarely, as an adjustment to an existing plan (see chapter 4.3). If it is to be worked on now, the Story's Agreement is finalized and agreed to by the Team, and the Story is accepted into the Front Burner to be Done and delivered.

These layers of prioritization are the same regardless of what the Scrum Team is developing, and simply represent the movement of Backlog Items up and through the Backlog. No matter the kind of prioritization, there are lots of factors involved, some of which are discussed later in this chapter. However, overall prioritization strategies differ, based on what the main goals of the Team are. There are three basic strategies a Team could have:

*   **Continuous Improvement**: This strategy is primarily for Teams doing Maintenance or providing features on an opportunistic basis; there is little (or no) long-term strategy to be considered when prioritizing.

*   **Defined Feature Delivery**: The Team has a fixed set of Features to deliver, often on a given date. The Goal of this strategy is to get *all* the Features *across the finish line* to minimally releasable at the time of Release; and this focus is constant and paramount in all prioritization efforts.

*   **Fuzzy Feature Delivery**: This is the *'I don't know what I want, but I'll know it when I see it'* type of delivery. When done well, it usually turns into a series of (internal) Defined Feature Delivery Releases, as the necessary Features make themselves known. When done poorly,

it could turn into a Continuous Improvement Delivery, with everybody *hoping* that there will be a successful endpoint.

Of course, it's not this simple – a Team can be doing more than one of these strategies at a time, or might not even have any notion of what its overall strategy is. Right now, though, I'd like to discuss the basic strategy for the second case, the Defined Feature Delivery, as it's the most interesting. The basic situation is that the Team has a set of Features that it needs to deliver, and these Features are initially represented by Epics in the Fridge. In order to help manage and monitor their delivery, these Features probably have StoryPoint budgets (see chapters 3.7 and 3.8).

In this situation, success is *defined* by delivering releasable versions of these features (probably with the highest value features being more robust) on or before the expected release date. It is very important to realize that *perfect is the enemy of good enough* and that the Team's job is to provide *Releasable* features – not *Complete* features. The difference between Releasable and Complete (at the feature level) is the wiggle room that we are managing with agility. The defining and refining of the definition and details of Releasable is the primary reason the Team works with SMEs and Stakeholders in an iterative way – with lots of feedback and conversations.

The overall strategy is to get any given Feature to minimally Releasable as soon as you can, and then *stop development* on that Feature. Once *all* the Features are minimally Releasable, the Team can come back and beef them up. If there is a question if a feature is minimally Releasable or not and there are other features to do, I recommend that you stop work on the feature that is *almost* (but not quite) there, and come back to it later. Remember that the Team needs *all* of the Features to be *good enough* before making *any* of them *perfect* (or even significantly better than good enough...).

I recommend that the Team focus on no more than one or two Features at a time, so that many of the Team Members are *in the same mental space* and can help each other out easily. Many Teams want to set the Team Members off to work on *their own* Features in parallel, but this is *precisely* the wrong approach for a couple of reasons:

- It can result in many features being *almost* releasable while a few others are overdone – the effort should have been better managed to get them all Releasable.

- It can result in *each* of the features being non-Releasable, while dropping one or two of the features could have allowed *all of the rest* to be Releasable.

Anyway, it's a bad idea... the Team should Swarm on each feature until it's Releasable in the same way it Swarms on a Story until it's Done (see chapter 2.6).

In order to do this, the Team needs two behaviors:

1. It must be able to switch from one Feature to another *as soon as* the first becomes minimally Releasable; this requires the Team to either have short Sprints or be comfortable with changing content within a Sprint (see chapter 4.3); and

2. The Team will need to have frequent reviews with SMEs and Stakeholders (probably more often than simply the standard once-a-sprint Product Reviews) in order to determine when a Feature is minimally Releasable.

Each of these behaviors is hard to do, and many Teams have problems with them. Nobody said agility was easy... and each of these behaviors is largely the responsibility of the Product Owner. It is the Product Owner who is *accountable* for determining when to switch from one Feature to another and it is the Product Owner who is *accountable* for moving each Feature up the S-Shaped Curve of value production I discuss in appendix A.5.

Managing the switching between features is not easy. Sometimes, a Team constructs a Release Strategy at the beginning of the Release that describes how the balance between Features is to be achieved and maintained. Often, though, this balancing act is managed *on the fly* by the Product Owner, using the Team and Stakeholders to provide advice on which Features need to be focused on in each Sprint throughout the Release.

Prioritization Factors

Unfortunately, it is not only Features that are implemented by Stories in a Sprint, and 'progressing towards release' is not the only factor considered in prioritization of Stories. The basic strategy discussed in the last section is very difficult to follow in most cases – not only is it simple, it is also simplistic. There are additional factors to take into account when prioritizing and reprioritizing Stories. These factors supplement and modify the prioritization that arises from the strategy described in the last section.

Underlying all prioritizations is the imperative to meet the Release Goal, if the Team has one. With that imperative in mind, each of the following factors is important at one time or another. Prioritization is a distinctly subjective, and human, endeavor, and should be undertaken with a lot of discussions, arguments, and analysis. There is nothing simple about it.

Stories with Business Value: First of all, there are other Stories (besides Features) that have Business Value. These Stories are those that some *external* Stakeholder values and wants done. The Features that are done as part of the Release Goal beget Stories with Business Value, but these are not the *only* Stories with Business Value. It is the Product Owner's problem to reconcile the different notions of business value that are *owned* by the different Stakeholders and decide which is most important – thus allowing final prioritization of the Stories.

Business Value Stories are the ones we're being paid to produce – they are the ones that the Stakeholders care about. In fact, since the term Business Value is hard to define, I simply define by saying that *'a Story has business value if (and only if) some external Stakeholder wants it done,'* and leave it at that. There are many types of Stories that provide business value, as we discussed in chapter 3.3:

- Stories that provide Capabilities/Features for a system,

- Bug fixes or maintenance Stories in other systems,

- Stories that help the sales or marketing people with materials, clients, etc.,

- Analysis Stories involving the Product Owner and other Team Members working with Stakeholders and SMEs to find new Stories,

- and so on.

In any case, one of the major issues in prioritizing Stories is how much effort will be used to mitigate the production of Technical Debt (see chapter 3.5), as this could be a major part of the effort the Story will take. Discussions about Prioritization often include comments like *'I want this one if it's not too much effort.'* Comments like these can become an evil pressure to cut corners and produce Technical Debt, and they should be avoided. If comments like these *are* said, they need to be discussed in a -spective.

Architecturally Significant Stories: Second, Stories could be prioritized based on Architectural Significance or other technical risk factors. Typically, the Product Owner needs help from the Team to determine this sort of prioritization. To me, and thus in this book, the word Architecture refers to the definition I heard from Grady Booch[1] years ago, that "architecture is the collection of decisions that have been made about *how* the software will be built." That is, architecture consists of decisions, not just boxes and arrows or high-level design.

---

[1] One of the original gurus in Object Orientation, went on to help develop UML.

Many Team Members believe that architectural decisions need to be made up front. This may or may not be true (I believe it is not), but what is *certainly* true is that architectural decisions should be made *only* in the context of doing some actual work. That is, the Team does an *actual* Story with Business Value that *forces* it to make the architectural decision that needs to be made.

Often, there are a number of Stories that all rely on the same underlying architectural decision. Whichever one the Team does first will cause the architectural decision to be made, so this Story is the Architecturally Significant one. This Story will be more Intrinsically Difficult and thus take more Ideal Effort than the ones that follow, so its size may need to be changed to reflect this (see chapter 3.7).

For example, if the Team Members need to know how to do logging, or error handling, they actually do a Story that forces them to do logging or error handling. As a result, they make a decision that works for now, and they have actual code that uses the decision to help deliver some value. If they're not sure that the decision was correct, so they think there's still a risk that they need to investigate, they do another Story that forces a decision about the new risk. By prioritizing this new Story (or not) the Product Owner (with input from the Team) indicates how much the Team thinks that architectural risk is worth.

There is always a balance between prioritizing purely on Business Value and prioritizing based on Architectural Significance. The Team is usually doing both types throughout the project, with the balance shifting from architecture-heavy Sprints to business-value-heavy Sprints as the Team moves through a release. That is, early Sprints in a release often put together a 'walking skeleton' (demonstrating the architectural decisions in running code) based on doing Architecturally Significant Stories, and the later Sprints focus on adding Business Value by adding 'meat on the bones.'

Dependencies: One of the more interesting, and contentious, prioritization issues is the issue of dependencies. These dependencies come in two types:

- **Feature Dependencies**: The Team must develop a feature (or part of a feature) in order to develop another part (possibly of another feature). Sometimes this dependency is technical, sometimes it is architectural, and sometimes it is because the feature will be easier to review if delivered in this order.

- **Technical Dependencies**: The Team may see dependencies on some Chores, such as cleaning up code, improving the environment, and so on. These dependencies are less obvious and harder to see. They are often thought of as overhead – and the Product Owner has no *real* reason to want to do them. But the Team *needs* them Done in order to be able to produce the business value Stories the Product Owner wants, and this is an interesting dilemma.

If everything was perfect, the Product Owner would just take *all* these Stories and place them in the Backlog so that the dependency goes away by doing them in the appropriate order. This can usually be accomplished for the Feature Dependencies, as they are easier to see.

Unfortunately, things are not always perfect when thinking about the Chores, so we have some other prioritization strategies that I discussed at the end of chapter 3.3, and I refer you back there for that discussion. Also, in chapter 3.8 I discussed using Tags and Themes to make it easier to document dependencies found in the Backlog, so they are easier to discuss later. Remember that the Team does Chores primarily to maintain its Capacity going into the future – not because the Team wants 'pretty code' – so this prioritization can get quite contentious.

People Availability: Something that is frequently overlooked is that there are dependencies based on people. It may be obvious that sometimes the work can *only* be Done if specific people are available, but Teams usually don't prioritize on this basis. What I typically find is Teams will try to get some work Done, and then are stymied because people aren't available – and then it's presented as an impediment.

Usually, though, it's a result of bad planning – not an *actual* impediment. Of course, people can be unexpectedly absent, which is an impediment, but Teams need to do more thinking about people's availability when they prioritize.

PlaceHolder Stories: Sometimes we prioritize Stories that really have no content yet, just so we can reserve their effort for later – these Stories are for managing the known unknowns – and are called PlaceHolder Stories (discussed in chapter 4.4). One of the most common types of PlaceHolder Stories is the 'Bug to be Named Later' Story, which simply reserves some Story-Points to be used to fix bugs (probably in other systems) that the Team will be obligated to fix during the Sprint. PlaceHolders can be used for other reasons, too. For example, the team may say *'Let's put a 16 SP Story in here to hold effort we'll use on support for the sales guys this Sprint.'*

Summary

A Team is constantly refining the Backlog in order to have Stories ready for Planning. The Team shouldn't have too many ready, as this is waste, and prioritizing which Stories need to be refined is a major concern.

There are a number of factors to consider when prioritizing Stories. Of course, your Team's prioritization is *your Team's* prioritization, so it's up to the Team and its Product Owner. If you consider the factors mentioned in this chapter you will have a good chance of having the conversations you need to have in order to do this prioritization successfully.

Discussion Questions

1. Is Backlog Refinement analysis? Or is it something else? Why do we use the word refinement here? What is the purpose of refinement?

2. Discuss the difference between a Done Story and a Releasable Feature. If all the Stories 'inside' a Feature are Done, does that make the Feature Done? Does it make the Feature Releasable?

3. What does if mean for a Feature to be minimally releasable?

4. Name several types of Refinement and describe when Refinement is completed.

5. What are we doing when we extract Stories? Where do they go and what are they being extracted from?

6. Discuss with your group to see if you can agree to a good rule of thumb for the number of Stories that belong in the backburner.

7. Who is responsible for moving things to the backburner? How is this decided and when are we saying it will be done?

8. Should sizing of a Story be re-done if the Story's Agreement changes? Is it proper to change the Story's size during a sprint? What is the impact of this and why would it be argued for? Against?

9. Do teams discover new capabilities in the System when doing work? Where do new capabilities go?

10. Why would a team do Chores?

3.10

Storyotypes

*Storyotypes are stereotypes of Stories; that is, they represent
exemplars or templates that apply to many of the Stories that
we find. We use Storyotypes to help decompose Epics, as well as
a tool to methodically capture, document, and reuse common
Agreements, especially the common Definitions of Done.*

In 2004, Gerard Meszaros introduced the Storyotype (stereotype of a Story) in the article "Using Storyotypes to Split Bloated XP Stories," which he presented at XP/Agile Universe 2004. Reading this article taught (or reinforced) three important things for me:

1. How to decompose a Use Case using only four Storyotypes (types of Stories), which augmented the knowledge I already knew about analyzing Use Cases;

2. That the right size for a Functional Story was 'one positive test'; and

3. That each Story should only have one focus (he explicitly separated cleaning up interfaces from adding functionality).

At about the same time, the Scrum community was starting to focus on the Definition of Done as we discussed in chapter 3.6. I quickly realized that the Stories of a given Storyotype had similar Definitions of Done, and that the Storyotypes could be used not only for help in decomposing Use Cases, but also as a way to capture common Definitions of Done for similar Stories.

In this chapter I will discuss Storyotypes and storyotyping. I believe that many Teams have, either consciously or unconsciously, already used many of these concepts, and I hope that a discussion of them will help your Team with its development efforts with Scrum.

Discussion

First of all, there is no definitive list of *common* Storyotypes. Each Team seems to develop its own Storyotypes, which are usually either examples or templates of Stories (and Epics) that contain common, reusable, information. This information could be of many different types: rules and standards based on CMMI compliance, security policies, Sarbanes-Oxley, FDA, FAA, or other regulations; there could be 'best practices' that are imposed by a process or architectural group within the Organization; there could be procedures that need to be followed when releasing a Product, and so on (see chapter 2.3).

It's not really about the Storyotypes themselves; it's about the *storyotyping*, which is an ongoing activity that finds (and documents) reusable patterns in a Team's Stories and Epics. In my experience, there are many kinds of Stories (and Storyotypes), including but not limited to: Coding Stories, Analysis Stories, Environmental Stories, Support Stories, and so on.

Each Team sees this differently, so I'm just going to present a few Stories and Storyotypes that illustrate the concept – your Team will do the rest on its own. Of course, I will show you Gerard's original four Storyotypes and indicate how Use Cases are decomposed, and my hope is that by seeing these examples you will have a good understanding of the concepts and can implement them yourselves.

Once a Team has its Storyotypes, they serve three primary purposes: to help the Team find new Stories and Epics for the Backlog; to help the Team decompose existing Epics into Stories; and to help the Team have consistent, high-quality, Agreements for those Stories.

The last two of these purposes are Backlog Refinement activities, which (as you recall) are activities that prepare Stories for Planning (see chapter 3.9). Storyotyping captures patterns within these Refinement activities, and I have found storyotyping to be a *natural* activity for most development Scrum Teams.

Once a Team has these patterns (Storyotypes) captured and documented, they can be used in other ways: to help train new Team Members, document Team lore, standardize Refinement practices across Teams, and so on.

But, for now, let's just talk about how storyotyping helps with Backlog Refinement.

Finding New Stories and Epics: I suspect that 80% or more of a Team's Stories are ones they've *seen before* and are, therefore, good candidates for storyotyping. Storyotypes make analysis and Epic decomposition easier by helping the Team know what they're looking for and also help a Team be more consistent. Storyotypes can also be made consistent across Teams, and is one of the few things that can help cross-team consistency without overly interfering with each Team's self-organization.

They are also useful to help prevent scope creep hidden in overhead activities. For example, a Team Member is less likely to independently agree to go on a sales call if he or she knows that there is a '**Sales Call**' Storyotype. The existence of the Storyotype will give the Team Member the courage to say to the sales guy: *'ok, we'll have to add a new Story for that sales call to the Backlog and talk to the Product Owner about prioritization...'* I find that the act of storyotyping reminds Team Members of the fact that *all* work is managed with the Backlog – that there is no magic, nothing is free.

Primary Use Is to Hold Common Definitions of Done: One of the Scrum Trainers I work with, Tamara Sulaiman Runyon, recently reminded me that there are basically four levels of Doneness, and the notion of storyotyping applies to all four. This is a subset of the overall storyotyping idea, and is one of the most useful and important parts – especially for Teams that are just starting to do (or think about) storyotyping.

> **Story Level:** For Coding Stories the Team wants to know what it takes to mitigate the production of Technical Debt, so that it will continue to produce Clean Code. This type of doneness can be captured in the Definition of Done section of each individual Story's Agreement, or it can be a more global definition, captured in Storyotypes. This is one of the main topics of this chapter.

> **Capability Level:** Capabilities actually get released to Users, so there is an inherent definition of *releasable* for a given Capability. This can be thought of as Doneness at the Capability level, and since a Capability is simply an Epic, it extends the Agreement on Done at the Story level. Therefore, it can be captured as part of the Epic itself, or more globally in a Storyotype of an Epic. Keep in mind, though, that this definition does not *guarantee* releasability – it merely documents what we what we think may provide releasability – the Capability will still need to pass its Validations to actually be considered releasable.

> **Sprint Level:** Yet another level is the Doneness for a Sprint. Most Sprints have some common Definitions of Done, which involve things like assuring the Sprint's Goal is met, determining what to get feedback on during the Product Review, moving the integrated code to a test lab, preparing necessary metrics and reports, and so on. These can be captured in a storyotyped 'Sprint Wrap-up' Story, where each of these common doneness requirements is part of the Acceptance Criteria section of the Wrap-up Story's Agreement.

> **Release Level:** A higher level of Doneness is for a Release. In the Release Sprint discussion in chapter 4.9 there is a description of what a Team does in order to release a Product; and it is similar from Release to Release. The commonalities can be captured in a storyotyped Doneness Epic, consisting of a collection of Stories, each of which contains one (or more) of the little things the Team has to do.

Each of these levels of Done is important, and it's natural for Teams to think about them. By capturing this knowledge in Storyotypes, it helps keep the Team from being *stupid on purpose* or forgetting things by being caught up in the moment. It also gives a clear topic to retrospect about, and gives a mechanism for documenting the improved knowledge of what Done is as the Team improves. In my opinion, having the Team think about storyotyping is a primary responsibility of the ScrumMaster, especially as the Team matures and moves from Storming to Norming (see chapter 2.4).

Storyotypes don't replace thinking: Even though Storyotypes are a great help for a Team doing Backlog Refinement, it must be stressed that the use of Storyotypes does not replace thinking. I admit that it's tempting, when the Team has Practices, for the Team to allow the Practices to dominate their development efforts. However, it is the ScrumMaster's job to make sure that the Team doesn't let the Practices overwhelm the self-organization, self-management, and analytical thinking of the Team.

In particular, even though the Storyotypes may provide a template for a Story's Agreement, the Team must still take a good, hard, look at the Agreement during Sprint Planning before they actually agree to it. The Storyotype is merely guidance, not dogma, and the Team must adapt it as necessary. (Note: In chapter 3.6 the 'Determine 'Buy an e-Ticket' Backbone' Story is one where the Storyotyped Agreement was changed based on the realities discovered at Sprint Planning.)

These Storyotypes are also an excellent topic for -spectives, as the Team is always learning about what works and what doesn't. The Storyotypes' Agreements should be constantly under revision as the Team inspects and adapts them. This is true even if the Storyotypes are common across multiple Teams. Even though these shared Storyotypes *constrain* what the Team may do, the Team should still feel free to strengthen the Storyotypes to meet its own particular needs.

Anyway, that's enough discussion for now. Let's just take a look at some sample Storyotypes.

Coding Storyotypes

First of all, there are Coding Storyotypes – those that represent Stories whose primary result is code. Because of the need to prevent Technical Debt (see chapter 3.5), storyotyping of Coding Stories (especially the Definition of Done) is often done. Typically, a Team will have a common Definition of Done that applies to *all* Coding Stories; and this definition could be mounted on the wall right next to the Team's Story Board. I usually refer to this simply as the [coding] Storyotype, and it could look something like the following figure, Figure 28.

Storyotype: [coding]
Size: *given in SPs*

Main Text: Written expression of what functionality needs
to be coded up.
<u>General Agreements</u>:
- SME (s) the Team will work with – have only one SME, if
  possible
- Coordinator for this Story, if appropriate
- Simplifying Assumptions: further information that limits
  the scope of the Story to make it manageable, that helps
  determine what is explicitly out of scope, and so on...

<u>Acceptance Criteria</u>:
- ❑ Description of the 'positive' acceptance test that defines
  the 'external' behavior that this Story represents – want
  only one of them
- ❑ User documentation is updated

<u>Definition of Done</u>:
- ❑ Did a half-hour of pre-factoring on the way in
- ❑ Passed Interface Design Review
- ❑ Passed Software Design Review
- ❑ Passed Review of Functional Test Cases (especially 'edge
  cases')
- ❑ Passed Review of Unit Tests
- ❑ XX% Unit Test Coverage
- ❑ Verified all Tests passing on Development Machine
- ❑ Tied up all 'loose ends'
- ❑ Passed Code Review
- ❑ Verified all Tests passing on Integration Box
- ❑ All Tests (Functional and Unit) added to Regression Test
  Suite
- ❑ Technical Documentation is Updated
- ❑ Did a half-hour of refactoring on the way out

Figure 28: the [coding] Storyotype

This is just an example, but I believe this is reasonably complete, with the
major ambiguity/variability being with the Definition of Done, which
changes from Team to Team, and from Organization to Organization. For
example, if the Team is following XP practices, the Definition of Done can be
greatly simplified, as the XP practices take care of many of the details
automatically. The Definition of Done may also include constraints based on
regulatory compliance, security issues, and so on (see chapter 2.3).

The [coding] Storyotype is sufficient for many Teams. However, Teams don't actually deliver code – they deliver features. I'm a Use Case kind of person, and think of most features as being Use Cases, so what I'd like is to know how to decompose Use Cases into Stories that I can use to produce a releasable version of the Use Case. This is the problem that Gerard talked about in his 2004 paper, so I'm partially reinventing the wheel here.

First of all, since I'm talking about Use Cases, which are a kind of Epic, there will be a Storyotype of an Epic called the [use case]. The [use case] Epic is the Bucket (see chapter 3.8) for all the Stories the Team will work on in order to build the Use Case (see Table 5 of chapter 3.4 for an example).

Remember (from chapter 3.6) that Epics representing Capabilities have Agreements that hold things that are inherited by *all* the Stories belonging to the Capability and also to hold requirements *at the Capability level* that will need to be satisfied before the Capability is considered Done, or Releasable. So, given that, here is a Storyotype for a Use Case.

Storyotype: [use case]
Size: a budget in SPs, see chapter 3.7

Brief: A few sentences summarizing the Use Case.

Agreement:

List the SMEs the Team will work with to implement this Use Case

List the Release Criteria for the Use Case; what needs to be done or implemented before the Use Case is considered 'complete' enough to release. Note that this list doesn't replace actual reviews, inspections, or tests to determine releasability...

Figure 29: The [use case] Storyotype

The 'Shop for Flights' Epic in chapter 3.6 gives an actual instance of this Storyotype, and you may want to go back and take a look at it now...

Once we have the Use Case, we can decompose it into Stories, which I'll be storyotyping next. In order to do that, though, I need to make sure that we understand what a Use Case is. By definition, a Use Case is a collection of scenarios, each of which represents a particular way to try to achieve the goal of the Use Case. Each scenario is defined by a single positive acceptance test, and follows a particular flow, or path, through the system. There are many ways to look at this, but I look at it in a fairly simple way and define a Use Case as containing a single Backbone Scenario and multiple Alternative Scenarios.

Because of the Release Criteria contained in the Use Case's Agreement, it may take more than simply implementing the Use Case's scenarios to make it releasable. For example, the Team may need to internationalize the Use Case, do usability testing, or do performance testing, before the Use Case can be released. However, in this discussion I will only look at the Storyotypes concerning scenarios that need to be developed.

The Backbone Scenario is an Architecturally Significant, end-to-end, flow that forms the core of the Use Case, and that the alternative scenarios supplement, augment or branch off of. Developing the Backbone Scenario causes most (if not all) of the significant design elements involved in the Use Case to be defined and developed in a minimal way. I think of the Backbone as being the Use Case's 'walking skeleton' – the major architectural decisions actually implemented in code.

In all but the most trivial Use Cases, the Backbone Scenario is too big for the Team to develop all at once, so it is an Epic of its own. It is a well-defined Epic, rather than a fuzzy Epic like the Use Case itself, but it is an Epic nonetheless. I like to think of the Backbone as being a scenario of 5-10 steps, each of which is its own Story. These will be the [backbone] Stories of the [backbone epic]. Let me give you an example this time:

[backbone epic] Backbone of 'Buy an e-Ticket'
Size: 48SPs (this is the sum of the SPs for the internal
   [backbone] Stories)

General Agreements:
- Simplifying Assumptions: One Way, Single Leg, No Seat
   Selection, Single Passenger, Full Fare, pay with VISA™,
   No Luggage ...
- If any other simplifying assumptions are needed to make
   this a single thread, make them, and add them to the list
   above

[backbone] Stories: (optional – Stories themselves are in
   Backlog)
1. [backbone] Capture Itinerary Information
2. [backbone] Get List of Flights from CUTLASS
3. [backbone] Capture Passenger Information
4. [backbone] Reserve Flight in CUTLASS
5. [backbone] Pick Flight and Pay for It
6. [backbone] Issue email Confirmation to Customer

Figure 30: A [backbone epic] Storyotype

Note that the primary purposes of the [backbone epic] are to define the simplifying assumptions that make it a single thread, and to hold the [backbone] Stories that make up the [backbone epic]. Each of these [backbone] Stories will inherit the simplifying assumptions so that there will be a single, end-to-end acceptance test that holds them all together.

Ok, so here's where we are so far. I've defined two Epic Storyotypes: the [use case] and the [backbone epic]. I've also defined a [backbone] Story, which is simply a Story that lives in the [backbone epic] and is part of the backbone itself. There are four other Storyotypes that I need to complete the picture; these closely follow the Storyotypes discovered by Meszaros, but I have added the [redo] Storyotype and given all of them my own names. They are:

- [alt] – a Story that develops an Alternative Scenario for the Use Case, following a different flow, or path, through the system, restricted to a single thread, or acceptance test;

- [beefup] – a Story that 'beefs up' or improves a business rule on an already existing path, adding an additional acceptance test;

- [redo] – a Story that changes a business rule that turned out to be wrong, including replacing the incorrect acceptance test; and

- [interface] – a Story for Cleaning Up the interface (or flow) for the Use Case itself.

The last one (the [interface]) is true genius, as it shows that the Story should have only one focus. Remember the mantra: *'Make it work, then make it fast, then make it pretty?'* Well, what Gerard was pointing out is that these are different Stories within the same Epic. Very cool. Not only that, but we need to do [interface] Stories much less often than the others. An [interface] Story applies to the whole Use Case, and is usually needed after three, four, or more other Stories are Done. The basic idea is that most Stories are implemented with a plain, simple, interface, and the interface is cleaned up every so often – this keeps the pace of development up, and actually makes the job of the interface designer easier.

Not only do these four Storyotypes help the Team decompose Use Cases, but each of them also adds a little something to the [coding] Storyotype's Definition of Done:

- The [backbone] Storyotype adds:

  ❑ Reviewed Architectural Decisions with the Team and Architectural SMEs

  ❑ Reviewed simplifying assumptions of [backbone epic] and connections between [backbone] Stories with Team

- The [alt] Storyotype adds:

  ❑ Reviewed business importance of [alt] scenario with SMEs and Team

- The [beefup] Storyotype adds:

  ❑ Verified Business Rule with SME

- The [redo] Storyotype adds:

  ❑ Verified new Business Rule with SME

  ❑ Modified unit and Acceptance tests to match new business rule

- The [interface] Storyotype adds:

  ❑ Reviewed interface design with UI SME and Team

  ❑ Conducted informal Usability Testing and made improvements based on it

That's enough for the Coding Storyotypes based on Use Cases. There are other Development Storyotypes, as well. Some of these Storyotypes are *mixins* – they can be used along with other Storyotypes in order to provide fthe "Tags" section of chapter 3.8). I will not go into detail here, but just give you a sampling of them:

- [bug] – a Storyotype to show that a Story is a bug fix. I define a bug to be a simple change that does not require an acceptance test; examples include correcting a misspelling in a dialog box or moving an interface element on the screen. Note that many things we typically call 'bugs' are more significant than this, and are actually Stories of other types, but I restrict the [bug] Storyotype for things that are relatively unimportant, easy to fix, and unlikely to recur once fixed.

- [arch-sig] – a Storyotype to show that a Story is Architecturally Significant; that developing this Story will cause an architectural decision to be made.

- [cleanup] – used to represent the Chores that clean up Technical Debt. This is so important that they are the subject of chapter 4.5.

- [hack] – used to mark a Story, producing production code, that is intentionally being Done at poor quality for some reason; it should always be accompanied by a [cleanup] Story added to the Backlog (see chapter 4.5).

- [user] – used to mark a story that has particular user significance, often used to capture user motivations or a discussion of Business Value.

- [user documentation] – even though the user documentation is augmented or updated as part of every Coding Story, there is still a need to clean up the documentation for delivery. There could be similar Storyotypes for cleaning up [training materials], [technical documentation], and so on.

- [spike] – a Story that (as quickly as possible) explores a tough technical or design problem in order to help make a decision. A spike only addresses the problem under examination and ignores all other concerns. Spikes are built to be thrown away, so their Definition of Done is compromised – without the need for a [cleanup] Story.

- [research] – a Story (or Epic) whose purpose is research. The idea is that each Story is time-boxed, with a review at the end; and the Epic is made up of a (seemingly) never-ending sequence of these Stories until the Team agrees the research is complete. I discussed this briefly in chapter 3.6.

- [sprint done] or [release done] – used to capture the criteria for Sprint or Release levels of Doneness as described earlier in this chapter. These could be either Stories or Epics, and (if Epics) contain *Story* Storyotypes like [finalize documentation], [finalize training materials], [transfer to test lab], and so on. And, yes, I know that I might be stretching a bit here – you're probably not really going to have such Storyotypes – but it's the idea that counts... the idea that you need to do this storyotyping somehow.

Ok, that's enough. As you can imagine, there are many other potential Coding Storyotypes a Team can come up with. For now, though, let's move on to other things.

Analysis Storyotypes

Well, now that we've talked about Coding Stories, let's talk about analysis. I don't think that analysis gets talked about enough in Scrum, probably because many Teams think that their Product Owner is supposed to bring them the Stories complete and ready to go. However, this is usually not true. The Team's Product Owner is not Superman – the Team should help him or her come up with the Stories... and not just because it's the right thing to do, but also to make sure they are Stories that the Team Members understand and believe they can do.

In fact, it is Ken Schwaber's guidance that the Team should spend 10% of its total time and effort on analysis and refining activities – not including Sprint Planning [S2, pg. 114]. Now, when I'm talking about analysis here, I'm not talking about the analysis that takes place *within* the Story that explains what the Story is all about. That analysis is an *intrinsic* part of development and is one of the conversations that we talk about when they say the Story is *a promise for a conversation*.

No, the analysis I'm talking about now is the analysis that *produces* Stories, and that finds the Capabilities that turn into the Epics that we extract the Stories from. That's the sort of analysis I'm talking about. Some of this analysis is done during Backlog Refinement sessions (as we discussed in chapter 3.9) especially if we get the SMEs to attend them. But that's often not enough.

So we have analysis (and Analysis Stories), which is done in many different ways; and now I'm going to talk about Storyotypes for Analysis Stories. Of course, by default I'm also discussing techniques that the Team would use when doing Backlog Refinement. This illustrates what I meant when I said that the *concept* of storyotyping is more important than the Storyotypes themselves.

I'm going to discuss two types, or levels, of analysis. The first type I refer to as Top-Level analysis, which is the finding of Capabilities – not the finding of the Stories within the Capabilities. The second type I refer to as Epic Decomposition, which is the decomposition of Epics to Stories, or the extraction of Stories from Epics – depending on how you look at it. I know that these terms aren't common, but I need a way to separate the levels in the following discussions – and there aren't any better terms to use.

In each case, however, I'm only going to give a brief overview of the topic, a single example of the basic Storyotype, and a discussion of possible Storyotypes that are similar.

Top-Level Analysis: The top-level Analysis Stories are ones that are used to find Capabilities. There are a number of ways to find these Capabilities – a variety of techniques to use – and I do not intend to explain how to do systems analysis here. Let me just say that some of the techniques I've used include Use Case Modeling, User Experience (UX) Studies, Innovation Games, Paper Research, Risk Analysis, and many others... these are *not* things you would expect to do in Backlog Refinement Sessions.

Therefore, they must be Stories, all of which have certain things in common. They all need to be time-boxed (to hours or days, not weeks or months), they all involve working with SMEs (or the artifacts of SMEs), and they all result in a collection of Capabilities (Use Cases, Features, Storyboards and Wireframes, etc.) that become Epics on the Backlog.

In other words, they all look basically like this.

Storyotype: [top-level analysis]
Size: time-boxed

As a <Team Member> I want <to know what the Stakeholders want this system (or part of system) to do> so that <I can start refinement and find Stories to work on>

General Agreements:
- Sources of Information.
  - SME (s) the Team will work with – try to get a representative sample, but have a workable number of them
  - Documents the Team will study/analyze – make sure this is a small, well-defined list
- Coordinator for this Story –the analyst or facilitator (if the analysis is game-based, for example)

Acceptance Criteria:
- ❏ All Capabilities found are entered in the Backlog as Epics
- ❏ The Product Owner worked with the Stakeholders and decided which ones are 'in scope' for the next release
- ❏ For the Capabilities that are 'in scope', the Product Owner worked with the Team, Stakeholders, and SMEs to 'budget' the effort to be spent (this could be done as an additional Story that is 'inside' the Epic itself)

Definition of Done: depends on the actual type of top-level analysis being done. This is usually a recipe, or set of tasks or milestones (including reviews), that will be performed in order to complete the analysis.

Figure 31: An Analysis Storyotype

Now, of course, we could go crazy with this and have each of the different kinds of top-level analysis be its own Storyotype. I won't do that here because the main purpose of this section is to *remind* you that you have to *think about* this stuff – that these Capabilities don't just show up – and it's our Team's problem to deal with. It's fine if somebody else is delivering the Capabilities to the Team, just keep in mind that the Team is responsible for delivering Product, not just writing code – so the Team *should be* really interested in this stuff.

Epic Decomposition: Epic decomposition is used to extract Stories from existing Epics, and figure out enough information about them so that further

Backlog Refinement (Sizing, Prioritizing, and initial Agreements) can be done. This can be done as part of a Backlog Refinement Session or as its own Refinement Story (see chapter 3.9). Remember that the goal of Backlog Refinement is that the Story becomes Ready – it winds up being less than a '10 minute' conversation away from being agreed to in Sprint Planning. Also remember that if the Stories we find have Storyotypes then further refinement will be easier.

There are really two issues here:

- What sort of analysis are we doing? and

- What sources/information/methods are we using to do the analysis?

For example, we could be doing different sorts of analysis such as Use Case analysis or UX analysis; we could be finding new Stories with usability or exploratory testing; or we could simply be looking for Stories in any-old-way. We could be gathering information by studying source material, working with Stakeholders, or evaluating the product itself. These are the variables that are involved in our analysis efforts, and must be captured in the Story's Agreements.

In all cases, the Storyotypes will look something like this, which is a Storyotype for finding the backbone of a Use Case by having a discussion with SMEs. In this case the SMEs are known up-front, but in a Story of this Storyotype in chapter 3.6, the SMEs were determined as part of the Story. This is an example of the Storyotype's information being adapted to the realities of the *actual* Story at the time of Planning.

Storyotype: [find the backbone]
Size: time-boxed

As a <Team Member> I want (to know the [backbone] of Use Case ABC> so that <I can begin work on the Use Case>

General Agreements:
- SME (s) the Team will work with – try to get a representative sample, but have a workable number of them
- Coordinator for this Story –the analyst

Acceptance Criteria:
☐ The backbone Epic is in the Backlog
☐ There is at least one valid [backbone] Story, based on this backbone Epic, in the Back Burner ready to be groomed for Planning

---

> Definition of Done: Meet with the SMEs and:
> ❑ Discussed the Use Case and documented the Results in the Wiki
> ❑ Generated, and validated, the backbone Epic for this Use Case
> ❑ Decomposed the backbone into at most 10 Stories
> ❑ Worked with SMEs and Team to prioritize and move at least one of these Stories into the Back Burner for further refinement

Figure 32: Another Analysis Storyotype

Ok, enough about analysis. Let's discuss other Storyotypes.

Other Storyotypes

There are many other Storyotypes than a Team could use. In this section I just want to give a list of them, with very short explanations of what they are and why they might be useful. So here's the list.

Planning Storyotypes

- [release planning]: I've talked about Backlog Refinement and Sprint Planning, but I haven't talked about Release Planning. This is a significant exercise that takes enough time that it must be prioritized, either as a part of the process or as a (collection of) Stories. I think that the [release planning] Storyotype represents an Epic, but I will leave that up to you.

- [sprint planning]: there might be additional sprint planning activities besides just the Sprint Planning session and the Backlog Refinement that we've talked about so far. You might want to have some Storyotypes for these additional activities.

Epic Storyotypes

- [use case], [backbone epic]: discussed already in this chapter.

- [placeholder]: an Epic that is used to hold a small bit of Kanban(ish) activity within the Sprint (see chapter 4.4).

- [perf]: for Performance Epics, discussed in the 'You Can't Always Get What You Want' discussion in the 'Other Topics' section of chapter 3.6.

- [theme]: for Epics that represent issues, dependencies, and the like. Used to document the theme that the associated Stories are connected by (see chapter 3.8).

<u>Infrastructure Storyotypes</u>

- [setup]: a Story for setting up environmental elements, like the 'Sam needs a Development Machine' Story.

- [team training]: Stories for training Team Members; there are significant hoops to be jumped through to get people trained, and these can be documented in this Storyotype.

- [add software]: Stories for updating existing machines with software. This takes planning, involves downtime, possible testing, and so on.

<u>Support Storyotypes</u>

- [sales call]: having a Team Member go with a Sales Person to meet with a client is expensive, and must be prioritized in the Backlog. This Storyotype exists to remind us of that.

- [trade show]: an even bigger problem is sending Team Members to attend Trade Shows...

- [train users]: our Team Members are often asked to train users on our systems. This takes significant time and effort, and must be prioritized.

- [support help desk]: a special type of Coding Storyotype...

As you can imagine, there are an almost infinite number of Storyotypes that a Team can come up with. Team Members are often complaining about the time they spend doing things that aren't 'my work' and Storyotypes give us a way to handle that. Some Stories of these types occur within a coding Epic, the example of the 'Buy an e-Ticket (Release 1)' in chapter 3.4 shows a support ([spt]) Story inside the [use case] – this support activity was considered necessary for the delivery of the Use Case's value.

Scrum says that *all* of the Team's work is either an intrinsic part of the Team's process or is managed through the Backlog. Storyotypes such as these remind us that there are lots of different kinds of work that need to be on the Backlog so that it can be prioritized by the Team's Product Owner. Remember: there is no magic, nothing is free.

Summary

Storyotyping is a useful concept to use to reuse knowledge and become more consistent. Storyotypes themselves are useful in order to document this knowledge. Storyotypes and Storyotyping help the Scrum Team in three ways:

- It helps the Team find Capabilities, Epics, and Stories that represent work the Stakeholders want and put them in the Backlog (usually the Fridge);

- It helps the Team decompose (extract Stories from) Epics in order to put Stories on the Back Burner; and

- It helps the Team with Story Agreements, which helps with Planning and moving the Stories to the Front Burner to be worked on.

In other words, storyotyping helps with almost all the major activities in Scrum.

Discussion Question

1. What is the difference between a mature Storyotype and a Tag? What is a Storyotype?

2. How can Storyotypes help and teams deal with external constraints from high-ceremony process demands such as SOX, security, or FDA?

3. The primary use of Storyotypes is to hold common Definitions of Done. What are the four levels of doneness ?

4. Can you create a Storyotype aimed at getting feedback during a product review? What would it look like and what would be common?

5. List six or more common storyotypes and see if you can provide concrete examples of each.

6. Describe a situation that you have experienced where the Team repeatedly made the same mistake, and eventually they figures out how to avoid it. How did they accomplish that? Would storyotyping being a similar mechanism for teams to use to avoid repeating mistakes?

Section 4: The Practices

Agile software development is primarily about conversations and feedback: Team Members are constantly talking to each other about production issues; the Product Owner provides feedback to the Team Members about Doneness and priorities; and the Stakeholders and SMEs provide feedback to the Team that makes sure their Results are correct and useful.

The Scrum Framework provides a small set of Practices that are *just enough* for the Team to manage these basic feedback loops. In addition, through the use of their self-organization, the Team can add new Practices or modify existing ones, as long as it remains true to the essence of Scrum and abides by the constraints, rules, and standards the Organization has imposed on the Team.

In this section I explore the basic Scrum Practices and discuss some typical additions and modifications that address common issues.

$$\boxed{4.1}$$

Planning Day

This chapter discusses the day that takes place between Sprints, which includes the Product Review, Progress Assessment, Team Retrospective, and Sprint Planning for the next Sprint.

All Teams are different, but there are a few things that are quite common. For example, many of the Teams I coach try to limit the time they waste; in particular, they try to limit the amount of time they spend *between* Sprints. In the Scrum Framework, this time is reserved for the Product Review, Team Retrospective, and Sprint Planning, and they often try to do all of these things in one day.

This is a reasonable thing to want to do, and there are two patterns I have seen be successful. The first pattern does it all in *one* Calendar day, and is the one I describe in this chapter. The second spreads the day across *two* Calendar days, with the Review the first afternoon, Planning the next morning, and the Retrospective in between – wherever it fits. In either case, one of the most important things to do is make sure that there is *enough time* between the Review and Sprint Planning in order to do a Progress Assessment and revise the priorities of the Backlog based on the feedback received at the Review.

It is recommended that the Backlog *should* be updated during the Review itself, when the Stakeholders are available (see [SG, pg. 11]). However, this may not be possible, for a variety of reasons. Maybe there's not enough time in the Review, maybe there's some significant analysis that needs to be done, whatever... This is why I recommend having time set aside for a Progress Assessment, which is when the Team would do the necessary updates. If it's not needed, that's cool... but you should probably have the time set aside... just sayin'...

In this chapter I describe this Planning day, and will explain it with an artificial timeline just to get my points across. Don't take this to mean that I think this timeline is the *only* way to go, or even the *best* way to go – I don't – it's for illustrative purposes only. Ken Schwaber suggests (for a 2-week Sprint) that Planning take 4 hours, the Retrospective takes 1.5 hours, and the Product Review takes 2 hours [SG, pgs. 8-12]. I'm suggesting a Team can do it in less time, but this is only because the ScrumMaster is holding frequent Intraspectives (chapter 2.3) and the Team is doing ongoing Backlog Refinement activities (chapter 3.9) – which lessens the load on the Team

Retrospective and Sprint Planning sessions. Each of these three sessions should be time-boxed, and their time-boxes should be respected. If *any* of them should be allowed to expand, it could be the Product Review, as the Stakeholder's feedback is the lifeblood of the project, and cutting it short could shortchange the Team, the Stakeholders, and the Product – but don't let the Review go on forever, either. In any case, it will certainly be an issue for the Retrospective if any of these sessions gets too long.

Product Review (10am to Noon)

The purpose of the Product Review is to get meaningful feedback from the Stakeholders about the Team's Work Results (Product). This Review is often called the Sprint Review, and is the most important in Scrum, as without this feedback Scrum won't work. For this reason, it is very important to get the *right* Stakeholders into the room for the Product Review. It is the Product Owner's responsibility to assemble Stakeholders that have the knowledge to give meaningful feedback and feel safe enough to give it.

In my experience it is sometimes necessary to separate the Stakeholders from their bosses, as their bosses may intimidate the Stakeholders from being open and honest when it comes to feedback. Not only that, but these bosses may want to focus the review on people, process, or progress, rather than product – and this is not a part of Scrum… just sayin'…

For these reasons I often recommend having a separate Executive (or Project) Review for the Stakeholder's bosses in order to discuss what they want to discuss, which usually includes Project Management discussions. This separation of the bosses from the Stakeholders allows the Product Review itself to be a discussion solely about the Product – which is what it's for.

Now, this advice about the Executive Review is *not* standard Scrum, but is a reasonable response to a particular Product Ownership issue that could (and often does) occur. As a ScrumMaster you may have this sort of problem and need this sort of solution. Just sayin'…

Anyway, back to the Planning Day.

In the Planning Day I'm describing here, the Review is held in the morning. Don't do it *too* early, because the Stakeholders need to be awake and alert. Also, if the session were held very early in the morning the Team (or Product Owner) might be tempted to spend the previous day getting ready.

I don't want the Team to spend very much time preparing for the Review; preparation should be part of the natural flow of things. But, many Teams can't help it; they feel a need to prepare a 'dog and pony' show, even if it's just a small one. So, I like the Team to prepare for the Review in the morning before the Review. By limiting the preparation to the morning before, the Team can spend no more than one or two hours getting ready, which is reasonable.

When preparing for the Review it is important to remember that the Team shouldn't demonstrate or review any Results that aren't Done; that is, the Product being Reviewed should be the result of Stories that have met their Doneness Agreements (see chapter 3.5). We like to say that there is *no partial credit* in Scrum – we don't Review something that isn't Done.

That being said, let's get real here... The Team may want to review a Story that's in progress in order to gather information that will help them finish it. If the Team feels that it needs to do this, make sure they are open, honest, and visible about it. Make sure the Stakeholders know that this Story *isn't* Done; that the Team is just taking advantage of the fact that the Stakeholders are available to get information that will help them finish it. And, I also recommend that the Team does this late in the review after the Stakeholders have reviewed everything that *is* actually Done. The Review is *supposed* to be a review, not a working session...

Once the Team is prepared for the Product Review, it's time to actually do it. There are a few things to remember. First and foremost, the Review is *owned* by the Product Owner. The Product Owner is accountable to the Stakeholders for the Team's performance, and the Product Review is for the Product Owner to review with the Stakeholders what the Team has done for them. Of course, most of the session *actually* consists of Team Members working with, and demonstrating things for, the Stakeholders.

Second, the Review is of the Team's Work Results, not the Stories. The Stakeholders are interested in *what* was Done, not *how* it was Done. Review the content, not the process.

There are many ways to conduct the Review and your Teams will find their own way, but I don't want the Team to bore the Stakeholders by telling them *everything*. The Product Owner (and Team) must keep focused on the following four *purposes* for the Review:

1. To have the Stakeholders gain and retain confidence that the Team is going in the right direction – that the Stakeholders are getting what they expect;

2. For the Team to maintain confidence that it is going in the right direction – that it is producing what the Stakeholders want and need;

3. To help the Stakeholders have realistic expectations for the Team's performance and their delivery of Product; and

4. To give the Product Owner and Team the input they need to have successful and productive Sprint Planning for the next Sprint.

There is no standard agenda for the Review, but here are a few things that that could (or should) be done in order to achieve the purposes listed above:

-   The Product Owner should review the Sprint Goal for the Sprint, and state whether or not the Team achieved it. This defines whether the Sprint succeeded or failed. The topic of what makes a good Sprint Goal is discussed, in detail, in chapter 4.2.

-   Review the Product the Stakeholders expect to see. The Product Owner and other Team Members should be in frequent contact throughout the Sprint with both Stakeholders and Subject Matter Experts, and know what they are worried about. Use this information to show them what they need to see so that their worries are either justified or assuaged.

-   Review the Product the Team isn't confident about. Sure, the Stories are Done, but were they right? The Team worked with *some* SMEs, but not *all* Stakeholders were involved. What do the rest of the Stakeholders feel about the Product? This takes some courage, but this is a Scrum Team, so we've got plenty of that, right? ;-)

-   Have the Stakeholders discuss (with the Team) potential Sprint Goals and new Backlog Items for the next Sprint (see chapter 4.2 for a discussion of appropriate Sprint Goals).

-   Ask the Stakeholders what they want to see in the next Review. Be inquisitive; take advantage of the 'face time' with the Stakeholders.

-   You may want to discuss the Team's Velocity for the Sprint with the Stakeholders, and what it means for the assumed Capacity and the Release Strategy. This should be done in an Executive Review, but it is sometimes appended to the Product Review. Make sure it is an add-on discussion, not a major topic.

Ultimately, the main purpose for the Review is to get the Stakeholders to understand that they are important. Without Stakeholder feedback things may fail – and they will certainly be worse than they could have been. It is their feedback that gives the Product Owner the necessary information to drive the Team in an agile way – and in the right direction.

Progress Assessment (Lunch, Noon to 1pm)

After the Team has its Review with the Stakeholders, go to lunch and let the Stakeholder's comments sink in – maybe the Product Owner needs to take the Business Owner and a couple of the key Stakeholders to lunch. This is a good time to discuss the overall progress of the Team, taking into account the Review just completed. This may be when that 'Executive Review' takes place.

The Product Owner may need to do some significant reprioritization of the Backlog prior to the Sprint Planning session that is coming up. Stories may need to be added. The Release Strategy may need to be revised based on the new realities that have surfaced. The next Sprint's Goal may need to be discussed. There are many things that might need to be worked on, and this is the time to talk about them with the Stakeholders and Team Members. These discussions shouldn't be done during the Product Review itself – the Review should have been restricted to discussions about the Product. This Sprint Assessment can be thought of as a special Backlog Refinement Session, with special emphasis on prioritization, rather than analysis, decomposition, sizing, and the like (see chapter 3.9).

If this assessment usually takes longer than an hour, it is a good reason to split the Planning Day across two Calendar Days, with the Product Review in the afternoon of the first day, Sprint Planning in the morning of the second day, and the Retrospective wherever it fits in between. This allows a good dinner discussion with the Business Owner and a few Stakeholders (and maybe a Team Member or two) about the redirection of the Team. In any case, remember that the final say on priorities *always* rests with the Product Owner; this assessment is merely providing information, guidance, and advice to the Product Owner, not direction.

Team Retrospective (1pm to 3pm)

After the Progress Assessment, it's time for the Team to take ownership of its process with a Team Retrospective, which is a discussion about teamwork and work practices. There are many techniques for Retrospectives[1]; I will briefly describe only one of them – the **Continuous Timeline** that was introduced to me by my good friend Linda Rising[2]. Here are the rules:

- The Timeline consists of cards on the wall, organized by the days in the Sprint; for example, for a 2-week Sprint there may be headings on the wall like "Day 1", "Day 2", and so on.

---

[1] See, for example, Esther Derby and Diana Larson, *Agile Retrospectives: Making Good Teams Great*, The Pragmatic Bookshelf, 2006.

[2] I have known Linda for almost 20 years. She is best known for her book: Linda Rising and Mary Lynn Manns, *Fearless Change: Patterns for Introducing New Ideas*, Addison-Wesley, 2004.

- Any Team Member may add cards at any time (but can't remove them). Each card describes an event that happened (work-related personal, whatever...) and they are color coded:

  o **Green**: an event that made the Team Member Happy;

  o **Yellow**: an event that caused the Team Member some Concern;

  o **Red**: an event that angered or frustrated the Team Member; or

  o **Orange**: an event that surprised the Team Member.

- The Timeline is available to all the Team Members to read and think about, and it is natural for them to start thinking (consciously or subconsciously) about the events that are represented – and what to do about them. This means that the Retrospective's discovery phase has a huge head start before the Retrospective begins.

- After the Team Retrospective, the Cards are removed from the wall, and the Timeline starts over again with the next Sprint.

- Note that if a Team Member posts a Red Card on the wall it may lead to the ScrumMaster initiating an Intraspective right away. For Teams that are Storming, I can imagine the ScrumMaster having many Intraspectives during the Sprint about the Events represented on the Timeline.

The Continuous Timeline is a good way to gather data for your Retrospective. But no matter how you do your Retrospectives, here are some things that are important to know about them.

First, I think the Team should *always* discuss the Team Values and compare them to the Team's actual performance (see chapter 2.1). This discussion can often be integrated into the Retrospective as a whole, and I think it's important to keep the Team focused on the Values. One of the most important Values to focus on is Respect, as it is one of the most difficult Values for many Teams to believe and have. However, in my experience, whenever a Team actually believes that everyone is doing the best they can it makes for a much better Team, and moves the discussions from blaming People to changing Practices.

Second, the Product Owner is a member of the Team, and *must* be present at the Team Retrospective; *all* Team Members must be present at the Team Retrospective – and it may be useful to have some SMEs there, as well. The Team Retrospective is a formal discussion for the whole Team to address its process – it's not about individuals or sub-teams. That being said, however, one of the major issues a Team may have is the relationship with its Product

Owner; so it may be reasonable to have a *part* of the Retrospective with the Product Owner *out of the room* in order to discuss such issues.

If there are Product Owner issues, it is the ScrumMaster's responsibility to discuss them one-on-one with the Product Owner before the Product Owner and the Team discusses them together. These discussions can be had after the Retrospective or, preferably, during a short break in the Retrospective. In this conversation the ScrumMaster should try to convince the Product Owner to work directly with the rest of the Team in order to resolve these issues. Unfortunately, the Team might have some fear of the Product Owner, so the ScrumMaster may need to act as an intermediary.

Within the Sprint the ScrumMaster should be having frequent Intraspectives with subsets of the Team in order to address issues as they come up. This is a different issue than the Retrospective, and is discussed in chapter 2.3.

Third, the Retrospective is not just a whine session. The most important thing to determine at the Retrospective is what worked well. It is very important that the Team doesn't stop doing what works for them; nothing upsets a Team more than sliding backwards. After the Team knows what it *doesn't* want to change, then the Team Members can think about what they *would* like to change.

Fourth, everybody on the Team needs to be *involved* in the Retrospective (not merely *present* at the Retrospective) – everybody needs to be respected. This is hard to do when there are quiet people and noisy people on the Team; if the Retrospective was simply a conversation, the noisy people would dominate.

So, Retrospectives are usually accomplished in two parts. The first part is to do discovery and data-gathering to determine what topics to discuss. Many topics will have been determined before-hand, either through the ScrumMaster's observations, discussions with Team Members, SMEs, and Stakeholders, involvement with the Continuous Timeline on the wall, or through other means... but I recommend there be some sort of writing session, interactive activity, or game, done within the Retrospective, as well. The purpose of this first portion of the Retrospective is to respect all Team Members by having their ideas put forth for discussion.

The second part is the discussion itself. Using the information gathered as an agenda (or at least a starting point), the ScrumMaster facilitates a discussion about the issues and what to do about them.

Fifth, when the Team Members do decide to change something, they must remember that Scrum's self-organization is not anarchy, the changes must adhere to whatever constraints, rules, and standards the Organization has imposed. Given that caveat, there are four types of change:

- <u>WIBNIs (wib'·neez)</u>: Changes the Team wishes would happen, but can't. For example: *'Wouldn't **It Be Nice If** the Stakeholders wouldn't keep changing their minds.'* WIBNIs should be discussed and the Team should decide how to deal with them, rather than continue to whine about them.

- <u>Decide Now</u>: Decisions the Team can make and implement immediately, such as a change to a Storyotype's Definition of Done that will be implemented in Sprint Planning later in the Planning Day. For example, the Team Members may decide that they need to do a Team review of the User Interface of a feature (at a whiteboard) before they start coding. If this change is considered important enough it may even form the basis for the next Sprint's Goal (see chapter 4.2);

- <u>Do Later</u>: Changes that are under the Team's control, but will take time and effort for the Team to implement. Examples could include improving the build process, beefing up test tools, rearranging the Team room, and so on. These changes must be written as Items and added to the Backlog, so that they can be prioritized and Done (the Team could discuss when it will be prioritized with the Product Owner, since the Product Owner is at the Retrospective); and

- <u>Not Us</u>: Changes that are outside the Team's control and must be accomplished outside the Scrum Team. In this case the ScrumMaster (often with the Product Owner's assistance) goes outside the Team to the Business Owner (and other Stakeholders) to get some help. If the fix will take a lot of time and effort, and the Business Owner can't get it fixed immediately, it is usually managed by the ScrumMaster Community as a whole – the Community of ScrumMasters is the primary change agent in an Organization using Scrum.

Useful Metaphors about Changing the Team's Process

There are two metaphors I like to think about when changing a Team's process. I learned these from an ex-boss of mine, Alan Shalloway of Net Objectives. These two metaphors are the 'Pick-Up Sticks' metaphor and the 'Trim Tab' metaphor, which I present to you now.

Pickup Sticks is a children's game that involves dropping a bunch of colored sticks on a table, and then removing sticks one at a time, without moving any other sticks, until the 'gold stick' is removed. This metaphor is useful to ScrumMasters because they may want to make a big change in a Team or Organization (represented by the gold stick), which will require many small changes before the big change can be reached.

As Alan reminded me, adults can only learn something they *almost already know*, and the sticks that are removed on the way to the gold stick represent changes that are small enough that the Team/Organization almost already knows them. It takes time to get to the big changes that are wanted, and making big changes is an incremental process. In fact, it's an agile process. Inspect and adapt along the way, but don't lose track of what is needed.

The second metaphor is the Trim Tab metaphor. Buckminster Fuller introduced this metaphor in 1972[3], and it is very relevant to us when considering change. First of all, you need to know what a 'trim tab' is. As Fuller put it:

"Think of the Queen Mary – the whole ship goes by and then comes the rudder. And there's a tiny thing at the edge of the rudder called a trim tab. It's a miniature rudder. Just moving the little trim tab builds a low pressure that pulls the rudder around. Takes almost no effort at all."

In other words, a trim tab is something that does something small but causes big things to happen as a natural by-product. When it comes to having teams change behaviors, the ScrumMaster should always be looking for the trim tabs, which are small changes in behavior, process, or environment that will cause the Team or Organization to move, change, or evolve.

There are many potential trim tabs that could be used. Some of the best ones focus on the Team Values I discussed in chapter 2.1 (focus, respect, courage, etc.), or provide changes in the Definitions of Done I discussed in chapter 3.6. It is my opinion that any trim tab that either causes more conversations or causes the Team to do work in smaller pieces is a good one. Let me tell you a story about the best trim tab I ever saw...

I was visiting a client site where I had previously established many Scrum Teams, and was coaching some of the newer ScrumMasters. One of the established ones – call him Dave – came up to me and said: 'Dan, come look at my trick.' Now, Dave was a seasoned Project Manager turned ScrumMaster, so I knew that any trick he had was going to be a good one. So, I went with him to witness his Team's Daily Standup.

The trick was very simple. For every Story that was completed, Dave gave a single M&M'S® candy to each person who had worked on that Story. The members of the Scrum Team had naturally developed a friendly competition to see who could get the most candy. I heard one of the senior Team Members talk about trying to fill a shot glass with M&M'S® in order to eat them all at once – in one big gulp.

I immediately saw why this is a cool trick: it encourages more conversations (more people working on the same Story) and causes smaller pieces of work

---

[3] Buckminster Fuller was a famous scientist/engineer and this discussion was in *Playboy*, in 1972.

(Stories get smaller so that more get finished). I asked Dave if he had any idea of what improvements this had caused. I was confident that Dave had an answer, because he was a metrics guy from way back.

He told me that this had caused a 25% increase in delivering releasable features over the previous two months. I took him at his word, as I had no time to discuss how he measured this. So, I asked him how much it cost, and he answered 'two dollars a week.'

Wow! A 25% improvement in feature delivery for $2 a week! For a Team that was already Performing before the trick... I've never heard of a better ROI or a better trim tab. Brilliant! Go Dave!

Anyway, in your Team's Retrospectives, first determine what works, and don't change that; in fact, do more of it. Then figure out what needs to change. Talk to the Team and look for trim tabs that will cause the changes. If you can't find trim tabs, use brute force. Good luck!

Sprint Planning (3pm to 5pm)

Finally, at the end of the day, the Team plans the next Sprint. The Team knows what the Stakeholders thought of the previous Sprint's work, there have been discussions with the Stakeholders and Team Members about the next Sprint's goals, and the Team Members know what changes they'll be making in their process based on their Retrospective.

The purpose of the Sprint Planning session is two-fold: to have the Team commit to a Sprint Goal, and to have the Team agree to do some Stories. The purpose of this layering of Commitment and Agreement is to provide some safety for the Team.

The Sprint Goal gives the Team some wiggle room when it comes to actually getting the work Done. It does this by defining the *success* of the Sprint in terms of this Sprint Goal rather than in terms of the Stories that have been agreed to. With this wiggle room the Team should be unafraid to agree to as many Stories as it can – the Sprint Goal provides a measure of personal safety to the Team Members. This wiggle room gives the Team the slack it needs to focus on doing its due diligence rather than worrying about how much work they have to do.

I fervently believe that the Sprint Goal should *not* be determined by how many Stories get Done. My suggestion is that the Sprint Goal should not require more than half of the agreed-to Stories to get Done. I have observed that in many, if not most, Scrum Teams the *de facto* Sprint Goal is *'do all the Stories that were agreed to,'* and I think this is a perversion of Scrum. This is making Sprint Planning very predictive, agility is lost, and Technical Debt (or an admission of Failure) is a possible – if not likely – result.

The Sprint Goal is what is promised to the Stakeholders, and it provides focus and helps prioritize the work within the Sprint. The Sprint Goal can have many forms, which are discussed in detail in chapter 4.2.

Sprint Planning is the formal discussion when the Team commits to a Sprint Goal and agrees to do a collection of Stories based on their Doneness Agreements (see chapter 3.6). Since the Team is trying to do Sprint Planning in two hours, it should be clear that this session is merely the culmination of a series of planning activities, as getting enough information to make an informed agreement is much too difficult to do in just two hours. In order for this session to be successful, there needs to have been frequent Backlog Refinement in order to have Stories that are Ready to go to Planning (see chapter 3.9).

I assume that you are familiar with Sprint Planning as a general concept. You are probably familiar with some version of Velocity-Based Sprint Planning, which is planning that bases its determination of 'how much a Team can do' primarily on the Team's Velocity and Capacity estimates[4]. However, you might not be familiar with Agreement-Based Sprint Planning, which I recommend and will briefly describe now.

Agreement-Based Planning (also known by the name 'Commitment-Based Planning') is relatively new, and is gaining traction amongst Scrum aficionados. One of the primary reasons we can do it with a modern Scrum Team is that the Product Owner is part of the Team, and can be expected to be an active participant in Sprint Planning from beginning to end. The Agreement-Based Planning process is reasonably simple, and the next chapter will give a more complete description of it. For now, let's just have a simple outline:

1. It all starts with the Product Owner having a prioritized list of Stories in the Back Burner, sufficient to fill the Sprint during Planning. Typically, based on StoryPoints and Capacity, you would want 125% to 200% of a single Sprint's worth of Stories available for Planning.

2. At the beginning of Planning, the Product Owner selects a single Story to work with. The Team (including the Product Owner) negotiates and finalizes the Doneness Agreement for this single Story, and the Team (without undue influence from the Product Owner, or consideration of the Story's size in StoryPoints) evaluates and agrees to do this single Story, if it can.

---

[4] Velocity-Based Planning is inherently flawed for complicated (or complex) work, but Teams keep re-inventing it anyway. See the 'Some Simple Statistics' section of Appendix A.5 for a discussion of why it *can't* work...

3. After a Story is agreed to, or if a Story is skipped because it can't be agreed to, the Product Owner gives the Team another Story to consider. This is usually the next one on the list, but the order may be changed because of dependencies, or to try to make things fit. Once again, the Team finalizes the Story's Doneness Agreement and agrees to add the Story to the list of already-agreed-to Stories. This process is repeated until the Team thinks the Sprint is 'full' and the Sprint Backlog is complete.

4. The Product Owner and the Team negotiate the Sprint Goal, which will be committed to and advertised to the Stakeholders. I like to do this last so that discussions about the Sprint Goal don't take time away from agreeing to Stories.

This form of Planning results in a committed-to Sprint Goal and a list of agreed-to Stories with Doneness Agreements (which are what the Team has actually agreed to). When done well, there should be no more than one extra Story on the backlog that has a *finalized* Doneness Agreement, and it is there only if the final Story considered wouldn't actually fit in the Sprint.

Summary

It is possible, and desirable for most Teams, to spend only one day between Sprints. In this day the Team has:

- Its Product Review with its Stakeholders, in order to get feedback about the Product;

- A Progress Assessment discussion, including select Stakeholders, SMEs and Team Members, in order to discuss the impact of the feedback from the Review;

- Its Team Retrospective, in order to refine and improve its Practices and Teamwork; and

- Its next Sprint's Sprint Planning session, when it commits to a Sprint Goal and agrees to do a collection of Stories.

There are two major things that are important to remember:

1. There must be adequate time between the Product Review and the next Sprint's Planning (e.g., Progress Assessment time) in order to digest the feedback and reprioritize if necessary; and

2. The Team must do frequent Intraspectives and considerable Backlog Refinement throughout the Sprint in order to make it possible to do this all in one day.

Discussion Questions

1. What are the advantages of have the Planning day all on one day? What if it spreads over two days?

2. Why should Planning Day not take longer than a single day, two at the most?

3. Why is the Product Review the most important ceremony in Scrum? Who needs to be there?

4. Why don't we want the Executive (or Project) Review to be combined with the Product Review?

5. Discuss how the Continuous Timeline can be used to prepare the Team for its Retrospective.

6. Why do I suggest that the Team always review the Team Values during the Retrospective?

7. Why must the Product Owner attend the Retrospective?

8. Discuss the four types of change that could result from a Retrospective. Give an example of each.

9. Who determines the Sprint Goal? When is it done? Why does it exist?

Agreement-Based Planning

This chapter gives more details about the Agreement-Based Planning practice that was introduced in the last chapter, including a discussion of the Sprint Goal.

In the previous chapter I talked about the Sprint Planning session that takes place between Sprints. The purpose of this session is to have the Team commit to a Sprint Goal and forecast a collection of Stories for the next Sprint.

In this chapter I will describe Agreement-Based Planning, which is my preferred method for Sprint Planning. Agreement-Based Planning results in two things:

- The Team forecasts which Stories they think they may be able to do in the next Sprint, and

- The Team commits to a Sprint Goal.

The main advantage of Planning in this way is that it takes into account the most current information available at the time of Planning.

General Strategy for Agreement-Based Sprint Planning

In the previous chapter (chapter 4.1) I gave a brief introduction/overview of Agreement-Based Sprint Planning. In order to assure that *this* chapter is self-contained, I will (essentially) repeat the overview here, and add more details and explanation in the rest of the chapter.

Agreement-Based Planning begins with the Product Owner having a collection of Ready Stories in the Back Burner sufficient to fill the Sprint. Typically, I would expect up to two Sprint's worth of Stories to be available, with a minimum of 125% of a Sprint's worth. See chapter 3.9 for a discussion of getting Stories ready for Planning.

At the beginning of Sprint Planning the Team discusses the Sprint's goals and priorities, and comes to an overall agreement about what is important. This is *not* determination of the Sprint Goal! It is merely setting a *tone* for the rest of the discussion. I have seen Teams waste a lot of time arguing over the specifics of the Sprint Goal, so I recommend the Team saves that for the end of the Sprint Planning discussion.

Once the overall agreement is reached, the Product Owner selects a single Story to consider first. The Team (including the Product Owner) negotiates and finalizes the Doneness Agreement for this single Story, and the Team (without undue influence from the Product Owner, or consideration of the Story's size in StoryPoints) decides if they can agree this single Story will fit in the Sprint. What they are actually agreeing to is the Story's Doneness Agreement, which is discussed in chapter 3.6. Basically, the Agreement becomes the formal definition of the Story, as it determines how the Team will know they are Done with it.

The Team may not be able to agree to do the Story, or might not even be able to agree on the Doneness Agreement. This makes the Story in question an Epic, by definition, and the Team must decide what to do. Typical choices include agreeing to an Analysis Story to analyze the Epic, extracting a smaller Story from the Epic to do instead (putting the remainder back on the Backlog), or skipping the Story altogether and moving to the next one (in chapter 3.4 I discussed an example of 'on the fly' decomposition of an Epic with the 'Pick Flight and Pay for It' Story).

After a Story is agreed to, the Team (with the Product Owner in the lead) has the option to reprioritize the Story list, and the Team considers the next Story. Once again, the Team negotiates the Story's Doneness Agreement and decides whether not to add the Story to the list of already-agreed-to Stories. This process is repeated until the Team decides the Sprint is 'full' and the Sprint Backlog is complete.

Here's a quick example of how this process could go...

> **PO:**   'Ok, guys, here's the first Story – it's heavy on the database work...'

> *(PO plus Team negotiates Agreement, Team agrees to do the Story)*

> **Team:**   'Ok, what's next?'

> **PO:**   'Here's another database-heavy one...'

> *(PO plus Team negotiates Agreement, Team agrees to the Story)*

> **Team:**   'Ok, what's next? ...but no more database-heavy Stories; we're full-up...'

> **PO:**   'Well, I wanted another one of those... let me reprioritize... here we go... do this one next – it's a new business rule.'

> *(PO plus Team negotiates Agreement, Team agrees to the Story)*

> **Team:**   'Got it. We have room for one more Story, but it's got to be a small one. And remember, no database-heavy ones...'

> **PO**:   *'All right, how about this 'clean up the interface' one?'*
>
> *(PO plus Team negotiates Agreement, Team starts a discussion...)*
>
> **Team**:   *'Sorry, that won't fit. We're done.'*
>
> **PO**:   *'Ok'*

Once the Stories are agreed to, the Team finalizes the Sprint Goal (remember that the Team *includes* the Product Owner). The Sprint Goal is a single, clear, benefit that will be achieved during the Sprint, was probably discussed with the Stakeholders at the previous Product Review, and will be achieved as a by-product of doing the agreed-to Stories. The Team finalizes and commits to the Sprint Goal, and the Product Owner announces this Goal to the Stakeholders. It is hoped that the Sprint Goal meets the Stakeholders' expectations (that's why the Team discussed it with them at the Product Review), but it is the Team's decision about the Sprint Goal that is final.

Depending on the predictability of the Team and the ambiguity of the Sprint Goal, I expect the Sprint Goal to be achievable without completing all (or even 'almost all') of the agreed-to Stories. It is the ScrumMaster's job to make sure the Team does not set a Goal that is too ambitious; I do not want the Team setting itself up for failure. I believe that the Team can be aggressive in the Stories it agrees to do, but not the Goal it commits to meet.

The purpose of the Sprint Goal is to give the Team some wiggle room when it comes to actually getting the Stories Done; it does this by defining the success of the Sprint in terms of this Sprint Goal rather than in terms of the Stories that have been agreed to. Without this wiggle room the Team may be inhibited and afraid to agree to as many Stories as it can – the Sprint Goal provides a measure of safety for the Team. It allows the Team to treat the agreed-to list of Stories as simply a forecast – not a commitment.

This completes the Sprint Planning. The process is quite simple, but leads to a number of issues that are tightly intertwined. I describe and discuss some of these issues in the following sections.

Stories Should Be 'Ready' for Planning

There are a number of things the Team should do before it can even begin Sprint Planning. The most important thing it must do is make sure that the Team is prepared, and understands what the Stories are about. In other words, *someone* on the Team knows about each Story; that is, each Story has its own champion (Story Owner) who represents the Stakeholder's needs and wants to the Team. This may require that the Product Owner coordinates the efforts of all the Story Owners.

This preparation is probably the result of significant Backlog Refinement (chapter 3.9) that has happened previously, which has moved the Stories to the Back Burner and made them Ready. The Team must make sure that the Product Owner is familiar with what has happened so far, and that each Story has its Story Owner. The Product Owner must be familiar enough with all the Stories (or trust the Team enough) in order for him or her to prioritize the Stories correctly.

Of course, it's not just the Product Owner that must be prepared; the Stories themselves must be Ready for Planning. This means that they're going to be small enough so that the Team feels confident that they're not Epics, and that the Doneness Agreement is well enough known so that the Team can know 'what they're getting into' with a minimum of conversation. This confidence about the Doneness Agreement can happen in a couple of ways:

- If the Story is a common one, the Team may do nothing until Sprint Planning. That is, the Team will almost surely know what to do, because they have seen Stories like this one before, at another time and another place... this process of recognizing similar Stories is called Storyotyping, and is the subject of chapter 3.10. What is important to know (for now) about Storyotyping is that it gives the Team Members a common Doneness Agreement that they can begin negotiations with.

- They could have finished some analysis already. That is, the Team (perhaps the Story Owner) could've worked with SMEs in order to already have a good idea about what the Doneness Agreement should be for the Story. If necessary, the Story Owner can be a SME who is an 'honorary' member of the Team throughout Refining, Planning, and Development of the Story.

In either case, this Doneness Agreement has not been *finalized* – that happens during the Sprint Planning session. What has happened so far is that the Doneness Agreement has been thought about and discussed, and notes may have been made for consideration and discussion during that session.

Reprioritization

As the Team Members conduct Sprint Planning, they move down the list of Stories (as prioritized by the Product Owner) discussing and agreeing to them one at a time. While doing this, they are also working with the Product Owner to reprioritize the list along the way, if needed. In fact, they may even be adding new Stories to the list as they go; based on discussions they're having about the realities of the situation.

Technically, this prioritization/reprioritization is 'owned' by the Product Owner, but in *reality* it is done by the Team as a whole, with the Product Owner having the final say – especially about Business Value. There are a number of things to consider when prioritizing and reprioritizing the Backlog. Most of these factors are in play all the time, and influence which Stories will be prioritized in the Sprint, and in what order.

Because prioritization is so important and complicated, we have separated out the considerations for prioritization into chapter 3.9, where it is discussed as a part of Backlog Refinement. For the purposes of Agreement-Based Planning, it suffices to say that the list may be reprioritized after each Story is agreed to, and the way it is done is up to the Team, with the Product Owner having the final say. The Team needs to remember to prioritize necessary Chores, either directly, through adoption, or with some version of the '70/30 Rule' – all of this is discussed in chapter 3.9.

One of the interesting twists on prioritization that comes about because the Team is doing Agreement-Based Planning is what happens when the Sprint is nearly 'full.' It may be that after a number of Stories have been agreed to some Team Members will say something like *'We think we might be able to fit one more Small Story in here'* or *'We really shouldn't have any more database-centric Stories, since our database skills are being stretched already'* or something similar. In situations like these the Product Owner (along with the Team) may need to reprioritize the remaining Backlog in order to bring Stories forward that might fit into this Sprint based on these limitations.

There is no universal truth here; there are many prioritization issues that are important at one time or another. Prioritization is a distinctly subjective, and human, endeavor, and should be undertaken with a lot of discussions, arguments, and analysis. There is nothing simple about it.

The Team Agrees to the Stories

As the Team moves down the list during Sprint Planning, it is agreeing to the Stories as it goes. This is actually an agreement to *all* the Stories in the list so far, so it's more complex than just agreeing to each Story individually. And this agreement is merely a forecast of what *might* get Done; it is not a commitment to what *will* be Done.

As the Team moves down the list, it does whatever it needs to do to help it decide if it can agree to the next Story. This could include opening a browser and looking at the code to make an assessment of Technical Debt, but it doesn't have to. This could include tasking it out and adding TaskHours, but it doesn't have to. It could include estimating the Story's effort in Effort-Points and considering the Team's WorkRate, but it doesn't have to. It could include a detailed Plan of Action about how the Team will actually get all the work Done – including this new Story – but it doesn't have to. It could include using an Estimation Game and simply asking the Team *'can we get all this Done down to here?'* but it doesn't have to. It could include some quick analysis or experimentation in order to reduce risk, but it doesn't have to. All that is *required* is an agreement to do the Story along with the others already agreed to. Everything else is just a means to that end.

The Product Owner can be a problem when the Team is agreeing. Since the Product Owner has *actual* power, the ScrumMaster must go to great lengths to make sure that the Team's agreement is genuine, and not coerced by the Product Owner. This issue is a constant one for the ScrumMaster, and a frequent topic during many Teams' Retrospectives.

The Team ignores the Story's StoryPoint size as a factor in agreeing to do the Story. However, when discussing the Doneness Agreement, it is reasonable to make statements like *'I thought you said this was a Small, and these Acceptance Criteria sure make it look like a Large.'* This won't influence the Team's agreement, but helps keep the Product Owner honest, and may also lead to a resizing of the Story – this could be important when doing Velocity calculations and making Capacity assumptions.

If the last Story that is investigated doesn't fit, the Team should quit Planning. The Team should not have very many planned out Stories on the Backlog, as this is considered inventory, and hence waste, based on Lean principles (see appendix A.5). Practically speaking, Stories that are planned out are *too easy* to choose in future Sprint Planning – just because they *look* ready to go – even if they aren't really the most important. This shouldn't happen, so make sure it doesn't.

Agreement and Technical Debt

As the Team is moving along, agreeing and reprioritizing, it may have to make a decision to do a Story with less quality than the Team Members know it should because the Stakeholders *really need it* and it won't fit if the Team *does it right*. In other words, the Team Members are agreeing to produce Technical Debt *on purpose*, and are *intentionally* watering down the Definition of Done (see chapter 3.6).

Now, there are people that argue that if we don't have time to do it right then we shouldn't do it at all – that not giving enough time and effort to the Story proves that we don't really want it enough. This is an honorable concept but, in my experience, it's not realistic. Often, doing the right thing is not the right thing to do for some legitimate business reason, so there must be a process to deal with it – the Team can't ignore this reality and still call itself agile.

Whether we like it or not, there are times that a Team will knowingly create Technical Debt in order to provide Business Value, and they will do it if the tradeoff seems reasonable to the Product Owner, the Team Members, and the Stakeholders. The bottom line is that the Product Owner has the *right* to request that the Team do this, and all the Team can hope for is that the Product Owner doesn't do it lightly.

In situations like this I want to make sure that the Team adds a Cleanup Story (chapter 4.5) to the Backlog, and put (and keep) it in the Back Burner, so that it's not hidden from the Team or Stakeholders. This Story will be a constant reminder that the Team made this compromise, and I hope it will make everyone (especially the Product Owner and Stakeholders) feel guilty enough that they will allow the Team to fix the problem they all caused.

Plan of Action

As the Team is moving down the list, remember that what is important is that the Team agrees to the *collection* of Stories as it goes. That is, at any given point the Team is agreeing to add the next Story to the list of Stories it has *already* agreed to.

In order to do this the Team may need to have a Plan of Action, which could look like an actual old-fashioned plan the way we used to make them. The Team may need to have conversations that go like *'Amir and Dan will work on this Story first, and then switch to this other Story. While this is going on Amy and Pam will work on these two other Stories, and Fred and Mark will Swarm as necessary.'*

The Team may need to task out the Stories in order to have a more fine-grained Plan of Action. In this case it winds up with a collection of Tasks for the Stories, but we must remember that it is *not* the Tasks the Team is agreeing to, it is the Stories and, specifically, the Stories' Agreements.

If the Team does task out the Stories, it may want to estimate the effort for the Tasks in something real, such as TaskHours. Even if the Team doesn't task out the Stories it may need to apply effort estimates to the Stories themselves, in terms of days, hours of effort, Ideal Engineering Hours or Days, EffortPoints, or whatever works for them. Just remember that this is *not the same* as the sizing of the Stories (in StoryPoints) that I discussed in chapter 3.6 – that is about the Story itself, not the effort it will take to get the Story Done.

This Plan of Action could be documented, or it might not be. The point is not to actually have the Plan, but to have the Team believe that there is a way that they can get the Stories Done – this will give the Team Members the confidence they need so that they will be able to agree to try to do it. It's all about the Agreements, not the Plan of Action. During Sprint Planning and the Sprint, it will be clear that Team 'has a little of the waterfall' in them when they start talking about the Plan of Action rather than the Stories them-selves. In particular, the ScrumMaster needs to make sure that the Team stays focused on the Agreements and the Stories during the Sprint, not the Plan of Action or the Tasks.

Appropriate Sprint Goals

As a part of Agreement-Based Planning, the Team should decide on a Sprint Goal, which will define the ultimate success or failure of the Sprint. The main purpose of the Sprint Goal is to provide a focus on something besides finishing all the Stories and provide wiggle room for the Team to work within. This is important for many Teams because, without it, the Team's *de facto* goal is to finish *all* the Stories they agreed to – and this pressure to finish *all* of them often leads to the unintentional creation of Technical Debt (see chapter 3.5). Having something else to focus on that *defines* success allows the Team to do their due diligence in order to get the Stories Done right.

The Sprint Goal should be determined by the Team at the end of Sprint Planning, even though it may be discussed with the Stakeholders at the Review. I like doing it at the end so that there isn't a long, protracted discussion about it. Since Sprint Planning is time-boxed, holding it at the end limits the amount of wrangling the Team can go through about it.

The Sprint Goal *defines* success, and can be about Product, People, or Practices. Most people think the Sprint Goal should be a subset of the Release Goal, or a milestone along the way, or something like that. I think that is too narrow a view. I think that the Sprint Goal is what is *actually* important in this Sprint, and this is not always about the Product. Let's just see some examples of Sprint Goals.

- 'Have something to Review' – the default Sprint Goal for *any* Sprint.

- 'Have a releasable version of <Buy an e-Ticket>' – indicating that, even though the Team is *almost* there, and everybody thinks it shouldn't take much more effort, make sure you get 'Buy an e-Ticket' ready to go – even if it means reprioritizing the other Stories in the Sprint or creating Technical Debt.

- 'Clean up Module ABC' – indicating that, even though functional Coding Stories have been agreed to, and are important, what is *really important* is cleaning up some Technical Debt.

- 'We will get this Product in the hands of users this Sprint!' – indicating that it is imperative that the Product go out the door. Do whatever it takes, including sacrificing features, quality, and work/life balance – but get it out the door. A Goal like this one defines the Sprint as a Release Sprint (see chapter 4.9).

- 'Bring the new people, Joe and Gina, up to speed' – indicating that speed of development may be sacrificed if it helps in knowledge-sharing with the new Team Members.

- 'Be up and running the first day of the next Sprint' – this is common for a so-called Startup Sprint (see chapter 4.9) and indicates that the Team needs to do *enough* analysis, have *enough* development environment, have *enough* training, and so on, so that it can begin production immediately. This is used to eliminate a long, up-front, setup period.

- 'No Technical Debt in this Sprint' – let's actually follow the rules and take no shortcuts this time, shall we?

- 'Everybody goes home by 6:00pm' – we need to get our work/life balance back, and stop working at an unsustainable pace.

- 'Nobody works alone this Sprint' – everybody Pairs or Swarms, let's just bite the bullet and get used to it...

- 'Keep Improving <Buy an e-Ticket>' – which indicates that the Team should just keep doing what it's doing, but *focus* on the 'Buy an e-Ticket' Capability...

Once the Sprint Goal is determined it should be announced to the Stakeholders, and it should be adhered to as a focus throughout the Sprint. Remember that this is what *defines* success for the Sprint, and must be the primary focus. It is the ScrumMaster's job to make sure the Team keeps focused on this Goal throughout the Sprint.

Sprint Planning and the Release Strategy

So, while the Team is focused on the Sprint Goal, the Product Owner must also keep focused on the Release Goal and Release Strategy, if appropriate. The Team's job is to produce quality Product at a Sustainable Pace, and it is the Product Owner's job to keep his or her eye on the Release. Attempting to achieve the Release Goal is inherent in the Backlog's prioritization.

This is one of the places where Scrum gets very interesting, and differs significantly from 'normal' project management. Achieving the Release Goal and carrying out the Release Strategy may require that the Team have a certain Velocity/Capacity, and everybody knows this. However, achieving this production speed should *not* be a formal Sprint Goal; it should be a by-product of doing the work.

How fast the Team does work (its Velocity or Capacity) is a reality determined by the Stories' Agreements, the Team's Abilities, Technical Debt, and so on (see chapter 3.7). This reality may not meet expectations and, as I said in chapter 1.1: *"when reality and expectations don't match, it is the expectations that must change."* Figuring out how to increase the Team's Capacity is a significant Retrospective issue that must be brought to the Team by the ScrumMaster; it is not a Release Goal that can be placed upon the Team by the Product Owner.

This exhortation is not just a theoretical one; it is based on pragmatism. It is an observed reality that when a Team's Goal is *be fast*, one result is the production of Technical Debt. There are few Products that can survive the production of Technical Debt for very long, and this is a truth that is hard to change. Basically, Scrum Teams *must* believe that the reality of the Technical Debt is more important than the reality of the Release Date...

Ok, I'll get down off the soapbox now... ;-)

Why I Like Agreement-Based Planning

There are two reasons that I like Agreement-Based Planning more than other Planning methods:

1. It minimizes the number of already-planned-out Stories on the Backlog which, in lean terms, is minimizing inventory. This is important because an already planned out, tasked out, and estimated Story just sits there saying *'I'm all ready to go'* when in reality it might not be ready, or it might not be the right Story to go next, soon, or even at all. Things happen, things change, and what we thought we knew previously is likely to be false as we move along.

2. This method of Planning does not rely on the StoryPoint sizing of the Stories, which means that the Agreements are based on the realities of the moment rather than what the Team used to think when it sized the Stories. Also, since the Team is agreeing to the Stories (and not their Sizes), they may need to do some investigation of the Technical Debt, find out if the right people are available, and so on, during Sprint Planning itself. These are usually things that they did not know when they did the Story Sizing, so they need to learn them during Planning.

The main problem with Agreement-Based Planning is that the Product Owner is a Team Member and can, therefore, be involved as a Team Member during negotiations. This apparent conflict of interest causes the possibility of undue influence by the Product Owner when it comes to the Team's agreeing to the Stories. This potential problem is a job for the ScrumMaster to manage, and is an inherent risk of Agreement-Based Planning. However, I believe that this risk is worth the reward of doing Sprint Planning based on the actual facts of the moment.

Discussion Questions

1. Why does the Team do Sprint Planning based on a Story's Agreement, rather than a Story's Size?

2. The Sprint Goal defines success for the Sprint. Doesn't success for the Sprint mean the Team got all the Stories it agreed to Done?

3. Give some examples of Sprint Goals that may seem a bit unusual to you.

4. Why might the Team reprioritize the Backlog during Sprint Planning?

5. The Team agrees to the Stories; the forecast belongs to the Team. How does the Product Owner participate in this agreement?

6. Discuss the difference between a forecast and a commitment.

4.3

Adjusting Sprint Content

One of the most common issues that arises with a Scrum Team is that the content of a Sprint needs to change during the Sprint. This happens for a number of reasons, and I discuss this issue in this chapter.

As I have discussed, Sprint Planning has two objectives:

- To have the Team commit to a Sprint Goal, and
- To have the Team agree to do some Stories.

It is also a *given* that the Team is obligated to do its due diligence, which means it does much quality work as it can while working at a Sustainable Pace – this is simply the Values in action.

If there's anything that I know for sure, it's that stuff happens. As Robert Burns (1785) said, "The best laid schemes of Mice and Men oft go awry," and nowhere is this more true than with Sprint Planning. During the Sprint it often happens that the Team can't finish what it agreed to do, its Sprint Goal changes, it finishes early, new important stuff shows up, existing stuff has to change, some of the Items the Team agreed to do aren't really important, and so on.

What do we do, oh, what do we do? I've seen more Teams agonize over this than almost anything else in Scrum. Well, the short answer to *'what does the Team do?'* is that *this is the reality in front of the Team, so just deal with it*, but this is somehow unsatisfying. These Teams want advice, not platitudes, so here goes.

There are six different situations here. Two of them are relatively easy to deal with:

- The Team finishes its Stories early, and
- The Team needs to remove something from the Sprint.

Two of them are straightforward, but painful:

- The Sprint Goal needs to change, and
- The Team is not going to finish what it agreed to do.

And two of them are potentially difficult to deal with:

- The agreed-upon Doneness Agreement for a Story needs to change, and

- The Product Owner wants to add something to an already full Sprint.

In this chapter I discuss these issues, from easy to hard.

Finishing Early

So, let me talk about the easy stuff first. One of the *best* things that can happen to a Scrum Team is that it finishes its work early in a Sprint. It amazes me that Teams are confused about what to do, but they are. So here goes...

If the Team finishes early, it seems to me there are two choices: take a holiday, or do something new. I have seen Teams take a half-day off if that's all the time they have left, and I applaud this. In most cases, however, the Team should just bring something new into the Sprint and do it.

By definition, the Items near the top of the Back Burner are Stories that are no more than one short conversation away from being agreed to; that is, the Team only needs to have a short conversation before it can start work on one of them.

So, the Team should work with its Product Owner to figure out which Story on the Back Burner to do. Maybe it's something the Product Owner wants, or maybe the Team gets to work on one of the Chores (like some refactoring or something) that has been put off until later. It should be one that the Team thinks might fit into the time remaining in the Sprint, so they finalize the Doneness Agreement, task it out, and just do it.

Yes, it is really just that simple... unless the Team can't find one that will fit in the time remaining in the Sprint. Then the Team can do one of two things: take a holiday, or just start a new Story, knowing that it will spill over into the next Sprint. In this second case the Story is actually part of the next Sprint, not this one.

Now, that really wasn't so hard, was it?

Removing Something that's Not Necessary

The second easy case is only one step more complicated. If the Team realizes that something on the Sprint Backlog doesn't really need to be Done, and the Product Owner agrees, then it should probably be removed from the Sprint.

If the Team has already started working on it, the problem is a little bit more complicated, as the Team needs to decide whether it's more effort to stop doing it (which will mean cleaning up whatever messes have been caused while working on it), changing it until it's right (see the 'Changing Something that it Already Agreed To' section in this chapter), or continuing to do it until it's finished or is in a good state to stop.

If the Team hasn't started it already, though, the decision should be easy. Just remove it from the Sprint Backlog and continue. If it turns out that this will cause the Team to finish early, then deal with that as I discussed in the last section. And, the Team shouldn't worry about what Story they will replace this one with... they don't need to figure out what to replace the removed Story with until they actually know that they have extra time – that's trying to solve a problem they don't have yet. ;-)

The Sprint Goal Needs to Change

The Sprint Goal defines the success of the Sprint, has been negotiated by the Team and the Product Owner, and has been advertised to the Stakeholders. Any of these three parties can suggest a change in Sprint Goal, but the Sprint Goal can't change without agreement from the Product Owner and the rest of the Team. There are a number of reasons the Sprint Goal could change, and here are a couple of examples:

- Maybe Gina, a new Team Member, has arrived, and the ScrumMaster suggests to the Product Owner and Team that the Sprint Goal should change from 'Have a releasable version of <Buy an e-Ticket>' to 'Bring Gina up to speed' – changing the focus from producing functionality to the Team's health for this Sprint;

- Maybe some significant Technical Debt has been found by the Team in Module ABC, so the Team thinks the Sprint Goal should change from 'Have a releasable version of <Buy an e-Ticket>' to 'Clean up Module ABC' – changing the focus from functionality to reducing Technical Debt; or

- Maybe the Product Owner and the Stakeholder have talked about an upcoming Trade Show and they think that the Sprint Goal should change from 'Keep Improving <Buy an e-Ticket>' to 'Provide a version of <Buy an e-Ticket> that can be demonstrated at the Trade Show' – changing the focus to indicate that providing a demonstrable version of the 'Buy an e-Ticket' Capability is more important than anything else, including the prevention of Technical Debt.

No matter who suggests the change, it won't be accepted until the Product Owner and the rest of the Team agree to it, and then it must be advertised to the Stakeholders. If the Team won't agree to a Sprint Goal change suggested by the Product Owner, the Product Owner always has the option to Cancel the Sprint (see chapter 4.9) and force a re-planning. In general, however, if agreement is not reached, the Sprint Goal simply remains unchanged.

Changing the Sprint Goal may cause a need to change the Stories the Team has agreed to do. If this happens, a re-planning session must happen, and the Product Owner and the Team must renegotiate the agreed-upon Stories. In drastic cases, this may cause the Product Owner to Cancel the Sprint, or the Team to call for an Abnormal Termination (see chapter 4.9). However, I think that a simple time-out to re-plan is usually sufficient. Make it quick, though, as the Time taken to re-plan is time that is not being spent actually doing Stories.

The Team Can't Do what It Agreed to Do

Now, for one of the more painful situations we have in Scrum. What if the Team just can't finish what it agreed to do? This situation may make the Team Members feel badly about themselves, and they may want to do these Stories no matter what...

Since the Team actually agreed to the Stories' Doneness Agreements, this means that they can't meet all the Agreements that they agreed to. So, there are only two basic things the Team can do: remove some Stories, or modify some Agreements. The second case actually has two options: the Team can split a Story and remove part of it, or it can decrease quality and produce Technical Debt. So, there are three options in total: remove Stories, split Stories, or increase Technical Debt.

Before discussing these options, we must all remember that the Team's agreement to the Stories is an agreement between the Product Owner and the rest of the Team. The Team has committed to a Sprint Goal with the Stakeholders, but it is possible (if not preferable) that the Stakeholders are unaware of what Stories the Team has *actually* agreed to. I think it might be reasonable to say that it's none of their business – their concern should be the Sprint Goal... but this may be an impossible dream for your Team.

The best of the three options is to remove Stories from the Sprint. I believe that it should be possible to remove (at least some) Stories without affecting the Team's achieving the Sprint Goal – remember that the reason there *is* a Sprint Goal defining the Sprint's success is so that the Team has the wiggle room it needs to allow it to fail to do some of the Stories. So, the preferable option is to just remove whatever Stories are necessary, while still achieving the Sprint Goal.

Luckily, the Stories that the Team hasn't started yet are probably the least important ones in the Sprint – they aren't needed to achieve the Sprint Goal – and can easily be pushed into the next Sprint. This will have an effect on the Team's Velocity for this Sprint, and that's a shame, but it's the reality we're dealing with. And yes, I know it is painful, but this is Scrum, not the playground. ;-)

The second best thing to do is to split a Story and remove part of it. This can only be done if we have a large, decomposable, Story that can be split. Generally speaking, we don't want to have Stories like this in our Sprint in the first place; but if we do, we could split one of them into two Stories and then remove one of them. This is not easy, but it can sometimes be done. The things we need to worry about when we split the Story are: that each of the sub-Stories still has a Doneness Agreement that mitigates Technical Debt, and that each Story still has enough Stakeholder value that it can elicit meaningful feedback.

The third case (taking shortcuts and increasing Technical Debt) is the least palatable, as it involves relaxing the Definition of Done and purposefully creating Technical Debt. The Team may need to do this because it *really* needs to deliver all the Stories, and the cost of not delivering them in this Sprint is higher than the future cost of the Technical Debt created (this shouldn't happen, but it does nonetheless...). This decision can't be made lightly, and is a decision that is owned by the Product Owner – but should probably be agreed to by the Business Owner, as well as other Stakeholders.

I hate this option! But some Teams think it's a good idea. If your Team is one of those Teams, just remember to add Cleanup Stories (chapter 4.5) to the Backlog (and they go in the Back Burner so that they are always visible – right in everybody's face – they never slip to the Fridge). Make sure that it is visible, and well known, that the Team created Technical Debt, and that the Team has promised the system, via the Cleanup Stories, that they will fix it. Additionally, make sure that all the Stakeholders (or, at least, the Business Owner) know that the Team has done so, and that they agree it's the best, if not only, way to go.

Changing Something that It Already Agreed to Do

Often, when a Team is in the middle of a Sprint, the Team realizes that the Agreement for some Story isn't actually correct. Sometimes a developer realizes this, sometimes a Subject Matter Expert; maybe it's the Product Owner. Whatever... Since this is the reality, the Team must do something about it. There are two cases: the case where the change is actually internal scope creep for the Story, and the case where it's just a simple change that takes no additional effort.

The second case is pretty simple; all we have to do is change the Agreement. If the change is something as simple as 'it's supposed to be green, not blue' and the Team hasn't already started working on it, it's no big deal, right? Just make sure that everybody on the Team knows about the change in case the change affects somebody else.

However, what if the Team has already made it blue and it will take a significant amount of work to make it green? Well, then it's not really a simple change anymore, is it? And so it will fall into the first case, that of a change that requires significant effort, and thus constitutes internal scope creep.

If it is determined that the necessary change is internal scope creep for whatever reason, then it is treated just like any other significant addition to the Backlog; that is, the Team goes into negotiations. This is what I will talk about next.

Negotiating New Work

It is not unusual that external realities cause requirements to change faster than the Team wants them to, putting pressure on the Team to modify its Sprint Backlog. Usually, this modification comes in the form of the Product Owner wanting to add something to the Backlog – at least that's the way the problem is usually put to the Team: *'here's something new we need to do...'* Sometimes this change actually comes from *above* the Product Owner, but it is the Product Owner's responsibility to bring it to the Team.

This discussion about new stuff should *not* happen in the Daily Scrum; the Team needs to have a scope negotiation discussion separately. The fact that there must be a scope negotiation discussion could be discussed at the Daily Scrum, but the discussion itself is not appropriate for the Daily Scrum (see chapter 4.8).

Now, it is clear that this new stuff must be something that needs to be worked on *right now*, or else it would be simply put it into the next Sprint. There are a couple of cases:

- It might have a brand-new piece of work, that just showed up, and it's more important than stuff being worked on in the Sprint;

- There might be an emergency, of a type that is recurring, like fixing a bug in an existing system or helping out on a sales call; or

- It might be a one-of-a-kind emergency, like helping out when the production server goes down.

Each of these cases is different, and I recommend different resolutions. What is common to the cases is the notion of having a good faith negotiation between the Product Owner and the rest of the Team. This negotiation should be refereed by the ScrumMaster, as managing the relationship between the Product Owner and the rest of the Team is one of the ScrumMaster's primary responsibilities.

So now let's look at the three cases.

Case one: there is a new important piece of work: This case is straightforward. If there is work that the Team hasn't started yet and it's about the same amount of effort as the new Story, and the new Story can be integrated into the current Sprint's work without undue hardship or changing the Sprint's Goal, then the Team just makes the swap – the new Story for the existing Story. The Story the Team hasn't started yet is pushed into the Back Burner, and the new Story that needs to be worked on gets moved into the Front Burner to be worked on in the Sprint.

Now, of course, this requires good faith negotiations between the Product Owner and the rest of the Team. Both sides are equal partners in this negotiation, and there should be no issues or problems with it. If there are problems with it, there is always the threat of an Abnormal Termination to get the parties to negotiate (see chapter 4.9).

By the way, if the need to integrate new, important, work into your Team's Sprint is a recurring problem, your Team may want to try mid-Sprint Planning sessions to help solve the problem (see chapter 4.9). This may reduce the need for constant negotiations, and make it more normal and natural to integrate this new work. If the Team wants to go all-out, and remove this problem altogether, try the Kanban(ish) variant of Scrum I discuss in chapter 4.7, but don't try and do that until the Team is mature.

Case two: an emergency of recurring type: The Team often gets called to deal with emergencies that recur, such as going on a Sales Call, or fixing a defect in a different system. The first few times the Team sees an emergency like this, it should be treated like new work; that is, the Team negotiates putting them into the Sprint. However, it doesn't make much sense to continue to negotiate every time once the Team realizes that this is a recurring issue. I don't want something that is just 'business as usual' to cause upheaval on the Team – that's just silly.

Once it is realized that this is a common 'emergency,' there are a couple of things the Team can do. The Team can set aside time, as part of its process, to just work on this stuff; for example, the Team might say: *'let's give ourselves four hours every day (as a Team) to Work on Bugs in the ABC System.'* What this does is separates these recurring emergencies from the Backlog altogether.

This has pluses and minuses. On the plus side, the issue is solved since there doesn't need to be a negotiation every time, and it only becomes an issue for the Team if the amount of recurring work exceeds the time they've set aside

– in which case it becomes an impediment, and the Team has to do some negotiating at that point.

On the minus side, the Team won't get credit for the Velocity that is being produced while doing this work. This is an issue because the Product Owner might need to know how much total Velocity the Team has in order to predict what the Team could do if it started doing different work altogether. The Team may also just want to get credit for the Velocity, mightn't it?

What I recommend in these cases is what we call PlaceHolder Stories, such as *'Let's just have two 'Sales Call Stories' to use in the next Sprint.'* These PlaceHolder Stories are Stories that hold StoryPoints to be used for as-yet-unknown work (see chapter 4.4 for more details).

Case three: the one-of-a-kind emergency: In this situation what you do is pretty simple; you just drop everything and go fix the problem. Once the problem is fixed, the Team renegotiates the Sprint. As usual, the negotiation must be carried out in good faith, and may result in an Abnormal Termination. This is the one case where I think the Abnormal Termination is a legitimate possibility, depending on how long it took to fix the emergency, and how willing the Product Owner is to renegotiate afterwards.

Summary

The issues we've discussed in this chapter are likely to happen to your Team. The basics of resolving them are pretty simple:

- Negotiate in good faith;
- Try to process-ize recurring stuff; and
- Cancel the Sprint or do an Abnormal Termination as the last resort.

Discussion Question

1. What are some of the options for a Team that finishes all the work in the Front Burner before the end of the Sprint?

2. When and Why would a Team change its Sprint Goal? Who do they need to tell about it?

3. It is very common that a Team has forecast more work than it can actually do. What should they do when they realize they can't finish all the work in the Sprint Backlog?

4. What should a Team do if some new, important, piece of work comes up, and they're in the middle of a Sprint?

PlaceHolder Stories

One of the most common issues for Scrum Teams is what to do about work that it expects to have to do during a Sprint, but doesn't actually know the details about yet, such as bugs in existing systems, or expected sales support efforts. In this chapter I introduce a method to manage these 'known unknowns.'

When I'm coaching or training there is one question that I invariably get, which is *'what do I do about the bugs I have to fix in other systems I'm maintaining? Every Sprint I get new bugs I hadn't planned for, and it throws my planning off. I get the same impediments Sprint after Sprint! Is there something I can do about it?'*

Well, I think that it's crazy that something that happens *every* Sprint throws your planning off – why are you surprised? When a Team winds up having the same impediments over and over again, management is going to stop paying attention to it – the Team is like the little boy that cried 'Wolf'!

What the Team is supposed to do is inspect and adapt and modify its process so that the surprises aren't surprises. Something that's just part of the normal way of doing business should never be described as an impediment – the Team's job is to modify its process so that the process adapts for it, and the recurring issue becomes part of the normal way of doing business.

General Budget/Planning Problem

This issue about bugs is just the simplest, and most common, example of a more general problem, which is the problem about how to manage the 'known unknowns'; that is, those general things that everyone *knows* will happen, but the exact details are unknown. Here are some of the most common examples:

- Fixing bugs in other Systems,

- Going on sales calls with virtually no warning,

- Helping the systems people with common hardware and software maintenance issues, and

- Doing the day-to-day things that managers find for Team Members to do, such as reviewing resumes or doing interviews.

Issues like these are quite common, and they cause Teams to have problems with their budgeting and planning for the Sprint. In general, what these things can do to a Team if it doesn't find a way to make it part of the normal way of doing business is throw off plans and cause the Team to need to modify its Sprint Plan (see chapter 4.3). Since this is such a common problem, there must be a simple way to manage it, and there is.

PlaceHolder Stories to Manage Budget

The solution is so simple that it's actually elegant. What I recommend is that the Team puts Stories in the Sprint Backlog in order to hold (or contain) a budget for the StoryPoints that the Team *knows* it's going to need to spend on these things. We call these Stories PlaceHolder Stories, as they hold a place in our Sprint Backlog for Stories in a general category that the Team doesn't know the details about yet.

There are two basic ways to do this. The first is to put Stories in the Sprint Backlog that will be replaced by the *real* Stories once they show up. For example, there might put Stories in the Sprint Backlog called 'SouvSite bug_1', 'SouvSite bug_2', 'SouvSite bug_3', and so on, each of which is a medium-sized Story that has been given a size of 4 StoryPoints. I call this the 'Bugs to be Named Later' pattern, and it's a fairly common pattern to use.

The second way to do it is to put in PlaceHolder Stories (actually Epics) that contain a number of StoryPoints that will be *consumed* as the actual Stories show up (these will be the Stories within the Epic).

For example, the Team may have a Story called 'SouvSite Bugs' which has been assigned a size of 20 StoryPoints. As the actual bugs show up they consume the StoryPoints (based on their StoryPoint size) and the number of StoryPoints remaining in the 'SouvSite Bugs' Epic is decreased accordingly. Some other example Stories of this type might be:

- 'Sales Support' – which may contain StoryPoints that the Team expects to spend on the sales calls they will be asked to assist in,

- 'Admin Support' – which could contain StoryPoints the Team expects to spend helping the admin folks, or

- 'Management Support' – which will contain StoryPoints the Team thinks will be required to spend doing things like reviewing resumes, interviews for hiring new people, and other management-type overhead work that the Team's people are required to do.

The Team might even go all-out and have an Item just called 'Chores' that will hold the 30% of the total budgeted StoryPoints that the Team expects to spend on Chores within the Sprint. There are lots of ways to do this, but they all involve putting Epics in the Sprint Backlog that hold StoryPoints that the Team is budgeting for future, unknown-but-expected, Stories.

There Must Be a Sufficient Back Burner

Of course, there is no guarantee that the Team will actually spend these StoryPoints that we have set aside. So we need to make sure that the Back Burner part of the Backlog has some Ready Stories that are 'ready to go' if the Team gets to the end of the Sprint and still has some unused StoryPoints left over – and also has the time to use them.

This shouldn't be a surprise; this is what the Back Burner is for, anyway. Remember that it contains Stories that are one short conversation away from being agreed to – these Stories are nearly ready to go.

So, if the Team has a robust Back Burner, as it is supposed to, then using this pattern of having the PlaceHolder Stories is no problem at all. Note that *robust* does not mean *big*. The Team must still make sure that there aren't *too many* Stories on the Back Burner, as this would be considered waste, from a Lean perspective. I discussed this issue earlier (in chapter 3.2), and the guidance still stands. So, the Team needs *enough* Back Burner to fill in any gaps that may be created in the current Sprint, as well as being ready for the next Sprint's Planning, but not many more than that.

Discussion

The problem I'm discussing here is quite common for Scrum Teams, and the use of PlaceHolder Stories is a very simple and elegant solution. There is a variant of Scrum that eliminates these problems altogether, and I refer to that variant as the Kanban(ish) variant, which is discussed in chapter 4.7.

Discussion Questions

1. Discuss what we mean when we say *known unknown*? Give some examples.

2. Discuss the use of a PlaceHolder Story to manage ongoing bug fixes.

3. What do you do with 'leftover' StoryPoints in a PlaceHolder Story?

Cleanup Stories

*Technical Debt is so important that we must manage it directly –
its management won't happen by accident or as a byproduct of
development. Since Technical Debt can't be seen except by
looking at the code, its presence must be made visible to the
outside somehow. To do this I introduce the Cleanup Story.*

As I stated in chapter 3.5, Technical Debt is an evil, invisible, killer of our product. I defined it as "deficiencies in the code, technical documentation, development environments, 3rd-party tools, and development practices, which makes the code hard for the Team to change," and it's hard, if not impossible, to test for.

In the discussions in this chapter, I will restrict my discussions to that portion of the Technical Debt that involves the Code. In other words, I'm going to discuss things like bad design, incomprehensible code, incorrect or insufficient documentation, a shortage of unit tests, and so on. Similar discussions would be relevant to other types of Technical Debt, but I restrict myself to the Code in order to keep the discussions simple and easy to understand.

Technical Debt is so evil, so insidious, that it needs to be treated differently from almost anything else that happens in software. There are a number of ways that Teams create, or find, Technical Debt, and I'll discuss them in this chapter.

Normally, when a Team Member finds Technical Debt, it gets skipped over because there isn't time to fix it. But the Team Member must do something – not ignore it – and that something is to either fix it (which the Team Member probably doesn't have time for) or create a Cleanup Story. Cleanup Stories are the topic of this chapter.

How Technical Debt Arises

There are a number of ways that Technical Debt happens. The most obvious is that the Team Members take shortcuts when doing work, or don't do something as well as they should have. They are supposed to follow the Definition of Done to prevent this from happening, but sometimes the Agreement just isn't good enough, or they don't do it quite as well as they should... stuff happens. Maybe it shouldn't, maybe none of us wants it to, but it does.

Sometimes the Team Members create Technical Debt on purpose, because they have to do some work and they don't have the time to do it right. Some people say this should never happen, but it does anyway. Imagine the Product Owner saying: *'we need to deliver this feature by tomorrow or it will cost us a ten million dollar fine, and I don't care if you just have to hack it in!!'* What would you do?

That's a rhetorical question, I hope. Of course you would just hack it in – you would intentionally create Technical Debt – because doing the right thing is not always the right thing to do. There could be a higher business reason that overrules quality, right? Of course there could be, and because of this fact Teams wind up with Technical Debt. It would be nice if Teams didn't have to do this, and some Teams don't, but if your Team does you've got Technical Debt.

Sometimes Team Members just *find* Technical Debt when they are wandering around in the code working on something. They don't know how it got there, but there it is – that's the reality of the thing. It could be simply that their concept of 'good enough' has changed since the code they're looking at was written, but the fact is that there is Technical Debt now.

Sometimes, when Team Members are actually doing the work, they run out of time and claim that they're Done even though they haven't actually finished everything in the Agreement. In other words, they are creating Technical Debt *accidently on purpose*; it was not their intention to create Technical Debt when they started the Story, but when they got into it, there it was. A typical example of this might be when they have finished the Story, but they didn't do as much unit testing as they agreed to; or they realized that there was Technical Debt during the Code Review, but didn't take time to fix it.

In any case, the Team Members have got to do *something* about it, because they need to live their Values – they need to respect their code and make the fact they found the Technical Debt visible. After all, it might not be found again until it's too late. So what do they do?

Cleanup Stories

When there is Technical Debt the Team should add a Cleanup Story, which is a special kind of Chore. Remember that Chores are things that are Done that do *not* provide Business Value; they often exist in order to help the Team maintain its Capacity (see chapter 3.2). There are Chores about things needed in the environment, and there are Chores about things needed for the Product. This last type of Chore is often to reduce Technical Debt, and is the type I refer to as a Cleanup Story[1].

So let's say the Team found, or created, some Technical Debt. There is this piece of the code that's 'stinking up the place.' The Team must live its Values, and the two Values that are the most important here are respect and visibility; the Team must respect its Product, and make the Technical Debt visible so that they can do something about it.

Basically, a Cleanup Story is a Story that *apologizes* to the code base about something bad that happened, and *promises* to fix it. For example, let's say that the Team hacked in some code by not unit testing and doing some fairly bad design – so that it needs re-factoring. Then what the Team should do is add a Story to the Backlog called 'Fix up module 123' that would explain what unit testing needs to be done and what code needs to be re-factored.

Or say that a Team Member is wandering around and sees some terrible code in module XYZ that needs to be redesigned. Then he or she should add a Cleanup Story called 'Redesign Module XYZ' which would explain what was found and what needs to be done about it. Or the Team Member notices that the code is hard to understand and adds a Cleanup Story called 'Document Module ABC' to request adding some inline documentation to explain the logic being implemented.

Maybe the Team was relying on some Subject Matter Expert, say an architect, to build a cool tool, or design something – and it didn't happen. Then that SME's Buddy on the Team (see chapter 2.5) would do the best he or she could, but there may be some Technical Debt lurking about. So, the Buddy puts in a Cleanup Story to make it visible, and goes to the Product Review to show what has (and hasn't) been done.

Now, the Team Member doesn't have to admit to creating the Technical Debt – even if it's true – there only needs to be documentation that it's there and what needs to be done to resolve it. I'm not asking anybody to be a martyr... and, besides, it's Chet's fault.

This is what Cleanup Stories do; they make it visible on the Backlog what has to be done to bring the code quality back to where it should be. The Cleanup Story always belongs on the Back Burner, so that it's always right in front of the Team and the Stakeholders when discussing prioritization and Sprint Planning, which forces them to either do something about it or ignore it *on purpose*. A Cleanup Story *never* gets put in the Fridge or Freezer or dropped out of the Backlog – It's always right there in the Back Burner making

---

[1] Cleanup Stories have been spontaneously invented by many different Teams. If I am adding anything new to the concept, it is that they never disappear from view in the Backlog – they remain in the Back Burner...

everybody feel guilty. Its *purpose* is to guilt the Stakeholders, the Product Owner, and the Team into doing something about the problem, forcing a repayment of the Technical Debt.

The basic idea here is that the Product Owner must be forced to make tough choices; '*do I want the Team to fix the Technical Debt, or do something else instead?*' If the Product Owner is technically incapable of making these decisions, maybe the Team should consider using one of the strategies for managing Chores I discussed in chapter 3.3.

A Dream

Now that I've described the Cleanup Story to you, let's see what happens when we knock two good ideas together. The first good idea is that Cleanup Stories are put in the Back Burner, and they never leave. The second good idea is that the Back Burner is limited in size, since it is (in Lean terms) inventory (waste) and should be minimized.

Hmmm...

If there is an absolute upper bound on the size of the Back Burner, say 25 Stories (2-3 Sprint's worth), and if the Team continues to create (or find) Technical Debt – and thus keeps adding Cleanup Stories – then the Backlog will eventually run out of space for any other Stories in the Back Burner.

Cool. Then by the definition of the Back Burner, this will mean the *only* Stories the Team has to choose from at the next Sprint Planning session will be Cleanup Stories.

In other words, by acknowledging that Team Members are creating (or finding) Technical Debt the Team is setting up a situation in which either Technical Debt gets cleaned up or the Team violates its process. This is a very interesting decision to make...

I like it. A man can dream, can't he? ;-)

Cleanup Stories and the Story's Agreement

As I described in chapter 3.6, a Coding Story's Definition of Done describes what the Team will do in order to avoid creating Technical Debt. Just following these rules, though, does not *guarantee* the quality of the code. The Team's idea of what is *good enough* may change; the rules may not have been good enough to start with, whatever.

The point is that following the process – doing what the Definition of Done requires – may not be enough to prevent Technical Debt. So, if a Team Member finds Technical Debt, a couple of things happen: a Cleanup Story is put in the Backlog, and a -spective of some sort must be held to determine if the Definition of Done needs to change in the future

As I discussed in chapter 3.10, Storyotypes are used to help catalog the Definitions of Done for different kinds of Stories, among other things. So as the Team captures and improves the Definitions of Done, the Team (probably via the ScrumMaster) needs to make sure the Storyotypes get updated so that the new information is documented and the new information can be spread amongst Team Members and between Teams.

Summary

When it comes to Technical Debt, the first (and best) choice is not to create it. In order to do this the Team follows the code's Definition of Done, and continuously inspects and adapts the Results to make sure that the Definition of Done continues to improve and remains good enough. However, if Technical Debt is created or found the Team needs to add a Cleanup Story to the Backlog to document it, request it be fixed, and make it visible.

Discussion Questions

1. What is Technical Debt? Where does it come from? How do we find it?

2. Why are Cleanup Stories usually considered Chores? Are there times they wouldn't be Chores?

3. Why do Cleanup Stories remain in the Back Burner?

4. Explain how finding Technical Debt can influence the Definition of Done.

$$\boxed{4.6}$$

Monitoring Sprint Progress

In this chapter I show two ways to measure the progress of a Sprint, the TaskHour BurnDown and the Checklist Item BuildUp. I discuss the pros and cons of each, discuss why I have a strong preference for the Checklist Item BuildUp, and show a work-around that allows it to be simulated with most tools.

Once the Team agrees to Stories for a Sprint, it starts work on them. During the Sprint the Team often wants to know if it is on track – how it's doing on the Stories it agreed to. There are many ways to do this, from simply observing the movement of Stories and Tasks across the Story Board to using complicated metrics.

In this chapter I present two simple metrics to measure and graph in order to help the Team monitor progress in the Sprint. Historically, the most common way to do this is the TaskHour BurnDown chart that is presented in most writings on Scrum.

> Note: the latest version of Scrum ([SG], July 2013) removed this BurnDown (along with the Product/Release BurnDown) from Scrum, but it was part of Scrum until 2010 (see [SS] pg. 5). This means that you will see this BurnDown a *lot* – it will likely be in your tools. I have always hated the BurnDowns because they are predictive and evil, and applaud their removal from Scrum.

In this chapter I show the TaskHour BurnDown and discuss why I think it is a bad idea to use it. Then I introduce what I think is a *much better* chart to use, the Checklist Item BuildUp.

Since these are fairly simple data and graphs to understand, I'll describe and discuss them quickly and give a common example. Since I have a strong preference for the Checklist item BuildUp, I will also describe how tools that produce TaskHour BurnDowns can be 'fooled' into creating a Checklist Item BurnDown that simulates the Checklist Item BuildUp.

The Sprint's TaskHour BurnDown

The most common way Teams measure a Sprint's progress is the TaskHour BurnDown chart. I assume you are familiar with it, and know that it displays *the estimated remaining hours of work for the Sprint*. It is calculated by re-estimating the hours remaining on the Sprint's Tasks every day, adding these estimates together, and charting the result on a day-by-day basis. It is called a BurnDown because the total estimated remaining TaskHours will 'burn down' to zero if all the Tasks get completed. Let me present an example of a typical BurnDown chart for a 2-week Sprint.

Example

The CatAir Team doesn't do a single Planning Day as described in chapter 4.1. It does its Review and Retrospective every other Wednesday afternoon, and its Planning on the following Thursday morning. It then immediately starts work. Its Daily Scrums are just before lunch.

Table 6 shows the progress of the first Sprint, held from 2/6/08 to 2/19/08 (Planning on 2/6, Review and Retro on 2/19). This table shows the Team's estimates on the number of hours remaining on the tasks, as collected at the Daily Scrum.

Table 6: Data for TaskHour BurnDown Graph

Sprint 1: Getting Started — Day (Feb 6 thru Feb 19)

TaskHour BurnDown Data	1	2	5	6	7	8	9	12	13	14
[enviro] Install Copy of CUTLASS in Lab										
Set up clean machine in lab	8	16	12	0						
Install CUTLASS on new machine	8	12	24	0						
*Smoke Test CUTLASS on new machine		6	8	0						
[analysis] Get Smart on CUTLASS Capabilities										
Analyze CUTLASS Documentation	16	20	30	24	0					
Prepare briefing for Team	2	12			12	0				
[backbone] Get List of Flights from CUTLASS										
Architecture and Design	40				44	6	4	0		
Write Functional Tests	16				18	12	0			
Code and Unit Test	96				108	96	60	48	12	0
[enviro] Set Up CatAir Website in Lab										
Set up website on test machine	30							12	6	0
*Test CatAir on test machine (time-box)								8	6	0
[analysis] Find Size of 'Check Status of Flights'										
Investigate 'Check Status of Flights'	18						12	12	8	0
Prepare briefing for Team	6						2			0
Total Estimated Hours Remaining	240	264	284	234	236	168	108	82	34	0

Task added after Planning

The way to read this table is:

- The Stories and Tasks are listed in the first column. The Stories in this table are prefaced by their Storyotypes in square brackets, like '[backbone]' – these Storyotypes were discussed in chapter 3.10.

- The column for Day 1 contains the initial estimates for the tasks, as derived at Sprint Planning. For a task that was added during the Sprint, its initial estimate is on the day it was added – their names are prefaced by an asterisk (*).

- A new estimate (of time remaining) is added at the Daily Scrum if the task was worked on since the previous Daily Scrum – so a 'blank' means the task was not worked on the previous work day.

- The 'Total' row adds up all the current estimates, either as changed or carried along from previously.

- Note that the estimates can go down, remain the same, or even increase. The estimates of time remaining do not depend on the hours actually worked.

Once we have this data, and daily throughout the Sprint, the Team can graph the TaskHour BurnDown Graph. Here is the result.

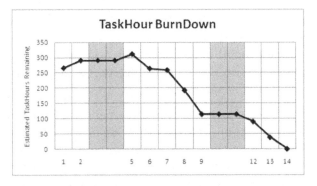

Figure 33: TaskHour BurnDown Graph

There are a few things to notice about this graph:

1. It goes up at the beginning. This often happens with a TaskHour BurnDown. The reasons for this are twofold: some of the tasks are harder than estimated, and there are often tasks that are discovered once the work begins. There are examples of each of these cases in the data presented.

2. Using a Task Hour BurnDown puts the focus on doing Tasks, which is not what the Team actually agreed to. The Team agreed to doing Stories, as defined by their Doneness Agreements.

3. The BurnDown graph indicates if the Team is 'on track' to complete *all* the agreed-to Stories. This is highly predictive, and puts the focus in the wrong place, as the success of the Sprint is defined by the Sprint Goal, not completion of the Stories (see chapters 4.1 and 4.2). In fact, this may put such a pressure on the Team to complete all the Stories that they end up creating Technical Debt (see chapter 3.5).

4. If the graph is available to Stakeholders, it can change their focus from Stories to Tasks, and this is unfortunate – they need to keep their focus on Stories being completed. If the underlying data is also

available to them, such as which Team Members are working on each Task, this allows them to meddle with the Team's self-organization.

So, the fact that this is a BurnDown graph is bad because it's predictive and can cause the creation of Technical Debt, and the fact that it is based on TaskHours is bad because it places the focus on Tasks instead of Stories. Either of these reasons is enough to convince me not to use this graph, so I like to use different data and a different graph for measuring progress within a Sprint, which I now present.

The Sprint's Checklist Item BuildUp

Just like the TaskHour BurnDown, the Checklist Item BuildUp's purpose is to show the Team its progress throughout the Sprint. Unlike the BurnDown, however, the focus is on the Doneness Agreements that were agreed to during Planning. The reason for this is that the Doneness Agreements are what the Team has actually agreed to.

In order to turn this into a graph, we convert the Doneness Agreement for each Story to a checklist; all items on the checklist must be checked off in order for the Story to be completed. So, by combining the Stories' checklists we can get the Sprint's Doneness Checklist. Thus, progress can be measured by simply counting up the number of checked off items, and comparing it to the total number of Checklist Items in the Sprint.

There are three basic ways to show this information: as a BuildUp graph that just shows the count of checked off Items, as a 'percent done' graph, showing what percentage of the total items are checked off, or as a BurnDown graph showing the items counting down from the total. We prefer the BuildUp graph because it is not as predictive as the BurnDown, so I will show it first. Later in the chapter I will show a BurnDown version that we can produce with most tools.

An Example

Table 7 shows the progress of CatAir's first Sprint, held from 2/6/08 to 2/19/08 (Planning on 2/6, Review and Retro on 2/19) – the same Sprint as for the TaskHour BurnDown example. In this table the Doneness Checklist Items are listed beneath the respective Stories, which are given including their Storyotypes (see chapter 3.10). The date that each Checklist Item was completed is given in the right column.

Table 7: Data for Doneness Checklist Item BuildUp Graph

Sprint 1: Getting Started	Date
Doneness Checklist Items	Completed
Story: [enviro] Install Copy of CUTLASS in Lab	
✓ Get CUTLASS Install from SirJeff	2/7
✓ Set up clean machine	2/6
✓ Install CUTLASS	2/10
✓ Do Smoke Test to see if it works	2/10
Story: [analysis] Get Smart on CUTLASS Capabilities	
✓ Get Documentation and other Sources	2/6
✓ Study, Analyze, etc. (includes exploration)	2/11
✓ Reported Results to Team	2/12
Story: [backbone] Get List of Flights from CUTLASS	
✓ Verified Acceptance Test is Working	2/17
✓ User Documentation is Updated	2/19
✓ Reviewed Architectural Decisions with Team	2/13
✓ Passed Design Review	2/14
✓ Passed Review of Functional Test Strategy	2/13
✓ Passed Review of Unit Tests	2/14
✓ Verified working on Development Machine	2/17
✓ Passed Code Review	2/17
✓ Functional Tests Written	2/18
✓ Verified working on Integration Box	2/18
✓ Added Functional Tests to Regression Test Suite	2/19
✓ Technical Documentation is Updated	2/19
Story: [enviro] Set Up CatAir Website in Lab	
✓ Set up website on test machine	2/18
✓ Set up Default Home Page	2/18
✓ Verified website is reached from Dev Machines	2/19
Story: [analysis] Determine Size of 'Check Status of Flights'	
✓ Get Documentation and other Sources	2/7
✓ Study, Analyze, etc. (includes exploration)	2/18
✓ Reported Results to Team	2/19

shows the Checklist Item BuildUp graph for the Sprint.

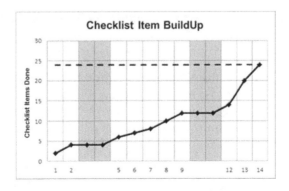

Figure 34: Doneness Checklist Item BuildUp Graph

The dates are given along the bottom, with the cumulative number of completed checklist items shown on the vertical axis. The total number of Checklist Items for the Sprint is given by the line across the top. The presence of this line is predictive, and can be a force for creation of Technical Debt, as discussed before. If it is, remove the line, and the graph will simply show the progress of the Team throughout the Sprint.

There are a few things to notice about this graph:

1. It never dips down; its direction is always upwards. This is because a Checklist Item will not become unchecked during the Sprint... if a Story has had a passing Code Review, there has been a passing Code Review – it can't be undone... just sayin'...

2. Using a Checklist Item BuildUp puts the focus on the Doneness Agreement, which is the right thing to focus on, as this defines Done for the Story.

3. If the Team is using Storyotypes (chapter 3.10), a Story's checklist can be largely determined by looking at the Story's Storyotype. This makes it easier to determine the Checklist Items, and easier for the Stakeholders to understand the BuildUp data and graph.

4. If the graph is available to Stakeholders, it focuses them on the Stories and Doneness, not the Team Members.

5. This graph still has the drawback that it is predictive; it has that line at the top that shows what the Team is climbing towards. However, this line could be removed if it causes the Team to create Technical Debt.

Discussion

The TaskHour BurnDown has been significant topic of conversation within the Scrum community for years. It is one of the things almost every Team I talk to wants to discuss. I created the Checklist Item BuildUp as a response to these discussions, and I'll summarize the reasons here.

1. The TaskHour BurnDown shows information that is about effort, and not product. That is, the focus is on Tasks, and not the Doneness Agreement. This re-enforces the *incorrect* notion that Scrum is about Team Members doing Work, rather than a Team developing Product.

2. The BurnDown chart goes *down* when showing progress – and this is counter-intuitive. Charts showing progress should go *up*. I know that this is a silly reason to object to it, but many people (and Teams) have expressed this concern to me. Many of them try to make their BurnDowns go up – which is hard to do, actually, because you don't

know where the 'top' is. In order to make it go up, in fact, many of them insist that the hourly estimates for tasks can't increase from one day to the next – and this is *terribly wrong*, as it intentionally denies a common reality.

3. The BurnDown chart often has a strange shape, with the chart going up in the beginning, and then going down, as we see in our example. This is irritating and hard to explain to Stakeholders, and often leads to management wanting 'better estimating' from developers, which isn't the point. Developers need to be better developers, *not* better estimators. We need better Results and better Agreements, and shouldn't be focusing on better estimates.

Since I am presenting a new chart, you would expect that it addresses the objections I just listed. It does. Just like the TaskHour BurnDown, the Checklist Item BuildUp's purpose is to show the Team its progress during the Sprint. Unlike the BurnDown, however, the focus is on the Doneness Agreement, and this is what the Team has actually agreed to. Therefore, it more accurately represents something of value to the Stakeholders.

The BurnDown Work-Around

Ok, so I've convinced you to use the Checklist Item BuildUp, but your tool automatically produces a TaskHour BurnDown. Is there a work-around? Or do you have to pop open Excel® to do it? Well, there *is* a work-around, and here it is.

Look at the information in Table 8. As you can see, it has the same basic *shape* as the data for the TaskHour BurnDown, but the Tasks have been replaced by Checklist Items, and the TaskHour estimates have been replaced by checkmarks indicating when the Checklist Item was Done.

Table 8: Data for Checklist Item BurnDown Work-Around Graph

Sprint 1: Getting Started — Day (Feb 6 thru Feb 19)

Checklist Item BurnDown Data	1	2		5	6	7	8	9		12	13	14
[enviro] Install Copy of CUTLASS in Lab												
Get CUTLASS Install from SirJeff		✓										
Set up clean machine	✓											
Install CUTLASS				✓								
Do Smoke Test to see if it works				✓								
[analysis] Get Smart on CUTLASS Capabilities												
Get Documentation and other Sources	✓											
Study, Analyze, etc. (includes exploration)					✓							
Reported Results to Team						✓						
[backbone] Get List of Flights from CUTLASS												
Verified Acceptance Test is Working										✓		
User Documentation is Updated												✓
Reviewed Architectural Decisions with Team							✓					

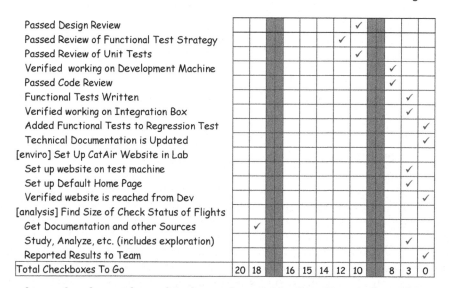

Passed Design Review								✓				
Passed Review of Functional Test Strategy							✓					
Passed Review of Unit Tests							✓					
Verified working on Development Machine										✓		
Passed Code Review										✓		
Functional Tests Written											✓	
Verified working on Integration Box											✓	
Added Functional Tests to Regression Test												✓
Technical Documentation is Updated												✓
[enviro] Set Up CatAir Website in Lab												
Set up website on test machine											✓	
Set up Default Home Page											✓	
Verified website is reached from Dev												✓
[analysis] Find Size of Check Status of Flights												
Get Documentation and other Sources		✓										
Study, Analyze, etc. (includes exploration)											✓	
Reported Results to Team												✓
Total Checkboxes To Go	20	18		16	15	14	12	10		8	3	0

In order to develop and use this data, what some of my Teams do is this:

- Enter the Checklist Items as Tasks within the Story. The actual Tasks are relatively unimportant, as I've mentioned before, and are documented by these Teams only as 'stickies on the wall.'

- For each Checklist Item (Task), give it an initial hourly estimate of 1 hour.

- When the Checklist Item is completed, change the hourly estimate to 0 hours, indicating that the Checklist Item (Task) is completed.

- Then the TaskHour BurnDown that is automatically produced by your tool is actually a Checklist Item BurnDown that has the right information and is something that the Stakeholders can understand.

Figure 35 is an example of what this Checklist Item BurnDown looks like.

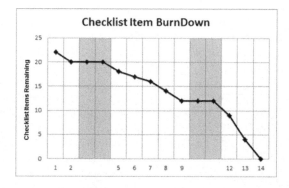

Figure 35: Checklist Item BurnDown Work-Around Graph

Note that it is predictive and burns *down*, and not *up*, but at least it's the right information. ;-)

Summary

The TaskHour BurnDown and Checklist Item BuildUp charts have the same purpose: to show how the Team is doing throughout the Sprint – to answer the Team's questions *'How much will we finish?'* and *'How are we doing?'* However, they do it by focusing on two completely different things:

- The TaskHour BurnDown focuses on the *effort* the Team is expending. It uses the Team's estimates of how much effort is remaining on their tasks to indicate if the total remaining effort is trending to zero.

- The Checklist Item BuildUp focuses on the Doneness Agreement for the Stories the Team has agreed to. It counts how many items have been checked off and indicates the daily progress of the Team.

Either of these charts does the job of determining how the Team is doing. However, only one of them actually focuses on what the Team has agreed to do and what provides value. I believe that the Checklist Item BuildUp (or BurnDown) has two good qualities:

- It measures what is important – the Product, and

- It is easy to calculate and explain.

Discussion Questions

1. Why do some people want to use the BurnDown graph?

2. Why is the TaskHour BurnDown a 'bad' thing to use?

3. How does the BurnUp graph work?

4. Do you think the BurnDown Work-Around could work for you?

Kanban(ish) Variant

There is another agile method, called Kanban, which is becoming popular for software development. In this chapter I describe its main strength, and how it can be integrated into a Kanban(ish) Variant of Scrum.

As much as I love Scrum, even I would have to admit that the basic Scrum Practices are not perfect. Nor are they intended to be. As I explained in chapter 1.1, the basic, out-of-the-box, Scrum Practices are merely 'training wheels' that allow Teams to develop their 'scrummish' personalities – their mental agility – while successfully developing Product.

One of the more commonly noted deficiencies in basic Scrum is that it plans its work a whole Sprint at a time – planning in batches. There are a couple of reasons this is a problem:

- This batch planning process may not be agile enough to cope with the actual rate of change of requirements.

- This batch process may not be appropriate for maintenance Teams or others that basically have a constant flow of (non-related) Stories being added to the Backlog.

In fact, chapter 4.4 on PlaceHolder Stories, the discussion of the mid-Sprint re-planning in chapter 4.8, and the discussion of renegotiating the scope of a Sprint in chapter 4.3 are all about resolving problems like these.

There is another agile process, called Kanban, which solves this problem and is becoming popular for software development projects and Teams. In this chapter I will describe Kanban, what I like about it, and how to bring the most useful parts of Kanban into Scrum.

Brief Description of Kanban

The 'Kanban for software' movement is led by David Anderson[1], and is gaining traction in the agile community. The main idea of Kanban that I like (and is separate from agility) is very simple and based on fundamental Lean principles: make sure the Team doesn't agree to *do* work until it is actually ready to *start* the work (see appendix A.5 for a discussion of Lean).

---

[1] http://www.agilemanagement.net.

In other words, eliminate the future planned-out work that causes problems for some Scrum Teams by planning just in time; only agreeing to do *new* Stories when the Team becomes available to work on them by *finishing* old Stories.

This leads to the notion of Work in Progress (WIP), which is a collection of Stories that are actually being worked on all at the same time. This WIP is a replacement for the Sprint Backlog, which is a collection of work that has been agreed to being worked on during the Sprint. Because the Team can only work on a few Stories at a time, this means that some of the Stories in the Sprint Backlog will not be started until later in the Sprint.

These Stories that are in the Sprint Backlog, but not yet started, are *waste* in the Lean sense – and can provide a drag on the Team. As I discussed in chapter 4.3, there are times when the Product Owner wants to modify the Sprint's content, and these Stories are in the way of doing that. In order to eliminate this problem, and make the Sprint more malleable and able to adapt to changing realities, a Team can replace the Sprint Backlog with a WIP list.

The primary variable in Kanban is the WIP Length, which is an upper bound on the number of Stories that are allowed to be worked on at the same time. Typically, the WIP Length is a small number like four or five, and the number of Coding Stories that are worked on at any given time is usually slightly less than the total number of coders (not developers) that are on the Team.

What does replacing the Sprint Backlog with the WIP do for a Scrum Team? Well, here's a short list of benefits:

- There is no prediction about what the Team will be doing later in the Sprint. The Team is actively working on *all* of the Stories it has agreed to do so far. This makes the Team more agile by reducing whatever predictive thinking may be present in the Scrum Team;

- If the Stories that are being worked on are small, there is little or no need to renegotiate what is being worked on when something comes up. This is because if the Stories are small some part of the Team will be finishing their current Story soon, and will be available to take on additional work as part of the normal WIP selection; and

- By its very nature, this process causes Team Swarming behavior, because of its focus on the 'single item flow' concept of Lean (see appendix A.5). That is, the subset of the Team that just finished its Story is now free to jump on the next Story that is elevated to the WIP. Also, the system lends itself to having a single coder on each TeamLet Swarming on a Coding Story, and having one floating Coder to help out.

Now, Kanban can be made much more complex than I stated here. It is not my intention to adequately, or accurately, define Kanban in all its glory. It is my intention merely to capture the essence of what I think makes Kanban good, and figure out a way to integrate it into Scrum. Take a look at chapter 2.6 for more information and guidance about how Swarming in a Kanban(ish) version of Scrum might look. If you want a very thorough discussion of integration of Kanban and Scrum, read Corey Ladas' book on ScrumBan.[2]

Integrating WIP into Scrum

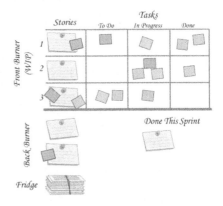

Figure 36: WIP as Front Burner

Well, now I've told you what the basic idea is, I better tell you what actually happens when integrating the WIP concept into Scrum.

First of all, we simply replace the Sprint Backlog with Work in Progress. In terms of the Story board, the Sprint Backlog is replaced with a fixed length Work in Progress, as shown in Figure 36, where the WIP length is three.

This picture makes it seem like a relatively simple thing to do, but it isn't really. It raises a lot of questions about process and practices, so I'll just make a list of the major issues/changes here (in no particular order):

1. Clearly, Sprint Planning changes. The Sprint Planning session at the beginning of a Sprint is used merely to establish the Sprint Goal, and the selection of Stories to work on is continuous, using on-the-spot Planning sessions that take place whenever a Story in the WIP is completed. When a Story is completed, the Product Owner and the Team reprioritize the Backlog and select the next Story to be done, finalize the negotiation about the Doneness Agreement, and then simply elevate the Story to the WIP and commence work on it. This may also cause the Team to reorganize the people across the Stories in the WIP.

2. The Back Burner must have Stories that are ready to go whenever the WIP has room to move a new Story up. This means there must be continuous Backlog Refinement, and probably requires the use of Analysis Stories (which must be selected into the WIP just like any other Story), just as before. However, the Back Burner can be

---

[2] Corey Ladas, ScrumBan and other Essays on Kanban Systems for Lean Software Development, Modus Cooperandi Press, 2008.

shorter than when the Team needed to have a full Sprint's worth of Stories to plan with. This is a good thing, as it follows the Lean principle of minimizing waste by having fewer Ready Stories in the Backlog at any given time.

3. Renegotiations during a Sprint are different, in practice if not in theory. Since there is less pressure to finish what was planned for it is easier to stop working on a Story that is in progress in order to go work on an emergency one. Not only that, if the Product Owner can wait a day or two for the new Story to start, then it can just be moved into the WIP as a matter of course.

4. Since the Team is not trying to accomplish a particular number of Stories within the Sprint, there is no need for Sprint BurnDown or BuildUp graphs. However, since the Team will still be Reviewing and Reporting on a Sprint-by-Sprint basis (see the next section), the Team still needs to keep track of which Stories have been finished in the current Sprint – and will be able to calculate a Velocity.

5. There needs to be a *robust* Definition of Done in the Agreements. It is tempting to relax the Definition of Done because there is no apparent time pressure within the Sprint. Don't let the Team do this! It can lead to gold-plating Stories (or scope creep inside the Story), which will steal time from the future, which will make it harder to be successfully agile in the long run.

6. Finally, it is easier for the Team to have a rule to manage Chores, such as the '70/30 Rule.' All the Team has to do is make sure that one third (or some appropriate percentage) of the Stories that are elevated to the WIP are Chores, and it's taken care of. Even easier, if the WIP Length is three (or whatever is appropriate), the Team just needs to make sure that one of the slots in the WIP is reserved for Chores.

This list may not be exhaustive, but it should give you a good idea of the changes you have to make to accommodate integrating the WIP into Scrum, and having the WIP, rather than the Sprint Backlog, be the contents of the Front Burner.

The Sprint Is Still There

It is important to remember that this is still Scrum – the Sprint is still there. However, its purposes have slightly changed, as the Team no longer plans the whole Sprint at one time – it is planned continuously by managing the Work in Progress.

So, what is Sprint for? Why is it still Important?

Good questions, with good answers, as follows:

1. The Sprint still defines the major Review Cycle. The Team still reviews the Results of the Sprint with the Stakeholders on a consistent cycle. As usual, there is no partial credit in Scrum, so only the Stories that were completed in the Sprint get reviewed. The Stories that are still in the WIP at the end of the Sprint are not reviewed. As usual, this consistent drumbeat of Product Reviews is comforting to our Stakeholders, and also allows the Team to produce the Sprint-based metrics (like Velocity) the Stakeholders are used to.

2. The Team still does Retrospectives at the end of every Sprint in order to improve its Practices.

3. The Release Strategy is still modified at the Sprint boundaries, based on the Product Review and Stakeholder needs.

4. Each Sprint still has a Planning session to choose a Sprint Goal, and it is used as guidance when the WIP is updated.

Basically, all that has changed by adding the WIP to Scrum is to change the 'choosing Stories to work on' portion of Sprint Planning from a batch process to a continuous one – thus becoming Leaner. The Team still does its self-organization to meet the Doneness Agreements they have agreed to – which is the crux of Scrum – and virtually everything else is the same as usual.

Discussion

It is very tempting to want to do this Kanban(ish) version of Scrum; at first appearance it is quite appealing. However, it is actually harder to do correctly than normal, basic Scrum, and should only be attempted once the Team is mature and it is clear that the benefits outweigh the risks.

It is beneficial to replace the Sprint Backlog with WIP when there is a need for constant re-planning within a Sprint. Managing the Work in Progress replaces the re-planning with constant planning and avoids unnecessary planning that later turns out to be wrong.

However, when using this variant it is tempting for many Teams to relax the commitment to using the Doneness Agreements to manage scope creep and Technical Debt inside Stories. This is because many people see Kanban as saying *'just do the Story until it's done'* rather than *'do it as quickly as you can, while satisfying the Doneness Agreement.'*

For basically the same reason, it is also tempting to commit to larger and larger Stories rather than break them into small bits. This *'just do it until it's done'* attitude can lead to never-ending Stories with significant scope creep inside them – look out for this!

However, if the Team can stick to the discipline of using the Doneness Agreements, then go ahead and let them try it. Since there are only a few Stories in the WIP, Kanban automatically leads to Swarming – where the Team (or sub-Team or TeamLet) works together on a Story until it is Done.

Unfortunately, it sometimes leads to stove-piping – the subdividing of the Team into permanent sub-Teams that work together. This is because when one sub-Team finishes a Story in the WIP, it is tempting to just assign the next Story to that sub-Team as the Story moves up into the WIP.

So, try to get the Swarming to evolve so that most of the Team is Swarming across all of the Stories. That is, when a new Story is moved up to the WIP, assign one person to work on that Story full-time as its Coordinator, and all the Swarmers on the Team start Swarming on the new Story as well. So, each Story in the WIP has a Coordinator, and the rest of the Team Members are Swarmers (see chapter 2.6). The TeamLets should be constantly changing; we don't want permanent sub-Teams.

In short, I think that this Kanban(ish) variant of Scrum is a good and natural thing to do when a Team matures, if the Team is encountering issues that result in constant re-planning and renegotiating. It is a good tool for a ScrumMaster to have in his or her back pocket to use for those occasions.

Discussion Questions

1. Why do some people think batch planning is a problem for Scrum?

2. Explain the basic idea of replacing the Sprint Backlog with a kanban WIP. What are the advantages and disadvantages of doing this on a Scrum Team?

3. How does a Scrum Team's planning process change when it becomes kanban(ish)?

4. Why do I recommend that becoming kanban(ish) is only for a mature Scrum Teams?

4.8

The Daily Scrum

The Daily Scrum is one of the most important parts of Scrum, as it allows for a daily inspect and adapt cycle. However, many people misunderstand the Daily Scrum, and treat it as a simple status update. In this chapter I will convince you it is much more than that.

Ahh, the Daily Scrum... Everybody who knows anything about Scrum knows the three questions:

1. What have you done since the last Daily Scrum?

2. What are you going to do until the next Daily Scrum? and

3. What impediments are standing in your way?

Well, the Daily Scrum is an absolutely necessary part of Scrum, but it's not really about the three questions. In fact, the three questions aren't even the most important part of the Daily Scrum, which is a formal inspect and adapt point in Scrum. As it says in [SG, pg. 10], the purpose of the Daily Scrum is "to synchronize activities and create a plan for the next 24 hours."

Like all inspect and adapt points, it has two parts: collecting information (inspecting), and doing something with the information (adapting). The three questions are only about collecting information; what the Team does with the information is what's *really* important.

In fact, I think that there's an important question missing. I like to ask a more open-ended question that gets us even more information that the Team adapts to. And that question is:

4. Is there anything else we need to talk about?

So let me tell you a little bit more about the Daily Scrum.

The Result Is Other Discussions

First of all, the Daily Scrum is about adapting to daily realities. This adapting usually involves scheduling other discussions either directly after the Daily Scrum or later in the day. One of the most important of these discussions is an immediate re-planning session based on who showed up to work, what SMEs are actually available to the Team, Technical Debt that was found yesterday, the work 'getting harder,' personal obligations Team Members have, and so on.

Because immediate re-planning is based on the current reality, the Daily Scrum should be held in the morning, because if it's not the Team might have to have another re-planning session tomorrow morning anyway, in order to react to tomorrow's realities of Team Member availability. People have different work hours, so this could be difficult. However, it is reasonable to have core hours for the Team (e.g., 10:00am to 2:00pm), and hold the Daily Scrum at 10:30am, for example. *Note: don't use the Daily Scrum as a way to force people to show up for work earlier than they want to. That violates the Team Values, and is just plain bad manners. On the other hand, the Team Members should be able to learn to live with core hours. Just sayin'...*

In any case, the Daily Scrum's primary purpose is to gather information and figure out what to do about it. It is important that the whole Team is there, including the Product Owner and the ScrumMaster (in their Team Member roles). Usually, if something needs to be done with the information that is gathered, the solution is to have another discussion – either immediately after the Daily Scrum or later in the day. A very common way of doing this is that the ScrumMaster (or Product Owner) keeps a list of sidebar discussions that will be had later, and then schedules them at the end of the Daily Scrum. Of course, some of these sidebars are held immediately, as if they were a continuation of the Daily Scrum.

The reason these discussions are not an *official* part of the Daily Scrum itself is because only the people that *need* to be involved in the discussions should attend them – one of the worst things that can be done to somebody is *trap* them in somebody else's discussion, so I want the Team Members who are not needed for additional discussions to leave and do some *real* work.

The Main purpose of the Daily Scrum is to determine if these other discussions need to happen; and if they do, to schedule and figure out who's going to be there. There are a number of types of discussions that we can have:

Re-Plan Existing Work. The most important kind of discussion (the one I just discussed above), and one that often directly follows the Daily Scrum, is a tactical re-planning session. This is the discussion where the tactical agility takes place; this is where the Team really exercises its self-organization and self-management.

The Team is Swarming (see chapter 2.6), and there's often re-planning to do on the Stories that are currently being worked on. The Team needs to know which Coordinators (or stay-at-homes) need help from the Swarmers and which Swarmers are available to help, and the Team Members need to know what they're going to do today. There's really no magic to this, it's just simply a discussion amongst the Team Members about who's going to do what today, who needs help, who's available, and so on.

When this discussion is over, all the Team Members walk away knowing what they're going to do today or, at least, what they're going to be doing *right now*. That's it, that's all, that's enough.

Impediment Removal. The second most common type of discussion that the Team may have after the Daily Scrum is an Impediment Removal session. In this discussion the ScrumMaster works with the Team Members who have impediments in order to help them figure out how to remove, or bypass, them.

In order to do this the impediment must be thoroughly discussed to determine what's really going on, why it is an impediment, what the Team wants done about it, and so on. The goal is to figure out what the Team's plan of attack is, and then have the Team go and execute this plan.

Often, the Product Owner will be involved in this discussion for one of two reasons: either the Product Owner will help remove the impediment; or the Product Owner will negotiate with the Team Members about the balance between effort spent on the impediment, effort spent on the Story that's being impeded, and the possibility that other Stories won't get Done. This could easily turn into a Scope Negotiation Discussion (discussed below) if the Story's Agreements need to be modified.

Intraspective. The ScrumMaster may have noticed or heard something that requires an Intraspective. Remember that the purpose of an Intraspective is to discuss a particular issue, activity, or event in order to figure out if changes in the Team's practices are needed (see chapter 2.3). Having an Intraspective is often an appropriate thing to do after hearing issues raised at the Daily Scrum.

Product-Focused Discussions. Of course, since the Team is Swarming on the Stories, the TeamLets that are Swarming will need to have discussions about their Stories. For example, they will need architecture discussions, design discussions, interface discussions, test design discussions, and so on. At the Daily Scrum they should tell the rest of the Team that they're having these discussions.

It is generally considered good team behavior to allow anybody on the Team to attend a discussion, as this is a good way to foster knowledge, get input from other smart people, and so on. Of course, these discussions don't necessarily take place right after the Daily Scrum; they can occur at any time during the day.

Scope Negotiation Session. As we saw in chapter 4.3, it is occasionally necessary to negotiate a change in scope with the Product Owner during the

Sprint. This can happen either because the Team isn't going to finish all it agreed to, or because the Product Owner needs to add or change scope. During the Daily Scrum, either the Product Owner or an affected Team Member should bring up the fact that a change in scope is necessary, and the ScrumMaster and the Team should figure out when to have a discussion about this.

This session may not need to be had immediately, or even right away. It all depends on how urgent the scope change is, how much time is left in the Sprint, how many Stories are not started yet, and so on. Of course, if the scope change causes a modification to the Sprint Goal, the follow-on discussions will have to include Stakeholders, as well.

Other Questions

Okay, so now you know why the Team has a Daily Scrum: in order to figure out what other discussions the Team must have during the day in order to get its work done. So let's go back to discussing the questions themselves.

I stated that there are three (or four) questions that I like to ask:

1. What have you done since the last Daily Scrum?

2. What are you going to do until the next Daily Scrum?

3. What impediments are standing in your way? and

4. Is there anything else we need to talk about?

Are these the only questions to ask? Are these even the best questions to ask? I don't know, that's really up to you and your Team. However, these are certainly a good set of questions to start with.

The Team could certainly add some questions about status, especially if they are calculating BurnDown/BuildUp Graphs or doing some other sort of daily metrics (see chapter 4.6). If the Team is asking questions like *'how many hours do you need on the task?'* or *'how many Checklist Items have you done?'* I think it's a *good* idea to do them during the Daily Scrum as it insures that everybody on the Team has at least *heard* the answers.

I must admit that I hate questions like: *'are we going to finish on time?'* because these questions invariably put pressure on the Team and create a force for Technical Debt. If you are a ScrumMaster and people are insisting that you use questions like these, I would push back. The Team is already doing the best it can (remember the value of Respect...), and these questions can only hurt. However, there are people that can't help themselves when it comes to questions like these; these people are focused much more on the Team's plan than they are on the quality of the product. All the ScrumMaster can do is discuss the issue with them and try to come to an accommodation that won't hurt either the Team or the Product.

Focus on the Story

Thus far, the questions we have been talking about have been focused on what an individual Team Member is doing. Another thing to do is change the focus entirely, and focus on the Stories themselves, rather than the people. For example, instead of asking the question *'What have you done since the last Daily Scrum?'* the Team might ask the question *'What has happened to the Story since the last Daily Scrum?'* This would be common when the Team is using the Team Swarm pattern, for example (see chapter 2.6).

This completely changes the focus of the Daily Scrum – and I think it's mostly in a good way. Now, rather than focusing on **People doing Work** the Daily Scrum is focused more on the **Team building Product**. Questions like these lead to the same need for additional discussions, but they get there in a different way. For large, or distributed, Teams, these questions also get there in a more effective, efficient manner – by focusing on things at the appropriate level of detail.

Of course, if the Team is asking questions like these, then it could turn out that the only people that are talking are the Stories' Coordinators, which has its good points and its bad points. On the good side the discussion is much more focused, and on the bad side there are people that don't speak – it's a tradeoff.

I think that there can be a balance. What I suggest is if you want to try this Story-based focus that your Daily Scrum has *each* person talk, with the Coordinators answering the questions:

1. What happened to the Story since the last Daily Scrum?

2. What will happen to the Story until the next Daily Scrum?

3. What is impeding the Story's progress?

and everyone else on the Team answering the question

4. Is there anything else we need to talk about?

In this way the Daily Scrum is more focused, but everyone gets to say what they need to say.

Who Attends, Who Talks?

The most common questions about the Daily Scrum, since the beginning of Scrum, have been: *'who gets to attend?'* and *'who gets to talk?'* I'd like to discuss these issues fairly quickly. At a conceptual level it's actually pretty easy: any Stakeholder can attend, but only the Team Members get to talk.

But that's not enough for most people, so let me be a little more specific, and discuss it in terms of the six roles that are involved in a Scrum Team:

- The ScrumMaster facilitates this discussion and, as a Team Member, answers questions just like everybody else. The ScrumMaster may have the additional responsibility of helping facilitate the scheduling of the additional discussions that will take place – but that could be done by the Product Owner or other designated Team Member.

- The Product Owner attends the Daily Scrum and, as a Team Member, answers questions just like everybody else. The Product Owner is not allowed to act as the Product Owner during the Daily Scrum, except to remark that re-planning or renegotiation discussions are necessary.

- All other Team Members answer the appropriate questions.

- The Business Owner and other Stakeholders may attend, but they may not speak.

- The Subject Matter Experts that are working with the Team may attend, and may speak as if they were Team Members (after all, they are Sprint Team Members...). However, it is not required that they do so, since every SME should be represented by a Team Member (the Buddy) who is accountable for the SME's work for the Team (see chapter 2.5).

That just about covers it, it's actually pretty simple.

Summary

The Daily Scrum is an integral part of Scrum, and has proven itself so useful that many other processes have adopted it. It is important to realize that it is not a status meeting; it is a conversation that discovers today's realities, and schedules appropriate additional discussions to deal with them.

Discussion Questions

1. The 'three questions' of Daily Scrum are used to collect information about the work the Team is doing. What does the Team do with that information?

2. Do the ScrumMaster and Product Owner attend the Daily Scrum? Why or why not?

3. Why would the Team need to re-plan existing work? How does the Daily Scrum fit in with this re-planning?

4. Impediments often come up at the Daily Scrum? What does the Team do about them?

4.9

Other Sprint Issues

This chapter contains discussions of some Sprint Issues that weren't quite long enough (or important enough) to be their own chapters, and didn't really fit anywhere else.

Startup Sprint

Agile development is all about delivering valuable Results early and often, in order to receive and incorporate feedback as soon as possible. Many of the Organizations I coach are *convinced* that it will take *months* before they can write any code that produces value. Is this a reasonable fear? How do we get past this fear? How do we get a Team writing code and delivering value as quickly as possible? And how quick can that be?

Let me describe the *Startup Sprint* pattern, which many coaches have used (and are using) successfully to get a Team up and running quickly.

The idea is simple: Take an initial Sprint (called the Startup Sprint) that has the following goal: 'Be up and running the first day of the next Sprint' and the following three Backlog Items:

1. 'Place some quality items on the Backlog';

2. 'Create a minimal environment dedicated to the writing of Clean Code'; and

3. 'Write a piece of real code, no matter how small'.

And, of course, make the Startup Sprint as short as possible. In my experience, this Sprint can be as short as one week, which is what I recommend. I think one week is good because it applies pressure on the Team to achieve the three Items listed above quickly and efficiently – I don't want the Team to do any gold-plating or unnecessary work in order to get to that first real code. Of course, there is continued work on environment and the Product Backlog in future Sprints, so we don't delude ourselves that we're finished in this Startup Sprint. In fact, we don't even delude ourselves that we've achieved the 80% solution, or even the 50% solution. We're just getting started... That's the point of the Startup Sprint. Get started, but do *real* stuff as you start and ramp up.

So what does the Team actually do in the Startup Sprint? Well, it works on the initial Sprint Backlog (Stories) shown above. Since the Team has this

Backlog, the conversations that we call Backlog Refinement and Sprint Planning can begin. Firstly, we elaborate upon each of these three Stories to add their Agreements, Tasks, and so on. This conversation is what is really important, and here's the way it might go...

The first Story requires the Team to do some up-front thinking in order to figure out what we're actually trying to build. The Acceptance Criteria (along with some notes on how to accomplish them) for this Story could be something like this:

- ❑ 'Add at least 10 good Items to the Product Backlog that have been validated by our Stakeholders' – Note: I suggest holding a one-day session with them to figure out what these Stories are – and Epics are ok for now...

- ❑ 'For at least one of these Items, make sure it is small enough and well enough defined that it is a 'small' Story – that the Team can develop it in one day once our minimal environment is in place' – *Note: it will probably take the whole Team to do this. In other words, split off at least one good Story from one of the Epics...*

The second Story is a little more straightforward and centers on how much environment is enough. The Acceptance Criteria might look something like:

- ❑ 'Configure everybody's machines'

- ❑ 'Set up a build box'

- ❑ 'Get the database server set up'

- ❑ 'Get the Team Room set up'

- ❑ And so on...

This Story could turn into an Epic, with each of these Acceptance Criteria becoming its own Story. That's ok, the idea is that the Team gets a minimal, though effective, environment as soon as possible.

Finally, the third Story is really simple. The idea is that when we have a 'real' Story to work on *and* a good enough environment, we will use that environment to do the Story and have some actual Code to Review.

So what does the Startup Sprint actually look like? Well, it's a week long. The Team spends half a day Planning and half a day with the Review and Retrospective at the end. This leaves four days for actual work. In two roughly parallel tracks (some Team Members may be Swarming across the tracks), the Team spends two days setting up the environments, and two days getting the Product Backlog together. Then, the Team (along with the Product Owner) will choose the Story to actually implement. Then it will get it Done. This takes a day or so, leaving the Team almost a day of float. It seems like a workable plan to me...

Anyway, I hope that this discussion of the Startup Sprint pattern helps you think about how to start a project quickly, and not let the beginning drag on forever.

Release Sprint

Imagine you are the Team's Product Owner at the Product Review and the Sales Manager says, *'That looks good! I can sell the heck out of that. Give it to me NOW! Ship that puppy!'* Now what? Are you going to say: *'I'm sorry, ma'am, we're not planning to deliver this System for 10 more weeks...'*? Of course not! You're in the value-delivering business, so you've got to figure out what you need to do to get the system shipped.

This could be a tough situation. What do you (the Product Owner) do? We have a Done Increment consisting of Clean Code (like we do at the end of every Sprint), and our Stakeholders think it's *feature complete* and want to get it released and out the door.

This thing is Done, we need to ship it, so we just put a 'Ship It' Story in the next Sprint, right? Or maybe we step outside the Scrum Framework and ship it before the next Sprint. I don't know... Let's think about this for a second. Let's have a discussion with the Sales Manager...

Well, what does the Sales Manager mean when she says *'Ship that puppy!'* anyway? Well, here is a list of things she might be expecting to see once the system is shipped:

- The product is available to users – it's moved from the Development Environment to the Production Environment. It provides value, doesn't break or blow up in users' faces, meets performance requirements, and so on. It has accurate documentation, and the Help Desk is prepared to answer questions about the new version.

- Marketing has new materials and the marketing plan is implemented, including advertisements, YouTube videos, Google key words, and so on.

- Sales is able to sell the new version. The Sales System is updated to manage the sales, new sales forms exist, the website's sales pages are updated, etc.

So, the 'Ship It' Story in the next Sprint might not be so simple, maybe it's an Epic, maybe it's even bigger than that. So, in order to get this thing shipped in the next Sprint, we decide that the Goal of the next Sprint will be: 'We *will* get this puppy in the hands of users this Sprint!' A Sprint with the goal of releasing product is called a Release Sprint[1]. A Release Sprint is different from other Sprints in a couple of ways:

1. The System is already believed to be *feature complete*, so there is no additional functionality that we *know* we need.

2. Anything we *discover* during the Sprint that is *necessary* for Release must also be *done* within the Sprint. This could be risky, as we don't really *know* what we'll find.

3. Since we'll be Releasing during the Sprint, there will be no Product Review before we release it. This means that the work done in the Sprint *should* be low risk and have frequent reviews (from SMEs) during the Sprint.

I can hear you saying: *'Ok, that makes sense, so what? Now what?'*

Well, now it's time to think about what might be done in this Sprint. What should be on the Sprint Backlog?

To understand what needs to be done, we need to understand the notion of Done for a Release – which is much different from the Definition of Done for a Story or Sprint. For a Story or Sprint, Doneness means the Team has done its due diligence: everything has met its Acceptance Criteria and Definition of Done, and the Definition of Done has assured that we have high quality Results – that we have Clean Code.

So, what does Done for a Release mean? Well, actually releasing something is not a Scrum ceremony; actually releasing something is done with Stories within a Sprint. Consequently, the definition of Done for a Release might not be clear, and you (the Product Owner) need to negotiate it with your Stakeholders.

Since you have been talking to the Sales Manager, you are not surprised by the expectations (listed above) that the Sales Manager has, but there are probably things on this list that your Team hasn't Done already.

So, anyway, where are you? What does your Team have left to do?

We know that the Team produced a reviewable Product Increment that was Done, it was reviewed, and the Sales Manager likes it – it is both *feature complete* and believed to be *code complete* based on that Review. However, it is unlikely that the Help Desk is prepared to support it, that Marketing has materials that reflect the latest and greatest features, or that Sales can manage the new Product – so it is not *actually* Releasable (fit for use) as it stands – it doesn't meet the Sales Manager's expectations. The difference

---

[1] For example, Mike Cohn's 2007 blog, http://www.mountaingoatsoftware.com/blog/correct-use-of-a-release-sprint.

between being Done (meeting the Definition of Done) and being actually Releasable is often called Undone Work – work that was not done, but maybe should have been.

Don't get me wrong. There are some Teams, in some Domains, that produce actually Releasable Products continuously; all they need to do is push the 'Ship It' button, and it's on its way. However, I don't *expect* this behavior from all Teams. In fact, I don't *want* it from most Teams. The essence of Product Ownership (at all levels) is to maximize ROI from Sprint to Sprint, and keeping *all* the Documentation current, or keeping the Help Desk, Marketing, and Sales continuously up to speed (on the off chance the Stakeholders will want to ship it) seems like a waste of time and effort to me – unless the Team is shipping every (or nearly) Sprint, of course.

So, what sorts of things might be in the Release Sprint's Backlog? What sort of Undone Work is there? Let's look at the Sales Manager's expectations and make a list:

- Exploratory testing to find what things need to be Done – what holes need to be plugged – in order to assure that the system doesn't blow up, the edge cases are handled, and there isn't something else going on we don't want it to do.

- Performance testing (this may need to be done in a test lab the Team doesn't control) to find defects and holes to be plugged.

- Interoperability testing (this may need to be done in a test lab the Team doesn't control) to find defects and holes to be plugged.

- Plug those holes and fix those defects.

- Finish User Documentation.

- Finish Maintenance Documentation.

- Finish Training Materials.

- Support Marketing and Sales as they finish their documentation and materials.

- Train the Help Desk to support the new system, and finish any documentation they may need.

- Move the System from Development to Production.

- Other stuff - it's up to the Team...

And, of course, there are *no* additional features that we plan to add – that we know about that need to be there – we believe it is *actually* feature complete.

Now, this stuff is potentially a lot of work, and if we want it to be completed in a single Sprint it is likely that the Team shouldn't wait until the last minute to *start* this work. The Release Sprint is when the Team does the *last bit* of this work before the Release. And since it all has to be Done, and reviewed, before the Sprint's actual Review, this Release Sprint may need to be more kanban(ish) than usual. This is true because the Team may need to grope their way through the Sprint as it tries to figure out what holes they need to fill as they get this Product (which is already feature complete) released and out the door.

I'm pretty sure that the totality of this stuff is more than one Sprint's worth of work for most Teams, so they will actually have to be closer to *releasable* – at all times – than they really want to be. This gives them that ability to be *only* one Sprint away from Release when the Business says *'Go!'*

In other words, in order to be (predictably) able to release the Product one Sprint after the Business has said it's good enough, the Team needs to practice Releasing – doing release activities – early on. This allows them to understand how much of each of these Release Activities it can defer to the Release Sprint, and how close to *actually* releasable they need to be at all times. Clearly, this practicing will take a whole Sprint, and most Organizations and Teams don't want to *waste* a non-Release Sprint practicing Releasing. This is a reasonable decision to make, because the ROI of spending a Sprint to practice Releasing may be seen to be less than the ROI of using that Sprint to add new features to the Product.

It may be a tough call for a Product Owner (and the Business) to make, but I still believe that you should practice Releasing at least once in order to reduce surprises and create reasonable expectations. It has been my experience that Teams that think they are only one Sprint away from Release are often actually three to six Sprints away, and the only way to know the truth is to do it and see. I think it is part of the Product Owner's due diligence to have the Team do the practice it needs to do in order to become predictable at going from *feature complete* to *released and out the door* in a single Release Sprint.

Sprint Length

Here are a couple more questions I get quite often: 'How long should my Team's Sprint be?' and 'Does the Sprint have to be a fixed-length?' I find that it's not enough to just say: 'Don't think too hard about it. If you're using a reasonable environment and language like Java or dot-net, use a Sprint Length of two weeks. That seems to work for most Teams, but some are using one week or three weeks. Just see what works for you.' Maybe they don't trust me enough. ;-)

First of all, let's look at the fixed-length part. There are two aspects of this: that the length of the Sprint shouldn't be changed after the Sprint starts, and that all Sprints should be the same length. I think the first part is straight-forward; it would be *cheating* to change the Sprint's length after it starts. If it was known that a Team would condone changing the Sprint length, there would be a temptation to change a Story's Doneness Agreement to allow for some internal scope creep. For reasons I have discussed before, this is a bad thing – the correct thing to do is add another Story to the Backlog.

As for all Sprints being the same length – that's a little trickier. I've already advised that a Startup Sprint could be only a week long, so clearly I'm not totally adamant that *all* Sprints should be the same length. However, since a Sprint can be viewed as a feedback loop, the Team needs to take the Stake-holders into account. Having a fixed Sprint length gives the Stakeholders a constant 'pulse beat' of the Product Reviews, which is comforting and breeds familiarity. However, having different Sprint lengths for specialized Sprints, to accommodate the Holiday Season, or for some other reason the Team and Stakeholders can agree on, doesn't seem to be a terribly bad thing to me.

So that covers the 'fixed length' issue. So I'd now like to discuss the issue of how long a 'typical' Sprint should be. This is a good question, and Sprint length is determined by looking at two factors that need to be balanced:

1. A Sprint must be *long* enough to actually complete Stories. That is, the Team needs to be able to get Stories Done. My guidance to Teams is that the Sprint length should be approximately three times as long as it takes to Swarm on an *average* medium-size Story and get it Done. For some reason, this seems to give enough 'squishiness' in the system to allow the Team to self-organize to get work Done. My experience is that a Story takes about 2-3 *calendar* days for a typical Team that is Swarming, so a reasonable Sprint length is two weeks. However, environments are different – some are easier (or harder) to work in than others – and I expect a Team's Sprint lengths to vary widely based on differences in the environment.

2. The Sprint length should be *short* enough so that the requirements churn is slower than the Sprint length can accommodate. That is, if the Sprint length is two weeks, then the Team is hoping that the changes in requirements happen slower than every two weeks – that Stakeholders can wait until the end of the Sprint to see their 'new stuff' Done. This is often untrue, and is a reason for the Team to shorten the Sprint length, shorten the planning cycle, or even move to the Kanban(ish) variant described in chapter 4.7.

I have seen Sprint lengths vary from one day to one month, and it's a rule of Scrum [SS, pg. 11] that it should *never* be longer than one month. Having both of these factors concerning Sprint length actually 'match up' is difficult for many Teams. In many of today's environment, it is typical that the requirements churn is too fast for the Sprint. There are bugs to fix in other systems the Team is maintaining, there are emergencies throughout the Organization we have to fix, and the Stakeholders are almost constantly changing their minds about what is important.

This is why the second factor is the less important, and Teams have developed methods for managing the fact that requirements need to be changed more often than once a Sprint. There are three chapters in this book (chapters 4.3, 4.4, and 4.7) that address this problem, and a Team may also want to try mid-Sprint re-planning sessions, which is coming up next.

Planned Mid-Sprint Re-Planning Sessions

Sometimes a Team's Sprint length is just too long for their Agreements to survive; the requirements churn is higher than the Sprint length can sustain. It is tempting to make shorter Sprints, but maybe that can't be done because either the Stakeholders can't handle more frequent reviews, or because the Team can't develop product any faster.

What does the Team do?

Well, Scrum is nothing if not adaptive. In fact, if the Team is not adapting to meet its realities, it's not doing Scrum. So, adapt... the Team could jump right to the Kanban(ish) variant if it's mature enough (chapter 4.7) or it could just have Sprint Planning sessions more often – perhaps once a week.

For example, say the Team has a two-week Sprint, from Monday to Friday two weeks later. Then the Team could plan *every* Monday, not just every other Monday. The first Monday the Team would fill its Sprint to 80% capacity or so, and the second Monday the Team Members would ask themselves the question, *'What do we add now?'*

I find that many Teams have spontaneously moved to this system, so it is a known pattern that is very successful. Therefore, it should be part of a ScrumMaster's toolbox to use with their Scrum Teams.

Cancelling a Sprint

The Product Owner may cancel a Sprint at any time, usually because the Sprint Goal isn't going to be met or because the Sprint Goal is no longer what is needed. In either case, the Sprint's work is evaluated to see what can be kept, and whether or not a re-planning is called for. This is not considered abnormal, but is simply an agile reaction to something that has happened. It should not be considered a 'bad thing' – it is merely a 'thing.'

Abnormal Termination of a Sprint

Not only can the Product Owner cancel a Sprint at any time, but the Scrum-Master can stop the Sprint at any time at the behest of either the Team or the Product Owner – this is called an Abnormal Termination. The Abnormal Termination has been a part of Scrum from the very beginning. As it says in [S1, pg. 136]: "The ScrumMaster can abnormally terminate the Sprint... The ScrumMaster can make this change of his or her own accord or as requested by the Team or the Product Owner" and the fact "that the Team has the power to cancel its own Sprint is very important" [SB, pg. 54]. If an Abnormal Termination is invoked, the Sprint is re-planned and all work in the Sprint is discarded, carrying the notion of 'no partial credit' to extremes.

In my experience, the Abnormal Termination is seldom invoked, but often threatened. The threat of an Abnormal Termination alerts management (in a very noticeable way) that something is going wrong and needs to be addressed. The most common use of the threat of the Abnormal Termination is when the Product Owner and Team are not renegotiating the Sprint Goal or Backlog in good faith (see chapter 4.3), and it can be called by either party. In essence, the threat is saying *'if you don't play nice, we'll force a do-over.'* It is imperative that renegotiating the Sprint Goal or Backlog should actually be *negotiations*, with the Team willing to consider the needs of the Product Owner, and the Product Owner realizing that the Team has the right to say *'No.'*

In any case, people should not threaten to use the Abnormal Termination unless they are willing to actually use it. The Abnormal Termination is quite disruptive, but does give the Team the ability to start over with a clean slate.

Stories that Are 'Too Big' for One Sprint

What should a Team do with a 'big' Story that can't be decomposed into small, manageable ones? Well, first of all, the Team should try harder to decompose it... but if that fails, the Team must accept the reality and deal with it.

If the Story is going to spill over the Sprint boundary into the next Sprint, so be it. The Team gets no partial credit for the Story in the current Sprint, and shouldn't discuss it at the Product Review – unless the Team explicitly states that the Story is not Done and the Team is simply taking advantage of the fact that the Stakeholders are in one place to help give some feedback to get the Story to completion.

Complicated Story Boards

I see a lot of complicated Story Boards on the walls of Scrum Team Rooms, and this bothers me. When I see a lot of columns in a Story Board it indicates to me that the Team is re-inventing a predictive process of development – and this tells me that they are not going through the self-organization and discovery processes as I believe they should be.

There is one particular thing I look for, and that is a column labeled 'To Verify' or 'Ready to Test' or something similar. This *really* bothers me, as it indicates that the code has to wait for testing after it's been coded. This usually means that the Coder of that Story has gone on to other things in the meantime. In other words, this Coder could end up context-switching if the Story fails its test, and the Coder has to return to fix it up.

If there's one thing I know for certain, it is that having a Coder context-switching from one Story to another is a *bad thing*... code is a complicated medium, and it takes a while to get into the right state of understanding that allows a Coder to write good code. In fact, two pieces of code will be messed up if the Coder has to return to fix something: the one the Coder has to return to fix, and the one the Coder has been working on in the meantime.

So, don't let a Coder context-switch! Have at least one Coder stay with the Story from beginning to end, with the other Team Members Swarming around helping get it Done (see chapter 2.6).

Discussion Questions

1. Some people think that specialized Sprints are a bad idea. After reading about the Startup Sprint and Release Sprint, what do you think?

2. Is it ok to change Sprint length inside the Sprint? Is it ok to change Sprint length from Sprint to Sprint? How about every once in a while for special reasons?

3. Assume your Team is doing 2-week Sprints. Discuss the differences, advantages, and disadvantages of having weekly planning sessions versus going to the kanban(ish) variant of Scrum.

4. Discuss the differences between Cancelling a Sprint and Abnormally Terminating a Sprint.

Appendices

This book focuses on People, Product, and Practices, but that's not all there is to know. In this section are a number of Appendices of 'random stuff' that doesn't fit well somewhere else. Most of this is referenced from somewhere in the body of the book, and I hope you find it interesting.

A.1

Glossary of Scrum Terms

Scrum uses many terms that are confusing to people, and these terms are used throughout this book. This glossary presents many terms and phrases that have become 'standard' in the Scrum community, as well as a few that are introduced in this book. This is not a complete list!

Abnormal Termination | A cancellation of the Sprint by the ScrumMaster at the behest of the Team. This is a self-organization 'thing' and is often threatened but seldom invoked – it is usually used by the Team as a way of saying *'you didn't play nice, so we are forcing a do-over.'*

Acceptance-Based Story | A Story whose 'doneness' is determined by Acceptance Criteria; the time an Acceptance-Based Story takes is a byproduct of getting to Done. (see Time-Boxed Story)

Acceptance Criteria | A description of the objective criteria the Team will use to determine whether or not a Story achieves the Value it represents. For functional Stories, this is usually a description of an Acceptance Test. (see Story Agreement)

Accountable | The accountable person is the individual who is ultimately answerable for the activity or decision; the accountable person can be *held to account* for the results of the activity or the making of the decision. There can only be one person accountable for any particular activity or decision. Often confused with Responsible. (see Responsible)

Agile Analysis | Any iterative and incremental method or practice that produces Epics and/or Stories for the Backlog.

agility | The act of basing actions on current reality, as opposed to being predictive or plan-driven. Agility has two primary facets: Physical Agility and Mental Agility. (see Physical Agility, Mental Agility)

Agreement | (Story Agreement)

Analysis Story | A Story that finds Items or Stories; a Story that conducts Agile Analysis. The most common Analysis Stories find functional Stories by one of various methods (working with SMEs, studying Change Requests, conducting Usability Analysis, etc.); however, there can be risk analysis Stories (finding risks and fears that need be dealt with), process analysis Stories (finding process improvements), and so on. (see Agile Analysis, Backlog Refinement)

Architecturally Significant Story | A Functional Story (producing actual, demonstrable user value) that causes the Team to make an architectural decision | which is then validated by the fact that there is existing, working functionality using the decision.

Architecture | The collection of decisions about how a system will be built – I got this from Grady Booch in the early 80's. (see Architecturally Significant Story).

Back Burner | Stories in the Backlog that are being groomed to become Ready for Planning. Usually thought of as being Stories that are 'near the top' of the Backlog and *becoming* Ready. (see Ready Story)

Backlog | A list of Items that represents everything that anyone interested in the product or process has thought is needed or would be a good idea. It drives development and discussions with Stakeholders. (also called Product Backlog)

Backlog Item | (Item)

Backlog Maintenance | (Backlog Refinement)

Backlog Refinement | The process of extracting Stories from Epics and/or refining Stories to make them Ready. There could be Refinement Stories, Sessions, or both. Backlog Refinement is also called Grooming, Backlog Maintenance or Story Time.

Bug | A simple change that does not require an acceptance test; examples include correcting a misspelling in a dialog box or moving an interface element on the screen. Often used (incorrectly, in my view) as a synonym for Defect. (see Defect)

BuildUp | A BuildUp graph is any graph that shows the completion of Backlog as a function of Time. Many people call these BurnUp graphs (see BurnUp, Checklist Item BuildUp)

BurnDown | A BurnDown graph is any graph that shows the amount of remaining Backlog (Items or Tasks) as a function of Time. Many people and tools use BurnDowns, but they have been largely deprecated from Scrum as they are inherently predictive, and not agile.

BurnUp | A BurnUp graph is any graph that shows the completion of Backlog as a function of Time. I prefer the term BuildUp, as I don't believe that burning something up should be a measure of progress... just sayin'... ;-) (see BuildUp)

Business Owner | A role defined to represent management outside the Team. In practice the Business Owner is either the 'lead' Stakeholder, the Team's Sponsor, or the Product Owner's Product Owner.

Business Value (BV) | A property of an Item that simply indicates that some external Stakeholder wants it done; it is very hard to quantify, even though we continue to try to do so.

Cancelling a Sprint | The Product Owner may cancel a Sprint at any time, usually because the Sprint Goal isn't going to be met or because the Sprint Goal is no longer what is needed.

Capability | An Item that provides value to an external Stakeholder; an Item that has Business Value. (compare to Chore)

Capacity | An estimate or prediction of the rate that a Team or Organization *will be able* to develop Product; it is used in Release Planning. Often confused with Velocity and WorkRate.

Checklist Item BuildUp | A BuildUp Graph that accumulates Checklist Items during a Sprint. (see BuildUp)

Chore | An Item that is done to provide value to the Team or Product, as opposed to an external Stakeholder; an Item whose value is other than Business Value. (compare to Capability)

Clean Code | 1) Code that is easy to change: that is extensible, modifiable, and maintainable. 2) Code that has little or no Technical Debt.

CleanUp Story | A Story that *apologizes* to the Code Base about something bad that happened, and *promises* to fix it. It usually documents what is wrong and indicates what needs to be done to fix it.

Code Complete | A Product Increment is code complete when the development team agrees that no entirely new source code will be added.

Coding Story | A Story that has Code as its primary result.

Coordination Team | (Product Owner Team)

Coordinator | In a Team Swarm, the Coordinator is the Team Member who is 'in charge' of the Story being worked on.

Commitment | One of the least understood of the Team Values; the Team commits to living the Scrum Values and doing its due diligence to get Stories Done. It is often used as a synonym for Sprint Commitment. (see Values)

Cross-Functional Team | A team is cross-functional if it has all the skills and knowledge necessary to do its work.

Daily Scrum | A discussion the Team has on a daily basis in order to collect 'today's reality' in order to deal with it.

Defect | Anything about a Product that is seen as 'wrong' by a Stakeholder; usually results in a new Item in the Backlog. (see Bug)

Definition of Done (DoD) | A subset of the Story Agreement, the Definition of Done is the description of the *objective* criteria the Team will use to determine whether or not a Story meets *internal* standards or constraints, as opposed to providing *external* Stakeholder Value. The Definition of Done provides the Standard of Care are to be used to 'guarantee' sufficient technical quality to be releasable. (see Story Agreement)

Definition of Ready (DoR) | The State a Story must be in in order to be Ready. (see Ready Story)

Developer | (Team Member)

Development Team | The subset of the Scrum Team that is actually producing Results; this may, or may not, include the Scrum Team's Scrum-Master and Product Owner.

DoD | (Definition of Done)

Done | A Story is Done when its Story Agreement has been met. The concept of Done has often been extended to Epics, Sprints, Releases, and so on... (compare to Undone)

Done Increment | (per Ken Schwaber, *Agile Project Management with Scrum*, Microsoft Press, 2004, pg. 12) *"the increment consists of thoroughly tested, well-structured, and well-written code that has been built into an executable and that the user operation of the functionality is documented... This is the definition of a 'done' increment."* An Increment is Done when all the Stories involved in the Increment meet their Doneness Agreements.

Doneness Agreement | (Story Agreement)

Due Diligence | A person, Team, or Organization has done its 'due diligence' when it has followed the appropriate Standard of Care in its work. For example, Team Members are doing their due diligence when Stories are actually getting Done, Product Owners are doing their due diligence when they make timely decisions while considering all the options, and the Organization is doing its due diligence when it creates a safe environment for the Team.

EffortPoint | A relative measure of the effort it will take to 'do' a Story. Often confused with StoryPoint. (see StoryPoint, Ideal Engineering Hour/Day)

Empirical Process | Any decision-making process based on knowledge and observation is called an empirical process. (synonym for agility)

Environmental Variables | Factors affecting effort that are not related to the actual Story. These include, but are not limited to, Technical Debt, Organizational Noise, and Team Ability.

Epic | 1) an Item that is too Complex, Unknown, Risky, or Big for the Team to agree to do all at once; 2) a named Container of other Epics and Stories.

Estimation Game | Any of a variety of consensus-based methods of estimating.

Executive Review | A Review for the business to discuss progress, process, or people issues. This is not a part of Scrum, but is often necessary for legitimate business reasons. (see Sprint Review, Project Review, and Product Review)

Exemplar Story | An example Item used as a reference point for Estimation. For example, we could have exemplar Small, Medium, and Large Stories as reference points for Estimating Story Size or Effort.

eXtreme Programming (XP) | An agile development process whose practices largely focus on the production of Clean Code. (see Clean Code)

Feature | Something a software product enables a user to do. (see Capability)

Feature Complete | A state of software indicating that no more features need to be added.

Forecast | The Team's best guess about how many Items will fit into the next Sprint. The Sprint Backlog is a forecast: not a plan, commitment, or promise.

Freezer | The portion of the Backlog that contains Items that are 'out of scope.'

Fridge | The portion of the Backlog that contains items that are 'in scope' but are not yet being actively Groomed for Planning. Typically, these Items are Epics or the un-decomposed remains of Epics.

Front Burner | The portion of the Backlog that the Team has agreed to work on 'now'. In Scrum this is usually called the Sprint Backlog; in Kanban this is called the Work in Progress (WIP).

General Agreement | The Part of the Story Agreement that contains information about which SMEs will be involved, who will be the Story Coordinator, what is 'out of scope' for the Story, and so on. (see Story Agreement)

Grooming | (Backlog Refinement)

Ideal Effort | The amount of effort it would take to build something if conditions were as they *should* be; there are no impediments of any kind, and you don't require any magic or miracles. (see Ideal Engineering Hour/ Day)

Ideal Engineering Hour/Day | An estimate of effort that assumes no disruptions or disasters; an Ideal Hour/Day is an Hour/Day that has no interruptions. (see Ideal Effort)

Impediment | Anything that is causing the Team to not be at its best. These could be fears, risks, or problems.

InBox | Items in the Backlog that have not yet been prioritized.

Interested Bystander | People who think that they are Stakeholders, but actually 'don't matter' to you, are called Interested Bystanders.

Intraspective | A discussion by the Scrum Team about its Practices or Teamwork that occurs *within* the Sprint: it is often precipitated by an event that 'didn't go well.' (compare to Retrospective)

Intrinsic Difficulty | The Intrinsic Difficulty of a Functional Story is inherent in the Acceptance Criteria, and is based on the complexity involved in the design activities themselves and the complexity of the resulting designs and algorithms

Item | A single unit of work on the Backlog, an Item is either an Epic or a Story.

Kanban | An agile development process based heavily on Lean Principles. The main strength of Kanban (from a Scrum point of view) is that its Planning is continuous, which makes it more likely to keep up with reality, and hence more agile.

Leadership Team | (Product Owner Team)

Lean Principles | Lean Principles focus on creating value while eliminating waste, thus making a Value Stream (process flow) more efficient. Two of the Lean Principles that are built into *good* implementations of Scrum are 'Pull, don't Push' and 'Minimize Inventory.'

Mental Agility | Having situational awareness and using feedback to make the decisions necessary to be agile. (see agility, Physical Agility)

Order | Refers to the order of the Backlog; the order that the Product Owner wants the Items worked on. (see Priority)

Organizational Noise | An Organization that empowers and nurtures its Teams is said to be a 'quiet' Organization, while one with many procedures, meetings, interruptions, and the like, is said to be 'noisy.' (see Environmental Variables)

Pairing | Pairing, a practice often associated with eXtreme Programming (XP), is when each Story is worked on by two Developers, working side-by-side at one computer, collaborating on the same design, algorithm, code or test. Many Teams have found it useful to rotate Pairs every 1-2 hours, which is referred to as Polygamous Pairing.

Physical Agility | A Team, Project, or Organization has Physical Agility if its processes provide the feedback necessary to enable agility. (see agility, Mental Agility)

PlaceHolder Story | A Story that holds a budget of StoryPoints to be used by Stories that are 'known unknowns'; that is the Team *knows* it's going to need to do these things, like fix bugs, go on Sales Calls, ...

Plan of Action | A tentative plan, developed by the Team, of how the Sprint might be carried out. The purpose of the Plan of Action is not to have a plan, *per se*, but to enable the Team to justify to itself that doing the work is possible. (see Sprint Planning)

Potentially Releasable Increment | (Done Increment)

Potentially Shippable Increment | (Done Increment)

Priority | In Scrum, the priority of an item is determined by when it will be done, not by how important it is. (see Order)

Product | 1) (in Scrum) Whatever the Team produces; the Team's Work Results; 2) (in popular use) A particular marketable/sellable/usable unit, such as 'website ABC' or the '123 Counting Program.'

Product Backlog | (Backlog)

Product Backlog Item | (Item)

Product Owner | The Scrum Team Member who is accountable to the Business for the value of the Team's Work Results.

Product Owner Team | A Scrum Team that consists of Product Owners from different Teams along with their own Product Owner. The purpose of the Product Owner Team is to coordination cross-cutting issues, foster communications, and enable collaboration across the Teams. (also called Leadership Team, Coordination Team)

Product Review | A Team session at the end of a Sprint where the Team reviews their Work Results with Stakeholders in order to get feedback on what to do next, what to do better, and so on. In practice, it often includes reviews of both the Product and the Project, but this is a mistake – it should focus *only* on the Product. (see Executive Review, Project Review)

Product Vision | The product vision statement is a quick summary expressing how the product supports Organization or Users.

Project Review | A form of Executive Review that focuses on Project Status. (Executive Review)

Quality Code | (Clean Code)

Ready Story | A Story that is small, well-defined and ready to take to Planning. Generally, this means that the Story's Agreement is a '10 minute discussion' away from being agreed to. (see Well-Defined Story, Ready Story)

Refactoring | Rewriting existing source code in order to improve its readability, reusability or structure without affecting its meaning or behavior.

Refinement | (Backlog Refinement)

Release | A movement of the Team's Product from the development environment to some other environment, for some other reason than development. Examples include alpha releases, beta releases, go-live releases, releases to a test lab, and so on. Actually Releasing something is not a part of Scrum; releasing product must be done through Stories – there is no 'release' ceremony in Scrum.

Release Sprint | A specialized Sprint whose purpose is to Release Product; it contains Stories specific to Release Activities and finishing Undone Work A Release Sprint usually contains no additional development. (see Undone)

Release Strategy | A term used to refer to all types of Release Planning, Release Monitoring, and the like. Not a part of Scrum.

Responsible | Responsible people are the individual(s) who actually do the work; responsibility can be shared. The degree of responsibility is determined by the person with the "Accountability". Often confused with Accountability. (see Accountable)

Results | (Work Results)

Retrospective | (Team Retrospective)

Scenario | An interaction with the System that consists of a single thread, and is represented by a single Acceptance Test. (see Use Case)

Scrum | An agile framework (or process) for Product Development, *not* Project Management.

Scrum Board | (Story Board)

Scrum Team | A cross-functional, self-organized, value-driven collection of Team Members united in the goal of producing high Quality Results at a Sustainable Pace. Two of the Team Members have special accountabilities: the Product Owner and the ScrumMaster.

Scrum Values | The Scrum Values are the following subset of the Team Values: Openness, Focus, Commitment, Respect, Courage, Visibility, and Humor. (see Values, Team Values)

ScrumMaster | The Team Member who is accountable for making sure that Scrum is used correctly, that the Team uses Scrum in a positive way, and that the Team is constantly improving its use of Scrum. The ScrumMaster is a servant leader and facilitator, not a manager.

ScrumMaster Community | The group of ScrumMasters within an Organization. This group is the designated collection of Change Agents in scrum. They have a Backlog (often virtual or invisible) of changes they would like to have in the Organization to make it more amenable to Scrum.

Self-Contained | (Cross-Functional)

Self-Organization | A Team has self-organization when nobody outside the Team tells the Team Members what to do, how to organize themselves. And so on. In other words, nobody outside the Team micromanages the Team. (see Tactical Agility)

Single Item Flow | Single item flow (also called 'single piece flow' or 'one piece flow') is a lean manufacturing concept that says that each individual Item will move through the manufacturing process *all at once* with no waiting between steps. On Scrum Teams, this means Stories don't wait for people who have skills they need – the people are available when they're needed. (see Team Swarm)

SME | (Subject Matter Expert)

SME Availability | This is an Environmental Variable that indicates whether or not there are Subject Matter Experts available who have the knowledge or expertise you need, when you need it. (see Environmental Variables)

Spike | An XP (eXtreme Programming) term that describes Stories that figure out answers to tough technical or design problems. Spikes address only the problem under consideration and ignore all other concerns. Most Spikes get thrown away, which differentiates them from Architecturally Significant Stories.

Sprint | A fixed period of time (less than a month) in which a Team produces Work Results for review. The Sprint length is defined by the interval between Product Reviews, is usually consistent across Sprints, and must not be changed once the Sprint has started.

Sprint Backlog | The Stories the Team has forecast it may be able to do in the Sprint. This includes their Agreements and (possibly) Tasks. (see Front Burner)

Sprint Commitment | The Team commits to its Sprint Goal and to doing due diligence in order to have all completed Stories meet their Agreements. The Team does *not* commit to doing all the Stories in the Sprint Backlog.

Sprint Goal | The Sprint Goal is a single, clear, benefit that defines success for the Sprint.

Sprint Planning | A Team session at the beginning of a Sprint in which the Team Members (including the Product Owner) discuss and negotiate amongst themselves and 1) *commit to* a Sprint Goal and 2) *forecast* the Stories they believe are possible to achieve in the Sprint.

Sprint Retrospective | (Team Retrospective)

Sprint Review | The Sprint Review is supposed to be a Product Review, but many Teams include other reviews, as well... this is usually *not* a good thing. (see Executive Review, Project Review, and Product Review)

Sprint Team | The Scrum Team *along with* any external SMEs who are (either officially or unofficially) members of the Team during the Sprint.

Stakeholder | 1) A person with a *legitimate* interest in the Product, Process, or Team. 2) Someone who the Scrum Team ignores 'at their peril.' 3) A person who reviews the Team's Work Results at the Product Review. *Note: while Team Members are stakeholders, the word Stakeholder [uppercase] is usually reserved for external stakeholders.*

Startup Sprint | The name of a pattern in which a specialized Sprint used to get a Team 'up and running' quickly, rather than dragging their feet *getting ready* to start development. A Startup Sprint usually includes Analysis, Team Training, Infrastructure and Environmental Work – and the development of something 'real' – and its purpose is to limit the amount of 'up front' work that takes place before actual Product is developed.

Story | 1) A request for something of value from a stakeholder. 2) A unit of work that is 'small enough' to be agreed to by the Team; an Item that is not an Epic. 3) (by others) A synonym for Backlog Item.

Story Agreement | An agreement between the Product Owner and the rest of the Team that defines when a Story will be complete (or Done). The Story Agreement consists of the Acceptance Criteria, the Definition of

Done, and possibly additional General Agreements. This notion can be extended to Capabilities, Sprints, Releases, and so on… (see Done)

Story Board | A Team tool that shows the tasks that are needed in the Sprint, organized by Story.

Story Owner | A Team Member (or SME) who represents the Stakeholder's interests in the Story to the rest of the Team during Planning and development.

Story Size | A measure of how much product will be produced by the Story.

Story Time | (Backlog Refinement)

Storyotype | A stereotype or template for a Story or Epic. Storyotypes are used to capture re-useful information common to many Stories; in particular, Storyotypes are used to capture common Agreements on Done (see chapter 3.10).

StoryPoint | A relative measure of the size of a Story. Often confused with EffortPoint. (see EffortPoint, Velocity)

Strategic Agility | Agility that changes 'what' the Team or Organization does in order to maximize Value or ROI. Strategic Agility is a Product Ownership responsibility. (compare to Tactical Agility)

Subject Matter Expert (SME) | Somebody with specialized knowledge or talent that is needed by the Team; this includes SMEs on the product, the environment, development practices, and so on. The term usually refers to SMEs that are 'outside' the Team, but not always.

Sustainable Pace | The rate at which a Team can work without burning itself out. Originally called "40 Hour Week" by Kent Beck as an XP practice.

Swarm | (Team Swarm)

Swarmer | In a Team Swarm, a Swarmer is a person who is moving from Story to Story, working with those Story's Coordinators and other Swarmers, in order to offer his or her expertise and efforts wherever they are needed.

Tactical Agility | Agility that changes 'how' a Team works in order to achieve its goals; this is embodied in the Team's Self-Organization. (compare to Strategic Agility)

Team | 1) The Scrum Team; 2) (by others) The Development Team; 3) (Ken Schwaber) A role, taken on by a group of people, that means that they are a Well-Formed Team.

Team Ability | Team Ability includes the capabilities of individual Team Members, the Team's frame of mind, and how well the Team synergizes. (see Environmental Variables)

Team Member | Any member of the Scrum Team, including the Product Owner and ScrumMaster.

Team Retrospective | A Team session at the end of a Sprint when the Team Members (facilitated by the ScrumMaster) discuss and agree upon ways they could improve their Practices, teamwork, environment, or Organization for the next Sprint.

Team Swarm | A method of working where a Team works on just a few Stories at a time. Each Story is finished as quickly as possible by having many people work on it together, rather than having a series of handoffs. The ultimate in Swarming is Single Item Flow, where the Team works on *only* one Story at a time, and finishes it completely before moving on to the next one.

Team Values | The Team Values are: Openness, Focus, Commitment, Respect, Courage, Visibility, and Humor. (see Values, Scrum Values)

TeamLet | The Team Members and SMEs who are Swarming on a particular Story. (see Team Swarm)

Technical Debt | Deficiencies in the code, technical documentation, development environments, 3rd-party tools, and development practices, which makes it hard for the Team to modify, update, repair, or deliver the Product. (see Environmental Variables)

Time-Boxed Story | Time-Boxed Stories have their Doneness defined by a time-box, and the actual Results produced are limited to what can be completed in that time-box. (see Acceptance-Based Story)

Undone | The phrase "Undone work" is often used to describe the work needed to move something from Done to Releasable; in other words, it is work that *maybe should have been* done, but wasn't. Deciding what work to leave Undone is a delicate issue. (see Done)

Use Case | A Capability that represents an interaction between a User and the System in order to achieve a Goal. A Use Case consists of multiple Scenarios, and usually requires many Stories to implement, so a Use Case is usually an Epic. (see Scenario)

User Story | A Story whose value is for the User of the software; popularized by eXtreme Programming (XP).

Validation | Validation is assuring that a Result (Capability) is fit for use; that it does what it *needs* to do. (compare to Verification)

Values | Scrum Teams are value-driven. The word Values, in common use, refers either to values in general, the Team Values, or the Scrum Values.

Velocity | The rate that a Team or Organization *has been producing* Product; calculated as completed StoryPoints per Sprint. It is often used as an approximation for Capacity and is often confused with WorkRate. (see StoryPoint, Capacity, WorkRate)

Verification | Verification is assuring that something has met its specification; that it does as it was *intended* to do. (compare to Validation)

Walking Skeleton | A subset of the System that demonstrates the basic architectural decisions; it is the result of many Architecturally Significant Stories.

Well-Defined Story | A Story whose Acceptance Criteria are known. (compare to Ready Story)

WIBNI (wib'·nee) **|** stands for **W**ouldn't **I**t **B**e **N**ice **I**f, and represents things that we wish were true, but aren't – so we must *get over* them; example is "wouldn't it be nice if we had more testers…"

Work in Progress (WIP) | In Kanban, the Stories that the Team is currently working on. (see Front Burner)

Well-Formed Team (WFT) | A team that is self-organized, self-contained, and value-driven. A Scrum Team is a well-formed team that has both a Product Owner and a ScrumMaster, and it is a primary teaching of Scrum that all teams (especially those working in complex domains) should be well-formed.

WFT | (Well-Formed Team)

Work Results | Whatever an individual or Team produces. (see Product)

WorkRate | The rate that a Team works; usually calculated as EffortPoints per Sprint, Ideal Engineering Hours/Days per Sprint, or something similar. It is used as an aid in Sprint Planning, and is often confused with Velocity. (see EffortPoints, Ideal Engineering Hours/Days, Velocity)

XP | (eXtreme Programming)

Discussion Questions

1. Read through these definitions, and discuss any of them that confuse you.

A.2

Product Owner Definition

This appendix discusses the definition of the Product Owner. The purpose is to show, based on first principles, that the Team's Product Owner should be the one and only Team Member who is accountable to the Business for the Team's Work Results. This definition is commonly misunderstood in Scrum, so this discussion is vital.

In chapter 2.1 I defined the Product Owner as "[the one and only] Team Member who is accountable to the business for the success of the Team – for the value of the Team's Work Results." This is the most current definition of the Product Owner – it is derived from [SS, pg. 4] – but it is not the only definition of the Product Owner. In [SB, pg. 34] the Product Owner is defined as "the person who is officially responsible for the project" and in [S1, pg. 142], the Product Owner is defined as "the person responsible for managing the Product Backlog so as to maximize the value of the project."

As you can see, the definition of the Product Owner has been refined through the years to clarify that the Product Owner is both a member of the Scrum Team and accountable for the value of the Team's Results. Because of the confusion inherent in such a changing definition, some people use the words Product Owner in different ways than I do. In particular, there are some who believe either or both of:

- The Product Owner manages the Backlog to maximize the value of the project, but need not be accountable, or

- The Product Owner need not be a Team Member.

In this appendix I'd like to start from Scrum's first principles and show that, in order to be successful, the Team's Product Owner *must be* accountable for the Scrum Team's product, and *should be* a member of the Scrum Team. After reading these two arguments you, the reader, will know why the definition was clarified and why I use the definition I use in this book.

The Basics

So, let me start with the basics, and look at the Product Owner role as it was first introduced to most of us. As I mention above, its original, succinct definition was that the Product Owner is "the person who is officially responsible for the project" [SB, pg. 34]. But there's more...

It is *also* emphasized that the Product Owner's decisions must be final. It doesn't get any clearer than this quote found on the same page [SB, page 34]: "For the Product Owner to succeed, *everyone* in the organization has to respect his or her decisions. *No one* is allowed to tell the Scrum Teams to work from a different set of priorities, and Scrum Teams *aren't allowed* to listen to anyone who says otherwise" [emphasis mine].

In other words, the defining characteristic of a Product Owner is that the Product Owner makes prioritization decisions that *can't be overruled* by anybody else, even their bosses. Their bosses can replace them if they continue to make 'bad' decisions, but they can't overrule them.

Few people who know Scrum disagree with this characterization of the Product Owner – it is one of the basic definitions of Scrum, and is very important for self-organized Teams. So, I'll just start from there and see where it leads.

The Product Owner *Must* Be Accountable

First of all, it's easy to show that the Team's Product Owner *must be* accountable for the Team's Product. Since, according to Scrum, no one is *allowed* to modify or change the Product Owner's priorities by talking to the Team, the Product Owner is the *only* person who can be held to account for what gets built.

Figure 37 shows it quite clearly. When Stakeholders want to modify the Team's priorities, they must go *through* the Product Owner. This is the very definition of accountability, that someone is accountable if (and only if) that person can be 'held to account.' It is clear that the Product Owner is accountable to the Stakeholders for the ultimate priorities that go to the Team, and thus for the value of what the Team builds.

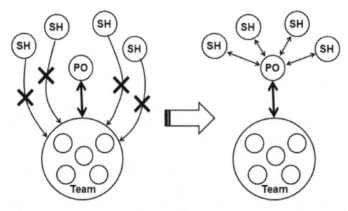

Figure 37: Stakeholders Go *Through* the Product Owner

The Product Owner *Should Be* a Team Member

Showing that the Product Owner should be a Team Member is a little bit trickier. It seems perfectly reasonable to think that an *external* Product Owner can give the Team the priorities and guidance it needs at Sprint Planning, and review the Results at the Product Review.

In fact, this seems to be the original intention of Scrum. The Team would get the Product Owner's priorities at the beginning of the Sprint, self-organize to achieve the priorities, and present the Results to the Product Owner at the end of the Sprint at the Product Review.

However, it didn't work out that way in practice. It turns out that the Team needs *frequent* prioritization guidance and advice *during* the Sprint. Let's take a look at a diagram to see what happened...

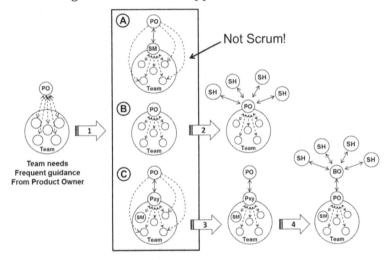

Figure 38: Evolution of Product Owner's Relationship with Team

In order to provide more frequent guidance to the Team during the Sprint, the Product Owner must have more frequent contact with the Team Members, as we see at the left-hand side of the diagram. This leads to a situation where the Product Owner is under a lot of pressure, and something must be done about it.

There are three patterns that arose within the Scrum community because of this pressure on the Product Owner. The arrow labeled '1' shows how the pressure on the Product Owner led to these patterns, which are shown in the box.

The first pattern that arose (labeled 'A' in the diagram) seemed quite natural and simply had the ScrumMaster provide daily prioritization advice to the Team Members. The end result was that the Product Owner and the

ScrumMaster each gave prioritization advice to the Team on an as-needed basis. This made perfect sense, but it was realized this was *not* Scrum. It puts the ScrumMaster in the position of acting like a manager – worrying about the Product and not just the Process and the Team. This is a *bad* thing, as it prevents the Team from self-organizing (the ScrumMaster became a boss, not a facilitator...). It's a pattern I still see frequently, and as a Scrum coach I *must* try to stamp it out every time I see it. So, this pattern is out, *out*, **out**!

The second pattern (labeled 'B' in the diagram) is also a natural evolution. Since the Product Owner is providing frequent prioritization advice to the members of the Team, the Product Owner starts spending more and more time with the Team. Eventually, the Product Owner has become a *de facto*, if not a formal, member of the Team. As arrow '2' shows, the end result is that we have a Product Owner on the Team who is directly accountable to all the Stakeholders.

The third pattern (labeled 'C' in the diagram) is also natural. In this pattern there is a 'leader' on the Team, called the Proxy Product Owner (labeled 'Pxy' in the diagram), who is *not* the ScrumMaster, who helps explain the priorities to the Team. Initially, both the Product Owner and the Proxy explain priorities to the Team, but this invariably leads to conflict as the Proxy and Product Owner will give different guidance in some cases. Since the Proxy is not *allowed* to give different guidance than the Product Owner, either the Proxy or the Product Owner must *stop giving* guidance.

So, in order to resolve the conflict and keep the Proxy in place, *all* the Product Owner's advice must be filtered through the Proxy (this transition is shows at arrow 3). This leads to a situation where the Product Owner gives prioritization guidance at Sprint Planning, and the Proxy gives ongoing advice during the Sprint.

This structure became so prevalent that it became clear that the role of Proxy was becoming essential to the understanding of Scrum as it was actually practiced. The Scrum community realized that this didn't make a lot of sense, as from the Team's perspective the Proxy was actually the ongoing Product Owner. So, rather than add the Proxy role to Scrum, the Proxy was dismissed from Scrum and the Product Owner was moved onto the Team.

In the language we see in this book, this means that the (Product Owner, Proxy) pair became the (Business Owner, Product Owner) pair – this transition is shown at arrow '4'. The end result, as you can see in the diagram, is that there is a Product Owner *on* the Team, accountable to the Business Owner, who is then accountable to all the Stakeholders. This is the basic pattern that I use when explaining Scrum.

I must make two points very clear, though...

First, I have nothing against the Proxy Product Owner as a concept. It served its purpose quite well, but it led to two different descriptions of Scrum that were *actually* the same from the Team's perspective; the only *real* difference was in the naming of the roles. There are still some Scrum experts using the 'Proxy' language, so when you hear the words Product Owner coming from them you should realize they actually mean Business Owner. I prefer the naming that has the Product Owner on the Scrum Team, and in the next section we'll see that this is also the decision that Ken Schwaber made in his 2007 book *The Enterprise and Scrum* [S2].

Second, this in no way means that the Business Owner is *not* accountable for the Team's product; it only means that the Team's Product Owner is a member of the Team. The Team's Product Owner is accountable to the Business Owner, and the Business Owner is often accountable to the Stakeholders and others above him. As I described in chapter 2.2, there could be a hierarchy of accountability, starting with the Team's Product Owner and running all the way up to the CEO, if necessary.

Appeal to Authority

I hope I have convinced you that the Product Owner *should* be the Team Member who is accountable to the Business for the Team's Product. If not, I'll just appeal to authority...

First of all, it has always been realized that the Product Owner was accountable. Remember that the Black Book defined the Product Owner as "the person who is officially responsible for the project" [SB, pg. 34].

Unfortunately, it was not clear at that time that the Product Owner needed to be a member of the Scrum Team, as well. As the discussion above shows, this realization took some time. Basically, Scrum is a pattern language, and it was out of balance. Adding the Proxy brought it back into balance, but added complexity.

Scrum inspected and adapted itself and realized that it was easier to just move the Product Owner onto the Team and reject the notion of the Proxy. In [S2], Ken Schwaber acknowledged this evolutionary move and explicitly stated the fact that the Product Owner *is* a member of the Scrum Team. In fact, he goes a bit further, and says that "The Product Owner and Scrum-Master are the first people on a Scrum Team." [S2, pg. 73]

Of course, he also reiterates that the Product Owner is accountable. Here is a great statement defining the Product Owner: "They [Product Owners] are responsible for managing the projects, Sprint by Sprint, to maximize value and control risk. They are accountable to senior management for the success or failure of the project. They are the single, wringable, neck. If members of senior management want to find out how the project is doing, they will call the Product Owner." [S2, pg. 6]

Summary

So, there we are. As I have just demonstrated, the Product Owner *must* be accountable to the business for the Team's Results, and *should* be a member of the Scrum Team. This is the definition used throughout this book. As I hope this appendix has convinced you, this is not just the current *official* definition, but the *correct* one as well.

Discussion Questions

1. Why is it a bad idea for Product Owner to be outside the Scrum Team and work with the Team Members through the ScrumMaster?

2. Explain why the Product Owner Proxy pattern shown in Figure 38 is fatally flawed.

3. Why did Ken Schwaber's description of the Product Owner role change as Scrum matured?

A.3

Evolution of Dan's Scrum

By Dan Rawsthorne

By its very nature, Scrum is an ever-evolving process. The answer to the question 'What is Scrum?' has changed since I first heard about it in 1995. In this appendix I describe the basic stages in the evolution of Scrum as I understand them.

This book is largely an exploration and explanation of Scrum as I understand it. Scrum itself has been around a long time, as software processes go, starting in the early 1990s with independent work of Jeff Sutherland and Ken Schwaber. Scrum has been 'inspecting and adapting' itself, as a process, ever since. There have been, and continue to be, many different interpretations of what Scrum is. Most of the differences are subtle and inconsequential, but some are not...

Since this book is about my understanding of what Scrum is (and should be), I think that you deserve to know how I came to have this understanding. This appendix explains how I experienced the evolution of Scrum – how the Scrum that's in this book came to be. It's not intended to be a history of Scrum; it's not intended to be well-researched; it's not intended to be accurate; it's just intended to be my best recollection of my story[1].

I hope you find it interesting.

My History

Before we get into the evolution of Scrum, let me tell you some of the high points about *my* evolution, what brought me to Scrum in the first place.

My first software development job was when I was a U.S. Army Intel Officer, back in 1983. I was working on a Symbolics 3600 LISP Machine using Flavors, in a laboratory-type setting, doing stuff I still can't talk about. One of the amusing things about this development is that we *called* our style 'agile development' because the word 'agile' was one of the US Army's primary buzzwords at the time – especially for us Intel guys[2]. What is even *more* amusing is that we *were* agile in the modern sense, with daily team discus-

---

[1] Unlike the rest of the book, the "I" in this story is Dan, not an amalgam of Dan and Doug.

[2] The US Army's AirLand Battle Doctrine was brand-new in 1983. One of its primary tenets was agility, which was basically defined as "reacting quickly to ground truth," which Intel is all about. See FM 100-5, *Operations*, HQ, Department of the Army, 20 August 1982.

sions and weekly demonstrations of working product to, and feedback from, our sponsors. The job was too good to last, and it didn't...

I got out of the Army and for the next 10+ years I worked primarily in Government Contracting. Most of the projects were waterfall, but many were agile – and some were both! I was normally the Team Lead or Project Manager (acting as Product Owner), and I had great teams. We did incremental development, had weekly demonstrations and renegotiations of scope with our clients, and my team wrote good Clean Code using C++. Along the way I learned the Rational Unified Process (RUP), Use Cases, and became a 'process geek.'

I met Kent Beck and talked about XP at PLoP94, and Linda Rising told me about this great talk about Scrum at OOPSLA95 (I missed the talk, I don't remember why). The major influence on me in the late 90s, though, was Ward Cunningham's WikiWikiWeb (http://c2.com/cgi/wiki), which had all the *good stuff* on agility and XP in it. It's still there; you should check it out...

In the late 90's I worked on a Military Contract developing an avionics system for a Helicopter. The contract was using RUP, and I was coaching the team to try to use an 'agile version' of RUP, rather than a 'waterfall version.' The team was using XP-ish practices as much as it could on the development side, and on the analytic side it was using the ICONIX method – which comes from Doug Rosenberg.

I worked with Doug quite a bit to understand and refine the method, and even drew the pictures for his first book[3]. In my opinion, the main thing to know about the ICONIX method is that it contains an incremental process for extracting scenarios from Use Cases that are accompanied by sequence and robustness diagrams. These scenarios made great inputs for our XP Teams.

In those days I didn't think a lot about Scrum, and what thinking I did do convinced me that Scrum and XP were basically the same. I thought that the main difference was that XP was focused on the coding (and was very prescriptive about it), while Scrum was focused on the Whole Team, including the analysts generating the Stories. This was a naïve view, but it was good enough for me at that time.

Anyway, the best part of this project was that I met Jim Sosville, a guy who's been working on government software projects since the late 60s. We used to go for 4-mile walks almost every evening, and we talked about all things agile. We discussed what we'd read on Ward's wiki, we discussed how to make big teams work, how to handle dependencies and inter-connected teams – we discussed it all. It was great! One of the great learning exper-

---

[3] Doug Rosenberg (with Kendall Scott), *Use Case Object Modeling with UML: A Practical Approach*, Addison-Wesley 1999.

iences of my life, and I'm still digesting some of it to this day. Jim and I still keep in touch, and as I'm writing this chapter he's out there somewhere, writing software, making the world a better place, and thinking big...

I then decided I was tired of government contracting work for a while and went to work for AccessVia, a company that produces signage software for retail stores. I spent a couple of years working there with Rod Claar to make agility work (stickies on the wall, the whole bit...) for the development of the software. It was a great few years, but I wound up getting 'dot-bombed' and that's what pushed me into being a full-time coach and trainer.

The first thing I did was work with Alistair Cockburn doing training in Use Cases[4]. This evolved into doing training and coaching about general agile topics, including Scrum and Agile Use Cases. I met Doug Shimp, who was also training with Alistair, and is my co-author of this book. Besides becoming one of my very best friends, Doug is the person who taught me that the essence of Scrum is not the practices, but the emphasis on the self-organization of the people. We have talked for hours and hours and hours about this stuff...

Basically, Doug's main lesson was that the Retrospective is the essence of Scrum, and without it Scrum is just another process. This opened my eyes, and in 2002 or so, I finally realized (or came to accept) that I could fit everything I already knew about agility into the Scrum framework – and nothing else would do. I started studying Scrum in earnest, and using it when I taught and coached.

Old Scrum (1997 to 2005)

So, I finally became a full-time 'Scrum guy' in 2002, and started studying Scrum for real. What did I find? I studied my copy of the Black Book [SB], I went to conferences, I joined users groups, I got CSMed by Ken Schwaber, and I talked to a lot of people. What I found, even at that time, was that Scrum had almost as many different versions as there were Scrum Teams.

I don't want to bore you with all the different versions that I found, so let me just tell you about what was actively being promoted by many coaches as correct. Here's a list of the basic features of what I call Old Scrum, followed by my comments:

1. The Product Owner was outside the Team, and only saw the Team at Sprint Planning and the Product Review. Because the Product Owner was often unavailable, there was a Product Owner Proxy on the Team, making day-to-day prioritization decisions for the Team.

---

[4] Based on Alistair Cockburn, *Writing Effective Use Cases*, Addison-Wesley, 2000.

2. The ScrumMaster was often acting as the manager of the Team. The ScrumMaster was sometimes the Product Owner Proxy as well, but it was more likely that the Proxy would be a Business Analyst who was not actually empowered – setting up confusing power dynamics.

3. The Team committed to a collection of individual Backlog Items (often called Stories) at Sprint Planning. This commitment was a contract between the Team and the Product Owner, and the Team was expected to do 'whatever it takes' to meet the commitment. In order to meet these commitments, the Team typically ignored quality coding practices, leading to code being 'hacked out' and Velocity eventually plummeting as a result.

4. Once a Sprint was started, the only way to officially change requirements in the middle of the Sprint (renegotiate the Sprint Backlog) was to have an Abnormal Termination, restart the Sprint, and re-plan.

5. The Product Review consisted of a demonstration by the Team to the Product Owner, and the Team's Results were accepted or rejected by the Product Owner at the Product Review.

6. Teams often found the Retrospective to be an annoyance, and were either ignoring it, using it as a gripe session, or had deprecated it from their process altogether through 'self-organization.'

7. The focus was on 'getting work done' rather than quality, and progress was measured using tools like the TaskHour BurnDown, Release BurnDown, the Enhanced Release BurnDown[5], and so on. These tools require knowledge of 'how much work is left' and are thus predictive and non-agile. Just sayin'...

This version of Scrum (what I am calling 'Old Scrum') was functional, but out of balance. Its pieces didn't fit together well, and Teams, Trainers, and Coaches were working hard to bring it into balance. There were many issues, including:

*   The ScrumMaster was often in a position of power, which made it hard for a Team to self-organize;

*   The Product Owner and Proxy provided contradictory guidance, and the Team was confused (see the discussion in appendix A.2);

*   The Team committed to a fixed amount of work, thus becoming non-agile once the Sprint Started;

---

[5] From Mike Cohn, see http://www.mountaingoatsoftware.com/scrum/alt-releaseburndown/

- The Team's commitment was seen as more important than doing quality work, so the code suffered;

- External Stakeholders were often not involved in the feedback loop, so the Team developed the 'wrong product';

- And so on...

Modern Scrum (2005 to present) .

In 2005 I became a Certified Scrum Trainer, and I was required to figure out what Scrum looked like – what was the *official version* of Scrum – so that I could train people on it. I found that Scrum had changed based on the issues given above, and what follows is what 'state of the art' Scrum looks like today – and it's basically what this book covers. The list parallels what I gave for Old Scrum, so that you can easily compare the Old versus Modern versions, point by point.

1. The Product Owner is a Team Member and is accountable for the Team's product to the Business and Stakeholders; the Product Owner works with the Team constantly (at least three hours a day is my recommended practice), so there is no need for a Proxy.

2. The ScrumMaster is a Team Member, with no formal power, who acts as a facilitator, trainer, coach, mentor, and so on. The primary purposes of the ScrumMaster are to facilitate self-organization, get impediments removed, and act as a Change Agent.

3. The Product Owner and the Team jointly agree to a collection of individual Backlog Items (often called Stories) at Sprint Planning. The Stories have Definitions of Done in an attempt to keep Quality up, and it is universally acknowledged that developing Clean Code at a Sustainable Pace is a basic responsibility of the Team.

4. Once a Sprint has started, the Product Owner and the rest of the Team can change the Sprint Backlog by renegotiating; various strategies have been devised for doing so.

5. The Product Review consists of a demonstration by the Product Owner and the rest of the Team to the Stakeholders. Normally, the individual Stories have been accepted by the Product Owner during the Sprint, and the Review is mainly for Feedback from the Stakeholders.

6. Retrospectives are used more often, and Scrum Teams' Retrospectives are much more self-organized than they used to be.

7. Predictive tools were slowly replaced by monitoring tools by most practitioners. For example, the Release BurnDown was replaced by a

Release BurnUp, which measured how much work had been done, the TaskHour BurnDown is replaced by the Checklist Item Buildup (see chapter 4.6) and so on. Eventually, as of late 2011 (see [SG]), the BurnDowns were removed from Scrum altogether...

Future Scrum (2014 to ??)

I think that Scrum as defined above is *almost* right, but I see a few things that could, or should, change. Let me make some predictions here. I'll guess that there are two things that are happening that will modify Scrum in the relatively near future:

Adopt Better Development Practices. Ken Schwaber, Jeff Sutherland, and many others are currently talking about the lack of good technical practices on Scrum Teams. Ron Jeffries and Chet Hendricksen have started an Agile Skills Project to work with others to figure out what skills (technical and otherwise) Developers need who work on agile teams.

I predict that a role similar to XP's Coach role will be introduced to Scrum. I have introduced a role called Technical Owner to some of the Organizations I coach, and it is working quite well. I think that this role will *not* be an extension of the ScrumMaster role, but that many people will try to make it so.

Specifically, I predict that Scrum Teams will adopt a new role (call it Technical Owner or Coach...) who will:

- Train, Coach, and Mentor Team Members on technical practices in order to avoid Technical Debt and make code easier to extend and maintain; these practices are probably going to be similar to the existing XP practices.

- Work with Teams to develop common Definitions of Done that will support these technical practices and make integrations easier.

- Work with other Technical Owners in the Organization to solve cross-cutting technical issues.

- Prioritize Technical Stories (called Chores in this book) whose main purpose is to mitigate and remove Technical Debt. Basically, the same way the Product Owner owns Business Value, the Technical Owner will own Technical Debt.

I believe that the need for this Technical Owner is obvious, but it will take approximately 3-5 more years before it becomes ubiquitous on Scrum Teams.

Adopt Continuous Planning. On current Scrum Teams one of the biggest problems is that reality changes more often than the Sprint does. That is, there is a need to change the Sprint Backlog more often than Sprint Planning allows. We see this need already evidencing itself in the many strategies that Teams have developed in order to renegotiate Sprint Agreements during a Sprint.

I predict that, very soon, many Scrum Teams will adopt Continuous Planning. They will still use Sprints in order to have the regular feedback loop with Stakeholders, but the Planning and Commitments will take place nearly continuously.

Specifically, I think that many Teams will adopt the Kanban(ish) variant that I describe in chapter 4.7, and will combine Swarming, well-defined Story Agreements, and continuous re-planning. Some Teams are mature enough to do this already, but not many. Therefore, I think all of this will happen in concert with the adoption of better technical practices.

Summary

So, now you know where I'm coming from. I hope it helps you understand this book a little better.

Discussion Questions

1. You have probably heard a lot about different versions of Scrum. Did Dan's discussion of 'Old Scrum' versus 'Modern Scrum' help sort it out for you?

A.4

Doug's Story

By Doug Shimp

I have had an interesting Journey. From painting as a boy,
through college and graduate school, to software development,
and finally to training and coaching at 3Back, my life has
brought me to this point. Here's my story...

For me, Scrum has been a pathway to understand agility and how to make teams better. 'Agility in all things' is a phrase that I like.[1] It reminds me that most of the interesting work we do requires some amount of agility and that interesting work often requires a good team. For me, Scrum is an agile pathway to better teams that can do interesting work. I have applied Scrum on projects and coached others to apply it. Coaching and training in Scrum has taken me on a wonderful journey. I have had an opportunity to work across many different industries and have been exposed to a myriad of development efforts.

Working on this book has helped me refine my understanding of Scrum. The book reveals how I apply it to problem solving for my teams. Every conversation and recommendation has been field-tested multiple times and applied to many different domains of development. Each time ideas were applied they were either polished further, removed or were found to be irrelevant in context. While the descriptions in the book are far from complete – as a 'unified theory' type of thing – I have found it to be very useful for my teams.

Recent History

People often ask me about my history and how I came to see things as I do through the lens of Scrum. Even though I first heard about Scrum in 1996, I like to tell my history by starting with today and working backwards.

I have been teaching, training and/or coaching teams in Scrum for the last eight years. Each year has brought me something new and provided new insights. I founded 3Back in 2004 with a focus on Scrum and the motto *'We Make Teams Better'* (I was helped immensely in doing this by Derek Wade,

---

[1] Unlike the rest of the book, the "I" in this story is Doug, not an amalgam of Doug and Dan.

one of the most brilliant people I've had the pleasure to work with). Each year has been an adventure in exploring new companies, working with existing ones and finding better ways to apply Scrum. People often ask me, "Is there something else besides Scrum?" or "What if X?" My answers are always, "Yes, of course, but Scrum just happens to be one of the cleanest methods I have seen. Scrum helps teams get better faster. Scrum can scale. Scrum can work in distributed environments. Scrum is proven. Scrum will probably work for you. Your Scrum will be different."

Before working at 3Back (Senior Consultant / Partner), I was a Director of IT, a Manager of Software Development, Methodologist and Developer (Smalltalk, C, FORTRAN, etc.). I had the pleasure of working in the financial industry and applying the concepts of Scrum. At that time, we did not apply Scrum anything like I do today. However, in hindsight, we were effective when we behaved Scrum-like. Sometimes we used heavier upfront methods that invariably brought things to a halt. This was done for lots of reasons, but the classic reason was 'we need to get everything perfect up front' before we move. The 'get everything perfect up front' approach would fail like it always did and we would go back to my favorite method of 'Just Get Stuff Done'. My boss and mentor in this was Sal Miosi, who is my favorite boss of all time. Sal taught me the art of brevity and focus. I have rarely encountered someone like Sal. Sal had an iron hard focus on reducing things to the point that they were simple and easy to accomplish. Sal's lessons have stuck with me.

Influences on Me

My family: my wife, my children and my friends … they ground and help me connect every day.

Sal, more than any other person that I have worked with, has an ability to focus despite chaos. Sal was the only person I have known to relentlessly write his messages and thoughts over and over until he could distill them down to a few small concise sentences. Sal used his concise messages to focus teams and work. Even though there might have been half a dozen directions we could go next, Sal would choose one and keep us moving. As a Product Owner, Sal's gift was the ability to focus effort. As a ScrumMaster, Sal always encouraged behavior that took the 'high road.'

Ken Schwaber was a big influence on me, as he encouraged me to look at emergence in a different way and brought me closer to Scrum. Ken says that he believes in emergence, and now I know what he means and why it is so pivotal to his work in agility. Ken also made it possible for me to start my journey into Scrum. I cannot thank Ken enough for both of these things. Ken is brilliant and his work continues to inspire me.

Another big influence on me is Dan Rawsthorne, my co-author on this book. Dan has constantly given me lessons in adaptive thinking. I could say *agile thinking* but it is not so much quick or nimble as it is building a 'model of thought' by constantly adapting to new information and constructing and reconstructing models to fit. Dan and I have had dozens of conversations that move from one subject to the next; often our conversations have challenged me to unhinge rules I had built for myself. Dan sees things from so many different angles. From agility, to methodologies, to raw analysis and pure math, Dan has improved my thinking in every single way. This book exists because of Dan's herculean effort to write up our accumulated conversations. And this book was possible because we had those conversations. Thank you Dan!

A longtime friend of mine is Ed Porter. Ed was the first person with a 'pure math head' that I ever met. He is incredibly strong at mathematical thinking. When it comes to object-oriented thinking and breaking problems down, Ed is the first person that comes to mind. He took the time and made the effort to help me master objects in Smalltalk. Ten or more weeks of relentlessly working, reading, coding, and applying it finally got me to say 'ohhhhh', the rest of our time is history. ;-) It seems to me, there are a few folks who are born wired to think with objects and the rest of us must learn to think that way.

I also learned a lot from Chemistry, believe it or not. The two major lessons chemistry taught me allow me to stay flexible and humble because the universe is so complex.

- The first lesson from chemistry is small molecule spectroscopy. Doing work in small molecule spectroscopy as a summer intern showed me that the amount of data that could be generated from the smallest molecules can overwhelm the computational power of the planet. There is more data than we know what to do with so we must learn to ask the right questions first. Just because you have a pile of data doesn't mean you *know* anything – it could be the wrong data.

- The second area of chemistry that greatly influenced my thinking process was protein crystallography, which I worked on in graduate school. Proteins are large, sloppy molecules that are always breathing and moving through time. They never stop! To understand a protein you have to realize that nothing about them is static; actually nothing at all is really static. Everything is moving through time and changing. What a mess ... Cool!

Painting

The first time I really learned how to estimate was from painting. I started painting when I was 14. I used to time myself in everything and write down notes. My first indoor painting job (in Wisconsin where I grew up, indoor work was ideal during the winter months) was a big lesson in estimating. I bid the job for painting the inside of a house. I offered to move everything in each room of the house, offered to use the best paint, and went to work. The end result was that I made about 8 cents an hour, well below the $3 an hour minimum wage at the time. My estimating really sucked on that one... ;-)

However, I did learn one important lesson, and that lesson was to *finish what you start, and do a good job*. My estimating may have been poor, but my work was good. My client on that first job referred me to dozens of her friends, and my estimating rapidly improved. Over time the business grew and my brother and I joined forces. Our company grew to 40 people working in the field, with union workers, industrial/commercial jobs and large projects – house painting became a thing of the past.

Here is what I learned about estimating from painting:

1. You will never know exactly how long it will take until you are done;

2. Actual costs of a job can help estimate a similar new job;

3. Throughput on a big job becomes the best indicator of whether you will make any money; and, most importantly;

4. Estimating is relative.

You can size your job in anything: windows, T-shirts sizes, door frames, time, whatever... For smaller jobs these numbers become stable and reliable very easily. For large jobs, like painting the pipes in a coal power plant, it becomes tremendously difficult no matter what numbers you have, so all you can do is take a guess, begin somewhere, and start relying on monitoring throughput to refine your estimate.

Besides estimation, another thing I learned from painting was the 'Definition of Done'. Anyone who has spent any amount of time working with their hands will have the 'Definition of Done' hard wired into their head. All tradesmen know *'If you don't know what Done looks like you will never finish.'* Knowing what 'Done' looks like is so important that it forms a recognizable pattern of thinking. Knowing 'Done' must be constantly enforced and reinforced. There are some simple questions you can ask to understand 'Done' when working on a Story or painting a wall, and they can be summarized by: *"If it were 'Done', what would it look like to you?"* When a good understanding of 'Done' is missing, projects both big and small fail or go sideways.

The lessons of estimating and done are crucial to agility, and I initially learned them through painting.

Self-Organizing Teams

There are two starter lessons on self-organizing teams that I picked up while exploring. The first is that rapid-fire micromanagement of another *person's* actions is often not possible and is not sustainable. And the second is rapid-fire micromanagement of a *team's* action interferes with their communication patterns and destabilizes internal synergy. In both cases it aggravates the people involved and limits the intellectual power available for work.

Each of the above patterns leads me to understand the power of self-organizing teams. These patterns were reinforced with observations from painting, software development, management, training and coaching teams. I struggle to say more than that since this area is so subtle and tricky to describe. Instead I will give a list of bullets to summarize a few of my lessons.

- When working with teams you have to start by understanding the behavior pattern you want.

- Set clear elevating goals. What is the overall job? What do we need to achieve?

- Don't micromanage unless you are a mentor and are invited to do so. As a mentor, help a little at a time as they struggle to learn.

- Struggling for mastery is central to learning.

- Don't be afraid to learn. Kindergarten skills over technical skills.

- Good teams are learning all the time.

- For Scrum teams there are three main things to deal with: the Product Owner's intent, the plan, and reality.

- Nurture your passion in what you do. Help your team nurture theirs.

- Rapid-fire micromanagement of people doing work is hurtful.

- How you deliver a 'message' matters – with both individuals and teams!

- Great teams are built by doing work together.

- We are wired to connect. Help us do that and we can do amazing things together.

- Make a habit out of reflecting early and often. 'How is that working out for you?'

You would never tell an experienced plumber how to use the wrench, unless you wanted to 'wear' that wrench on the way to the emergency room. Why would you tell an experienced developer how to code? The best way to get a job done is make space and allow people to learn. Great teams figure out hard problems and optimize themselves to get the job done.

Conclusion

At this point I will stop writing. There are dozens more lessons that I could write up and dozens more people that helped me grasp those lessons. My last lesson is 'no head works alone'. I no longer worry about where I get an idea from or if I am smart enough. My ideas come from everywhere and every person that I have had the privilege of interacting with. Each interaction is an opportunity to learn and improve. Being on a Scrum team is a deeply personal social experience. Scrum has allowed me to accelerate my learning curve – it can do the same for you.

Discussion Questions

1. Doug has some real good ideas about self-organization. Please go re-read them and discuss...

Odds and Ends

Scrum is a simple framework that is fairly non-prescriptive.
Understanding Scrum and how to make it work requires a lot of
knowledge 'outside' of Scrum. In this appendix I summarize
some of this knowledge.

This appendix is a brief summary of some things that are useful to know when exploring Scrum. They are in an appendix, rather than the book itself, either because they are not central to Scrum, didn't fit nicely into the book's structure, or are applicable to the book as a whole. This doesn't mean they are not important, so here they are.

Project Complexity

In chapter 1.1 I said that *"solving complex problems requires brainpower, not recipes"* – and that I'd discuss what 'complex' meant later, in this appendix. Well, here is that discussion, which I will discuss in the context of projects. One of the common refrains I hear about agile versus waterfall processes is that the waterfall is for simple software projects, while agility is for complex projects. Often, this is explained through the use of the Stacey diagram[1], see Figure 39.

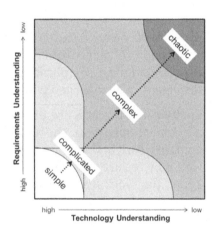

Figure 39: the Stacey Diagram

I like the basic visual depiction of the Stacey Diagram, but I don't like the fact that it represents *only* the areas of Requirements and Technology. I think things aren't quite that simple; I think that there are lots of other relevant factors. The way I look at it, projects involve doing all sorts of stuff – any of which can cause complexity – not just requirements and technology.

I'd like to discuss the concept of project complexity from a slightly different angle. You may remember the following quote that was brought to us by Donald Rumsfeld on February 12, 2002, when talking about difficulties that

---

[1] Ralph Stacey, Strategic management and organizational dynamics: the challenge of complexity. 3rd ed. Harlow: Prentice Hall, 2002.

were arising in Iraq: "There are known knowns; there are things we know that we know. There are known unknowns; that is to say, there are things that we now know we don't know. But there are also unknown unknowns; there are things we do not know we don't know."

Now, many people derided this statement as being gobbledygook, but that was unfortunate – as this statement is actually profound. At the very least, it is profound gobbledygook. In my discussion of complexity, I use the concepts of known knowns, unknown unknowns, and so on, to describe the progression of project difficulty – from Simple to Chaotic.

First of all, there are Simple projects, in which everything is known. The Team knows what it needs to do, how to do it (strategy and practices), and how much effort it will take. Everything is a *known known*. These are projects that are amenable to predictive processes, like the waterfall.

Of course, even in Simple projects, little things go wrong: things are harder than the Team thought they would be, the strategy has to be changed a bit, or they just take longer than expected. We call these things *complications*, and say that some piece of the project *'got Complicated on us.'* Simple projects may have a *few* complications, which can be managed with focused applications of agility (often called SWAT Teams and the like), but when *lots* of little things get complicated, we actually have a Complicated project – and this needs to be managed with agility.

Complicated projects are projects with lots of complications, most of which are *known unknowns*: the Team Members know what they need to do and are fairly sure of the strategy to use, but may be unsure of the exact practices (but they're sure it can be done), or exactly how long it will take. On a Scrum Team, the work *inside* a Sprint is supposed to be merely Complicated; the Team Members know what they should do (the Doneness Agreements of the agreed-to Stories in the Front Burner) and they have a strategy for getting all of them done (or else they shouldn't have agreed to all of them), but they are often unsure of either exactly how to do them, exactly how long they will take, or how to manage changes in the strategy. This complicatedness of the Sprint is resolved by the workings of the Self-Organizing Team itself.

Throughout the Sprint, but especially during the Product Review, Stake-holders add new Items to the Backlog. Many of these new Items were previously unknown to the Team, which makes this project Complex – there are *unknown unknowns*. New Items being added to the Backlog are *unknown unknowns* that have just become *known unknowns* to the Team. In other words, Scrum projects are inherently Complex across Sprints.

Through the action of adding new Items to the Backlog, reprioritizing the Backlog, and agreeing to do the next Sprint, the Team takes a Complex project and extracts a (merely) Complicated Sprint to do work on. Usually, the sub-project of releasing a collection of features (called a Release) is a Complex project – the Team knows what features to release, but is using agility to flesh out the details along the way.

Sometimes the new Items added to the Backlog actually *contradict* stuff the Team already knows, or stuff the Team has already done. In this case the project is called a Chaotic project, where there are things we know, that *'just ain't so.'* In other words, the truth is changing – the ground is shifting under the Team's feet. Usually, the lifecycle of a Software Product is Chaotic, as Releases tend to 'redo' things that were done in previous Releases.

So, in developing a 'normal' software Product, agility is the *only* way to survive. The Backlog is changing to reflect the overall Product Lifecycle's Chaos, and the Product Owner is prioritizing and the Team is agreeing to do work. In this process, at any given time, the Team is working on a Release that is merely Complex, in a Sprint that is merely Complicated, executing Stories that are supposed to be Simple.

To state this in another way, Teams work on Simple Stories, which combine to form a Complicated Sprint, which combine to form a Complex Release, which are part of a Chaotic Product Lifecycle. This is the reality of agile Product Development with Scrum.

Lean Principles

One of the major influences on modern agile software development has been Lean Manufacturing, which was pioneered by Toyota[2] and focuses on creating value while eliminating waste. Lean principles are used to improve the flow of Simple (or merely Complicated) processes. Remember that these are processes in which there are known Definitions of Dones and strategies for achieving them, but the details and necessary effort may be unknown. Lean principles have been applied to software development for decades, but the book that popularized the effort was the Poppendieck's book in 2003[3]

The fundamental idea behind Lean thinking is that doing work for *any* reason other than the creation of value for the end user is wasteful and should be eliminated (we must 'cut out the fat' and make the process lean...). Analysis of this simple idea has led to many Lean Principles that apply to agile development, and extend beyond the Simple and Complicated projects to include the Complex and Chaotic as well. Here is a list of the ones referenced in this book:

---

[2] See Yasuhiro Monden, *Toyota Production System, An Integrated Approach to Just-In-Time*, Third edition, Norcross, GA: Engineering & Management Press, 1998.

[3] Mary and Tom Poppendieck, *Lean Software Development: An Agile Toolkit*, Addison-Wesley Professional, 2003.

Pull, don't Push. This is simply the notion that one should look at the Process (called the 'Value Stream' in Lean) from the User's or Product's point of view, rather than the Developer's. We think of the Product as *pulling* itself from the Team rather than the Practices *pushing* it out from the Team. One of my development maxims is 'Let the Product Lead' which is equivalent to 'Pull, don't Push'. This idea is based on the fundamental Lean idea of focusing on Value and that anything else is waste.

Minimize Inventory (Waste). The basic Lean principle is to eliminate waste, so the basic improvement technique is to find waste and eliminate it. Inventory is work that has been done by one process, and is waiting for another process to do more work on it. In the standard waterfall process, design documents are inventory waiting for design, design documents are inventory waiting for development, code is inventory waiting for testing, and so on. While it is waiting to be worked on, this inventory is getting old (think of a stack of metal parts getting rusty) and some of the inventory items may be unfit for use before they actually get worked on. Not only that, but in Complex and Chaotic systems the inventory items may, in fact, have become wrong; but their existence provides inertia – the pressure to do them *just because they are there*. The most obvious inventory items in the Scrum process are the Stories in the Back Burner that are waiting to be selected to be worked on – but there are other inventories, as well.

Single Item Flow. One way to minimize inventory is to do 'Single Item Flow', in which the Team works on only one thing at a time, working on it from beginning to end. There is no inventory (internal to this item) in this type of development, as there is no waiting between steps in the process, so it is ideal from the point of view of the Product – each piece of end-to-end work is done in an ideal way. However, it often seems wasteful or inefficient as (at any given time) there can be some people sitting around doing little or nothing. I usually view complete end-to-end 'Single Item Flow' as an idealization, something to be simulated but not actually done. However, it is often possible to combine small pieces of process into bigger pieces that are then done 'all at once' as Single Item Flow. For example, we can use this principle to see that integrating analysis and testing into development is better than doing analysis, waiting for coding, and then waiting for testing...

Delay Decisions until the Last Responsible Moment. I think it is clear that wrong decisions are waste. What is not so clear is that the earlier a decision is made the more likely it is to be wrong – since there is less information to base the decision on. This leads to the Delay Decisions until the Last Responsible Moment principle. In practice, it is almost impossible to know when the Last Responsible Moment is, and people often wind up delaying decisions for way too long. This is a tough balance, and leads to the practice of making decisions fairly early, and then constantly analyzing them for continued correctness as new information comes in. Unfortunately, a decision (once made) has its own form of inertia, just as inventory does. It takes an agile mindset to re-make a decision – and this is one of the major discriminators between 'agile' and 'predictive' thinking.

Agile Manifesto

In 2001 a group of developers got together in Snowbird, Utah to talk about what they believed. The result was the Agile Manifesto[4]:

Manifesto for Agile Software Development

We are uncovering better ways of developing software by doing it and helping others do it. Through this work we have come to value:

Individuals and Interactions *over* Processes and tools
Working Software *over* Comprehensive Documentation
Customer Collaboration *over* Contract Negotiation
Responding to Change *over* Following a Plan

That is, while there is value in the items on the right, we value the items on the left more.

Figure 40: The Agile Manifesto

This did three great things for the agile software community:

1. It talked about values, rather than practices, which allowed the conversations about agility to include both practices and people, and allowed for discussions of interesting questions like *'does RUP enforce agility, or merely allow it?'* and *'Is it possible to have an agile waterfall process?'* and so on.

2. It gave Preferences, rather than dogmatic guidance, which allowed for a wide range of projects that could call themselves Agile, depending on how they balanced the preferences. These practices could be a disparate as the Rational Unified Process (RUP), Dynamic Systems Development Method (DSDM), Kanban (see chapter 4.7), eXtreme Programming (XP), Scrum, and many more.

3. It firmly established the word 'Agile' as the generic term for this wide-ranging family of tools, teams, and Organizations.

Although agile software development had been around a long time[5], this is arguably the most significant milestone in the area of software agility.

---

[4] See http://agilemanifesto.org/
[5] See Larman, Craig, and Victor Basili, "Iterative and Incremental Development: A Brief History," IEEE Computer, June 2003, pages 2-11.

Benefit/Cost Curves

When doing project work, there are many rules of thumb that I know and believe in. You have probably heard of Pareto's Principle, also called the '80/20 rule,' which (when restricted to projects) states that *'by doing 20% of the work you can generate 80% of the benefit'.*[6] Unfortunately, Pareto's Principle only applies in hindsight, when we can look back at the project and see that the *right* 20% of the work *would have* supplied 80% of the benefit (which is usually referred to as Business Value or BV).

But we don't live in that backwards world; we live in a forwards world. I can imagine that in a *very* Simple (trivial?) project it would be possible to have a 'perfect plan' that delivered BV close to the 80/20 curve, but I think that the plans for *most* Simple or *any* Complicated projects would (at best) deliver something approaching 80/50 – which is the curve in Figure 41. That is, these *plans* could deliver 80% of the Business Value for the first 50% of the work.

Why is it 80/50 and not 80/30 or something else? Well, it's because 80/50 is the average of *perfect*, which is 80/20, and *random*, which is 80/80. That's all there is to it...

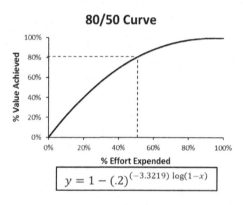

$$y = 1 - (.2)^{(-3.3219)\log(1-x)}$$

Figure 41: The '80/50 Curve'

Of course, in a Complex project, where many things are unknown in the beginning, no such plan *could* exist. In this case, I believe that an *average Product Owner* (rather than a plan) could achieve 80/50; that is, by properly reprioritizing the work, the Team could achieve 80% of the Product's overall Business Value for the first 50% of the work.

Why would you care about this? Good question. Basically, I'm leading up to taking a look at the standard S-Shaped Curve from software project management theory, which I have reproduced in Figure 42[7]. This S-Shaped Curve shows the delivery of a software project's Business Value (assuming a *perfect plan executed perfectly*) as a function of percent of Effort Expended, and is divided into three roughly equal sections:

---

[6] See, for example, http://www.projectsmart.co.uk/pareto-principle.html.

[7] See Denis F. Cioffi, "New Tools for Project Managers: Evolution of S-Curve and Earned Value Formalism," A Presentation at the Third Caribbean & Latin American Conference on Project Management, 21–23 May 2003.

- **The first third** of the expended effort is used to provide the architecture and infrastructure for the system. This is done in the context of delivering Business Value (see architecturally-significant and infrastructure Stories from chapter 3.4), but the major result is architecture or infrastructure.

- **The 'second' third** of the effort is used to provide Business Value using a greedy algorithm, doing the work that provides the most Business Value first. Generally, we think of this third of the effort as providing the must-haves for the system, and the system should be minimally releasable at the end of this third.

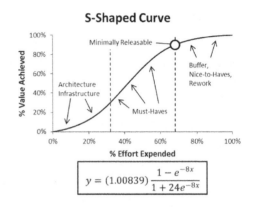

S-Shaped Curve

$$y = (1.00839)\frac{1 - e^{-8x}}{1 + 24e^{-8x}}$$

Figure 42: The 'Standard' S-Shaped Curve

- **The 'final' third** of the effort is intended to be used to provide nice-to-have functionality. In practice, however, it is often used as buffer and rework because something doesn't go right; initial budgeting is wrong, mistakes are made, new requirements are found, and so on.

In a Scrum Project the development of BV might not exactly follow the S-Shaped Curve because the Team doesn't normally do *all* the architecture and infrastructure up front. However, as I mentioned in chapter 3.9, Teams often build a Walking Skeleton in the first few Sprints of a Release, in order to provide the architecture and infrastructure to support the features being released.

Not only that, but for any given Capability that is being delivered in a release, it is considered good practice to do its Architecturally Significant Stories first. In chapter 3.10 I called these [backbone] Stories. So, while the S-Shaped Curve might not be *exactly* right for the Project as a whole, it is probably reasonably correct one Capability (and maybe Release) at a time.

It is the Product Owner's job to keep the Team on the S-Shaped Curve as it moves along, and this is done by constantly reprioritizing the Backlog to do the appropriate Stories next. We have reason to believe this can be done because the final 2/3 of the S-Shaped Curve (the non-architecturally-significant Stories) has *almost exactly* the same shape as the 80/50 Curve. In other words, if we discount the Architecturally Significant Stories, the prioritizing between must-have and nice-to-have Stories is the same as on the 80/50 curve – and I believe a competent Product Owner can do it. In other words, a competent Product Owner is as good as a perfect plan executed perfectly; this is one of the *real* reasons agility works... By the way, the fact that these two curves match up this way is *magical*, and points out one of the ways the truths of standard project management and of agility mesh together.

Some Simple Statistics

I'd like to talk about statistics in order to help you understand what to expect from Teams with different kinds of Projects. In particular, I'd like to answer the question: *'how consistent should we expect Velocities to be?'*

Let's say we have three Teams. Each has a Velocity of 10 Stories/Sprint and an average of 30 hours of effort for each Story. What makes our three Teams different is that the first Team's Stories are Simple, the second Team's Stories are Straightforward, and the third Team's Stories are Complicated. That is, even though all the Stories on each of the Teams take the same *average* effort to complete, they have differences in many factors affecting actual effort, such as Technical Debt, Team Ability, Organizational Noise, etc. (see chapter 3.7 for a discussion).

Statistically, this means the Stories have different effort distributions, as in Table 9. The distributions shown are Beta Distributions, which are often used to simulate effort distribution. They are based on having estimates for the minimum, average (mean), and maximum amounts of effort required. If you've seen these distributions before you may also be familiar with the mode, which is where the 'hump' of the curve is.

Table 9: Distributions for Simple, Straightforward, and Complex Stories

Beta Distribution, B(α, β)	Parameters
Distribution for Simple Stories Work Hours Distribution	min = 25 mean = μ = 30 max = 40 mode = 28.75 α = 2 β = 4 σ = 2.67 (std dev)
Distribution for Straightforward Stories Work Hours Distribution	min = 15 mean = μ = 30 max = 60 mode = 26.25 α = 2 β = 4 σ = 8.02 (std dev)

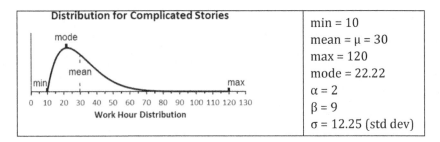

Distribution for Complicated Stories	min = 10
	mean = μ = 30
	max = 120
	mode = 22.22
	α = 2
	β = 9
	σ = 12.25 (std dev)

As you can see, these curves are *not* the standard 'bell-shaped' curves we are used to. That's the Normal Distribution – this is the Beta Distribution.

However, the Central Limit Theorem says that if we look at the aggregate of many of these things, the aggregate becomes Normal. This happens quickly – it turns out that 5 of them are enough, as we see in Figure 43. This graph compares the actual (Beta Distribution) for 5 Complicated Stories taken as a group with the Normal Distribution with the same mean and standard deviation.

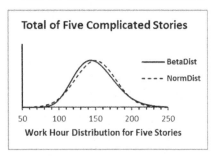

Figure 43: Beta Normalizes

Since we know that 5 Stories are enough for the Normal Distribution to be applicable, we can do some straightforward analyses of what to expect in a Sprint, and in a Release, based on the Normal Distribution. Since each of our Teams has a Velocity of 10 Stories in a Sprint, we'll take a look at what the distribution of effort is for each of our Teams for those 10 Stories.

Once we have this information we will have an idea of how much variation to expect for the Velocities from Sprint to Sprint for each of our Teams. To do this I will use some simple rules of Statistics:

- If we aggregate N Stories with mean = μ, then the aggregate has mean = Nμ.

- If we aggregate N Stories with standard deviation = σ, then the aggregate has standard deviation = $N^{1/2}\sigma$.

In other words, the mean increases with N, but the standard deviation increases with the square root of N. So, let's look at N = 10, a Sprint's worth of Stories for each of our Teams.

For our Team doing Simple Stories, μ = 30 and σ = 2.67, so for 10 Stories μ = 300 and σ = 8.45. This leads to the accompanying distribution (Figure 44), with the 95% Confidence Interval[8] for finishing 10 Stories being 300 ± 16.6

---

[8] For Normal distributions, the 95% confidence interval is μ ± 1.96σ.

hours, or 300 ± 5.5%. This isn't so bad, as the variation is less than one Story's worth of effort, and the Team can probably do *exactly* 10 Stories in a Sprint with a high degree of confidence. But that's what I would expect if the Team is doing Simple Stories... ;-)

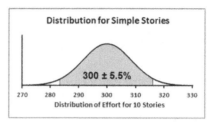

Figure 44: Simple Stories

What about our Team doing Straight-forward Stories? For this Team we have $\mu = 30$, $\sigma = 8.02$, so for 10 Stories we have $\mu = 300$ and $\sigma = 25.35$. When we do the Normal Distribution for this we get the 95% Confidence Interval for finishing 10 Stories being 300 ± 49.7 hours, or 300 ± 16.6%. This is a swing of about 1.6 Story's worth of work, and it is unlikely that the Team could manage this amount of variability without either causing Technical Debt or working at an Unsustainable Pace. Therefore, I would expect this Team to complete 8-12 Stories in a Sprint.

Finally, what about the Team doing Complicated Stories? For this Team we have $\mu = 30$, $\sigma = 12.25$, so for 10 Stories we have $\mu = 300$ and $\sigma = 38.7$. When we do the Normal Distribution for this we get the 95% Confidence Interval for finishing 10 Stories being 300 ± 75.9 hours, or 300 ± 25.3%. This is a swing of about 2.5 Story's worth of effort, so I would expect this Team to complete from 7-13 Stories in a Sprint.

Analysis of these last two Teams, doing the Straightforward and Complicated Stories, demonstrates why Agreement-Based Sprint Planning (chapter 4.2) is preferable to the Velocity-Based Sprint Planning that is often described. Trying to squeeze 20-30% more into a Sprint (which is what would sometimes happen if the Team was doing Velocity-Based Planning) will inevitably lead to creating Technical Debt and/or working at an Unsustainable Pace.

Ok, so that's the analysis for a Sprint. What about for a Release? I'll make it short... if I make the assumption that our Teams are releasing once a Quarter – or every 6-7 Sprints – then this means that they expect to produce 60-70 Stories in the Release. Doing the analysis (like the above) for 60 Stories, I get:

- The Team doing Simple Stories will likely do its 60 Stories in 1800 ± 40.6 hours or 1800 ± 2.3%,

- The Team doing Straightforward Stories will likely do its 60 Stories in 1800 ± 121.7 hours or 1800 ± 6.8%, and

- The Team doing Complicated Stories will likely do its 60 Stories in 1800 ± 185.9 hours or 1800 ± 10.3%.

Even the worst case has a variation of barely over 10%, which is quite reasonable for a span of three months – this is manageable. The variations from Sprint to Sprint might not be much *fun* for the Team doing Complicated Stories, but their variation is definitely manageable at the Release level. The main conclusion of this analysis is that *only* the Team doing Simple Stories can be managed based on its Velocity at the Sprint level, while *all three* Teams can be managed with their Velocities at the Release level. This is a very important conclusion, and leads to many of the recommendations in this book.

Discussion Questions

1. Explain why complex projects *require* agility.

2. Agile is not Lean, and Lean is not Agile. However, there are lean principles that are useful for Scrum. List some of them.

3. Why is the Agile Manifesto important?

4. Discuss why Velocity takes a while to settle down.

A.6

Estimation Games

*In chapter 3.7 on Sizing I mentioned that Scrum Teams normally
use Estimation Games to Size their Stories. In this Appendix I
define and discuss this topic.*

An Estimation Game is a way for a group of people to reach consensus on the size of something in a rapid, effective way. They are often used on Scrum Teams because the interactive nature of the Game is consistent with Scrum's notion of self-organization. One of the most popular Estimation Games is Planning Poker[1], which is often used by a Team to estimate the relative size of a Story.

Before the Team can estimate Stories, the Team needs to be prepared:

- There needs to be an exemplar Story; one that is well-understood by the Team and has a known size. For the 'CatAir Website' this could be the Medium-Sized Story 'Get List of Flights from CUTLASS.'

- Each Team Member needs to have estimation cards giving the valid estimation values.

Then, the basic script for estimating a Story's (relative) size is simple:

- The Product Owner gives the description of the Story to the Team. The Team Members may have a short (time-boxed to 1-2 minutes) Q&A session with the Product Owner to get more information.

- Each Team Member privately selects the card that represents his or her estimate of the size relative to the exemplar.

- Once all Team Members have all made their choices, all the cards are simultaneously shown to the Team.

- If estimates differ, the outliers explain their estimates and the Team may have a short discussion.

- Then, each Team Member privately re-estimates the Story's size, and the whole process repeats until either consensus is reached or it is agreed that consensus won't be reached.

---

[1] First described by James Grenning in 2002 and popularized in Mike Cohn, *Agile Estimating and Planning*, Pearson Education, 2005. Planning Poker® is a registered trademark of Mountain Goat Software. LLC.

This is a very simple script, and there are a number of interesting issues that arise. These issues are tightly intertwined, and I will discuss them one at a time.

Various Scales

An Estimation Game normally results in assigning a StoryPoint size to a Story. These values are then used when calculating the Team's Velocity every Sprint. One of the issues that comes up is what scale to use for the StoryPoints. There are many scales that can be used, and here are three common scales that are in use on Scrum Teams:

Figure 45: Estimation Cards

- T-shirt sizes, with XS = 1, S = 2, M = 4, L = 8, XL = 16, 4XL = 128,

- T-shirt sizes, with Small = 2, Medium = 4, Large = 8, 4XL = ?

- Fibonacci sizes, 1, 2, 3, 5, 8, 13, 20, 40, 100.

Personally, I prefer the second scale; but that is because what I'm looking for is a size – not a big discussion. When the Team uses a scale that has many different values to choose from, it invariably leads to serious discussions of the Story – including design and development issues. For example, if you're using the Fibonacci sizes there will invariably be arguments about whether the Story is a 3, a 5, or an 8.

This is not a bad thing; in Scrum we like lots of discussions. It's just that I prefer to have the big discussions about the Story during the development of the Story, not during the sizing of the Story. This is a style thing, though. Many Teams use the 'sizing exercise' during Backlog Refinement in order to discuss implementation of the Stories. There is no right answer on this one...

What to Compare

Note that in the Estimation Game script the Team Members estimate the Size of the Story compared to the exemplar. This is not very precise – there are many things that the word 'Size' could represent. For example, Size could represent Effort, Complexity, Difficulty, Risk, or just about anything else – it all depends on what sort of thing you're looking at and what it is you're trying to compare.

In chapter 3.7 when I was discussing Story Size, I suggested that the Team use or Ideal Effort (or Intrinsic Difficulty) as the thing to compare when estimating StoryPoints. I also suggested that the team could use EffortPoints if you needed to estimate Actual Effort for some reason – perhaps when doing Sprint Planning. This 'what to compare' issue is actually a non-trivial one, and could lead to a slight extension of the Estimation Game script.

When the Team Member selects the card that represents his or her estimate of the Story's Size relative to the exemplar, it must be clear what is being compared. In other words, there is an implied, if not explicit, question being asked such as: *'What is the size of* 'Story ABC' *relative to the* 'exemplar' *with respect to* 'XYZ'*?'* where 'XYZ' could be Actual Effort, Complexity, Ideal Effort, Intrinsic Difficulty, or whatever. At the end of this appendix I present a complicated Estimation Game that that explicitly uses this construct.

Affinity Analysis

In the Estimation Game that I described above, all Stories were compared to a *single* exemplar that represented a medium-sized Story. Another way to do this is to have *multiple* exemplars, giving examples for each of the various sizes.

For example, when looking at Stories for the 'CatAir Website,' there might be the following three exemplars:

- Small – 'Add Passenger to Itinerary'
- Medium – 'Get List of Flights from CUTLASS'
- Large – 'Pick a Flight and Pay for It'

Then, when the Team has a collection of exemplars like this the question naturally changes to *'which of the exemplars is the Story most like, with respect to...?'* rather than *'how does this Story compare to the exemplar...?'*

When the Team does it like this it is called 'affinity analysis,' because the Team is looking to see how things are alike rather than how they are different. There is another form of affinity analysis that a Team could use, especially at the beginning of a Project, when exemplar Stories don't yet exist. In this situation the team looks at *all* the Stories in the Backlog and groups them into 'piles' such as the 'small pile,' the 'medium pile,' and the 'large pile.'

The Stories are then given the Size that is associated with the pile they're in. What I like to do at this point is take a look at the piles and say *'okay, look at each pile and find me the* **most typical** *small Story, the* **most typical** *medium Story, and the* **most typical** *large Story that you can find'* – then the Team Members will have the exemplars they need to do affinity analysis in the future.

Is It Just about Stories?

So far I've been describing the Estimation Game in order to give relative sizes (in StoryPoints) for Stories. This is not the only thing the Team can use an Estimation Game for. I like the Team Members to carry around their Estimation Cards and use them to help focus *any* discussion.

For example, if there is an architectural discussion going on the Scrum-Master could have the Team Members do a quick Estimation Game on the question *'how important is this architectural decision?'* and help focus the discussion by finding out who really cares about the decision. Estimation Games can also be used to estimate how big risks are, or fears, or whatever.

Estimation Games can be used with our Stakeholders, too. I will use one with my Stakeholders when trying to size Capabilities. *'How big is this Use Case?'* Is a question I'd like to have an answer to when doing Release Planning, and an Estimation Game is a good way to do it.

Why It Works

There are lots of reasons that Estimation Games work; you can go look at James Surowiecki's book *The Wisdom of Crowds* (Doubleday, 2004) for a thorough discussion. You can also think of many of the games found in *Innovation Games* (Luke Hohmann, Addison-Wesley, 2006) as forms of Delphic Estimation[2], which has been common in software for decades.

But I just look at it in a more simple fashion. The reason Estimation Games work is that they appeal to the self-organization of the Team. It changes the question from *'What is the right answer?'* to *'Why do we disagree?'* – which is a much more focused question. This focusing of the question and making it about the Team rather than the problem itself, is what makes the Estimation Game so powerful.

A Complicated Example

Now that I've shown you a *simple* version of the Estimation Game, let me show you a *complicated* version for estimating the size of Stories in Story-Points. I'm not saying that this is better, only that it's more complicated. What it does is bring some other factors into the game. It uses affinity analysis rather than simple comparison, it takes Architectural Significance into account, and it treats different kinds of Stories differently. For some people, this looks *more professional* and thus is *clearly* more correct. In practice, it doesn't make much difference to the Team's work, but it may make things more comfortable for your Team and Stakeholders.

---

[2] http://en.wikipedia.org/wiki/Wideband_delphi.

In this version of the Estimation Game, I'll start off with three exemplar Stories:

- Small – 'Add Traveler to Itinerary' (2 SPs)
- Medium – 'Get List of Flights from CUTLASS' (4 SPs)
- Large – 'Pick a Flight and Pay for It' (8 SPs)

And then we have the Script:

1. Start off with the Story we're estimating, call it 'Story ABC'

2. If 'Story ABC' is a Functional Story, ask the question: 'Which exemplar Story is <Story ABC> most like, in terms of Intrinsic Difficulty, given that the codebase is clean, the best people work on it, and so on...' and assign 'Story ABC' the same number of SPs as this exemplar.

    a. If 'Story ABC' is Architecturally Significant, and you haven't already taken this into account, double the StoryPoints in order to account for making the Architectural Decision...

3. If 'Story ABC' is a non-Functional Story, but has a well-defined Acceptance Criteria, then ask the question: *'Which exemplar Story is <Story ABC> most like, in terms of Ideal Effort, given that the codebase is ready, the best people work on it, and so on...'* and assign 'Story ABC' the same number of SPs as this exemplar.

    a. Note that what I'm doing here is making sure that all the StoryPoints are the 'same size' in terms of Ideal Effort (on average), even though the Team is comparing different things. Intrinsic Difficulty isn't always the right thing to compare...

4. If 'Story ABC' has ill-defined Acceptance Criteria, it gets time-boxed in order to limit the damage *paralysis* or *internal scope creep* can do to the Team.

    a. I like to time-box in terms of StoryPoint's worth of effort in order to allow the Team some wiggle room, such as 'Do 2 StoryPoints worth of Exploratory Testing on page ABC' – and the Team should monitor the situation during the Daily Meeting.

Summary

Estimation Games are commonly used by Scrum Teams, as they are seen as a manifestation of self-organization and self-management. As I have just described, there are many variations and uses of these games. My experience is that Teams like these games and will invent their own uses for them. As a ScrumMaster I encourage this behavior, and I think you should, too.

Discussion Questions

1. Explain how Estimation Games can be used to have a serious discussion about a Story.

2. Discuss why Estimation Games work.

3. Discuss how the 'complicated' Estimation Game could be used in your Organization.

Index

70/30 Rule. 111, 219, 258, *See* Chore

80/20 rule 320

80/50 Curve 320

A

Abnormal Termination 277

definition 281

Acceptance Criteria ... 136, 173, 281, 290

and Story Size 161

definition 136

for ill-defined Stories 151

for Sprint Wrap-up Story 185

for Startup Sprint Stories............... 270

Acceptance-Based Story 102

and Done 102

definition 281

size of 150

Accountability .... *See* Responsibility

and Management ... 24, 37

and the Product Owner.......... 20, 36

can't be shared 31

definition 281

Actual Effort

three parts of 151

Affinity Analysis.......... 329

Agile Analysis

definition 281

Agile Manifesto 319

Agreement 12, 49, 51, 98, 136–47, 218, 316, *See* Doneness Agreement

and Backlog Refinement 173

and Sizing 173

as Checklist..... 82, 139, 264

as Time-Box 144

compromising........ 145

Daily Scrum............ 263

definition.............. 135

documenting SMEs.. 73

for [coding] Storyotype 186

for Capability 185

for Coding Story... 136–38

for Epics 143–44

for Mature Team ... 142

for Non-Coding Story 138–42

for Ready Story 171

for Release............. 185

for Sprint 185

good one 135

inspect and adapt .. 186

monitoring....... 245–53

needs to change ... 228, 231

no partial credit..... 203

Pulls Results............ 85

renegotiate............. 52

retrospecting on 146

risk for kanban....... 258

Sprint Planning 211, 218

standardized with Storyotypes...... 173, 184

verification, not validation 146

versus Task 82

Agreement-Based Planning........ 162, 211, 215–25, 324, *See* Sprint Planning

benefits................. 224

overview 215

results 215

simple description . 211

Analysis Story 113, 116, 138, 159, 174, 178, 184, 216

and kanban 257

definition.............. 281

example 116

Refinement as........ 174

Storyotypes 192–96

Architecturally Significant Story 116, 179, 189, 191, 321

and Sizing.............. 331

definition.............. 282

example 116, 144

part of Walking Skeleton 293

prioritizion of 178

versus Spike ... 116, 289

Architecture

and S-Shaped Curve 321

definition....... 178, 282

review.................... 128

time-boxing 144

B

Back Burner80, 81, 96, 97, 98, 99, 100, 115, 119, 139, 168, 171, 173, 175, 195, 196, 198, 211, 218, 228, 233, *See* Backlog

and kanban 257

as waste 172

Cleanup Story221, 231, 241

definition 93, 282

for Maintenance...... 94

limit inventory...... 172, 174, 215, 318

PlaceHolder Story.. 237

Ready Stories 93

Backbone Scenario..... 189

Backlog........... 10, 91–103

any stakeholder may add Items............ 92

definition 91, 282

drives development 91

informs Stakeholders 91

manages Team's unallocated time 91

multiple lists............ 92

prioritization 11, 92

prioritization Buckets 92

Refinement

definition 11

stakeholder needs and wants.................. 11

work to do someday 11

Backlog Item ...... *See* Item

definition 282

Backlog Maintenance. *See* Backlog Refinement

Backlog Refinement .. 162, 171–81

activity..................... 96

Agreement 173

definition 282

Fears, Risks, and Issues 109

Session 193

Story...................... 195

Storyotypes 183–86, 192–96

Tasks...................... 173

Beedle, Mike 6

Booch, Grady...... 178, 282

Bucket ... 165–69, *See* Epic

and Use Case 188

definition 166, 168

Buddy-Up pattern 72

Daily Scrum 266

discussion 72, 79

Technical Debt....... 241

Budget for 'known unknowns' 236

Budgeting for a Use Case 157–60

Bug

definition 191, 282

BuildUp 245–53, 258, 264, *See* Checklist Item Buildup

Checklist Item........ 253

definition 282

BurnDown ... 245–53, 258, 264, *See* TaskHour BurnDown

definition 282

Release 304, 305

TaskHour247, 253, 304

Burns, Robert 227

BurnUp..........*See* BuildUp

definition 282

Release 306

Business Owner........9, 18

as Product Owner ...68

basic responsibilities 21–22

definition .. 18, 65, 283

versus Product Owner 69

Business Value 192

Benefit/Cost Curves 320–22

Capabilities are Items with................... 109

Capability.............. 283

Chore..................... 283

comes from Stakeholders 108

creating Technical Debt 221

definition 178, 283

intrinsically subjective 109

making Architectural Decisions........... 179

prioritizing based on 178, 179, 219

Product Ownership .41

technical dependencies ...180

tension with reducing Technical Debt ...72, 128, 240

Buy an e-Ticket

Backbone Story 139

decomposed into Stories...............119

progress report........99

Size of 159

C

Cancelling a Sprint......276

definition 283

Capability ... 110, 111, *See* Epic

a Progress Report 99

and Definition of Done 185

definition 105, 283

development example 118

discussion and examples 107

example...................95

example Storyotype 188

has Business Value 109

in WBS 106

move to Fridge 98

progress on.............99

showing progress ..100

S-Shaped Curve 321

Use Case 117

Capacity.............109, 157

assumption............153

assumptions 220

definition 149, 283

how to increase 224

Release Strategy....204

StoryPoints 157

Technical Debt.......125

used for prediction 157

Catalina Air.............8, 106

examples 95

'Shop for Flights' Epic
...........................143

Work Breakdown
Structure...........106

Charter 11

Checklist Item........ 82, *See*
Checklist Item BuildUp

and Agreement 138

and Daily Scrum.....264

definition 248

Checklist Item Buildup306

Checklist Item BuildUp
...............245, 248–50

BurnDown
Workaround251–52

data for.................249

definition 283

Graph of 250

improvement over
TaskHour
BurnDown.........250

Chore.................107, 111

"70/30 Rule"..........111

adopt a 110

and kanban............258

as one Epic 236

Cleanup Story 132, 241

Constrains when
Capability 110

definition......105, 108,
283

dependencies on ...179

discussion and
examples...........108

examples 108

in WBS 107

necessary...............219

Orphan Task 110

prioritization of.....110,
132

Stories....................113

Technical Debt.......128

to maintain Capacity
..........................109

using 'spare time' for
..........................228

with Business Value
..........................110

Clean Code 185, 269, 271,
272

and Definition of Done
.....................136–47

and Modern Scrum305

and Scrum Team......49

and Technical Debt
.....................123–34

definition.........48, 283

Cleanup Story 72, 145,
239–43, 243

Agreement.............221

always in Back Burner
..........................241

creating Technical
Debt 231

is a Chore..............132

is an apology..........241

Technical Debt.......240

CleanUp Story

definition...............283

Coach

ScrumMaster as......10,
60–61

Cockburn, Alistair 115,
303

Code Complete...........272

definition...............283

Coding Story

Agreement.......136–38

and kanban 256

definition.......136, 283

Storyotypes 186–92

Swarming................77

Cohn, Mike 116, 327

Commitment 25, 210, 219

definition...............283

Commitment-Based
Planning................. *See*
Agreement-Based
Planning

Conscience

ScrumMaster as
Team's.................45

conservation of crap.....52

Constraint........... 187, *See*
Organizational
Constraint

Organizational ..48, 50,
199, 207

versus Impediment ..47

Constraints

Organizational 47

Continuous Timeline ..205

Coordination Team

definition...............283

Coordinator ...... *See* Team
Swarm

and kanban 260

definition.........75, 283

discuss status at Daily
Scrum..........80, 265

'in charge of' TeamLet
....................75, 283

not Product Owner ..78

not ScrumMaster 79

part of Storyotype 187,
194, 195

part of Story's
Agreement 136,
137, 139, 140

re-planning 262

Single Item Flow 78

when a Story is Done
.... 81
Cross-Functional Team 17
definition 26, 283
discussion 27
CURB 117

D

Daily Scrum 261–66
definition 284
follow-on discussions
.... 262
inspect and adapt
point 261
recommended four
questions 265
the three questions
.... 261
Defect .. 94, 146, 233, 273
definition 284
Definition of Done 87,
138, 145, 183, 185,
186, 192, 291, 305,
306, 312, 317, *See*
Agreement
analysis Story example
.... 139, 194, 196
and Due Diligence ... 87
as a Trim Tab 209
coding Story example
.... 137, 187, 190
definition 136, 284
externally constrained
.... 146
factor in Story Size 145
infrastructure Story
example 140
limiting scope creep
.... 140, 141
not good enough ... 242
research Story
example 141
Retrospecting on ... 146
risk for kanban 258
Storyotypes 243
Technical Debt 243

the Retrospective .. 208
watering down 220,
231
Developer......... *See* Team
Member
Development Team... 105,
131, 162, *See* Scrum
Team
definition 284
DoD .... *See* Definition of
Done
Done..88, 94, 96, 101, *See*
Agreement
and Epic.................... 93
definition 284
for Release 272
for Stories 101
Increment 89, 271, 284
part of Backlog 94
Done Increment 89
definition 284
Doneness Agreement 211,
212, 216, 218, 231,
248, 253, 275, *See*
Agreement
Due Diligence 10, 20, 127,
136, 210, 272
and Clean Code 137
and Definition of Done
.... 87
and Quality Results 135
and Sprint Goal...... 222
and Sustainable Pace
.... 19
and Technical Debt.. 13
definition 284
for Product Owner 274
for Team 227

E

Effort Distribution Graph
High-Performing Team
.... 152
Team in Trouble 153
EffortPoint. 161, 163, 173,
221, 328
and Technical Debt 156

definition 284
Sprint Planning 219
Empirical Process
definition 284
Environmental Drag
definition 152
Environmental Variables
and Velocity........... 154
definition 150, 285
must be managed.. 155
Epic.. 93, 98, 99, 113, 172,
216
Agreement 143
as Bucket166, 168, 188
as Container 118–20
CURB 117
definition 117, 285
examples 118
Fears, Risks, and Issues
.... 109
in Fridge........... 98, 176
not yet decomposed
.... 157
organize the Backlog
.... 119
Placeholder 236
progress on.............. 99
readjusting StoryPoint
budget 162
Research................ 141
'Ship It'................... 271
simple definition 93
Storyotypes 184
StoryPoint budget for
.... 157, 160
Estimation Game....... 109,
149–63, 151, 220,
327–32
and Comparing
Velocity............. 160
and Use Cases 159
complicated example
.... 330
definition 285
Executive Review 202,
205, 288

definition 285

Exemplar Story 327–32

  and Comparing
    Velocity.............160

  definition 285

Exploratory

  Story 144

  testing 40, 120, 138,
    146, 195, 331

eXtreme Programming..8,
  49, 113, 125, 130, 319

  and Pairing 76

  definition 285

F

facilitator

  ScrumMaster as.......45

Feathers, Michael......126,
  131

Feature

  definition 285

Feature Complete 271

  definition 285

feedback.... 12, 14, 15, 20,
  22, 65, 69, 212

  basis of agility........199

  from Product Review
    .... 185, 201, 212

  in Modern Scrum...305

  in 'old' Scrum.........305

  incremental delivery
    provides............175

  it's all about the.......88

  lifeblood of project 202

  long feedback cycles
   107

  meaningful 89

  need for provides
    definition of Work
    results.................90

  products provide 89

  Scrum won't work
    without it 202

  Stakeholders provide
    .... 70, 204, 277

  Startup Sprint 269

Story elicits
  meaningful........231

  to define Releasable
   176

Forecast. 11, 13, 171, 215,
  217, 219

  definition...............285

Freezer 95, 97, 99, 101,
  119, 168, 171, 173,
  174, *See* Backlog

  as Trash Can 94

  definition.........93, 285

  no Cleanup Stories.241

Fridge 94, 95, 96, 98, 118,
  119, 168, 171, 173,
  174, 175, 176, *See*
  Backlog

  definition.........93, 285

  no Cleanup Stories.241

Front Burner....81, 94, 96,
  97, 98, 99, 100, 115,
  119, 168, 175, 198,
  233, *See* Backlog

  and kanban............258

  definition.........93, 285

  for Maintenance......94

Functional Story 183, 282,
  286, 331

  definition...............102

G

General Agreement....*See*
  Story Agreement

  definition.......136, 285

  example.................137

H

Hendricksen, Chet 306

High-Performing Team

  Effort Distribution
    graph for...........152

Hohmann, Luke ...70, 109,
  330

I

Ideal Effort 179, 328

definition.......150, 286

Estimation Game

  example 331

Ideal Engineering
  Hour/Day

  definition...............286

Ideal Engineering
  Hours/Days............221

Ideal Time

  definition...............151

Impediment.....21, 23, 26,
  44, 73, 234

  and Business Owner 65

  and Daily Scrum....261,
    264

  and hyper-
    performance.......63

  and Ideal Effort......286

  and PlaceHolder
    Stories...............235

  and -spectives..........52

  and Technical Debt
    ....124, 132

  and the Leadership
    Team 39

  definition...............286

  difference in Values as
   26

  fear of changing Code
    as 49

  Organizational 21

  People Availability as
   180

  progress on..............50

  Removal of.............263

  ScrumMaster removes
    ... 10, 13, 45, 52, 79,
    305

  SMEs not delivering.72

  versus Constraints ...47

Impediment Manager

  ScrumMaster as.......45

InBox95, 96, 97, 171, 173,
  174, 175, *See* Backlog

  definition.........93, 286

Infrastructure Story...113,
  145

Storyotype............197
Innovation Game
  Buy a Feature..........*70*
  Product Box.............*70*
  Remember the Future
 70
Innovation Games70, 109,
  193, 330
Interested Bystander ...22
  definition 286
Intraspective 45, 201, *Also
  see* Retrospective, *See*
  -spective
  after Daily Scrum...263
  definition 46, 286
  discuss Values during
 26
  during Norming.......60
  during Performing...62
  during Storming 57
  frequent 47
  script for............46, 60
Intrinsic Difficulty......161,
  162, 328
  definition 286
  Estimation Game
    example............331
INVEST Criteria...........114
Invisible
  ScrumMaster Becomes
 63
Item.....10, 11, 12, 13, 91,
  105, 111, 113, 165,
  173, *See* Chore, *See*
  Capability, *See* Epic,
  See Story
  adjusting Sprint
    content.............227
  agreement good
    enough 135
  and reinventing
    detailed
    requirements......92
  and Single Item Flow
  ....78, 289
  and Technical Debt 124
  as Epic 117

  as Story 113
  becomes Epic.........117
  Bucket 166, 168
  called 'Chores'.......236
  definition 91, 105, 286
  Getting to Done.......13
  have all levels of
    fidelity.................11
  in Freezer 98
  in Fridge 98
  initially identified 94
  moving through
    Backlog, examples
   95–97
  moving to Back Burner
 172
  on Leadership Team
    Backlog 41
  prioritization strategy
 175
  prioritizing 92, 171
  provides Value.......113
  Refinement of 171
  Sizing is complex issue
 163
  Stakeholders add new
 97
  Tag..........................165
  Tagging 165–69
  Theme 166

J

Jeffries, Ron 94, 115, 130,
  306
Just in Time 256

K

Kanban 80, 196, 274
  brief description....255
  continuous Planning
 255
  definition 286
  main strength........255

  Kanban(ish) Variant.6, 80,
  81, 98, 233, 255–60,
  275, 307

L

Leadership Team.38, 286,
  See Product Owner
  Team
Lean Principles 4, 220,
  255, 286, 317–19
Legacy Code 126, 131

M

Maintenance 175
  Documentation 273
  of Code 127
  Project 94
  Story 178
  Team 11, 255
Management Team......38
Marco, Tom..............152
Mature Team
  and 'by the book'
    Scrum....................7
  and comparing or
    combining
    Velocities 161
  and Future Scrum ..307
  and Storyotyping ...186
  and Swarming..........81
  and the Back Burner
 172
  and the kanban(ish)
    Variant..............233
  and the ScrumMaster
    ....10, 21, 57–63
  and Tuckman Maturity
    Model 43
  as ScrumMaster
    changes modes...52
Mental Agility....5, 7, 255,
  281
  definition 286
Meszaros, Gerard......183,
  190
Minimize Inventory
  as Lean Principle....286

moderator

    ScrumMaster as.......10

Modern Scrum ....xvii, 305

moral authority

    ScrumMaster has ...20, 54

must-have

    and S-Shaped Curve 321

    scenario 158, 321

N

nice-to-have

    scenario 158

Non-Coding Story

    Agreement 138–42

O

One Piece Flow.*See* Single Item Flow

order

    versus Prioritization.92

Order

    definition 286

Organizational Constraints

    definition 47

    discussion 47–48

Organizational Noise

    as Environmental Variable 150

    definition 150, 286

Orphan Task .... 110, *See* Chore

P

Pairing 77, 81, 223

    definition 76, 287

    polygamous 77, 287

Pareto's Principle 320

People over Practices

    preference for 4

Physical Agility 281

    definition 287

PlaceHolder Story......180, 196, 234, 235–37, 255

    definition.......236, 287

Plan of Action 219, 221

    definition...............287

Point Person .... 76, *See* Coordinator

Poppendieck

    Mary and Tom 317

Portfolio Management.39

Potentially Releasable Increment

    definition...............287

Potentially Shippable Increment

    definition...............287

preferences

    Agile Manifesto 319

    People over Practices 4

    Pull, don't Push..........4

    Quality over Quantity 85, 224

    Reality trumps Expectations 4

    Self-Organizing Teams 4

    Team developing Product 4

    Team Members over JustaCoders, etc..58

Prioritization.................42

    and Stakeholders.....70

    by Product Owner ...69

    definition.................92

    during Planning218–19

    Factors for 177–80

    for managing the work 27

    initial.......................52

    into Buckets........92–94

    need a single............92

    Strategy for......175–77

Priority

    definition...............287

Process

    three parts of.............3

Product. *See* Work Results

    all about Feedback ..89

    definition.........90, 287

    discussion 87–90

    Potentially Shippable 87

    what Stakeholders want....................88

Product Backlog ....*See* Backlog, *See* Backlog

Product Backlog Item .*See* Item, *See* Item

Product Manager in Scrum.................24–25

Product Owner .9, 18, 31–42

    accountabilities 19

    as Team Member ..34–35

    basic responsibilities 19–20

    definition.. 18, 31, 287, 295–300

    determines Chores and Capabilities 110

    examples 35–38

    finds 'right' Stakeholders 202

    is also ScrumMaster 54

    ownership responsibilities....41

    relationship with Team 32–34

    single, wringable, neck 31, 49, 299

    versus Business Owner 69

Product Owner Team ..38, 40, 38–41, 67

    Backlog 40

    definition...............287

    responsibilities.........40

    sharing SMEs 67, 73

Product Review14, 40, 72, 96, 177, 185, 201, 202–4, 297

    and Product Owner .35

and Sprint Goal 217

definition 14, 287

discussing 'undone'
  Stories 277

in Modern scrum...305

in 'old' scrum.........304

major review cycle 259

making Technical Debt
  Visible 241

'missing' SME 73

'owned' by Product
  Owner...............203

preparing for 202

primary feedback
  mechanism 70

purpose 202

purposes for 203

Stakeholder
  participation 69, 70,
  98

Product Roadmap . 11, 12,
  70

Product Vision.. 11, 12, 70

definition 288

Progress Assessment 204–
  5

adequate time for . 212

digest feedback 212

Project Complexity.....315

Project Manager in Scrum
 24–25

Project Review 202

definition 288

Pull, don't Push 85

as Lean Principle ...286

definition 318

preference for 4

Q

Quality Code .....*See* Clean
  Code

Quality Results 20, 23, 43,
  69, 75, 135, *See* Clean
  Code

and Due Diligence . 135

R

RASCI Matrix 23

Ready

definition 171

Ready Story11, 52, 93, 94,
  109, 171, 175, 211,
  215, 218, 237, 258,
  Compare to Well-
  Defined Story, *See*
  Back Burner, *See*
  Backlog Refinement

definition 288

reality

adapt to it.....227, 231,
  277

business...................14

can't ignore 220

changes 143, 306

make it visible ... 25, 32

of Technical Debt ..240

too many skill sets...19

unacceptable to
  business 32

Reality Trumps
  Expectations..........224

realization that..........4

Refactoring

definition 288

Referee

ScrumMaster as 45

Refinement ...*See* Backlog
  Refinement

Release......................317

BurnDown 304, 305

BurnUp 306

definition 288

Goals 12

Strategy 12

Release Goal 178

as target 172

Release Planning ... 11, 12,
  41, 68, 95, 99, 156,
  288

Capacity.................283

Estimation Games .330

out of scope for book7,
  11

Storyotype.............196

Release Sprint 80, 89

definition 288

Release Strategy

definition 288

Respect

defined 25

Responsibility ....*See*
  Accountability

definition 288

Shared 28

Results. *See* Work Results,
  See Work Results

Retrospective .. 14, 46, 48,
  162, 169, 205–10, *See*
  Team Retrospective,
  See -spective

CatAir Team...........246

definition 46, 288

discuss values 26

during Norming 60

during Performing ...62

during Storming.......57

Identify and resolve
  issues 46

in Modern Scrum...305

in 'old' Scrum.........304

increasing Capacity 224

Product Owner
  boundaries..........35

Startup Sprint 270

Roadmap.......*See* Product
  Roadmap

S

Scenario

and Budgeting for a
  Use Case 157–60

definition 288

Schwaber, Ken...6, 32, 87,
  193, 201, 284, 291,
  299, 301, 303, 306,
  310

Scrum

"Future".............306–7

"Modern" 305–6

"Old"..................303–5

as training wheels 5

definition 288

is a simple
  development
  framework 1

is an ever-evolving
  framework 4

moving aggressively to
 58

out-of-the-box 7

pre-emptive
  optimization 7

soul of........................5

Scrum Board......*See* Story
  Board

Scrum Team ..... *See* Team

definition 289

Scrum Values

definition 289

ScrumMaster.. 10, 18, 43–
  55

accepted by Team ...53

accountabilities of ..20,
  23, 43, 54

and Clean Code issues
 48

and Product
  Ownership issues 49

and sub-roles...........44

as Change Agent......53

as Coach 60–61

as Mentor..........61–62

as Swarmer..............79

as Trainer 57–59

basic responsibilities of
 20–21

becomes 'Invisible'...63

definition 18, 289

facilitates Team's self-
  organization........50

facilitates, doesn't
  manage 46

how to find 53

is also Product Owner
 54

main issues to deal
  with...............48–52

'makes it work' 45

modes.....................52

removes Impediments
 152

scrummish personality ..5,
  7

Self-Contained Team....27

definition...............289

Self-Organizing Team1, 17

definition........27, 289

discussion 27

patterns of task-
  organization........59

preference for 4

-spectives................47

Swarming................80

Shalloway, Alan 208

Single Item Flow 78, 83,
  256, 292, 318

definition........78, 289

multiple TeamLets...78

Single Piece Flow........*See*
  Single Item Flow

SirJeff... 8, 95, 96, 97, 106,
  107, 120, 249, 251

Slack 152

SME .... 71–73, 289, *See*
  Subject Matter Expert

and Sprint Team 76

and Stakeholders.....70

and Swarming..........78

basic responsibilities of
 22

Buddy 72

external 79

internal 79

is Consulted 23

SME Availability

as Environmental
  Variable.............150

SME Availability

definition...............150

SME Availability

definition 289

-spective52, 128, 243, *See*
  Intraspective, *See*
  Retrospective

and Technical Debt 132

major tool for self-
  organization........47

Spike..........................116

definition...............289

Storyotype 192

versus Architecturally
  Significant Story
  ....116, 289

Sprint

Abnormal Termination
  of......................277

adjusting content
  within..........227–34

and Doneness 185

and Intraspectives ...46

and kanban......255–59

and Product 90

Backlog ....*See* Sprint
  Backlog

cancelling...............276

definition........12, 289

fundamental process
  flow.....................12

gets meaningful
  feedback 89

Goal .... *See* Sprint Goal

in kanban 259

length of 274

monitoring progress in
 245–53

Planning.......*See* Sprint
  Planning

Release .....*See* Release
  Sprint

Retrospective.........*See*
  Retrospective

Review ....*See* Sprint
  Review

the Leadership Team
 39

Time Between..201–13

Sprint Backlog..11, 12, 81,
  98, *See* Front Burner

agreed to do............ 13
Agreement-Based
    Planning.... 212, 216
and kanban 80
continuous planning
    307
definition 135, 290
in 'modern' Scrum. 305
in 'old' Scrum......... 304
inventory and waste
    256
modifying 228, 232
PlaceHolder Story.. 236
replace with WIP.. 256,
    257
work to do now 11
Sprint Commitment ... *See*
Commitment
definition 290
Sprint Goal 13, 185
and Abnormal
    Termination...... 277
and Cancelling a Sprint
    276
and kanban 257
and Product Review 70,
    204
and Progress
    Assessment....... 205
and Sprint Planning 210
and Velocity 223
appropriate 222–23
changing it............. 229
de facto 210
defines success of
    Sprint 13
definition 13, 217, 290
for next Sprint 204
provides 'wiggle room'
    .... 210, 222, 230
versus Release Goal
    223
Sprint Planning 12, 13, 70,
    173, 201, 212, 215–25,
    227, *See* Ageement-
    Based Planning

and agreeing to do
    Stories............... 219
and Backlog
    Refinement... 14, 52
and Cleanup Stories
    .... 221, 241
and EffortPoints 173
and Epic
    decomposition.. 120
and kanban............ 257
and mid-Sprint Re-
    planning.... 233, 276
and Product Owner . 35
and Release Goal... 223
and Resizing Stories
    145
and SMEs............... 139
and Sprint Goal...... 222
and Story Agreement
    135
and Storyotype's
    Agreement........ 186
and Technical Debt 220
and the Back Burner 93
and 'warning' SMEs 174
and WorkRate 156
appropriate Sprint
    Goals for 222–23
as 'batch process'.. 255
conversations
    overheard at 142
definition 211, 290
for Startup Sprint... 270
getting ready for ... 217
in 'old' Scrum......... 304
purpose of............. 210
Sprint Retrospective . 290,
    See Team
    Retrospective
Sprint Review
    as Product Review. 202
    definition 290
Sprint Team............ 71, 76
    definition 290
Sprint Wrap-up Story . 185
S-Shaped Curve 320

Stakeholder . 9, 14, 15, 18,
    21, 23, 69–71
and Product Owner .. 9,
    11, 20, 27, 31, 33,
    65–68, 78
and Release Planning
    12
and the Backlog. 91–92
basic responsibilities 22
Business Owner as... 68
can add Items to
    Backlog 71
definition ... 18, 22, 65,
    69, 290
help identify SMEs... 70
interaction with Team
    ... 12, 13, 20, 22, 46,
    51
interested in Product
    69
most important role in
    scrum 9
provide feedback..... 70
Team of 68
versus stakeholder .. 91
work with
    ScrumMaster 73–74
Startup Sprint............. 119
definition 290
discussion 269–71
Goal for 223
length 275
Stay-at-Home Coder... *See*
Coordinator
Story............................ 75
Agreement .... *See*
    Agreement
Analysis ... *See* Analysis
    Story
Architecturally
    Significant .... *See*
    Architecturally
    Significant Story
becomes an Epic.... 117
becomes as Epic 120
changing Size 161

Cleanup ... *See* Cleanup Story

Coding .... *See* Coding Story

definition 113, 290

examples 116

extension of User Story 113

extracted from Epic 173

from Idea to Done . 115

in Back Burner 98

in Front Burner 98

Infrastructure113, 116, 145

Infrastructure Storyotypes....... 197

moved to Back Burner 173

Non-Coding .. *See* Non-Coding Story

Pairing on 76, 287

Placeholder 236

PlaceHolder 235–37

promise for a conversation 115

Ready. *See* Ready Story

refined 171

request for value ... 113

requiring SME 72, 73

Research 141

right size 183

simple definition 93

single focus 183

small and well-understood 114

status 82

Swarming on 59, 75, 76

Story Agreement . 136–47, *See* Agreement

definition 290

Story Board

and Definition of Done 186

Complicated 82, 278

definition 291

Story Owner 217

definition 291

Story Size

definition 291

Story Time ..... *See* Backlog Refinement

StoryBoss *See* Coordinator

Storyotype... 49, 116, 119, 173, 181–98, 186

Analysis 192–96

and Definition of Done .. 136, 183, 185, 243

and Doneness Checklist 250

and the Retrospective 208

Coding 186–92

decompose Epics ... 184

definition 291

don't replace thinking 186

find new Stories 184

finding reusable patterns 184

have consistent Story Agreements 184

Release Planning ... 196

Tag 166

used for documenting practices 184

used for standardization . 184

used for training 184

Storyotyping. 48, 137, 147

and Backlog Refinement 184

definition 184

is a natural activity 184

StoryPoint

allocated for Chores 111

and PlaceHolder Story 235–37

and Sprint Planning 211, 216, 220

and the Agreement145

and the 'Buy an e-Ticket' example . 119

budgeting for Epics 157–60, 168

complicated estimation 330

definition 149, 291

estimation scales ... 328

for Architectural decisions 331

for Time-Boxing 144

Sizing during Refinement 173

versus EffortPoints.156

Strategic Agility

definition 291

Subject Matter Expert . 18, 71–73

basic responsibilities22

can't trust them 71

definition 18, 22, 65, 71, 291

expert in any domain 71

not accountable to Team 71

work with ScrumMaster 73–74

Sustainable Pace ... 15, 18, 20, 31, 41, 223, 227, 289, 291, 305

and Due Diligence.... 19

and Slack 152

Sutherland, Jeff . 6, 58, 59, 125, 301, 306

Swarm ..... 13, 50, 59, 177, 221, 223, 256, 260, 263, 275, 291, *See* Team Swarm

Swarmer *See* Team Swarm

and kanban 260

definition 76, 291

mostly Swarmers 80

Pairing 77

Polygamous Pairing .81

professional 78–79

re-planning 262

Stay-at-Home Coder 77
when a Story gets
Done 81

T

Tactical Agility
    definition 291
Tag 165–69
    definition 166
TaskHour BurnDown 245–
    48, 250, 251
    data for 246
    Graph of 247
task-organization ... 50, 59
Teacher
    ScrumMaster as 45
Team
    can't do what it agreed
        to do 230
    cross-functional..... *See*
        Cross-Functional
        Team
    definition 291
    formal hierarchy...... 67
    fundamental
        development unit 17
    fundamental
        obligation 227
    maturity ....*See* Mature
        Team
    no specialized
        development roles
        18
    people with skills..... 17
    Product Owner paired
        with Business
        Owner................. 66
    Product Owner Stands
        Alone 66
    self-organizing*See* Self-
        Organizing Team
    simplified view 9
    size discussion 19
    values*See* Team Values
Team Ability

as Environmental
    Variable 150
    definition 150, 292
Team developing Product
    versus People doing
        Work..................... 4
Team in Trouble
    Effort Distribution
        Graph for 153
Team Member 10, 18
    accountabilities 23
    definition 18, 292
    ScrumMaster as 45
    versus JustaCoders, etc
        58
Team Retrospective ... 201
    definition 292
Team Swarm .. 75–83, 265
    definition 75, 292
    examples 76–78
    managed in Daily
        Scrum 80, 262
Team Values................ 25
    definition 292
    discussion 26
TeamLet *See* Team Swarm
    and kanban............ 256
    beginning to self-
        organize 59
    definition 75, 292
    not permanent sub-
        Teams 260
    the Daily Scrum 263
Technical Debt 6, 123–34,
    185, 186, 210, 220
    affecting effort
        distributions 322
    and Due Diligence ... 13
    and Performance... 153
    and Velocity 153
    as Environmental
        Variable 150
    changing Story Sizes
        161
    Cleanup Story . 72, 145,
        191, 239–43

considered in Sprint
    Planning... 117, 219,
    224
    definition 124, 292
EffortPoints 156
    increasing, on purpose
        231
    mitigating 136–38, 146,
        178, 222–23, 229
    prioritization of 132
    putting pressure on
        Team................. 264
    Retrospecting on ... 146
    risk in kanban 259
    StoryPoints 160
    Technical Owner.... 306
    tension with providing
        Business Value .. 128
    versus Clean Code ..49,
        283
    versus Speed.......... 224
Theme 165–69
    definition 166, 167
this book
    out of scope.............. 7
    purpose 5
Time-Boxed Story 161
    and Done 102
    definition 292
    size of 151
Trainer
    ScrumMaster as. 57–59
training wheels *See* Scrum
Trim Tab 208, 209, 210
    definition 209
Tuckman Team Maturity
    Model 43, 57
Tuckman, Bruce 43

U

Undone 273, 284, 288
    definition 273, 292
Usability
    analysis 281
    experts 18, 71

study.........................89

testing ..143, 146, 189, 191, 195

Use Case.... *See* Capability *and* Budgeting .157–60

decomposing with Storyotypes.......183

definition 292

User Story 113, 114

definition 292

V

Validation

versus Verification.146

Validation

definition 292

Values..*See* Scrum Values, *See* Team Values

definition 293

Velocity ..99, *See* Capability

as Indicator............154

calculated in kanban 258

comparing 160

definition 149, 293

distributions 323

flatten cost of change curve 125

including Chores....111

not a Sprint Goal....224

PlaceHolder Story ..234

plummeting in 'old' scrum 304

statistical analysis ..322

Technical Debt 125

used to estimate Capacity ...157, 204, 220

Velocity-Based Sprint Planning.................324

description.............211

Verification

definition...............293

versus Validation ...146

Verification versus Validation 146

viscosity of the code description of Technical Debt ..123

Vision..*See* Product Vision

Visioning...........11, 12, 70

W

Walking Skeleton........321

definition...............293

WBS*See* Work Breakdown Structure

Well-Defined 113, 307, 331

and Velocity...........161

definition.......136, 293

Well-Formed Team........28

definition...............293

WFT ...... *See* Well-Formed Team

WIBNI

definition...............293

wiggle room ..7, 110, 176, 210, 217, 222, 331

WIP.*See* Work in Progress

Work Breakdown Structure

collection of Epics ..118

for Catalina Air Project 106

Work in Progress 256, 257

benefits.................256

definition...............293

Work Results ....17, *See* Product

definition...............293

WorkRate

definition.......156, 293

EffortPoints............156

measure of Cost.....157

Sprint Planning 219

X

XP *See* eXtreme Programming

The best methodology's Scrum

It makes waterfall planning look dumb

    If your requirements are fragile

    Then your team must be agile

Where the whole is much more than the sum

    – Alger Rollins, student, 2011

Made in the USA
Middletown, DE
16 March 2019